UNEQUAL FREEDOMS
The Global Market as an Ethical System

UNEQUAL FREEDOMS

The Global Market as an Ethical System

John McMurtry

KUMARIAN
PRESS

Dedicated to the bearers of the civil commons.

Unequal Freedoms: The Global Market as an Ethical System

Published 1998 in the United States of America by Kumarian Press, Inc., 14 Oakwood Avenue, West Hartford, Connecticut 06119-2127 USA.

Published 1998 in Canada by Garamond Press Ltd., 67 Mowat Ave., Suite 144, Toronto, Ontario M6K 3E3

Printed in Canada
Cover illustration: Jill Glessing
Cover design: Tearney McMurtry
Editor: Robert Clarke

Library of Congress Cataloging-in-Publication Data
McMurtry, John, 1939-
    Unequal freedoms: the global market as an ethical system / John McMurtry
    p. cm.
Includes bibliographical references and index.
ISBN 1-56549-087-8 (pbk. : alk. paper)
1. Free enterprise—Moral and ethical aspects. 2. Competition, International—Moral and ethical aspects. 3. Competition—Moral and ethical aspects. 4. Profit—Moral and ethical aspects. 5. Markets— Moral and ethical aspects.   I. Title.
HB95.M385 1998
174' .4-—dc21   98-40415
                                         CIP

Contents

Part II: Market Theory and Practice: Arguments Pro and Con

Foreword

This book began in June 1995. I had just read a keynote paper to the Westminster Institute Conference, "Surviving Globalization: Economic, Social and Environmental Dimensions." Garamond Press director Peter Saunders and his colleague, Bob Mawhinney, convinced me to develop the paper into a short book. I agreed, and set about to complete the manuscript before returning to other projects. I did not realize that for the next three years the research for this work had other ideas for my life.

After thirty months of round-the-clock research and writing, the raw manuscript was over twelve hundred pages in length. I explained to Garamond while I wrote that the work was driven by deeply unsettling discoveries and new pathways of understanding which were taking me into uncharted seas. Garamond remained patient, while I continued in the white heat of the journey. The final manuscript was far beyond the limits of the planned single volume, and Garamond was obliged to select its text. The result is *Unequal Freedoms: The Global Market as an Ethical System*. For the many people who have kindly awaited the results, I hope the book explains as much as I have learned from its long journey.

Although I have written extensively on Karl Marx's thought, I decided from the outset to let the theory of the market wash through me as an ordering of thought whose principles I would see afresh, beginning from the doctrine's origins in John Locke and Adam Smith. I also resolved to track the implications of the doctrine's assumptions and tenets into the actual consequences and shocks of their impact on the lives of peoples and environments as they happened. In this way I hoped to link theory and practice across the divide presently separating them in academic economics and value theory.

These commitments to understanding the global market regime as a living value system propelled me unavoidably into a research that cut across disciplines at every turn. I became immersed ever more deeply in

1

the sea-changes of the "restructuring" of the world which was transpiring as I wrote. For long periods I felt like I was drowning in the velocity and magnitude of the declared "market revolution" and the accumulating rooms of files recording its effects on societies and ecosystems in every region of the globe.

A themal objective of the study throughout was to link these systemic social and environmental changes back to the underlying value program driving them. Although there is a shared assumption among economists of opposing schools that the market system we live under is regulated by economic laws independent of our choice and values, such an assumption fails to recognize a very basic but overlooked truth. No market decision is ever made that is not an expression of the market value system, however automatized it may have become by unthinking repetition and the force of coercive repetition. This study lays bare this hidden ethical infrastructure, follows the consequences which systematically flow from it, and raises to view the resources of social agency beneath it which can steer the world system out of its rapidly deepening life crisis.

My investigation has been assisted at every turn by an edgeless range of people and institutions. The Department of Philosophy of the University of Guelph provided senior seminar and graduate course slots to share the research I was pursuing, as well as permitting me to balance these more advanced research venues with my teaching of introductory Social and Political Issues, using selections from the same research text. For publishing preparatory articles prior to this book which worked out key links in its argument, I am grateful to *Informal Logic, The Journal of the Philosophy of Education, Praxis International, The Journal of Applied Philosophy, Social Justice* and *The Journal of Business Ethics*. For providing research support where needed for both travel and inputting text, I am indebted to the Social Sciences and Humanities Research Council.

As the research and writing of this work unfolded, I was also continuously assisted by many individuals. Bob Good, who had read some of my published work on the global market, first introduced me to the country's best informed think-tank on contemporary banking, the Committee on Monetary and Economic Reform. COMER's Chair, Bill Krehm, was a tower of strength in supporting the long repressed value-theory approach to economic principles, as well as in spelling out in detail, along with William Hixson, the nature and impacts of post-gold-standard banking policies on society. I came through this research to understand that the money-creating and interest-demanding process of both domestic and global markets is at the hidden base of our deepest economic problems. I also came via Bob Good's loans of his library of Canadian Centre for Policy Alternatives publications to find a reliable source of ongoing economic news selected out of view by the corporate chain media. The *CCPA Monitor*'s editor, Ed Finn, also took a strong interest in my ongoing research and published portions of it as I wrote it. These publications linked me further to the public initiatives of the Council of Canadians' Maude Barlow and Tony Clarke, who were strongly supportive of my work as they pursued their own heroic ground-level investigations of the corporate invasion of Canada.

The theoretical work I was immersed in would have been very lonely as no fellow academic I knew of was engaged in a project remotely similar. The global market was not understood as a value system, and neither value theorists nor social scientists critically approached it as one. But I found Adam Smith, himself a moral philosopher by training, pursuing a similar inquiry with the market system in its early stages at the end of the eighteenth century, and Karl Polanyi continuing this ethical overview of economic philosophy from a more critical historical perspective one hundred and seventy years later in *The Great Transformation*. Their composure and insight within such a sweeping task constantly reaffirmed me in the project, and Polanyi made me look in particular at society's "life substance" from an infra-class perspective. What I conceptualize here as "the civil commons" seeped upwards at the same time and I came more and more to understand it as an overlooked substructure of history which demanded a concept to name it. The same can be said for what I analyse in this book as the "life ground" and "the life sequence." They are recoveries of what has been lost as much as they are new concepts, and they have become for me the long missing value-bearings and evolving social agency which we require to bring the corporate market system under human control.

Many other people have assisted me on many different fronts in providing pieces of the puzzle. Alex Michalos first alerted me to the systematic exclusions of human and labour rights from the Canada-U.S. Free Trade Agreement as a philosopher-social scientist running for public office. Donald Buckingham then laid out in a long unpublished manuscript the legal parameters of the NAFTA and its paranthetical recognition of international environmental agreements. Ted Shrecker sent me a steady supply of valuable documentation exposing systemic job losses and other suppressed consequences of the new borderless trade.

Howard Woodhouse and David Walmark dropped off many indicators of the life slippage as they were recorded. Terisa Turner and Bill Graf continuously shared with me their own valuable research into the neo-liberal agenda in Africa and the non-industrial world. Barbara Sims gave me a copy of the Multilateral Agreement on Investment as it was leaked from the OECD as well as subsequent documentation, while Linda McQuaig faxed valuable documentation from the World Bank which I depended on. Bob Gould and Bob McMurtry supplied important documentation on relationships between public health-care and military policies and government banking respectively. Freeman Boyd and Ann Cavlovic—who were students in successive graduate Philosophy of Economics courses—provided me with documentation on agricultural trends and marketable pollution credits. Harry Glasbeek sent me his valuable legal scholarship on corporations, and was an extremely supportive reader of the book manuscript for Garamond. Gordon Laxer was also a careful and strengthening reader, who in the darkest days of the study insisted in the strongest terms that it must be published. Susan George responded to correspondence and text with sustaining generosity of support, translating my analysis of the MAI into French for submission to the French National Assembly. Jerry Cohen, as always, detail-critiqued anything I sent to Oxford with characteristic analytic exactness and counterargument. Michael Valpy, Frances Russell and Murray Dobbin helped to sustain my efforts with support and publication of central links of the argument as it was completed. David Korten was strongly responsive. All of these variously helping hands provided me with resources I could not have done without.

The very onerous tasks of inputting, copy-editing and proofing my work were performed with unfailing conscientiousness by Jennifer Sumner, Judy Martin and Garamond's Robert Clarke. My partner Jennifer Sumner also sustained me through frequent bouts of despair during the endless night corridors of labour. Terisa Turner, Leo Panitch, Stephen Clarkson and Tony Clarke responded to the results of my research with memorable generosity of time and insight with their commentaries at the 1998 Learned Societies Conference. Underneath us all was what I conceptualize here as the civil commons, whose shared infrastructure makes social self-understanding possible.

John McMurtry
May 1998

Publisher's note: The preceding foreword was written for the Canadian edition of the book. Since then, Kumarian Press has published an United States edition. We are proud of the collaboration of the two publishing houses on this excellent and thought provoking work.

Introduction:
An Overview

Understanding How We Live:
Recognizing Value Programs

This study began in the Himalayas. I had been inside the Dalai Lama's monastery, listening to the monks' chanting. When I went outside I was startled to hear a radio blaring another, more mundane, mantra. We all know the words: "We must compete in the new global marketplace."

In the Himalayas, where older value programs still rule, many variations of a deep cross-cultural theme proclaim, "We must compete," "There is no alternative," "There will be casualties, but we must stay the course."

I was in the Far East to study spiritual value systems, and in a searching discussion with the Dalai Lama, we explored this problem of life-blind social value systems. "The Chinese will not listen," he said. "There is no talking with them.... They are certain their program is right, and attack whatever disagrees with it." He was referring to the Chinese genocide of Tibet—the destruction of its people, its culture, and its environment for the value program known as "modernization." "They destroy Tibet and call it progress."

We know that human groups can be organized to perform the most heinous actions on a systematic basis, fully confident that what they do is necessary, and for an ultimate good. Some think that all of these actions merely represent a ruling-class problem. An ascendant group reaps privileges and demands that everyone else continue the program that yields these special payoffs. That analysis does not, however, go deep enough to comprehend the operation of a *value program* across class lines.

In the pure-type case, which will be our definition of a value program, all people enact its prescriptions and functions as presupposed norms of what they ought to do. All assume its value designations and value exclusions as givens. They seek only to climb its ladder of available positions to achieve their deserved reward as their due. Lives are valued, or not valued, in terms of the system's differentials and measurements. All fulfil its specified roles without question and accept its costs, however widespread, as unavoidable manifestations of reality. In the strange incoherence of the programmed mind, the commands of the system are seen as both freely chosen *and* as laws of nature, or God. Those who are harmed by the value program are ignored, or else blamed for falling on its wrong side, because its rule is good and right. Its victims must, it is believed, be at fault. A value program's ideology is in great part devoted to justifying the inevitability of the condition of the oppressed.

This is a common pattern that holds across nations, classes, races, and individuals. From ancient caste systems to contemporary genocides of "development," we can see the life-blind destructions of value programs in motion holding entire peoples in thrall. But it is not "human nature" that is the problem. The problem is not in how we are constructed, but in the inert repetition of the mind, a condition that does not question socially conditioned value programs.

To be indoctrinated is to internalize a structure of thinking by habitual repetition, allowing for no question, alternative, or critical exposure. Typically, people carrying on inside a closed value order do not recognize what they are part of, largely because the demands of that order are incessantly routinized as the requirements of daily life and presupposed as "the way things are" and "must be." It may also be dangerous, or at least risky, to question a value regime at all, even when people say "everyone is free to speak." The non-conformer is stigmatized as being against the social order. Often—and here is the basic confusion again—the value regime's prescriptions are not considered as *values* at all, but are thought to be even more basic than ethical standards, like physical laws. At the same time they are also thought to be freely chosen by the virtuous. So, to be free, one must stand up against whatever opposes the conventional values. This sort of thinking is a contradiction, but the contradiction is not noticed. People are apt to believe that a practice is simultaneously free, expresses a law of nature, and is ordained by divine authority. The incoherence of these assumptions of a value program cannot register *within* it, because its nature is to be closed to any possibility that it could be wrong. This is a strange and fateful pattern of humankind, a herd-pattern operating beneath consciousness, a pattern that bedevils history and civilization. But it is not inalterable, or immutable. It is always an unexamined value system.

Values, when joined into an overall structure of thinking, whether conscious or largely unconscious in formation, make up a value system. A value system connects together goods that are affirmed and bads that are repudiated as an integrated way of thinking and acting in the world. For example, we can begin a life-grounded value system by affirming clean air and effective regulations to protect it as good, and repudiating preventable practices of releasing life-poisoning effluents as bad. So far, providing the value system is life-grounded, we will see nothing that can go wrong with it.

But suppose the value or ethical system holds that a certain ethnic group is superior and another group inferior. Suppose it then assigns certain people rights and excludes other people on the basis of this first major premise of value. We are apt to criticize such a value system as itself bad. To do so, we have to expose it first, because racists and other group supremacists usually pretend that they are guided by other values, such as "freedom" or "western civilization." A value system surrounds itself with an armour of protective rationalizations, purporting to hold certain values while actually holding to others. We have to penetrate to this underlying program of value, to uncover it beneath the stories it propounds. We have to expose its underlying operating principles. This is what it "truly means."

Let us consider a more subtle example. In the "dynamic new economies of Southeast Asia," various newspapers and development journals report, the World Bank, the United Nations' National Development Bank, U.S. development experts, national government ministries, and "bold local entrepreneurs" are developing an "economic takeoff innovation." The innovation is prawn farming, which has already been established as a "major developing-world export" produced in coastal Asia, the Philippines, China, Taiwan, Thailand, Burma, southern Bangladesh, and India. In Vietnam bomb craters make ideal pond receptacles for prawn farming. Hundreds of thousands of hectares in these countries are devoted to "the pink gold." The trade has already captured "80 percent of the world market," and "exports have soared" to hundreds of millions of dollars of "needed foreign currency earnings." According to one report, "Profits for producers are ten times higher than they had been in growing rice in the same fields."[1]

All the basic guidelines of the global market value system are realized in these initiatives: efficiency of factor allocation, comparative advantage, increased export earnings, rise in market share, increased GDP performance and annual incomes, and, above all, vastly increased returns on investment in an area of chronic underinvestment.

In this case, as long as one stays within the money parametric of this value system, who could quarrel with its claim of great success? But problems invisible to this value system remain real for the lives and life-systems reduced and destroyed by it, whether they are factored into its structure of value judgement or not. In fact, what really occurred here on the deeper level of life's well-being is a story of loss and disaster. Most of the highly fertile soil of the sea coasts and Mekong Delta area allocated for the high-price prawn crops in eight densely populated countries was rapidly degraded and sapped of nutrients, oxygen, water-holding capability, and tree roots by repeated cycles of salt-water flooding. Ground water was polluted and rendered unsafe for drinking. Large-scale prawn plantations moved in with the support of tax-incentives for investment. They secured peasants' plots by rent or purchase, flooded the land, pressured peasants to sell their livestock so it did not consume prawn stocks, and moved on to other profitable sites as soon as the land was exhausted. Whether small-plot farmers had rented, sold, or used their own small plots for prawn farming in dynamically increased market activities and transactions, they were all left with desertified land to live on. It had been sown with salt as surely and destructively as if an invading army had done it deliberately as a punitive raid. Yet everything that transpired consistently expressed the market system's principles of preference and worth.

There was, moreover, "no government interference" and "no dependence of the poor on the state" in this process. There was "free movement of capital across past barriers" and "very strong profit showings." And, in general, there were no "barriers" or "obstacles" to "the maximization of shareholder value" or to the "freedom to move investment to wherever investors receive the most competitive returns." Throughout and after the life desolation of ecosystems and communities, the global market value program was fulfilled more or less perfectly.

What goes wrong in such a case? Nothing is decided or done in the entire sequence of money investment, market transactions, and profit returns that is a matter of "saying one thing and doing another." We are apt to think a value system goes wrong because there is a gap between what its agents and proponents claim to adhere to as values, and what they in fact *do*. That is not the problem here. The project complies with the doctrine's principles and carries them out to the letter. The problem is, rather, that the market metric does not include natural resources or self-subsistence plots as values in its value calculus. Goods that do not carry a price tag do not enter its value ledger. What the market *does* designate as value—money or its equivalent— is all that counts to its "bottom line." This value undergoes a spectacular rise by its investment in prawn farming. And so as far as its ethic goes, the entire process is clearly "bringing new prosperity and freedom to the peoples of the world."

Although human and ecological life has been devastated, these are "externalities" to the market value system. As long as investment capital continues to have "freedom of movement" across regions and borders and gains rapidly by the process, all is well in this value universe.

Is the life depredation in this example an unfortunate exception in the workings of the global market's "invisible hand"? The case fulfils the most basic principles of the value paradigm of the global market. There are no deviations or anomalies to their normal operation. So the underlying value question persists. Does this system of allocating scarce resources for production and profit contain a deep-structural blindness that is always at work in its value designations and exclusions? Are there defects—not of poor implementation, or of inconsistency and miscalculation, of political interference, or of social shortcoming, of unions or poor training, or of any other factor that advocates of this global paradigm of value rule might blame for failures—but of the *very market structure of value itself?*

These questions are not yet asked.

When we approach a value structure as global and as universally practised as "the market value system," with an immense edifice of technical experts, government ministries, national and international banks, transnational corporations, and international trade regimes all promulgating and implementing its prescriptions, we are faced by an especially difficult value program to investigate and question. Still it is important to make the effort to do this investigation, this questioning. If a value system is simply presupposed and obeyed as the given structure of the world that all are made to accept and serve, it can become systematically destructive without our knowing there is a moral choice involved.

In the case of a value system that governs our daily lives and the world as a whole, we need to understand the regulating principles in order to know what we are doing. We need to expose the guiding principles of work, association, distribution, and progress to reflective examination and question. This seems an obvious enough undertaking. It is the ancient move beyond "the unexamined life" long ago proposed by Socrates. It is, more basically, the way in which we become conscious beyond the instinct of a beast or the program of a machine. It is more than a question of individual self-understanding or a personal value code. It is a matter of a **social value code**, the form that human liberty takes in an entire community. With a **global value system**, it is the way of life that all of humanity adopts as the structure of its being. Without conscious reflection on this way of life—what it stands for and what it stands against—humans become merely functions of a blind value program.

Still, who is not bound by the value goal of "competing to find a place in the new international marketplace"? Who has yet examined the determining value system we are serving? What investigation has asked whether its overriding principles violate the most basic requirements of social and planetary life? "We didn't *know* what was going on" is a familiar refrain from past obedient conformities to "a new order." Yet, in that familiar case, the value program behind what was going on in this case was rapidly adopted by people as their own. The inhuman consequences they were complicit with followed from the value principles they triumphantly presupposed and obeyed. By and large, those who "did not know what was going on" accepted all the principles of value that played out as choreographs of mass life destruction. What is at work in such cases is a denial of consciousness at the most fundamental level—a resignation to the herd turns of a value program that is permitted to substitute slogans and conditioned reflexes for thought.

A vast and elaborate system of harm can follow from life-blind principles, but remain unrecognized as a value problem. The all-consuming energy to ensure that we succeed at a value program can exclude our ever questioning it. Since everyone knows that the "market" itself does not err, it follows that whatever life-reductive consequences flow from the implementation of its "fundamentals" must be "necessary costs." The only appropriate choice and action for both the individual and society, then, are to compete hard at fulfilling its demands to ensure that its harms fall elsewhere and not on one's own society or self.

When it is acknowledged or repetitively proclaimed that the global market is "brutally competitive," this is then, not conceived as a value problem, much less an issue to resolve in order to accept the value system that the market expresses. On the contrary, this "brutal" property of the market's processes and effects is seen as all the more reason to ruthlessly reorder society to succeed at its prescriptions. There is no escape from the circular reasoning that imprisons such a value system. One can observe the closed circuit at work daily in the discourse and first principles of such an ideology, and its metaphysic is that of the social value program. It is and must be because it is and must be because it is and must be.

From the standpoint of reason or common sense such a global value system ought to be of concern for all who live in this turning point of the world's evolution. But the value program behind the whole project remains assumed; it is the standard of all other values, and cannot itself be evaluated. If reason and common sense are themselves understood in its terms, there is no vantage point available to judge it as limited or wrong. Across nations, races, and classes, people are too preoccupied in meeting the demands of the system to be conscious of it as constituting their own frame of mind.

A value program's rule invariably alters the lives of different individuals and classes in different ways. Some become wealthy beyond limit, and many more starve. What is most interesting for the analysis of this social value system is that those who are oppressed by it aspire to exchange places with those who occupy positions of wealth. This general fact can be observed in the popularity of lotteries, which, if the best were to occur, would net their winners great sums of undeserved money-demand, becoming more and more unearned money-demand without end or limit. This is a phenomenon that ambiguates class analysis as an ultimate framework of understanding. It reveals that the stable determinants of motivation, the values at work, are similar across individuals and classes whose current interests may be diametrically opposed. All assume the value program determining their lives as a given ground of choice, whatever their position, if all are motivated to prefer its rewards for themselves. Such issues as others' desert, or need, or capacity fulfilment beyond this value of more money for themselves do not normally enter the value preference or judgement. The sequence of value, having ever more money for oneself if one can legally have it, is given as good, and all seek to be its exclusive beneficiaries. This is a symptom of a value program, which lies behind the phenomena of different positions within its distributions. It grounds and motivates across individual differences, classes, and opposite outcomes as a common value foundation, and is typically assumed as the structure of reality itself. For example, economists explicitly deny that any "value" judgement is at work in their analyses, even though they presuppose a value system in every step of analysis they make. Since it is a value program that is at work here, operating beneath consciousness like a system of conditioned reflexes or mechanical function, it follows that there can be no consciousness of it as a value system. It is presupposed in the same way that a physical law is presupposed, and we will see that this is how economists conceive of the market's conventions.

Overthrowing the ruling occupants of these positions does not change the value program. Others replace the favoured occupants. They continue to conform to the value program, which itself continues to be presupposed as given, and cuts across class or other divisions. The life-blind program will continue in another articulation, no less blind to life value and its intrinsic requirements.

There is a mind-set and fixed assumption that the market is the best known form of society, and therefore whatever occurs in accordance with its requirements is bound to be the best we can hope for. But the *global market* is by no means the same as "the market" as it is represented. To reduce all alternatives to a single option is another marker of a value program. The global market is not the classical *capitalist market* from which it derives, as we will see. In turn, a capitalist market has almost nothing in common with a *producers' market*. These three very different types of market have evolved and diverged over centuries into entirely distinct types of socioeconomic forms. The last two kinds of market are different forms of life in every significant characteristic.

Few true producer markets survive in the industrialized world other than as exotic tourist attractions. They have been replaced with non-producer "chains" and "supermarkets," terms intimating a different order of life. In a producers' market, individual vendors produce the goods they or their representatives are selling, usually as a family or an intimate circle. They produce goods for personal purchase and derive their income from the difference between their sum costs and their sum prices. No single defining feature of this traditional kind of market applies to a "chain supermarket." Even the use of money as an exchange medium is different in form: "pocket money" is the medium of the producers' market; and banks or credit-created loans are the basic medium of the capitalist market.

The principles of the local food and craft market in which producer and seller are one and the same could hardly be more dissimilar in nature from the capitalist market. Goods sold are the self-made, individual product of the vendor. The "profit" is not derived from capital invested, but from the sale of the direct producer's own labour embodied in the product sold. The article sold, in turn, is not prepackaged or advertised. It is brought to market direct from its place of growth or creation. It is, perhaps, fresh food or skilled handicrafts. It is for human need, not for demand-created want. Its site of sale is not on privately owned property, but in a public place shared with others. Its good expresses local culture and conditions and is not homogeneous across regions and nations. Prices are immediately comparable and negotiable on a face-to-face basis. Relations of transaction connect to a web of community, where all can be seen without a door or fence between. And, perhaps most significantly of all, the sellers of the producers' market are the opposite of capitalists in one essential respect. They live by their own productive work, rather than from the returns on money, loans, or stock ownership.

The use of the term "the market" for an ancient and transcultural form of local social life, as well as for the corporately structured competition for capital and profit in a borderless global economy, is a value confusion of such magnitude that it is metaphysical in nature. But the distinction between near opposites is consistently repressed in economic models, classrooms, and the corporate media and actively cultivated in public representations and value appeals. This pervasive pattern of inversion of meaning is inherent in the theory and practice of the global market. It is the power train between an underlying value program and people's understanding of its meaning and implications that drives the wheels of its social acceptance. The continuous inversion of reality and representation, which we will observe ahead, begins with the very concept of "the market" itself.

"I had to leave France to study man," the anthropologist Claude Lévi-Strauss once said, as if being inside one's society of everyday life made comprehension difficult. Perhaps Lévi-Strauss recognized a peculiar fact. Presupposing and identifying with the value system in which one has been indoctrinated day in and day out as a native member of a society form a mental block against recognizing it as a value system, just as the fish cannot recognize the sea. The value system is presupposed as the structure of being, and so impartial observation of it from a standpoint of exposing its inner logic of determination requires an act of philosophical excavation. This block to a critical understanding of one's own social value system is a transcultural problem. It militates against reflective thought the more that any alternative to the ruling value order is inconceivable to the normalized mindset. Social members can be so constituted by this social system of which they are cultural products that each person's own very meaning and identity are framed by the value order that everyone has learned to think in terms of. Each person sees and interprets within its frame of valuation as both onlooker and recipient. Each presupposes its goods of achievement and bads of failure as both evaluator of others and evaluator of self. That is why I have chosen to use the term "value program." A value system or ethic becomes a *program* when its assumed structure of worth rules out thought beyond it.

In this day and age we tend to think that we are beyond subjugation to a social value program, that we are no longer tribal, but cosmopolitan "world citizens" in a global concourse of contrasting ways of life and social belief systems. But this is naive if a single value program rules across all different expressions of that concourse. What could such a value program be, it may be replied, when we are all so different as individuals and peoples? The test is: Who among these different individuals and peoples do not now presuppose the global market value system as normal? Who do not see its system of production and exchanges as what necessarily regulates one's work and afterhours, its goods as what one must seek more of, its functions as what one must perform to be accepted, and its requirements as what one must compete against others to fulfil?

Do we now live within a globally ritualized social value system, sanctified by the spells of the "invisible hand," "market miracles," and "sacrifices" in continuous revelation of a new world religion? Certainly religious conceptions and worldviews are the traditional organizing frameworks of social self-conception in terms of which a social order understands itself. Certainly since at least the Old Testament, the Vedanta, and the I Ching, individual members of society have comprehended themselves in terms of these larger social orders of meaning and fate. We may again imagine that we are beyond these collective superstitions of social order as God in the apparently postreligious, scientific realm of the global market. Here, surely, all such religious mists of illusion and superstitious beliefs in divine plans and magical, invisible forces are dissolved and disappear. But there is a theocratic character to the global market value system not recognized by its adherents, even as they continually invoke "the invisible hand." Is market ideology a covert religion whose theology is economics? Are its this-worldly rewards and punishments its moral disciplinary apparatus? Is there an awed fear to ever question the jealous God of its commandments? Do the market's underlying prescriptions and prohibitions form the ancient pattern of society worshipping its own structure as divine totem? This further, basic issue of an "economic theology" raises the question of religion itself as a level of analysis.

Some marginalized religious thinkers have, interestingly, been among the most ethically explicit critics of the global market value system. They have focused on this system's deprivations of those with the least. They have in their "preferential option for the poor" represented an ancient tradition of the Old Testament prophets and, in particular, the teachings of Jesus. Recent "social justice" and "liberation theology" movements have emerged on this basis. To feed the hungry, protect the homeless, clothe the naked, and, in general, care for those on the wrong end of the market's distribution system have formed the vital purposes of another kind of value system that is grounded in social identification or love. In the East as well contemporary Buddhist, Islamic, and Hindu "speakers for the oppressed" have challenged the market value system from a religious standpoint.

These vital sources of criticism of the global market value code are designated as "meddling in affairs about which they know nothing" or "communist" in inspiration. Stigmatizing any and all critics of a social value program is, as we know, a standard defence mechanism whereby an unexamined value program remains unexamined. If a value system has become closed, one dare not criticize its accepted principles of assigning payoffs or deprivations, lest one be put in league with the system's designated evil. All social value programs are instituted and reproduced by this age-old reaction pattern, which is, in turn, itself maintained by avoiding exposure to conscious reflection. This process of confining consciousness within the closed loop of a social value regime continues until it is recognized to be in contradiction with the clear testimony of reason and the senses. Whether by violent upheaval or cognitive recognition, the old mind-set eventually becomes open to question. Either its adherents adjust to life realities that the value system has excluded from view or they cease to be in touch with society's evolved levels of comprehension.

It is this system-bound blindness to destructive consequence that marks any value program as pathological. It rules out comprehension of the life-harms it causes by in some way not recognizing them as avoidable harms.

"When a firm makes a profit," declares the Holy Father, Pope John Paul II, "this *means* that productive factors have been *properly* employed and corresponding human needs have been satisfied."[2] The Holy Father proposes a general value claim closed to fact. Profit is good by definition. It uses "property" and it "satisfies needs" by the necessity of its authoritative declaration. The norm is the fact. What the Pope says is, in principle, just what is presupposed by professional economists and others who assume this value program as the social good. A firm's profit *means* "properly employed." A firm's profit *means* "satisfaction of human needs." Although evidence puts John Paul II's universal assertion into clear doubt, this is not an issue that disturbs the metaphysic of a value program. Its presupposition as true rules out what rebuts it. Since the norm is good, so also must be the fact that it validates. If we insist upon counterevidence—say, that the pursuit of profit in the actual world widely leads to a denial of human needs—the evidence itself is interpreted through the fixed value framework in a way that discredits the evidence and its bearer.

In this case, for example, "theologians of liberation" in the same church, such as Father Leonardo Boff, have argued vigorously for an essentially opposite claim—namely, that the profits of private corporations of all kinds across the world have precisely *not* employed the productive factor of society's labour and resources "properly" and have systematically ignored or violated the "human needs" of workers. The fact-charged view of the liberation theologians is that the conditions of over two billion people living under this value system are "a living social and human hell."[3]

As we know, the very essence of a value program entails an avoidance of any recognition of what might call it into question or refute it. In this case, not only factual grounds but also grounds of principle exist for rejecting the Pope's categorical assertion of profit's "satisfaction of human needs." How can a value system that seeks money profit for the self as its overriding motivation be consistent with the founder's injunction to the rich man to "take all that you have and give to the poor." Despite these factual and principled grounds for value doubts, the Vatican still rules against such questions. It denounces these value-critical voices as "deviations ... which use in an insufficiently critical matter, concepts borrowed from various currents of Marxist thought."[4] The Vatican simply expels from the realm of what can be discussed the issue of human needs as not being satisfied by the for-profit use of productive factors. The response does not include the evidence of contradiction between representation and reality. Rather, it relocates the problem in those who assert that it exists. It puts that displacement into effect by the standard mechanism of stigmatization. "Marxist" in those societies where liberation theology challenges the established oligarchies is a term that can mean death to those who are so labelled, including liberation theologians.

The four important forms of inquiry that are particularly pertinent here—the metadiscipline of philosophy, the target discipline of economics, the power-mapping discipline of political science, and the spiritual discipline of theology—are all principal allies in a comprehensive analysis of this subject-matter. To bring the full metaphysic, internal logic and power-apparatus of the global market's value system to light, we must move freely across subject-borders. Still, a central problem leads us beyond the humanities and social sciences altogether. This is the medical-biological paradigm of "the immune system" and the patterns of "pathogenic invasion" it recognizes and responds to.

In raising the issue of "social disease" we may immediately wonder: What is "normal" for a social body, and what is "pathogenic"? Is there a principle of distinction between these conditions of life that is not merely subjective? The evolved value judgements of medical science between disease and health provide a life-ground for answering such questions. In most cases, we know the objective differences between being afflicted by a disease and not being afflicted. The objective distinctions of medical science regarding healthy and diseased states provide, for the most part, uncontroversial value bearings across individuals and cultures. At the bottom of these transcultural distinctions between the good of health and the bad of disease is a basic value fact. People in general, in all social orders, prefer to be fully alive, and they perform countless functions and avoidances to ensure they continue that way. There is no "cultural relativism" about whether unpolluted water to drink or freedom from hunger or having a place to sleep is of value or disvalue. This list of universal values and disvalues is, in the final analysis, about as long as all the conditions we can name as being necessary to the preservation and growth of our embodied being.

To examine a social value system, then, we need to look to the actual effects of its implementation to check how well or badly it scores on these factors of life. If its harms to life are serious and systemic, then we must ask why its rule of law does not prevent these systemic harms. But can "the rule of law" prevent them? All this requires deep-structural investigation. As the findings, arguments, and conclusions are developed here, it becomes clear that the law on all levels of governance, from local to national to international, is an essential framework of value diagnosis and resolution. It also becomes clear that distinctions between paper law and effective law, between subordinate law and overriding law, between what is legally regulated and what is not are basic to understanding the actual regulatory framework of global life as a whole. It is a commonplace that the rule of law is civilization's basic mode of protecting life, and—to this point—humanity's only collective way of limiting violations of it by private and self-serving interests. It is commonly agreed that no human actions or agents should be "above the law." But do we know whether the life values that have been traditionally safeguarded by law are now, in fact, still protected by law? If there has been a sea-change of confusion in the world between the requirements of the market and of society's common interest in which legal systems have shared, where are the footings of social restraint to represent the interests of life that the market does not compute? These questions touch on the core of life security of every state in the global market—but are not yet publicly asked.

Distinguishing between Representation and Reality

We might think that, since government is society's empowered representative of "the common interest," its proper function is to confront and regulate any social value program whose operations or consequences may come into conflict with the common life interest. This should be an established vocation of government on which we can rely. But, here again, we find that governments and their leaderships now assume that the value system of the global market is to be the proper order of social organization, and that societies must be made to adapt to this order as the needs and demands of the global market require. The market is not now seen as a structure to serve society. Rather, society is seen as an aggregate of resources to serve the global market.

This pattern of confusing the common interest's requirements with those of the price-and-profit-driven global market is of the greatest possible importance and significance. If the common interest is not protected and advanced by government as distinct from the global market's demands, then what is left to serve the shared life-interests of society? What becomes of community goods which are not priced and by their nature can only be safe-guarded or provided by government? There are certainly such goods—enforced regulations to preserve the air, water, and life-environment from fouling and exhaustion, for example, and social programs to protect people's lives and development from starvation without employment, or illiteracy without public education. All of these are public goods that the self-regulating market by itself is in principle not able to provide by its price system. If government-funded institutions and operations are not devoted to this vast life-sphere, which is outside the global market's capabilities to serve because it always sells for a price and a profit, then what takes its place? What publicly accountable institution with jurisdiction across a society can provide and protect this great and complex civil life-fabric evolved over centuries? The answer is, there is none. For not one public good ever has been or can be provided by profit-seeking investors by the nature of its value system. If powerful special interests seeking only their own wealth-security and gains are dominant, a condition in which humanity almost always finds itself, then what is there but independent, sovereign public authority answerable to the common interest to rein them in and to provide where they cannot? What assurance can there be in the global market that any good whatsoever that is not profitable to produce will survive? These are not questions that the market value system asks, or has answers for. But if the questions are not asked, in their absence we lose all awareness that there is a problem.

The proof positive that a value program has become the actual sovereign of society, and the state an instrument of it, is the refusal of public authority to decide or to implement or even to uphold a law or institution in the public interest except as it conforms to this value program's demands. The proof positive becomes more and more evident the more that, to satisfy such demands, citizens of a society or their sustaining environment lose a previously enjoyed life-security and well-being.[5]

Before eventual collapse or overthrow, the most extreme damages to civil and environmental life are rationalized away, and even justified in carrying out the demands of the "necessary" program, which is assumed *a priori* as the properly ordering framework of society. As such, no end of depredations and destructions that the value program wreaks upon life can register as problems with it. These problems, on the contrary, are interpreted from its standpoint as arising from people failing to adjust to its requirements. Whatever fails to comply with these requirements must therefore undergo further abolition, eradication, discipline, and restructuring to ensure the fulfillment of the program's fundamentals. The value program becomes in this way society's final ruler and judge, and the life of society's peoples and their environment become, in effect, enslaved as its instrumental and disposable functions.

A life-blind social value program sustains itself by uncritical identification of its demands with the public good, including the good of those who resist its imposition. In this case, what is good for the market's expansion and control of civil life is assumed to be good for society. The good of one is equated with the good of the other at the very base of this value system's assumptions. Actual life needs and requirements not taken into account in its value measures, accordingly, disappear from view.

If in the past, it was, "We must burn your body, but it is for the salvation of your immortal soul," today, it is, "We must axe your supports of life, but it is for the good of making the economy competitive."

If a value program's principles are disconnected from life's needs—whether of citizens for nourishing food and human conditions of work, or a civil society for clean air and biodiverse surroundings—then a social value program can become deadly in its impact. For its nature is to rule out any feedback loop of correction by its prior assumption that it is the only normal and acceptable system of social life-organization.

It may seem quixotic to think that a value program now embodied in transnational trade regimes overriding national law and prescribing only obligations of market access, price, and money demand could ever find its way back home again to human and planetary life's intrinsic requirements. It is difficult to see where any accountability or obligation to human, civil, and natural life beyond turning money into more money for money lenders and investors still exists for this value system. What can unlock it, and bring it back under the control of the life code of value? Beneath the questions and the arguments there is a still wider base upon which this discourse depends, an underlying life-ground that has been with us all along, resting beneath any value program. It is the connection of life to life's requirements as a felt bond of being that crosses boundaries of membranes, classes, peoples, and even species. This life value ground is at bottom what reacts against pathological social value programs with their depredatory sequences of value demand even when they are socially instituted. The defining feature of value programs is that they are blind in principle to the harm they cause. Only something deeper than their socially conditioned framework of perception can recognize and respond to their assaults.

We may think there is no such "value ground" or "life-code," complying predictably with a value program that rules out any alternative to itself. But the irrepressible expressions of the life-ground and its sequence are familiar. They erupt in the face of the most pervasively conditioned social doctrines. We cannot bear to see the bomb victims even if we are told their plight came to "protect the free world." We are disturbed by the sight of malnourished and homeless families, even if we are instructed that they must "adapt to the new reality." We react viscerally against torture and systematic violation of human life. The sight of rainforests being razed, toxic effluents flooding into lakes, rivers, and oceans, oil-tanker spills and pillaged life-habitats, species rendered extinct or ravaged in countless masses by routine operations of a ruling value system—all these sear us to the core of our being, even if they result in GDP gains. Something about destroying life's vital ranges in any form demands human concern and response, even when it does not seem to touch our private interests directly. Certainly we may learn not to see or to connect in this human-natural way, and our systems of public communication may condition us accordingly. But, sooner or later, we are electrified into action. This nameless value ground develops as our humanity builds, and has done so for millennia. This shared value ground is lost, however, to the extent that a value regime successfully conditions and overrides it, depriving it of connections to the wider community. This is the value malaise that is now felt across the world, the "moral crisis of civilization" we name with no clear comprehension of its roots.

The "life-ground" is the standpoint of this investigation. It locates debate in concrete regions and ranges of people's lives, places in which the elements of everyday existence are deprived and people are terrorized by relations of power and the value system they express. By reconnecting values and normative inquiry to the disciplining base of the real world and, beneath that, its regulating value system, we re-enter the life-field in which received discourses of "freedom" and "democracy" are laundered out of sight.

This is a "reconnective research," the paradigm of understanding required to pull together the intelligible unity of what afflicts us, and what can be done about it. We often forget that reality happens in a connected way in order to happen at all. The problem is to follow its organizing pattern across boundaries of unseeing.

Just as the life-ground of value is expressed in "the life-code and sequence," so what we call "the civil commons" is the instituted bearer of this life-code. The nature of the civil commons can be expressed as follows: *It is society's organized and community-funded capacity of universally accessible resources to provide for the life preservation and growth of society's members and their environmental life-host.* The civil commons is, in other words, what people ensure together as a society to protect and further life, as distinct from money aggregates. But global market doctrine not only does not distinguish these opposed values. They are treated as identical values. For even the sceptical, the civil commons is the only alternative for survival. But whereas the market offers commodities for a price to those able to pay, the civil commons guarantees access of all to the goods required to safeguard and advance life-capacities. These are wholly distinct and often opposed logics of value. The civil commons acts directly to serve and fulfil vital life needs and capacities by its nature, and does so by ensuring the universal accessibility of goods that protect and enable human and environmental life. The healthy family is a prototype of this pattern; but its principles become universalized with the true progress of civilization.

For example, public health care and education for all people of a society without barriers of social caste or market cost are major institutions of a developed civil commons today. They are shared life-capacities and—so far as they satisfy the criterion of the civil commons—they enable all of its members to flourish as individuals on their common life-base. Universally accessible benefits of society as it evolves into ever higher levels are so basic to a truly human existence that we are apt not to see what we are standing on and living from as individuals—collective sewage disposal and sanitation facilities across society, water and power installations to serve every dwelling, life-protecting regulations and inspections of all building structures and workplaces, society-wide pollution monitors, evaluation, and controls, central squares, sidewalks, bridges, and other universally accessible routes, social safety protections, laws and personnel to serve all citizens and residents, public airwaves, communication sites open to everyone, free access to parks, play areas, and wilderness, libraries, postal services and public services across distances that the market cannot serve, social assistance to the unemployed, the poor, and the old. The civil commons is the vast social fabric of unpriced goods, protecting and enabling life in a wide and deep seamless web of historical evolution that sustains society and civilization.

From the standpoint of the civil commons, the standard disjunction between individual rights on the one hand and community rights on the other hand is a shallow and false opposition. The individual's right to the resources of life—health-care, learning, clean air and water, and so on—is grounded in the community's ability to provide them. None of this need registers on a value program for which the only values are those that can be transacted in the market. As the life-ground that gives us our shared air, sunshine, water, plant life, and earth is privatized, polluted, or depleted to "keep the economy going," the civil commons is ever more needed to preserve and enable life, not to "save costs" for market commodity transactions. In such cases we see the conflict in principle between the logic of the civil commons and of the market value system.

The roots of the civil commons predate the market by millennia. The civil commons is, indeed, found in the origins of language itself. We secure and develop language through education, whether informal or formal. Through literacy, cultural heritage, and the opening word across the community fabric, the civil commons gives individuals the opportunity to express themselves—and it does so without a market exchange required for any step of its life-advancing process. Language provides access to the shared field of meaning and communication upon which our species' raised plane of consciousness depends. It is a universally accessible good whose resources, like all goods of the civil commons, enable the safeguarding and furthering of life without the mediation of market price or profit. This dynamic is lost on the market paradigm of value, and is defunded, privatized, instrumentalized, and, in general, ruled out of the market calculus as being of no value except as it promotes market activities.

The civil commons is, if we can see past the value program that now attacks it, the underlying life-organization of society. One might say that to attack the civil commons is to attack civilization itself and, beneath that, our common life-ground—individual, social, and environmental. But the civil commons is not recognized for what it is because the value program rules out universally accessible goods of life from its system of worth. In consequence, the value program now expropriates and attacks the civil commons at its edges, trunk, and roots, "privatizing," "axing," and "developing" so that its life-spaces and functions are stripped across society with no sense of loss. What is not recognized as being of value becomes valueless. Because the current market program cannot see past its own demands for ever more market activities of society, it cannot recognize the substance of what it annihilates.

This is a problem we have observed many times before in history—in, for example, the massive environmental depletions and collapses that have attended the great falls of past civilizations. Left behind, their historically celebrated triumphs are desertified landscapes. Environments cannot speak for themselves, so we must observe the inscription of their destruction in the facts. Babylonia, Egypt, Mesopotamia, the Indus Valley, Persia, South China, North Africa, the plains of India, Mexico: all were once fertile and forest-mantled grounds of species-rich life. All are now lifeless deserts, step by blind step stripped of their capacities to reproduce and differentiate by social value programs. Their bearers and leaders were—and still are as the process spreads—certain and complaisant of the necessity of their instituted patterns of life-rule. They declined to observe that razing and depleting the grounds of existence sooner or later has limits.

The plot is old, and always ruinous. One would have to be locked into the closed loop of the value program to fail to see such a pattern today, global in its sweep and powers. What Freud called the death instinct is, in macrocosm, a social value program, structured to avoid stimuli that do not fit it, compulsively reproduced at whatever cost to life is required to repeat its sequence. This death-compelling pattern of repetition is recognizable and preventible from the standpoint of the "life-code" and its social-bearer, the "civil commons." But authorities now regard the evolved resources of the world's civil commons to monitor, recognize, and respond to the advancing violations and despoliations of human life and its biophysical support systems by market-industrial culture as too great a "regulatory cost burden." They are thus defunded, unenforced, or institutionally dismantled to satisfy the value program. The stated goal is to "be competitive in the world market." What we will analyse as "the money-code and money-sequence" is the value program behind such declarations. Its "self-regulating" principles of "growth" and "development," we will see, entail violent consequences.

These life-harms only emerge to public consciousness in disconnected fragments and pieces. To connect these broken pieces into unitary pattern and to respond to their threat to social and environmental life-organization are, in the end, the collectively funded tasks of the civil commons. But authorities are increasingly stripping the civil commons of its financial support, scientific personnel, and powers to regulate the borderless private interests bearing the global market program. In this way, a social value system can close itself off against society's self-protective intervention and continue to depredate local and planetary life by its unaccountable sequences of utilization and expansion.

The underlying logic of the global market's value imperialism is simple enough. Because advocates believe that its system provides for people's lives better than any other that can exist—which is every value program's master assumption—then it follows that any other value ground or formation that is other to or resists it must be overridden. This metalogic of the global market program can be tested across all its representations, with astonishing implications. One of its unrecognized implications is the liquidation of the civil commons itself, a matter of profound significance. This value entailment is, however, presupposed rather than exposed or questioned. The underlying premise is that the "private sector is efficient," whereas "the government is inefficient." Since this premise is not qualified, it leads to the conclusion that whatever the market does is good, and whatever government does is bad, unless it can be shown to serve the market. On the basis of this unrecognized value metaphysic, it follows that whatever government does that does not serve the market is best swept away for "greater market efficiency."

There is clearly a systematic pathology to such a value system. The mainstream assumption is that this system of life-organization is something we must all adjust to for our future prosperity. Yet understanding the pattern at work here does not by itself provide a cure. We also need to explore "solutions" or, rather, resolutions to this unrecognized value derangement.

The global market value system is driven by a set of principles that overrules the deeper life-code. The life-code sequence remains available to us still, but is under severe stress and challenge. Our condition is not hopeless, but it is serious and misunderstood. Socially connective recognition, response, and development beyond a life-destructive value program has occurred for societies in the past, and eventually they have reordered themselves to overcome the most virulent and closed patterns of social organization. Examples are the absolute right of kings and oligarchies, the genocide of indigenous peoples as a given law, human slavery as a desirable organization of social production, and the subjugation of girls and women as the "natural" property of men.

Even today within many social groups, these value programs remain unexamined structures of premise for the closed loop of judgement. At least two of these life-destructive programs are not incompatible in principle with the market value system itself. Nevertheless, the action of non-market values at work in civil society have largely repudiated and abolished these structures of social life-organization. Exposed as value programs of terrorization and destruction, these structures were recognized as grotesque deformations and, in time, responded to as such. In every case, their pathological patterns were recognized from inside the regimes of their value ordering, even when they were pervasively represented in moralizing terms as forms of "freedom," "civilization," and "progress" (the very categories of final worth we hear today). But how in actual practice we could reform these value programs, which their adherents always militantly presuppose as forms of the Good, is never a matter we can foretell. From the outset, though, we can always act in consciousness from the life-ground we bear as evolved humans, recognizing these value programs for what they are.

This recognition comes only with difficulty, because it requires freedom from the habituated mind-set of the social system. No action is more demanding of human thought and will across daily life, and activists often disastrously overlook the depth of structural hold at work within social value programs.

Choices are not even raised in the social field of a presupposed value program if they conflict with its premises, which are assumed without question. The caste superior cannot recognize the choice of equality, because it conflicts with his deeper presupposition of inherited rank. The market believer cannot recognize the choice of universally accessible life goods, because it conflicts with his prior assumption that people should always pay a market price. The grounding rule of the market, self-maximizing choice, is indeed attributed to "human nature" itself. The people who do directly reject it are considered irrational or dissembling, and in this way a program of value rules out whatever is not consistent with it in the most casual operations of consciousness.

The principles are interlocked. Challenge the theoretical basis to the system—that human nature itself seeks to exchange to acquire more for the self—and the reply is that this works to everyone's benefit by the "invisible hand" of maximally efficient market allocation. Challenge the ideal of "equilibrium" between supply and demand as a theoretically invented state that never in fact exists, and the reply is that econometric equations are necessary to portray the relationships between variables. Question the failure in market theory and practice of any distinction between money-demand and need, and the answer is that this is a normative issue for moralists and politicians. Let ethical advocacy or political policy become involved in determining economic planning to overcome this chasm between market demand and life-requirement, and the response is to denounce "interference in the market." Argue that the unpriced goods of the environment are laid waste by a value program that excludes their value from its metric, and the rejoinder is that these costs are "externalities." The rightness of the value principles that explain the system to itself are always assumed as self-evidently true. Counterargument can be dismissed as a failure to understand their meaning. Another principle always rationalizes these fixed assumptions as immune to any evidence or reason opposing them. This tendency "locks in" a value program, which forever regresses back into itself as a self-certifying system.

Exposing the value programs we live within at the social level of life-organization is a requirement of value citizenship. In a period when computer programs determine the arrangements of the material world, the failure to examine and question the social value program behind these countless restructuring programs is a kind of collective enslavement. If we do not question the master program that drives and directs the entire elaborating system, what else can we call it? If all of us are subject to its rule, and we all presuppose that we cannot alter it, in what way are we not subjugated to its order, like so many servomechanisms?

Class analysis conceives of this subjection as a situation in which a minority rules, and the majority of society produces a surplus (or profit). On the one side are the owning exploiters, and on the other the non-owning exploited. This dualizing diagnosis contends that this class oppression is to be overthrown by a revolutionary reorganization of society.

However essential it is to understanding the implementing logic of ruling value programs, class analysis does not go deep enough. What joins people's mind-sets, motivations, and compliance across classes remains unexposed—even though its underlying program is at work everywhere, structuring self-identity itself. The position a person occupies within a value program's grid of functions and roles may indeed be one of gross class exploiter or grossly exploited, or many other possible positions between. But individuals within these various roles still accept and defend the system as necessary and given, seeking to hold or gain a more advantageous position within its structure.

Across this overarching order rules a deeper structure of social meaning, an underlying common value framework that does not superimpose on top of class relations and is the opposite of "superstructural." On the contrary, it is the regulating, order of selection and exclusion, in terms of which class divisions are formed and historically articulated.

Thus the value sequence of the market comes to underlie the operations of contesting class demands and politics. The name of the game of the money sequence of value is to maximize money or money-equivalent holdings as a good in itself as a condition in which life's requirements do not restrain choices by any recognized override of value. Although countless upsurges occur against the pattern's manifestations, they do not challenge the value ground. The value system instructs people to see their preferences as "rational" and proclaims the value ground's unlimited expression as "liberty." Class divisions in the distribution of payoffs and punishments, and positions and powers in the competition for this good, are clearly at work. But underneath these differences is, again, the unexamined framework of value presupposed by all as normal: an automatized preference to seek and accept more money as an unquestioned good, and to rule out less as non-sensical.

This prevailing program of thought and behaviour can have absurd as well as harmful consequences. For example, the resulting mind-set can demand simultaneously that governments must pay off their debts and citizens must pay lower taxes. The debts, by definition, result from the government having insufficient current revenues to discharge them. Lower taxes, by definition, reduce the revenues that government receives. To demand or prescribe both is a self-contradiction, yet that is what governments and voters across North America have been doing. The first principle of the market value system, self-maximization in money value terms, repels such wider-order contradictions from its calculus.

"It is a new world out there," counsel the adapters to the requirements of this value regime. "We must compete." The pattern is indeed world-wide. In the European Union itself, the historical ground of the civil commons' universally accessible goods of life security and human development, the same program of value is now being implemented not by tax cuts, but by the more systematic normative device of international treaty. "Structural adjustment" in the new reality is imposed by the terms of the monetary union of the Maastricht Treaty, which is being reordered to require on pain of penalty of .2 to .5 per cent of GDP that governments downsize their social budgets under a new iron ceiling of deficit-ratio-to GDP of 3 per cent.[6] In predictable accordance with this global value program's principles of worth, the requirements of life have no pride of place in this transcontinental prescription. Rather, what rules, even in European statecraft, are the requirements of the money sequence of value as the ultimate regulating principle of value. What does not serve this value program must be reduced and eliminated—even if it is the public employment of citizens at socially enabling, non-profit tasks, the protection of the lives of those without money demand, the educational development of the young to more comprehensive understanding for its own sake, and a more biodiverse and toxin-free environment. These life-goods, so far as they are ensured across a society, require commodious tax revenues to fund them. Since they do not sell in the market for a price or profit, they are beyond this value system's understanding. By the internal logic of the doctrine, therefore, they are predictably cut back by its prescriptions with no limit and conceived as "unaffordable." As more money is then made available for market activities by extinguishing the funding of public life-goods by the market law of selection, all who think and act in terms of this value program conclude that society is more efficient and freer—even if ever more of its citizens are unemployed, the culture is reduced to mass-marketing television, and life is lived in increasingly impoverished life-conditions.

In the current global market, this freedom from requirements to protect or enable human and environmental life includes the right to invest for transformations of money into more money without any productive outcome. Investment in the speculative or "paper" economy is now many times greater than in the production of goods and services. The market value program considers this redirection of investment desirable because money sequence returns can quickly bypass the complicating barriers of the life as the middle-term between money input and output. If returns beyond investment can be maximized with no employment of labour or output of use values involved, it follows that a complete decoupling of the money economy from society in international cyberspaces of ever more voluminous circuits of money gain is a self-evident choice-path of value. The sea-change movement of society's capital wealth into this more "rational" sequence of the money code of value is, therefore, predictable once the technical means of its pursuit are made available and governments release the market into the free movement of capital unconstrained by external regulation. This freedom of the money sequence of value from government interference, in turn, is assured if the requirements of the common interest and the market are seen to be identical. The key to comprehending what is otherwise difficult to compute from a life standpoint is that these upheavals in world organization all follow as predictable entailments of this global value program.

The articulation of this closed system of choice reveals an unmistakable bias towards those who live from turning money into more money. This is the structure of the "money code and sequence," and it underlies the motives and personalities of its temporary occupants who variously express its more fundamental ground. The value program itself is the problem to track and investigate, to confront and alter, rather than its passing phenomena and bearers. Its hold is much deeper than those in its leading positions, who may be most of all enslaved to its prescriptions. Its ruling precepts and logic are our quarry here, and what is worth bearing in mind is the acceptance of its value-ground across economic classes. Even the majority who are never bearers of the greatest transformations of money into more money in this sequence's endlessly expanding rounds will automatically comply and affirm the rules of its game if they are positioned to receive its payoffs. It is precisely this unexamined acceptance of a social value game and, thereby, its mode of organization, investment, distribution, and reward that exercises the deepest hold on society. It reaches beneath its winner and loser divisions into the organizing framework of individual and social normality itself, and the frame of mind presupposed by acceptable choice. Such a condition can give rise to an unlimited stripping away of social and environmental life-organization, with no recognition by those operating within its value system of any deeper problem outside its internal losses and rewards.

Social life, like organic life, can evolve through pathogenic challenge. It can develop a permanent "resistance" to pathological or life-destructive value sets by the processes of social recognition. Here too, the value bearings of social bodies can underlie class divisions. But is this evolving "resistance" to a value program's past disorders now in the throes of programmed reversal?

If people uncritically identify this value system with the common interest of society, the more it is "free from any external interference" the freer it is to revert to the reversal of history and civilization itself as "structural rigidities" in the way of the market's "unfettered growth."

Is this the pattern that is now unfolding in front of us? With unlimited technological resources, mass communication powers to propagate its necessity, and transboundary prerogatives of purchase and sale to overcome all past drawings of the line against it, what holds back such an unconditional program of value from total occupation of global society?

From life-organization at the cellular level to the macrobodies of national and transnational life-regulation, we can discern a common theme of survival and development. There is always a mode of life-and-death distinction between life *representation* and life *reality*. At the cellular level, for example, the carcinogenic pattern of growth and development represents itself to the surrounding cell community as sound and normal. In reality, however, it has no commitment to any organic function of the body, but only to its own autonomous repro-duction and spread. A body becomes diseased when it does not rec-ognize this fateful distinction between life-representation and life itself, a condition that certain fashions of thought now accept as our ines-capable lot. Because the life-order does not recognize this difference, it does not respond to the element that invades it and appropriates its nutriments for its own replication and spread. It does not interfere with what is accepted as a self-regulating reproduction of the system. The pathogenic pattern in this way can eventually take over one vessel and organ after another of the life-body with its non-contributing growth, and cumulatively impede, deplete, and destroy the vital capacities of the life-host to function as an effectively interconnected and mutually productive whole. The entire process of this carcinogenic invasion and spread, in other words, depends on the life-body's systemic failure of recognition and response.

A value program can, we will find, operate in this way as a pathogenic code and sequence on the social level of life-organization, increasingly blocking, depleting, and invading vital life functions of the social and environmental life-host in reproductive fulfilment of its own life-disconnected sequence of demand. Here too, the whole process of cumulative invasion and breakdown depends on the failure of recognition of the distinction between representation and reality. The pathogenic program is not seen for what it is. The reproductive marker of the disease is not displayed to the life-community. The bonding of surrounding members to recognition of the destructive sequence does not occur. The communication of the message of the pathogenic reproduction is not disseminated across the life-system. The response of the life-community is not set in motion to act in unison on behalf of the requirements of the life-organization. One after another the lesion and failure of the life-fabric occurs. The crises continue until a decisive, overwhelming intervention on behalf of the life-code and life-sequence emerges, or the system eventually collapses.

A cardinal, underlying theme runs through this book. Are the *representations* of the market system true to the world and their own claims? Or is their *reality* different from and opposed to their appearance? In the age-old distinction between appearance and reality lies the meta-argument of this investigation.

Notes

1. I am indebted to John Stackhouse's reportage in "Prawn farming Holds False Promises of Instant Riches," *The Globe and Mail*, July 13, 1996, p.A1.

2. Michael Novak, *Business as a Calling: Work and the Examined Life* (Glencoe, Ill.: Free Press, 1996), quoted in David Olive, "Michael Novak the Profit Prophet," *The Globe and Mail*, book review, July 13, 1996. Emphasis added. One might wonder how John Paul II's claim here is consistent with his assertion that "rights of workers are more important than the maximization of profits." The answer seems to be that under his conceptualization of profit, workers' and owners' rights cannot conflict. The quote above is from Gregory Baum, *Compassion and Solidarity* (Toronto: Anansi, 1992), p.94.

3. Leonardo Boff reports the following figures: according to conservative estimates, five hundred million people are starving; one billion persons live in absolute poverty; five hundred million live with no work and a per capita income of $150 a year; and two billion people have no dependable water supply. Boff, *Introducing Liberation Theology* (Mary Knoll, N.Y.: Orbis Books, 1986), pp.2-3.

4. Leonardo Boff, *Church: Charism and Power: Liberation Theology and the Institutional Church* (New York: Crossroad Press, 1986), p.vii.

5. There seem to be countless daily examples of this ruling presupposition of value expressed by governmental and quasi-governmental bodies who plan reductions of public goods of every kind—to fulfil the more ultimate and sovereign good of "competing in the international marketplace." A less visible but no less telling manifestation of this value program is within the adjudications of higher courts of justice themselves. In the Ontario Court of Justice in 1996, for example, judges agreed that whatever the rightness of the claim of the Lubicon to their unceded territory, and

whatever the destruction of their livelihood and culture that would be imposed by deforesting their traditional lands by commercial logging (in this case, by a Japanese transnational corporation, Daishowa Inc.), the Lubicon's right to boycott the purchasers of the logging corporation's paper-bag products "must give way to the appellants' right to trade." Ontario Court of Justice, Divisional Court, in *Daishowa Inc. versus Friends of the Lubicon*, Court file 418/95, October 1995, p.11. This decision was reversed on appeal by the Ontario Court of Justice in April, 1998. Daishowa responded that "the land would be logged anyway." ("Memories of the Deal," *Globe and Mail*, April 16, 1998, p.A2.

6. "The Burdensome National Debt," *The Economist*, Feb. 10, 1996, pp.68-69.

Part I
Behind the Invisible Hand

The Problem: A Question of Freedom

The Pursuit of Freedom: An Irony of History

History has a well-known habit of producing the opposite of what its justifying ideologies assert. The justifying representation of the world says it is "rational," or it is "Christian," or it is "free." The existing reality discloses that the world is ruled in an opposite way. We recognize this contradiction very well with societies distanced or opposed to our own, but we are inclined to assume that our society is somehow exempt. Social orders, in general, condition their inhabitants into not seeing what is there—for example, not seeing the suffering of the jobless or families who do not have enough food to eat, even if they number in the millions of our fellow citizens. This tendency not to see seems to increase the more what is not seen contradicts the accepted view that no alternative exists to the status quo.

Conflicts between justifying ideologies and the hard realities of social oppression are pervasive through history. Why does the gospel of love and sharing promoted by Jesus end in religious fundamentalists seeking more repression and money riches? How can the great classical thinkers of antiquity—Socrates, Plato, and Aristotle—introduce critical reason to humanity while all the while supposing that slavery for the majority is a necessary good for society? Why does the doctrine of the Buddha, which renounces attachment to the illusory self for boundless communion with all that lives, come to be the religion of state rulers who kill and torture their own citizens? What can account for the transformation of the doctrine of Karl Marx, which calls for the permanent liberation of humanity from bosses, into the ideology of some of history's most autocratic dictatorships?

The Postmodern Response

Postmodern thinkers have suggested a contemporary explanation to this problem that has had enormous intellectual appeal. Their position is that all doctrines pretending to be universal, necessary, and good for humanity are dictates of empowered dogma whose logic is to seek erasure of difference and plurality. In place of absolutist, immutable, and general structures of understanding or rule, they propose decentred autonomy of the local, the contingent, and the particular.

In the postmodernist or poststructuralist view, life and meaning are irreducibly perspectival, polyverse, and resistant to any necessary or obligatory order. To emancipate us from such reductive structures, they urge a radical opening to the diversity of our discourses and practices. This embrace of difference leaves behind all global doctrines and structures as so many forms of "terroristic totalitarianism."

Yet at the same time as the difference-affirming postmoderns boast of their contesting of all totalizing ideologies, the most powerful ideology ever of an inevitable, global, and necessary system of social organization has been rapidly implemented across the globe. Opposing every alternative to it as an enemy of "freedom," it has proclaimed itself a "new world order" to which there is "no alternative." Postmodern theory and practice would seem to be in absolute contradiction with such a global system of rule. But is the postmodern celebration of difference and plurality unconsciously imitative of the very "free consumer" of this world system who, with enough money, can select whatever difference is for sale in the market? Is this why the critiques of "revolutionary poststructuralism" have, in the main, been directed at everything except the actually ruling structure of the world?[1] Is postmodernism itself, despite appearances, just another ideology justifying the global market in a new way?

As with other social-value programs, the doctrine of "the global free market" itself does not recognize its ideology as ideology, but rather conceives of its prescriptions as a form of natural necessity. It is promulgated, indeed, as a *"post-ideological"* recognition of law-like truth. Yet, at the same time, any opposition or attempted alternative to this necessary truth is militantly attacked. The truth of the global market order is even believed to be final and eternal, "the end of history." Its rule is declared "inevitable." Its axioms are conceived as "iron laws." Societies that dare to evade its stern requirements are threatened with "harsh punishments" and "shock treatments." Ordinary people everywhere are required to "make necessary sacrifices" to its demands. Miracle economies and future prosperity are then promised to those who compete hardest to win.

Such absolutist conceptions do not seem plausible in an open and scientific culture. Surely in our free and competing marketplace of ideas we must have contrary opinions to such a doctrine. In a 500-channel universe of "unprecedented freedom of choice," some critical evaluation of these claims must find a place. Do we not live in an age whose hallmark is to be "suspicious of all absolutes" and "dedicated to diversity and freedom?" How can such conflicts between what is claimed as our values and what is our reality be so overlooked by market doctrine?

The Freedom of No Alternative

The mass media, as we know all too well, increasingly occupy the eyes, ears, and brain circuits of people's lives everywhere. Yet in the daily barrage of media we come across few—if any—voices that doubt the truth or goodness of free trade or the global economy or new world order. We are unlikely to come across any elected mainstream political party that challenges the necessity of ever more economic restructuring, worker shedding, and painful cuts to public health programs, universal education, and social security.

Do we hear even those who prize the liberal ideal of *"alternative conceptions of the good"* come forward to speak against this closure of public discourse to any other structure of social belief? Can we find in even the leading journals of philosophical enquiry a scepticism of such prescriptions for the entire world? Certainly we hear that there are opponents of the new global market order out there— "union bosses," "hard-line communists," "protectionists," "people afraid to compete," "tree huggers," Marxists, and so on. What they argue, however, is unclear because it seems always to be told to us by those who know how "ideological" and "out of touch" these criticisms are. So where in the mainstream across the world today is the doctrine of the "laws" and the "judgements," the "sacrifices" and "the miracles" of the market, *not* presupposed or advocated as the structure of the real?

In posing this question, we should be aware of significant distinctions. Some fields of assertion and representation affirm the doctrine of the universal necessity and goodness of the free market by little more than continuous repetition of the words "freedom," "democracy," and "competitiveness." More sophisticated arguments at the other end of the spectrum, especially among the learned of the academy, take greater care to justify market concepts of freedom, pluralism, and democracy in various different ways. At the one end of the spectrum, the slogans attach to definite policies or world conditions, while at the other the concepts are elaborated so abstractly that they no longer seem to refer to actual states of the world. Still, what they have in common is their presupposition of the market value system as necessary and without viable alternative.

Other voices, from extreme rightist to liberal or even social democrat, also express the global market ideology. Yet here as well a shared set of often unexpressed assumptions regulates the public speech of believers as a normative framework of acceptable position. These assumptions need not be expressed. Rather, they are normally presupposed as grounds of rational discussion. A number of more specific commitments follow, with variations, from these presuppositions—for example, the need for more prisons or weapons development or less welfare and social entitlements. There may be many different elaborations of these particular issues, but beneath that seeming variety a common ground of value orders discussion. As a result we find the mind-set of the market belief system at work all around us in varying forms and articulations, from the theory of neoclassical economists to the editorials of the nations' leading newspapers to the cocktail chatter of the business community. It is the basic grammar of the market value program, and it stretches far beyond its advocates in its regulation of what is assumed to be right and wrong in social discourse across the world.

Even critics of the market value program seldom transgress its bounds of true belief. Political parties that hope to find election funding assume the guidance of its logic as a given, which they must, as their duty, translate into effective governance.

The Pursuit of Freedom

The problem, in short, involves a kind of absolutist dogmatism. Usually, whenever a supreme doctrine of what is necessary and good for all people has been instituted as unquestionable, the result has been the destruction of people and social fabrics. In the past, doctrines far less global in power and representation, and never so unanimously subscribed to by the world's private wealth-holders and governments, have destroyed millions of people under the pretext of their "inevitability," their "harsh judgements," their "iron laws," and their destiny of "future prosperity." Now, when we see evidence of the same tendencies being set firmly in place, surely we need to step back and consider what is unfolding before us. We need, to begin, to examine the claims and logic, the value assumptions and conclusions, of this regulating metaphysic if we are not to fall prey to a global dictatorship ruthlessly determining how we and everyone else live.

Such a claim may seem extreme. But what individual's life— the university student, the ordinary pensioner, the middle-income worker—is not now being compelled "to adjust to the new reality" out of fear of the future? What government, what party leadership, what business representative does not now argue that we require social "slashing" and "cutbacks"? Do even democratic pluralists object to this single global system? Do even the past's staunchest critics of historical determinism and inevitability say a word about this new version of what they once deplored as inhuman?

In the face of these paradoxes of reality and ideology, the adherents to market theory and practice are apt not to see a problem. They attribute any problems to people falling short of the market's demands. If exchanges between buyer and seller are voluntary and for the bargainers' mutual benefit, they must be free and beneficent. If capitalism produces more commodities than any previous alternative system, it must be history's most prosperous and beneficent order. If the state protects the individual's private property and rights, how can the system not be the framework of individual liberty?

The Founders of the Theory and Their Revisionists: From John Locke and Adam Smith to "Value-Free Economics"

The doctrine of the "free market" has its classical moral-theological foundations in John Locke's *Second Treatise of Government*, published over three centuries ago, in 1690, the year after the English Revolution deposing King James II. Locke's work opposed the divine right of kings with the absolute right of private property, which Locke believed was conferred by God. Locke's epochal argument conceived of the laws of property as inviolable and as sanctified and protected by "He who has given mankind the world in common."[2]

Locke's declaration of the God-given right of private property was then developed into the fully fledged market theory in the founding classic of the faith, a monumental treatise by Adam Smith entitled *An Inquiry into the Nature and Understanding of the Wealth of Nations*. Smith was a scientific deist and professor of logic and moral philosophy at the University of Glasgow. He published his great work in 1776, the year of the American Revolution. His treatise is, with Locke's work as its property-theory ground, the theoretical foundation upon which the scholastic and popular edifice of the entire free market theory rests. The discussion had two central ideas: first, the advantages of production and exchange free of royal charter and government interference; and second, the revolutionary idea that the self-interested pursuit of profit promotes the social good. These are two of the three great pillars of the market doctrine's general system of value and justification. The other, and first, principle is the "sacred and inviolable right of private property" advanced by Locke and later appropriated as a basic premise by Smith and all his successors. Smith's classic formulation of the first principles of the "free market" as a dynamic system have continued as the received doctrine for over three hundred years to the present ideology of the "global economy," although with radical changes in meaning which have been overlooked by "neo-classical" and current advocates of the theory.

Those profound deviations from Smith's theory include four themes:

1. the "marginalist revolution," which grounds market value in "utility" or buyers' willingness to pay, a *subjectivization of value* that replaced Smith's, Ricardo's, and Marx's "labour theory of value," which understood the value of a good in terms of the human labour required to produce it;

2. "econometrics" and other formalist devices, which increasingly substitute *mathematical symbols and equations for observed facts and social relations in economic analysis*;

3. the "monetarist economics" made famous by Milton Friedman, whose regulating social objective is *to preserve the value of owned money* in place of Smith's overriding emphasis on "funds destined for *the employment of productive labour*";[3] and,

4. "political economy" becoming depoliticized as a subject category by the claim of *value-free* economics, which falsely claims to have removed all political or value judgement from its analysis.

None of these theory-cleansing operations on market doctrine, which, in effect, remove its human content, results in direct disavowal of Smith's fundamental principles of the market as a value system. Smith's first principles are, together, the enduring framework of an underlying theory of ultimate, universal, and axiomatic value that persists through all the theory's formalized abstractions of methodology and application. Professional economists since Smith have, however, strangely declared or assumed their "value neutrality," despite their grounding in the principles of Smith's and Locke's openly moral philosophy. This is one of the interesting mysteries of the doctrine, although it has, as we shall see, a quite mundane explanation. If you pretend to be strictly neutral and scientific, others are more likely to accept your value assertions as objective laws.

In practice, though, professional economists merely assume Smith's moral principles as givens and work from them as regulating premises of all their analyses. For example, the positions of a "value-free" or positivist economics still presuppose as given and self-evident the value system of private property rights, the pursuit of self-interest and profit, and the monetized production and exchange of needed goods as the foundational, regulating norms of their analyses. Indeed, no mainstream economist ever rejects, criticizes, or in any way questions these general principles of decision, conduct, or social distribution. To contest any of these value absolutes is taboo. Insofar as any thinker or text or school does not conform strictly to these governing principles in the conduct of their analyses, they to that extent fall outside the ultimately moral and theological doctrine we are considering. Interestingly, even Karl Marx was prone to the economists' later illusion that economic analysis could be value-free.[4]

The Moral System of a Market Exchange

Adam Smith was quite conscious of the main normative principles governing his work, because he was actively advocating them as principles of good conduct and government during a time when they were not, as now, so widely assumed as given by the nature of the physical world.

The full moral system of a market exchange is a complex, wide-ranging matter. The value premises, regulating principles of decision and action (both individual and social), the consequences of choice in rewards or punishments represent a vast system of ethical prescription and rule. Here we can begin only to peel back the layers of assumption to reveal the most basic moral presuppositions underlying the apparently value neutral world of market transactions and their analysis.

Every market transaction, for example, presupposes the principle of private property as a prescriptive right. People can exchange goods or services with security in the marketplace only on the basis of this private-property right and the effective enforcement of its claim against anyone else who might like or need what is held as private property. Indeed, market transactions of purchase and sale can only occur on the basis of this coercive right and the further prescription of an instituted medium of money value. These rights and values and their enforcement—with violations treated as moral crimes—together constitute a rigid system of normative command that almost everyone on the right or wrong side of the law seems to recognize as binding and morally obliging. Thus all churches or morally orthodox faiths prescribe the requirements of property as laws of God. Moreover, the criminal and civil codes of states across the world enforce these moral commandments, construing their violation as grave and severely punishable offences. These moral prescriptions surrounding private property are paradigmatic moral prescriptions.

The first principle that "value neutral" or "positivist" economists assume as the very foundation of their analyses and derivations is, then, a fundamental moral commandment whose violation is assailable by strict penalties and ascription of guilt. This principle is not only a principle of value or ethics, but also a strictly *moral* principle: it tells us how to act, and it assigns punishment for any violation of its prescription.

This seemingly fundamental moral norm of instituting and preserving private property is, however, by no means assumable as a given. It is not a "natural" condition or structure of the physical world that can be studied in the way that a physicist studies established laws governing the workings of the cosmos. It is, rather, a profoundly important moral institution open to choice and rejection. The first Christians, for example, repudiated strongly the principle of private property as being socially irresponsible and a violation of Jesus' teachings. The Acts of the Apostles of the New Testament reports:

> Not a man of them claimed any of his possession as his own, but everything was held in common. They never had a needy person among them, because all who had property in land or houses sold it, brought the proceeds of the sale and laid the money and ... it was then distributed to any who stood in need.[5]

Similarly, most First Nations peoples have always regarded private property, in particular in land, as an offence against nature and community, accepting only personal possession for use. For example, Tecumseh, the famous Shawnee war chief, once stated: "The land was never divided, but belongs to all for the use of each. That no part has a right to sell, even to each other."[6] The rightness or wrongness of the right to private property has been a moral and theological issue fought over for centuries.

The private property principle is thus not a premise that we can accept in a "value free" way. It is an ancient and profound moral issue. Accepting it means taking a side in this foundational moral issue—the side of private property. This is a moral commitment of the greatest significance, whether it is owned up to or not; and the moral commitment broadens and deepens as the right to private property extends its claim of enforceable right: from self-made possessions to personal possessions made by others, to objects used or managed in the production of use-values for sale, to objects never seen or touched at all. In the current global market this moral commitment extends to billions of units of money-demand used by some people only to possess ever more hundreds of millions of money-demand for themselves.

The "right to private property" is a complex possibility, and admits of many meanings. If its moral claim is not limited, its enforceable right against others is consistent with the right of an individual to buy and use up or sell the life-means of entire societies, and leave those societies to destitution—which has occurred in the cases of Native peoples, Third World agricultural communities, and company towns.

The right to private property can only be presupposed without question as a given order of nature by a profound moral blindness. The principles of social value systems can become so conventionally accepted and presupposed in people's thinking that they become no longer aware of them as principles of value at all. For instance, just as unreflective language-speakers are regulated by the grammatical rules of the native language to which they have been habituated in their speech acts since birth, without being aware of the conformity to them in all that they say, so naive moralists may be regulated by norms of value by which they have been socially conditioned, and imagine that they are being value neutral. Naive moralists accept all such principles of value as if they were the necessary and inalterable framework of social existence. They then readily imagine that people all freely enter into transactions of buying and selling goods by a money medium, and that all people do so in voluntary exchanges of what they possess. They might further imagine that people choose to compete to sell their working lives to others, and that all people seek terms in their transactions that are most advantageous to themselves. Pre-reflective economists accept each of these foundational normative principles of conduct as a value-independent fact. This mind-set sees the negation, rejection, or violation of these moral principles as "irrational" or as "rejecting free society."

To expose this underlying moral absolutism to consciousness is not merely a philosophical exercise. To lay bare our presuppositions and assumptions, in particular those governing how we live, is what humans as humans do to be conscious beings. More specifically, such consciousness is required of the market agent who, as the market theory declares, makes "free and responsible choices."[7] If we are not aware of the principles of freedom, choice, and contract in accordance with which we are said to be thinking and acting, but merely presuppose them as a program of behaviour described as "axiomatic" or "rational" or "the way of the free world," we are not thinking as free or independent or responsible agents. If we are to be truly free and independent agents, we are obliged to recognize the principles that provide the foundation of our thoughts and actions. If we are also rational free agents, we are further obliged to clarify the commitments that our principles of value are forming for us. Our principles of conduct and thought may be good or bad, or they may, as we shall see, allow for contradictory meanings that are repressed from view. But whatever their value and content, they require comprehension and the recognition of alternative possibilities if they are to be the principles of free agents.

Individual Freedom and the Neutral Market State: Are These Coherent Norms?

Despite claims of value neutrality, the market doctrine would seem to propose the tenet of *individual freedom* as its ultimate and unifying value. Thus, for example, it is because the right to private property, the pursuit of profit in investment, the competitive production of goods and services, and the unhindered exchange of these in the market are all conceived as basic requirements of individual freedom that contemporary adherents to market theory and practice assume or urge each and all of them as imperatives for society. This freedom is the supreme and universal value from which market theory and practice derive their ethical force and meaning. This condition is more clearly the case now than in Adam Smith's day. Smith's emphasis was, as the title of his work implies, more on increasing consumption or the "wealth of nations" than on individuals' merely increasing money-demand for themselves as an end in itself.[8]

Adam Smith, however, asserted freedom for one class. His principle of freedom for manufacturers and merchants was restricted in its application to their own freedom from state interference by monopoly or trade barriers. He did not extend this principle to "the race of labourers," as he called those dependent on wages to survive. All that they could do within the logical space provided for them in his theory was, if hired by a "master," obtain a better means of subsistence through the lower prices achieved by competitive production and sale. Smith never presumed to argue that acquiring greater means of subsistence from the wages of one's master represented freedom for the working classes.

Smith's successors generally claim both that the market confers freedom on everyone in it, including those who have nothing to sell but their working lives, and that a value neutral state is to enforce this system of freedom. This new conception of the state as a mechanism that is "impartial with respect to competing conceptions of the good," including apparently the good of citizens having enough to eat, is an almost unanimously presupposed norm by "liberal" and "democratic" theorists today.

To advocate a market system as now understood is to rule out any social limit both on inequality of wealth or on any dispossession of other people's means of life by the mechanisms of private-profit maximization. These implications are not much examined, but they follow straightforwardly from its principles. Nevertheless, those who espouse this market system as the basis of a democratic society suppose that the state, which institutes and enforces this system and the unlimited property rights of its richest citizens against all others, however poor, is still "neutral" and takes no sides "between competing conceptions of the good."

Although this position becomes manifestly absurd in light of the entailments of the market principles that the state "neutrally" enforces, the trick is to avoid seeing the implications of the principles. This is how a value program becomes closed and conventionalized in its acceptance of the absurd in even learned circles. The prevailing notion of the market-state advocates that the state apparatus enforces the systematic enforcement of life-determining principles of what is good; but at the same time it asserts that the state does *not* take sides in such issues—that the state holds a neutral position between competing conceptions of the good. This presupposition of opposite positions as simultaneously true has an underlying ground—the assumption that market principles come before judgements of what is good. Here again we begin to touch upon the repressed metaphysic of the doctrine.

The Case of Friedrich Hayek

One of the most influential and eminent advocates of free market doctrine in the twentieth century, Friedrich A. Hayek, both denies and asserts the idea of an ultimate, universal value for society's members. He says, "All that I shall have to say is derived from certain ultimate values." He declares that "our most precious inheritance" is "liberty" and argues at length in favour of the basic value of market freedom for human societies of all kinds.[9] Hayek defines this ultimate freedom:

> It is necessary in the first instance that the parties in the market should be free to sell and buy at any price at which they can find a partner to the transaction and that anybody should be free to produce, sell and buy anything that may be produced and sold at all.[10]

Hayek argues a few pages later in the same text that "nothing but partial scales of values exist—scales which are inevitably different and often inconsistent with each other."[11] Moreover, he argues that "totalitarianism" occurs when a state adopts a "single aim" or "unitary end" to "organize the whole of society."[12]

Clearly, for Hayek market freedom is somehow *not* "a single aim" and this market ideal is not a "unitary end to organize the whole of society." But Hayek nowhere explains why he makes these sweeping and unjustified exceptions, nor is he troubled by the contradictory claims in what he asserts. Hayek sees no problem, in short, in holding to liberty and the free market as "ultimate values" and our "precious inheritance" and at the same time rejecting ultimate values or moral aims for society. Perfect absurdity in market theory is, as we will increasingly see, not a problem to its value program because it is assumed as the structure of the world is assumed, without any alternative to it except by demonic usurpation.

If we think of a moral system as a set of principles held to prevent harm and promote good, with penalties in consequence of violation of its principles or laws, it is clear that the market order is a moral system. This remains so even if its adherents block its moralistic nature from their minds when purporting to be scientific and value neutral. Locke and Smith had no such problem in advocating the market as a moral system, and Locke in particular thought of the "natural laws" of private-property acquisition and protection as laws authorized by God, to whose recourse humankind could appeal by violent rebellion if those laws were broken. Smith too was a devout believer and a deist. His central concept of "the invisible hand"—referring to the market's providential operations in supplying goods in short supply by the mechanism of money-prices—invoked a theological model of an immaterial hand guiding the market's operations. Behind the selfish operations of profit-seekers in the market, Smith implied, there stood the invisible design of the "sublime Maker" whose ever-present and omniscient plan guided all transactions for the public interest. "We may admire," Smith says, "the wisdom and goodness of God even in the weakness and folly of men."[13] Smith's market theory was, in short, a theodicy which demonstrated God's "providential care" in even the competing wills of self-seeking profiteers. Their activities in pursuing profit where market supply was weakest fulfilled His design of providing more goods where there were fewer before.

The founders of the market doctrine were thus explicit in commending the market as a moral system and in ascribing its authority and powers to God's design and will. That is ultimately why they thought "interference with the market," to use the current phrase, was a violation of its divine design and a transgression against reason.

But their successors, excepting those from the Christian Right, deny or conceal this underlying theological framework of their doctrine and its moral absolutism. Yet even the term "free" to characterize the market, a term now everywhere used by purportedly "value neutral" analysts, is the most fundamental moral category of our time. "In God We Trust," we might also note, continues to be stamped on every coin of the world's leading market state. The "invisible hand" is, moreover, more frequently invoked by economists and planners in their analyses than by Adam Smith himself. Yet market theorists do not acknowledge the moral and theological logic of the principles, concepts, and operational signs of market theory and practice.

Professional economists and political theorists, it seems, like to think of themselves as rigorously impartial to the system of values and theologic moralisms embodied in the market theory and practice. The more systematically regulated they are by these values as universal absolutes, the less likely they are to recognize them as a value system with the underpinnings of a fundamentalist theology. The reason this is so seems to be that if they were to openly acknowledge the nature of these commitments they would lose their authority as disinterested experts telling us, for considerable salaries and emoluments, how we must live within the framework of the ruling economic order.

Notes

1. Jean François Lyotard, who coined the term "postmodern," writes: "I will use the term modern to designate any science that legitimates itself with reference to a metadiscourse ... some grand narrative, such as the dialectics of Spirit, the hermeneutics of meaning, the emancipation of the rational or working subject, or the creation of wealth." See Jean François Lyotard, *The Postmodern Condition* (Minneapolis: University of Minnesota Press, 1984), pp.xxiii–xxiv. As one may see from Lyotard's pantheon of oppressive totalities, the three-century tradition of the specifically capitalist market structure—now prescribed to the world as its inevitable grand narrative—manages to elude his attention in vague abstraction.

2. John Locke, "Of Property," chapter IV, *The Second Treatise on Government* (New York: Liberal Arts Press, 1952), pp.16-30.

3. Adam Smith, "Of the Accumulation of Capital, or of Productive and Unproductive Labour," chapter III, *An Inquiry into the Nature and Understanding of the Wealth of Nations* (New York: PF Collier and Son, 1909), p.279.

4. In his famous first Preface to *Capital*, for example, Marx says in canonical statements: "It is a questions of these laws, of these tendencies working with iron necessity towards inevitable results. ...My standpoint, from which the evolution of the economic formation of society is viewed as a process of natural history, can less than any other make the individual responsible for relations whose creature he socially remains, however much he may subjectively raise himself above them." *Capital*, vol. I (New York: Progress Publishers, 1967), pp.8, 10. Here we see that Marx and positivist economics are agreed on the premise that economics studies law-governed phenomena and can be, therefore, as value-free a science as physics.

5. Acts of the Apostles, chapter 2, verses 44-45.

6. Quoted in T.C. McLuhan, ed., *Touch the Earth* (New York: Simon and Schuster, 1972), p.85.

7. See, for example, Milton Friedman and Rose Friedman, *Freedom to Choose* (New York: Harcourt Brace Jovanovich, 1980).

8. Adam Smith writes: "By diminishing the funds destined for the employment of productive labour he necessarily diminishes the annual produce of the land and labour of the whole country." Smith, *Inquiry*, p.279.

9. Friedrich A. Hayek, *The Road to Serfdom* (Chicago: University of Chicago Press, 1944), pp.vi, 52.

10. Ibid., p.37.

11. Ibid., p.59.

12. Ibid., p.56.

13. Quoted in Robert Brank Fulton, *Adam Smith Speaks to Our Times* (Boston: Christopher Publishing House, 1963).

The Market
as God

The Problem of Evil

Problems arise for the market theology, as for traditional theologies, regarding the beneficent operations of the ruler's invisible hand and the justice of the rewards and penalties it metes out to the worthy and the unworthy. The economic choices made by people in their competition among one another to meet the market's demands seem often not to relate coherently or fairly to the consequences for them of the operations of market forces. Rewards, for example, seem to be preposterously slanted towards those with considerable wealth, almost all of it unearned by any productive activity on their part. Similarly, punishments seem almost entirely to fall on the poor. Even though the laws of the invisible hand are said to constitute a "maximally rational system of resource distribution,"[1] great numbers of people remain impoverished and underemployed amidst great wealth—up to 30 per cent even in "miracle economies."

Proponents of the market doctrine attempt to explain this anomaly away by introducing a no-nonsense defence of their theory of invisible hand rule. They classify problems such as the starvation of humans whose labour is not bought in the free marketplace or the pollution of a community's air and water as *"externalities."* These conditions are "externalities" because they are not costs of doing business and so do not compute into the market model. In consequence, they are not problems to be resolved by the market doctrine. The resolution of such problems, these proponents conclude, belongs to another realm of responsibility—the realm of subjective "morality" or, if such problems become a public issue, the realm of "politics." The doctrine adheres to a stern impersonality in these matters. Its concern is strictly restricted to the costs and outputs measured in business ledgers and GNPs or, as such measures are now called, GDPs.

This move to other, separate realms of responsibility and action may seem to limit the market doctrine's universality and necessity as a system of life rule, but this is only an appearance. If these separate, independent realms ever impinge on regulation of the market, market doctrinaires assail them as overstepping their bounds. The doctrine prescribes at the highest levels of its advocacy that decisions in the political realm, for instance, must "not interfere in the market."[2] Moreover, the doctrine stipulates that the first requirement of government is to ensure that the property rights, free exchanges, and profit opportunities of the market remain secure and protected. What appears to be a limitation on the absolute rule of the market turns out, on more careful examination, to be only a delegated requirement to the state to maintain it.

For example, people without money may be starving in masses, but production and distribution of the goods that people want and need are, according to the doctrine, exclusively the domain of the free market. One must never interfere with its production or its prices on moral, political, or any other grounds. When the Conference of Catholic Bishops and the moderator of the United Church dared to criticize the damaging effects of free market policies on the poor and the unemployed from a moral viewpoint, a thunderous condemnation greeted their concerns.[3] Above all the doctrine prescribes as its ultimate article of prohibition that a government must never in any way plan the production and distribution of the goods and services that those in society require to survive. This is the most basic violation of the market's laws and is certain to end in state tyranny.[4]

The free market is, in this way, the ruling Good of the doctrine, and its usurpation by "planning" or "state interference" constitutes, in consequence, the opposing force of Evil. To choose one is always virtuous; to choose the other is always bad. To test this generalization,

seek any society with social planning of distribution that is not denounced by market believers as undermining human freedom, self-
reliance, and other virtues. The market doctrine's binary opposition of
absolutes is, for modern example, the regulating structure of Friedrich
Hayek's classic free market text, *The Road to Serfdom* and, in differently conceptualized form, Milton Friedman's *Capitalism and
Freedom*. In its more familiar and contemporary public form this binary opposition opposes "the free market" on the one hand to "totalitarianism" on the other, with "state meddling" of any kind receiving
increasingly demonic attributions as it approaches the sheer cliff of
substituting government or other structures for the production and
pricing of human goods by the market.

What then remains of the freedom, independence, or power to
act of governments "elected by free individuals in a market society"?
In the theory and practice of the market, governments are elected by
the independent choices of the same "sovereign, free individuals" who
produce, sell, and choose consumer goods. But the doctrine stipulates
a strict limit on what governments are permitted to do. They are
prohibited from directing production in any way, regulating any price,
or in any manner interfering with profit maximization, property accumulation, the sale of labour, or any other prescription of the market's
regulating principles of belief. "Interference in the market" is, in a
word, apostasy, and its mere consideration as an option is heretical.

From this point of view the political or government realm as a
whole is only legitimate to the extent that it represents the private producers and consumers of the market operating within the laws of its
controlling invisible hand. Only an agent of evil forces, even if elected
by the majority, would—as in Chile's 1973 nationalization of foreign-
owned copper mines—violate these market relations of proper social
order. Those who do so, whether in Latin America or Southeast Asia,
are severely punished as the enemies of "freedom," "progress," and
"civilization." This is why at the height of the Cold War U.S. President Ronald Reagan represented the Soviet Union as "the Evil Empire." The characterization was not merely bully-pulpit bombast. It
followed logically from the market value program. Even if only a local

satrapy compared to the United States in matters of international empire, the Soviet Union had a form of social organization that, to a large extent at least, rejected market relations both at home and abroad—and this condition was sufficient to qualify it as maximally evil in the moral calculus of the global market system. The very practice of non-market social relations across a society, however small and impoverished the society, qualifies it as satanic to this value system.

Thus market ideology has labelled even Third World countries with per capita incomes among the lowest in the world but social orders meeting the primary needs of their peoples—Vietnam, Sandinista Nicaragua, and Cuba, for example—as demonic threats by their very existence. These implausible attributions did not and do not invite hilarity because they are expressions of the market's moral metaphysic. By definition—and the more clearly so the more they develop an attractive alternative—the market's regulation of society is good a priori, and social relations that reject market regulation are wicked.

The Regulating Principles of True Belief

Many adherents to the market doctrine—including televangelists, the religious right, and U.S. presidents—explicitly defend and advocate its rule and laws as the moral commands of God. Others advocate and justify it as akin to a natural or biological system, which develops by competitive laws of survival and exclusion. Still others presuppose it as a scientifically self-evident mechanism of human production and exchange. There are many interpretations of the market's certain truth; but what all the doctrine's believers—from the fundamentalist evangelist to the metropolitan newspaper editor, from the political head of state to the academic economist—have in common is an underlying set of absolute principles.

This unifying belief system of contemporary global society is made up of ten commandments of social order, which, although they may not be explicitly expressed or acknowledged, constitute an overall value program. Together they make up the ordering normality that societies across the world are expected to obey if they are, for instance, to "attract investors" and "survive in the world market."

1. Private property is good in all things, without right to limit its legal acquisition in any possession.

2. The money-price system optimally distributes goods and services through society.

3. Protectionism of domestic production of any kind is bad, and to be repudiated wherever it is counselled or raised.

4. Government intervention in the market is bad unless it promotes profitable market activities.

5. Profit-maximization is the engine of social well-being, and is not to be hedged in by public regulation or ownership.

6. Individual consumer desires are permanently increasing, unlimited, and a good in their satisfaction.

7. Freedom to buy and sell in money exchanges is the basis of human liberty and justice.

8. Pursuit of personal maximal income is natural, rational, and required for society to work.

9. Economic growth is permanently desirable and necessary, with no inherent environmental or human limit to the conversion of life into saleable commodities.

10. The great majority who have only their labour and service to sell must do so if we are to continue to live in a free and prosperous society.

In the dominant value program, each one of these basic prescriptions is held to be necessary and certain. They are, as in any absolutist moral doctrine, prescriptive, universal, overriding, and subject to punishment for their violation. Unlike the ten commandments of Judaic-Christian religion, however, these principles of proper organization of social life are now prescribed to or assumed by almost all states of the world as the ordering framework for their reproduction, and the inevitable requirement of their survival in the new global order.

What is perhaps most astonishing about these overriding principles of society's proper rule is that they remain unquestioned even by those who are known to be most sceptical of generalizations about what is true and right. The "scientific rigour" of the mainstream economist presupposes them all as given. The methodological doubt that philosophers bring to the existence of their own bodies here remains generally silent and without a question. Not even the liberal and antifoundationalist defenders of "pluralism" and "diverse ideas of the good" find any reason to notice or object to these absolutist prescriptions of the one and only right way for the world. This value program is the unseen moral absolutism of our age.

The global market doctrine in one form of expression or another promulgates these principles as immutable and overriding. Their authority is presumed as transcultural and above East-West or North-South divisions. All persons and societies everywhere must obey them to survive, or, in proportion to their delinquency, suffer the severest penalties and sacrifices—and, if necessary, armed attack.

The Confusion of Moral Commandments and Physical Laws since Ricardo

Despite these absolute commands of social order, believers in the market doctrine since Ricardo have supposed that they are not moral principles or prescriptions at all. This supposition is an ancient form of socially conditioned error, and it arises from a primitive conceptual confusion—the failure to distinguish between social norms and the physical laws of nature.

When people conceive of their surrounding social order as being prescribed by the very structure of the world they are experiencing something as old as humanity itself: an idol of the tribe. Tribes have invariably worshipped their particular forms of life as ordained to be so by their particular tribal gods. Today the market order is such a god. Its difference is its claim to universal authority for all peoples and societies on the planet for, apparently, all time. This absolutization of a social structure as the proper order of the cosmos is sustained by a narrow and peculiar use of empirical method. Since the market's regulation of social order can be verified by all those living within it as, indeed, *being there*, its adherents often mistake this contingent condition for a necessary order of the world. They decline to observe that this order is there because any transgression of its regulating principles is prohibited as an attack on the immutable laws of progress and freedom.

David Ricardo, the most influential classical economist after Adam Smith, was subject to this confusion. His error is quintessential in the market doctrine. He mistakes customary norms, which are obeyed in particular historical circumstances, for necessary, universal, and inevitable laws.

Consider the following statement, made in 1817 in response to Great Britain's "Poor Laws." Until their effective repeal in 1834, this Speenhamland legislation, as it was also called, provided for social assistance to rural labourers of England. The bread-price equivalent that these labourers received was required to ensure that they did not starve. Their prospective deaths without it, in turn, arose from the condition of their disemployment and uprooting by the new capitalist agricultural industry, which destroyed the old agrarian communities and the traditionally secure farm jobs of the working poor. This social assistance went to those without enough to stay alive, whether they worked or not. Ricardo wrote: "The *principle of gravitation* is not more certain than the tendency of such laws to change wealth and vigour into misery and weakness."[5]

Ricardo was a banker, and despite his superior understanding of the laws of the market's mechanisms, several aspects of his paradigm position typify the free market doctrine and its undergirding moral theology. In the first place, he interpreted the principles of the doctrine as revealed laws of nature. In this case, Ricardo's logic is representative of the believer's assumption of the market as an inalterable, progressive, and universal order whose principles of efficiency can no more be flouted than can Newton's laws of motion. Capital investment requires human labour to be set in motion and to work hard for masters. In turn, to stay alive and reasonably well workers must compete to sell their labour to capitalists, and work as hard as they possibly can on the job to earn their wages and sustain the circulation of capital. If a government interferes with these market operations by providing enough food rations for the poor to stay alive without competing for employment or working with sufficient vigour for employers, wealth production will plummet and labourers will become lazy dependants.

Whether or not such a system is either necessary or desirable as a means of creating "wealth" and sustaining "vigour" is an issue open to question. But Ricardo, as economists and others since, simply presupposes that this order of rule is the given order of nature. Nowadays various authorities tend to use the value terms "increased productivity" and "willingness to work" in place of "wealth" and "vigour." But whatever the terms, they continue to imply a steep moral command. "Wealth" is saleable consumer commodities, and is good. Obedient wage-labour to create them and a profit for masters is "vigour," and that also is good. Both goods must be pursued, or there can be no more "wealth" and "vigour" than an object can fall upwards. The ruling good is the economic system that enforces these moral commands.

Ricardo's position implies a deism, the popular intellectual religion of his day. The deist idea consisted in the certitude that a rational God is immanent in the design of the world's natural and economic order. If the plan is not complied with, disaster follows as surely as objects fall downwards. The plan is an eternal, necessary, and universal force. But Ricardo, unlike Smith, drops the religious trappings in his work, while retaining its content of absolute commands. In this way he forms a conventional moral-religious position of the time into an economic physics, a "science" of productive order that requires people to be without food so they will work hard for masters' profits, or starve.

The fundamental confusion here between a current system of ruling power and a law of physics seems to arise from the coincidence that the regime that economists presuppose and prescribe as a moral imperative is also the reliable ruling order of their surrounding society. Because the morally obligatory goals of "wealth" and "vigour" in the prescribed senses of commodity production and wage-labour for masters are clearly evident as conditions in the surrounding society—so long as workers are without any alternative means of life-support—

these moral prescriptions are thought to be laws of nature that are *provable by observation*. The good that is imposed in the form of masters ruling, willing workers working to avoid starvation, and the "wealth" and "vigour" of society flowing in consequence of this regime is made a necessity of nature by the success of its coercion.

Socrates, Plato, and Aristotle had much the same kind of thoughts about slavery, which was a structure of reality that was both necessary and good. But they never lost sight of the normative content of this structure, which was imposed as a form on the world. They never imagined it was merely a "value-free fact." On the contrary, they conceived it as a moral order of human rule, and justified it as such. The "scientific" market doctrine since Ricardo pretends that the normative nature of the market system does not exist. Ricardo and others present that system as if it was given as a set of laws to be discovered from the order of nature. Since its operations of wage-labour, commodity production, and profit can be observed as verifiable facts, they conclude that therefore these conditions must not involve values or value judgements at all, for those facets cannot be observed and proved as facts. It is, therefore, this naive doctrine assumes, "positive" versus "normative" analysis. It is "fact" versus "morality." It is "what can be verified" versus "what ought to be."

What this extraordinary non-sequitur from coercive social rule to physical law ignores is that just because certain prescriptive goals can be made to prevail over others and can be widely observed to do so does not mean that their successful imposition reveals a verifiable scientific truth. Otherwise, a concentration-camp society could prove to us that its system was merely the verifiable operations of "natural laws." This was, indeed, precisely the view of those who imposed concentration camps on countless people in Germany, South Africa, and elsewhere for extended periods of history. In the current sweatshops of the new global market order, where children and women may work for seventy hours a week for a few cents an hour, the employers' defence adopts the same logic of justification. "It is," as one told me in India, "a working out of the laws of nature."

Observation verifies that what people are forced to do under threat of death or destitution, they will eventually do. After countless thousands of unemployed people were hanged for vagrancy in Tudor England, for example, those initially choosing not to sell their labour to masters dramatically declined. When people are released from such life-or-death constraints, they do not necessarily choose to re-enter the nature-given order of good proclaimed by masters. But none of this observation yields us a value-free law of nature such as Ricardo's "the principle of gravitation." Rather, it shows us an enforced normative order—and it is an order that does not work to govern behaviour when people are not compelled by the threat of death or family starvation to obey its commands.

From the Market System to the Cosmic Order

A second aspect of Ricardo's statement that has since typified the market doctrine's "scientific" declarations is the assumption that the historically contingent and particular structure of commodity production by wage-labour for profit reveals a universal order; and that all production and distribution systems must conform to this order to be in accord with natural law.

This sweeping non-sequitur of inference follows from the metaphysical nature of the market doctrine. Ricardo's model here is the aforementioned "principle of gravitation," a principle that applies to all places, times, peoples, and events—even to the original gaseous state—and rules always as the immutable structure of earthly existence. Yet the market system, whose laws Ricardo conceives as having consequences "no less certain than the principle of gravitation," was then confined to small regions of the world and was not remotely universal in its governance. Almost all of the world governed by the law of gravity was quite outside the laws of private capital investment for money profit. Even Britain itself had been organized in other ways for almost all of its history.

How could Ricardo possibly take the law of gravity, which is universal and invariant, as his model for a recently governing and regional local market system? More interestingly still, how can economists since Ricardo sustain this absolutist ethnocentric dogma by continuing to assume the universal and unconditional nature of the market's principles of operation? Current economists, indeed, go even further than Ricardo, divesting their models of any reference to concrete reality and differences by formalist assumptions and econometric derivations. Timeless and universal necessity, we might note, is the logical mode that fundamentalist religions always assume in their prescriptions of how things are and ever will be in the changing and various world.

By translating a historical social formation into an absolute condition—into a universal and necessary order of human relations—economists took the second great step of a fundamentalist theology. They conceive their own idealized, contemporary order of production and distribution as a cosmic, globally binding order that prescribes universal truths "no less certain than the principle of gravitation." That all people everywhere must therefore submit to its demands follows as a global imperative. To interfere in its inevitable universalization with laws of welfare support for the poor, for example, is certain to result in loss of "wealth" and "vigour," as Ricardo proclaimed.

No traditional religion has declared more absolutely the universality and necessity of its laws and commandments than the proponents of the global market doctrine. Ricardo's implied position has become explicitly advanced as "the global economy." Being the revealed design of God and natural necessity, its prescriptions are rapidly instituted across the world as "inevitable," and it would appear that no society anywhere has any longer any choice but rapid adjustment to the new global order.

Punishments for Disobedience to Market Laws

Yet a third feature of Ricardo's assumption of the necessary and universal rule of the market's laws is perhaps the most remarkable of all in the doctrine's checkered career as an absolutist creed. The very "laws by which wages are regulated, and by which the happiness of far the greatest part of every community is governed," asserts Ricardo, are also recognized to be *transgressible*.[6] Unlike the principle of gravitation, they had already, as Ricardo knew, been long violated by the income supplements of the poor law or Speenhamland system. That is why Ricardo declares the grave consequences of the market order's violation—certain loss of "wealth" and "vigour." But if so these laws are clearly not, in even Ricardo's understanding of their nature, akin to the law of gravity, which cannot be transgressed. Its attraction and repulsion of masses knows of no exception. Yet here is the Speenhamland income-support system transgressing the wage-laws of the market, providing income outside of market value to the labour factor of production, thereby interfering in the price system of workers for capital's employment. The differences between the laws of nature and the laws of the market are perfectly clear from Ricardo's own description; yet he also asserts that their unavoidable necessity is the same, when it is precisely in this necessity that they plainly differ. The laws of the market can be transgressed, while the laws of nature cannot be. The scientific Ricardo fell prey, it seems to a fundamental logical confusion.

The certainty of the operation of market laws rested most clearly for Ricardo, as for economists since, in the harsh conse-quences that befell societies that sought to "interfere" with them. Ricardo emphasizes this point, as do economists and policy-makers today. Societies "must adapt to the tough new international market-place," or they will "be punished by the market," "suffer job cuts and lower standards of living," have to make "enormous sacrifices," or—most categorically—"*will not survive*." Ricardo was clear about these consequences. The labour market was "a flow of human lives the supply of which was regulated by the amount of food put at their disposal."[7] Those who did not sell their labour in this market starved. This was as it must be. There must be no interference in the laws of supply and demand; and labour, like any other commodity, must be regulated in its supply by employers' money demand, and nothing else, if the system was to work.

Ricardo's scientific conceptions have once again adopted a theological vestment in recent years. Economic seers such as George Gilder—Ronald Reagan's moral beacon during his presidency, when the market doctrine came into its own as the world's ruling fundamen-talist creed—conceived of the invisible hand's rewards and punish-ments in explicitly theological terms. "Under capitalism," Gilder wrote in *Wealth and Poverty*, "the ventures of reason are launched into a world ruled by morality and Providence.... Capitalism entails faith in the compensatory logic of the cosmos."[8] Gilder did not emphasize the punishments and sacrifices and pains so much as the rewards and favours of the market's providential order. But even in his upbeat version of the doctrine, the penalty of impoverishment to unbelievers remained the clear ultimatum of his title.

Perhaps the most tell-tale feature of a fundamentalist religion is the terrorism of its moral prescriptions. If you ignore or do not comply with them, then you are liable to the harshest punishments, to be administered by the invisible hand of the Supreme Ruler. Unlike the New Testament God, the market God is jealous and unforgiving. The penalties are strict: poverty, malnutrition, starvation, death, or, as the current lexicon of terrors warns us collectively, "social shock treatments," "slashings," "axings." The more that "sacrifices" are demanded, and the more that humanity is subjugated to the "demands of the market," the more terrorist the prescriptions seem to become. In the 1990s the starvation conditions of a quarter of the world's population, and the unemployment of a third, became a daily warning to all that they could be next.[9] As the World Bank, an austere vicar of the global market order, warned, "The harsh reality of the global market is that policy failures are punished hard." The Bank was referring to the sudden fall into unemployment of 15 per cent of Mexico's working population and the fall of real wages by 30 per cent, a harsh punishment imposed on workers for the sudden departure of transnational mobile capital from the country.[10]

The global market order is not sparing in its punishments. Most people in the world seem to have been disobedient, according to its judgements, because most people are suffering cutbacks to their life-incomes and entitlements. Business economists and market advocates are quick to remind the majority that they have "lived too long beyond their means." Their reproof, needless to say, does not apply to the much increased incomes of corporate chief executives, banks, and transnational investors during the same period. They apparently, have come by their increased fortunes in grace, by the operations of the market's invisible hand. Others must adjust to meet the market's demands. If this adjustment involves pain and sacrifice, this is a price that must be paid, for those who do not listen to the market will not survive. Often entire societies have transgressed the market's world order, and they cannot escape the consequences of its laws. They must bear the punishments of the market for not "getting the fundamentals right."

The rare exceptions to continuous sacrifices and punishments for societies across the world are the "economic miracles"—in Chile and South Korea, for example. But here too the punishments and sacrifices experienced as a result of not complying with the market's prescriptions have been severe, including, in Chile, mass murder and torture to get the society back on track. As well, the number of people in poverty has doubled since the miracle began in Chile, and the poorest citizens have suffered a 40 per cent reduction of life-income.[11] But the laws of the market are not to be tampered with, or there will be still more punishments and sacrifices.

Under free market rule, societies face two great moral choices: the correct choice, of not interfering or meddling with the operation of its laws, and the wrong choice, of intervention. Interference in the market is the worst of society's temptations, and it is a choice that will be warred against to the death if it seeks to replace market laws. Orthodoxy above all repudiates the right of humans or societies to alter or reform market laws. This is the cardinal sin of socialism, and must suffer the sentence of inevitable misery and extinction, if necessary by the armies of "the free world."

The Underlying Principles of the Market Theology

A theological doctrine, like a science, is an organized system of ideas intended to make sense of reality through the principles it advances. A fundamentalist theology has a number of established features:

1. It posits an invisible Supreme Ruler whose order of rule and laws are conceived as universal, inevitable, and absolute.

2. This order of rule and its laws are conceived as immutable and inalterable, and any interference in their nature or structure is construed as abhorrent.

3. The Supreme Ruler rewards those who are disciplined in their adherence to this order and its laws and is unforgiving to those who rebel against, violate, or fail to submit to its inevitable design.

4. The rewards granted by the Supreme Ruler are happiness and prosperity, which are distributed to all subjects in proportion to their competitive satisfaction of the order's demands; the punishments are poverty, degradation, and suffering, which inevitably befall all those who flout, shirk, or do not adapt to the Ruler's commands.

5. There are perfect states of equilibria of the Ruler's eternal order which do not exist and are never attained, but which all the Ruler's subjects must understand as the optimum states towards which the system tends if not interfered with by the atheist plans and insubordinations of governments and unbelievers.

6. If necessary sacrifices are made by a society to ensure that its fundamentals are right and in proper adjustment to the Supreme Ruler's re-structuring demands, then prosperity or miracles will transfigure that society by the workings of the Supreme Ruler's invisible hand.

7. Whatever facts of life disaster may seem to contradict the necessity and validity of the Ruler's order of rule only appear to conflict with them, and can always be explained and corrected by more rigorous understanding and application of the order's discipline, austerity and sacrifices.

8. Those who doubt or criticize the perfection of the design of the Ruler, the justice of the order's distribution of goods or punishments, and the global inevitability of the system's rule are repudiators of the only hope for human salvation and prosperity, and are to be known as heretics and subversives.

9. Although denominations and sects may fight among one another to determine and declare what the Supreme Ruler truly prescribes and prohibits to His subjects, they are united in their abomination of all that obstructs, creates barriers to, or builds protective walls against the Ruler's laws.

10. Any and all societies, parties, or governments that seek to live by any alternative order of social life-organization than ordained by the Supreme Ruler are forces of evil opposed to the freedom of humanity, and are to be warred against until expelled from the community of nations and eradicated.

For each logical space in which the term "the Supreme Ruler" or "the Ruler's order and laws" occurs, substitute the term "the global market." In this way, we can test whether and to what extent global market theory and practice fulfils the principles of a fundamentalist theological doctrine in its underlying structure of belief. The underlying theocratic metaphysic at work here is not recognized by such adherents to the market creed. What is revealed here are underlying principles of the doctrine's theory and practice. Like the workings of a grammar, the underlying principles regulate claims and behaviours beneath conscious beliefs and self-descriptions.

The freedom of choice of individuals within the market system's laws of property, supply, and demand and profit maximization are consistent with a determining theological absolutism behind the doctrine of "free choice" for consumers, sellers of labour, and other market agents. Consider, in comparison, the central and regulating doctrine of "free will" within the medieval theological framework. The doctrine of free will explicitly required that all that a person chose within the Supreme Ruler's laws and edicts was voluntary and individually responsible, that these actions were judged by the Supreme Ruler's representatives on earth as satisfying or not satisfying His demands, and that they were accorded either rewards or harsh punishment by the design and operations of His invisible hand. Significantly, the global market doctrine also asserts each of these principles, albeit by means of different, contemporary slogans.

The principal difference in theology between the global market and the absolutist church of yesteryear is that the judgements, rewards, and punishments of the global market do not wait for an afterlife beyond the death of the body for their administration by the invisible hand. Rather, they are meted out swiftly and decisively at the end of a business cycle or even a working day and are therefore conceived to be scientifically graphable. Economists are the priesthood of these theocratic fate-lines and structural readjustment programs are their militant crusade. Central banks and finance ministries are the theocracy's obedient arms and offices of state, adjusting societies and peoples everywhere to its necessary commands.

The Place of Free Will in the Market Theodicy

The basic feature of fundamentalist theology is that the order people must obey given by a higher and inviolable design. There is a strict line between humanity's freedom to *follow* the Supreme Ruler's commandments and the Supreme Ruler's sovereign power to *prescribe* these laws.

So it is too with market theory. If people or societies who do not meet the demands of the market subsequently suffer or die from the workings of its operations, this is a harsh price that is not much talked about. Market doctrine rules out any human or social responsibility for the laws of the market, for they are prior to and independent of society, as are laws of nature and God. This is the acme of the creed. The laws are conceived of as absolute, immutable, and obligatory prior to their recognition by science.

Market theory appears, therefore, in fundamental contradiction with its declaration of human freedom as its ultimate and overriding good. How can people be self-determining if they have no voice, say, or responsibility in the most basic principles of the way their society produces and distributes their means of life?

The market theory's doctrine of individual freedom provides the answer. If an individual is to reap rewards rather than severe punishments from the invisible hand, free choices must rest within the moral commandments of the market's rule, in particular the command not to interfere. Ultimately, it is the market that is free from human interference. Its laws are what is sovereign and absolute.

Robert Reich's Conversion

The most rigorous analysts of the market's laws declare repeatedly that a free society is "subverted" (Friedman) and "totalitarianism" is ensured (Hayek) if the laws are not understood as an inalterable framework of freedom on earth.

One of the most urbane and informed members of the first Clinton administration was Secretary of Labour Robert Reich, a Harvard professor. Reich was uninhibited in his warnings of how the recalcitrant majority must now adapt to the inviolable order of the new global reality or fall by the wayside towards Third World conditions. As a farsighted analyst of economic trends, Reich was well aware of the punishments that had already begun for his fellow Americans through the workings of the global market's laws of maximum cost reduction, job elimination, and ever more competition for the lowest common denominator of tax, labour, and environmental expenses. In the new world order, he observed frankly, "the majority of Americans are losing out." By the majority, he meant "four-fifths of the population."[13] But Secretary Reich, in accordance with the doctrine, did not infer from the increasing reduction of real incomes, secure jobs, and future prospects that anything could be amiss for that great majority of Americans he was in office to represent. He took the unfettered movement of goods and capital across borders to be a good by definition and saw its costs in reduced livelihoods to four-fifths of his fellow citizens as a necessary sacrifice to a higher design. The new order unfolding was "inevitable" and therefore not preventable or modifiable by even the most powerful government in the world. He submitted in attunement with the times to its rule and passionately urged adjustment, even though 80 per cent of Americans were, by his own calculation, "losing out" under it.

Indeed, Reich denounced "barriers" or "obstacles" to the universalization of this project precisely as it was attacking the living standards of most of his people.[14] Reich was a paradigm expression of the global market value program in action. He presupposed its laws as gravitational—as global, necessary, and overriding even the life-needs of the republic's people.

In invocation of the waiting punishments, Reich warned that if Americans did not adapt to the rule of the new global market order, "America may simply explode into a microcosm of the entire world. It will contain some of the world's richest people, and some of the world's poorest people.... There will be no national purpose, and no pretense of one."[15]

His solution to the unprecedented defeat of America's majority and its standard of living was more "symbolic analysts"—people who work with symbols rather than "routine producers" on assembly lines and "in-person servers" in the service industry. Reich's solution could not solve the problems he raised, nor those he did not raise—for example, where the jobs for "symbolic analysts" would come from, when such jobs represent a small percentage of all employment in even the world's most advanced information economies.

Like other progressive members of the faith for whom unemployment is a problem rather than a punishment, Reich proposed retraining for jobs that did not exist. This is the market doctrine in its New Testament form, not seeking to punish or blame the unemployed, but to offer deliverance based on faith rather than evidence. In the past, whatever was perceived as to deviate from or to endanger "the American way of life" was attacked by state denunciation and force of arms. Yet here the attack was, on the contrary, pronounced to be "inevitable" by the corporate media, the government, and the U.S. elites who had always declared themselves vigilant to defend the American people against their enemies. In the end Reich spoke out against the process of laying off workers in the tens of millions to increase shareholders' profits in the new world order. In *The New York Times* on March 8, 1996, he bravely advised the American people to "reorganize the corporations to put greater emphasis on the interests of their workers." But by then the new order which he had proclaimed with such panache was in place, and Reich was obliged to resign from office within the year.

The Doctrine of Infallibility

Market theory introduces the logic of social Darwinism before Darwin. Darwin reproduced the struggle for survival, in which masses of the species die as a matter of course, to the non-human realm, in which selection is not by man-made design. The market theory has not developed such a distinction between life-realms. Smith is certainly not alone in the tradition. Ricardo was also occasionally frank about the costs to the labouring race when the demand for their work was low. Starvation of oneself or one's family was the price in a truly "free and efficient market" for not selling one's labour to a master, and it was precisely the incentive to avoid such misery and starvation which made Ricardo so adamantly opposed to external income-support systems such as the Speenhamland poor laws.

From the beginning of its annunciation by Adam Smith, the invisible hand was known to result in large-scale miseries and starvation of working people even while it achieved profits, efficiencies of production, and lower prices. Smith writes: "But in civilized society ... among the inferior ranks of people ... the scantiness of subsistence can set limits to the further multiplication of the species; and it can do so in no other way than by destroying a great part of the children which their fruitful marriages produce.[16]

It did not occur to Smith or Ricardo that starvation, even mass starvation, could count as an argument against the truth or beneficence of the invisible hand of the market. On the contrary, they saw it as the effective mechanism whereby market laws of supply and demand worked with the labour factor of production. They did not much concern themselves with the life or death of the "inferior classes." Like the Social Darwinists they preceded by a century, they thought this to be a "natural law." Even continuously declining real incomes for the poor and the middle classes in the world's richest society today have not disturbed the most eminent adherents to the doctrine in their certitude of the desirability of the free market's beneficent rule.

The certitude and the dominance of market doctrine have increased in intensity as crises become more acute—for example, the demands for ever more deregulation, lower taxes, reduced environmental standards, wages cuts and elimination of social security systems as environmental breakdowns and social insecurity increase. All this occurs as the champions of the program make their claims for horizonless "efficiency," "productivity" and "progress." It seems that the more reality kicks back, the more the doctrine has become closed to the critical check and kickback of reality.

An intense certitude and demand for absolute rule in accordance with perceived divine design are characteristic of fundamentalist faiths, particularly in dark times. Of note here, however, is the closure of the market doctrine at its most "scientific" and "rigorous" levels of advocacy and defence to any possible disproof of its principles. If a theory rules out any possibility of factual disconfirmation, it is not a scientific or even rational theory, but a closed dogma. But which basic principle of the market doctrine is now open to evidence or argument that could show it to be mistaken? What extreme accumulation of wealth at the top of society, or destitution and misery for the majority of society, can indicate to this system of thought that something is wrong with its invisible hand of distribution?

On a more basic level still, what degree of destruction of planetary life-conditions—air, sunlight, water, earth, and species—can be accepted as "externalities" imposed on society at no cost to the private corporations responsible for them before the market's calculus of value recognizes a structural problem? It seems there is no verified fact that can count against the truth and desirability of the market's regulating principles. If this is true, the doctrine is a closed metaphysical loop.

A learned discipline ceases to be a learned discipline when it rules out rational challenge to its established theoretical paradigm. Without the resources for self-criticism of its model of understanding, a project is dogma and its promulgation propaganda. Interestingly, a group of eminent economists themselves who do not yet accept the doctrine's current presupposition of infallibility made a public declaration of this closure. Some forty-four dissenting economists from North America, the U.K., and Western Europe concluded in 1994 that the orthodox school of economic theory has become so closed to critical doubt or alternative that they jointly signed a "Plea for Pluralistic and Rigorous Economics." Their plea declared, with no discernible effect, a "profound concern with the drift towards ideological conformity in economics as demonstrated by the monopoly of one viewpoint in the academic journals."[17]

The Invisible Hand Revisited

In his important work *The Great Transformation*, the social theorist Karl Polanyi referred to the market system of the classical doctrine as a "gargantuan automaton" that its growing army of propagandists sought to impose on society even at the cost of millions of lives of those subjected to its command. Their "militant creed," Polanyi argued, sees even the protection of the living social substance as an "interference" in its freedom of operations for which no human sacrifice is too much:

> Hobbes' grotesque vision of the state—a human Leviathan whose vast body was made up of an infinite number of human bodies—was dwarfed by the Ricardian construct of the labour market. Only the penalty of starvation was deemed capable of creating a functioning labour market.[18]

Polanyi specifically explained the "poor laws," which Ricardo railed against as a calamitous "interference" with the free market system, as a "temporary moat erected in defense of the traditional rural organization." He saw welfare assistance as an interim protection of innumerable human lives that were being thrown into jeopardy by the new cash-crop system invading the countryside and "making agriculture a perilous industry." Polanyi looked to what had happened to the post-Ricardo hand-weavers of India when their produce was replaced by the cheaper, machine-made cotton goods of England's mills. Their "village community had been demolished" and they "had perished by the millions." Such "laws of economic competition," he held, wrought devastation and degeneration. They are, he argued, "a utopian experiment of a self-regulating market" that is intolerant to any guard of human society's existence. To demand the removal of the Speenhamland poor-relief system, he argued in particular against Ricardo, was "demanding the withdrawal of the right to live proclaimed by Speenhamland."[19]

Polanyi provides a very different, opposing social morality to that embodied in Ricardo's "classical" market system. He advocates the positive norm, not yet accepted by market doctrine, that humans have a right to live.

What could make the value program of this "gargantuan automaton," whose "freedom" from any human or social intervention or control is the first commandment of its doctrine, so certain of itself as history's final order for regulating social life-organization? This value system's principles of command have become ever more universal, more unconditional, and more militant as it has grown in world power. The once-abhorred ideas of "inevitable" and "global" rule have become accepted mantras that heads of state repeat as final prescriptions to be obeyed. But is there a real hand behind the invisible hand—whose real market power could help to explain the global absoluteness of this doctrine?

In the doctrine of the "perfect competition" of self-seeking producers and sellers in perpetual contest for buyers, the competition has necessary outcomes. Each cycle brings forward market "winners" who sell at a profit and leaves behind market "losers" who do not. The winners, in turn, vie against one another for "larger market shares," which, according to the doctrine, they achieve in proportion to their "greater efficiencies" compared to competitors. According to the logic of the doctrine this reiterated pattern, over time, takes the efficiencies and productivities of surviving market agents to ever higher levels. These ascending productivity levels, in turn, require ever renewed and improved machineries and methods. These continuous advances in marginal productivity, again in turn, demand greater and greater capital investments and labour-force co-ordination to organize and manage as the process inexorably reiterates its cycles.

Eventually more and more of society's overall volume of production of goods will be controlled by larger and larger producers who possess enough investment capital and economies of scale to compete at ever higher levels of unit-output efficiency and distribution capacity. Although these outcomes have been demonstrated empirically—and economists have had little disagreement on the pattern that has emerged—this element of "oligopolist tendency" has been widely ignored in the promulgation of market doctrine.

The reason for this reticence is not difficult to understand. Oligopoly and monopoly refute the doctrine's essential premise of open competition among producers and sellers. Market theories of the business firm, which take for granted market concentration as the very basis of the modern corporation, acknowledge the tendency towards oligopoly and monopoly. The market's requirement of productive efficiency makes the "combination of personal capitals" into even larger unities of integrated management and control a necessity for access to large amounts of capital, economies of scale, and unit-cost price reduction. The ever-larger corporation is, thus, a legally recognized as well as economically driven structure of modern market production. Indeed, the laws of property and liability themselves have had to increasingly adjust their concepts of individual responsibility to the fiction of the *"corporate person"* to legally enable the increasing concentration of capital ownership that has developed in the modern economic order.[20] Adam Smith, after all, thought a corporate structure or "joint stock company" was inappropriate to a free market order except for "uniform functions."[21]

This long-term qualitative shift towards ever larger corporations with ever larger market shares, a shift that now leaves up to 100 per cent of regional markets in the hands of one firm (such as a newspaper), and up to 90 per cent of the world's market in the control of a handful of firms (such as in automobile production, the oil industry, mass communications, computer software, and increasingly other global-scale production systems) has led to what economists refer to in the abstract as an *"oligopolist structure of the market"*—namely, a relatively few large firms that control market production and supply. Controlling market supply, as these firms aggregately do, with correspondingly large shares of market demand required to stay solvent, the market becomes, to this extent, "their market." The classical model of perfect competition in which many producers compete for many buyers and none can control or influence supply or demand is, in this situation, no longer a model that corresponds to reality. It is an ideological inversion of the truth: it conceals the conditions of the market's structure in a form of representation that makes it appear to be the opposite of what it is. This is the model of the market that is still presupposed.

Worldwide oligopolist corporations systematically condition market demand by global advertising; they control supply by international cartels and tacit agreements; they exercise dominion over distribution networks by mass purchase agreements and technical integrations across regions and borders; and they influence national and state governments by investment decisions, political donations, and firms of lobbyists shaping public policy and government expenditures. They exercise control, then, over the structure of both market supply and demand in a host of ways that no other firms in the market can duplicate. These all too real tendencies contradict the free market model in principle, because the model requires a large number of independently acting firms and buyers who are sufficiently small as not to be able to influence control or significantly influence supply or demand. The invisible hand that adjusts supply to demand is largely wielded by the oligopolist firms that control supply and demand across the globe.

The free market's immutable and necessary rule is, in reality, the rule of transnational conglomerates exercising ever more dominant control over the market's operations. For example, an estimated 60 per cent of international trade and 25 per cent of all world trade take place within these multinational firms themselves.[22] The market has already largely passed to intrafirm supply and demand cycles, in which both facets are under the single executive will of one firm. At the same time, the largest 300 transnational corporations control 25 per cent of all the world's productive assets, 70 per cent of all international trade, and 99 per cent of all direct foreign investment.[23]

These conditions contradict the market doctrine's claims of democracy and freedom depending on the competition of individual agents with none in a position to influence or determine market supply or demand. Neoclassical and other proclaimers of the free market's virtues pass over the existence of an oligopolist market in silence. As John Kenneth Galbraith observes:

It should be noted that exponents of the neo-classical system, while they have long deplored the monopolistic and thus pathological tendencies of oligopoly in principle, have never done much about them in practice. There was cancer, but one did not operate. Remedy became tantamount to talk of socializing, regulating or breaking up the firms that composed the dominant part of the economic system. This was not remedy but revolution.[24]

Thus the "free market" that decrees absolute commandments of non-intervention in its workings is ruled in the end by its "dominant part." Behind the deified design of its "invisible hand," to which all alike must submit, lies a very real and human centre of market command--the bloc fortunes of several hundred billionaires who own as much wealth as almost half the globe's population put together, the interlocking directorates of multinational corporations, and global intrafirm trading empires that dominate the market's base of supply and demand. These ruling positions of the global market hierarchy, in turn, are in lockstep with a presupposed value program governing their decisions and action as a closed, regulating paradigm of mind and reality. Moving down the great automaton's chain of command, the remainder of the positions operate within it as subordinate functions. Whatever their rank in the hallowed system, all enact its commands as elaborations of its demands to reproduce and enlarge. Those who preside and function for a time as the bearers of its reproductions and expansions do not question their roles as roles, but defend its mechanisms as the final structure of their lives' value. At the top of the great mechanism that centralizes and subjugates all life as it moves through time, the new global "market-winners" see themselves as champions of free, individual competition.

Functionaries of its value program "know" that all is for the optimum in accordance with the market's demands, which have come to constitute the organizing value set of both individuals and social orders. These regulating principles of value are, in turn, the human identity-structure as a program. One cannot get underneath what one is. The program cannot see itself, nor can it do other than enact its sequences as the necessary condition of survival and life success. In this way, the circle reproduces itself in widening arcs.

Societies have long tended to worship their received orders of rule as God and to conceive the regulating logic of their daily lives as given by the moral order of the cosmos. But they do so only as long as the representations of it are accepted. In the case of the global market system, an architectonic of argument and everyday benefits reaches back over centuries to justify its rule. These conditions build a solid foundation of tacit consent underneath the system of corporate oligopoly and state coercion.

The belief structure of the market has come a long way. Its organizing principles of social life and reproduction are now for the first time universally propagated and implemented without resistance of government regulation or foreign state opposition. What these principles lack is the test of critical examination at every level. We must make it our task to question and expose this metaproject that orders, restructures, and develops our existence.

Notes

1. In Chile, for example, often cited as a "market miracle," experts estimate that "approximately 30 percent of the population lives (apparently permanently) on the margin of the miracle." José Burneo, *Americas Update*, May/June 1994, p.8.

2. The standard principle here is that government is properly confined to those functions where, in Adam Smith's words, "profit could never repay the expense to any individual or small number of individuals" to provide what the market requires (such as police and armed forces to protect private property from domestic or foreign transgressions, and judicial systems to adjudicate proprietary disputes and criminal proceedings). Smith's words here, which occur at the end of book IV, chapter IX, are cited by both Hayek (*Road to Serfdom*, p.39) and Friedman and Friedman (*Freedom to Choose*, p.29). Smith's famous text, however, is ambiguous on whether a public good can exist for proper government activity that has no function for the market. Global market practice increasingly deems that there is not any public good that does not properly serve the market. To this extent, its position seems "totalitarian" by Hayek's own criterion.

3. "Ethical Reflections on the Economic Crisis," Message from the Administrative Board of the Canadian Conference of Catholic Bishops, Social Affairs Commission, 1983. See Bishop Remi de Roo, *Cries of Victims-Voice of God* (Ottawa: Novalis, 1986), for an account of "the storm" of attacks, including from the Archbishop of Toronto, which greeted this statement on the "scourge of unemployment" following from self-regulating market policies. The most persistent theme of the criticism was that the bishops, not being economists or businessmen, had no right to speak on economic affairs.

4. This is the essential argument of Hayek's *The Road to Serfdom* and is posed against the competition of producers and sellers competing within a money-price system. Hayek is typical in confronting us with an all-or-nothing choice. "Nothing indeed seems at first more plausible ... than a judicious mixture of the two methods of planning and competition--[but] a mixture of the two means that neither will really work and the result will be worse than if either system

had been consistently relied upon." Hayek, *Road to Serfdom*, p.42.

5. David Ricardo, *The Principles of Political Economy and Taxation* (London: J.M. Dent and Sons, 1965), p.63; emphasis added.

6. Ibid., p.61.

7. Karl Polanyi, *The Great Transformation* (Boston: Beacon Press, 1967), p.64.

8. George Gilder, *Wealth and Poverty* (New York: Basic Books, 1981), p.27.

9. Pierre Sané, "Amnesty International's Report Card from Hell." *The Globe and Mail*, Dec. 10, 1993, p.A21.

10. "Mexico's Woes," *The Globe and Mail*, July 8, 1995, p.A7.

11. *The New Internationalist*, August 1993, p.28.

12. William Greider, *Secrets of the Temple: How the Federal Reserve Runs the Country* (New York: Simon and Schuster, 1989), p.423.

13. Robert Reich, *The Work of Nations* (New York: Vintage Books, 1992), p.282.

14. Ibid., pp.8, 312.

15. Quoted in Maurice Banfield, "Capitalism and the Nation-State in the Dog Days of the Twentieth Century," *The Socialist Register 1994* (London: Merlin Press, 1994), p.100.

16. Smith, "Wages of Labour," book I, chapter VIII, *Inquiry*, p.84.

17. The "Plea" was published in *The American Economic Review* and quoted in Bernice Shrank, "Blind Reviewing," *The Canadian Association of University Teachers Bulletin*, March 1994, p.11.

18. Polanyi, *Great Transformation*, p.64.

19. Ibid., pp.86-8, 160.

20. I am indebted here to Harry Glasbeek, "Democracy for Corporations: Corporations against Democracy," Corporations at the Crossroads, Meredith Lectures, Toronto, May 1995.

21. Smith, book V, chapter I, part III, article I, *Inquiry*, pp.481-83.

22. Kimon Valaskakis, "Wanted: A GATT Agreement that Covers Workers," *The Globe and Mail*, April 22, 1994, p.A11.

23. Maude Barlow and Bruce Campbell, *Straight through the Heart* (Toronto: Harper Collins, 1995), p.45.

24. John Kenneth Galbraith, *Economics and the Public Purpose* (Boston: Houghton and Mifflin, 1973), p.17.

Part II
Market Theory and Practice:
Arguments Pro and Con

Freedom, Private Property, and Money:
From John Locke to the New World Order

John Locke on the Right to Private Property

The most fundamental principle of the market doctrine is the grounding of human right and freedom in private property. This principle is foundational because one cannot have a market at all unless individual agents first privately own what they buy and sell.

John Locke's *Second Treatise on Government*, published in 1690, is the founding statement and justification of the right to private property and to protection of that property by public law and force. Locke argues that the right to private property and to its secure protection is the foundation of all government legislation and duty, of all individual rights, and—if violated—of the right to rebel against the state or sovereign. Market doctrine since Locke has presupposed his position as canonical.

Locke bases his central argument for the right of private property on a number of unquestioned premises, all of which deserve careful reflection (we set aside here Locke's presupposition of God).[1] The first premise is that God has "given the earth to mankind in common" (25). This is, interestingly, a communist premise, which has strangely eluded free market theorists since. It is also a premise implying that no other species except human beings has any rights at all to the earth, an idea that the doctrine has since presupposed without question, however absolute its anthropocentric bias.

What alters humanity's initial "common ownership" of the planet for Locke is that God has also "given mankind reason to make use of it to the best advantage of life and convenience" (26). This appropriation, Locke assumes without reason, is "private and individual." This second premise goes against all of the reliable anthropological evidence that we now possess. But this false basis of private property right as well has not detained market believers from their certitudes of doctrine.

Since "every man has a property in his own person," Locke continues, "the labour of his body and the work of his hands are properly his" (27). Given that the product of labour is the private property of its producer, Locke concludes that whatever the individual "removes out of nature—and has mixed his labour with—is his own, and thereby makes it his property." He adds, "No man but he can have a right to what that is once joined to, at least where there is enough and good left in common for others" (27).

Locke declares another limiting condition to the right to private property based on what one has "mixed his labour with." The first requirement is that there must be "enough and as good left over" for others. The second is that nothing to which a private property claim has been fixed "can be allowed to spoil." He states, "Nothing was made by God for man to spoil and destroy" (31). Both these limiting conditions on private property seem ethically sound, but only Locke's most dubious premises survive today.

With his underlying framework established, Locke summarizes:

> He that in obedience to this command of God subdued, tilled, and sowed any part of the earth, thereby annexed to something that was his property, which another had no title to, nor could without injury take from him... He [God] gave it [the earth] to

the use of the industrious and rational... and labour was to be his title to it. (32, 34)

Locke's argument, so far granting all rights of private property to labour, then moves to the historical introduction of money, which negates this original foundation of right. Men (sic) can now buy one another's labour and the products of that labour, without having to "mix their own labour" with what they "rightfully" own. Locke's original labour basis of private property right is thereby rejected. Property can now be held by inviolable entitlement with no work to produce it at all. This is the first contradiction of Locke's private property doctrine.

"The invention of money," Locke also says, "and tacit agreement of men to put a value on it introduced—by consent—larger possessions and a right to them" (36). Locke nowhere proposes a limit to how much larger or smaller these possessions can become. His position thus permits a rightful inequality of private property without limit.

Locke gives three arguments for his new position. First, men have given their "consent" by "tacit agreement" to the value and use of money, and they renew this consent every time they use it. Let us consider, though, Locke's use of the terms "agreement" and "consent." To consent or to agree to something implies that one can refuse to consent or agree to it. But how can one refuse to agree or consent to the value of money if acceptance of its value is required to buy and sell the means to stay alive? It is more accurate to say that after money was historically instituted as the general currency of value, people were compelled to accept its value in exchange for necessities. Agreeing to money's transactions, Locke concludes, men agree to the results of these transactions—however little labour now counts for property title, and however unequal private property holdings become.

Second, money accumulation can continue and increase without limit in the hands of its private possessor because the largeness of its possession "never occasions" the perishing of anything useless within it. Money is "some lasting thing that men may keep without spoiling" (47).

Third, Locke suggests that the earlier condition specified for the limit of private property, that "there is as good and enough left over for others," is cancelled by the introduction of money as a common currency of private property's purchase:

> But since gold and silver, being little useful to the life of man in proportion to food, raiment, and carriage, has its value only from the consent of men--it is plain that *men have agreed to a disproportionate and unequal possession of the earth*, they having, by a tacit and voluntary consent, found out a way how *a man may fairly possess more than he himself can use the product of*. (50)

As the added emphases show, Locke's argument approves of inequality with no limit on the grounds of the tacit agreement to use money. He does not explicitly state the implication that this inequality can be unlimited, nor does he recognize the further implication that this unlimited inequality conflicts with the earlier condition of good and sufficient amounts of the earth's resources being left over for others. For without a limit to the accumulation of money or a limit to the land and resources that money can buy, it follows that the earth's land and resources can become the private property of those who have money with no limit to their "unequal possession." Locke never posits any bound to the unequal possession of the world through money and never alludes again to his earlier limit of leaving "as good and enough left over for others." We can only conclude that the "tacit consent of men to use money" negates this earlier requirement. This is the second unexposed contradiction of Locke's private property doctrine.

The doctrine's philosophical foundation thus justifies the market theory's basic principles of private property, of money transactions to purchase it, and of inequality of possession with no limit. Given this justification, they are thereafter presupposed. From Smith on, no economist, classical or neoclassical, or other proponent ever supposes these principles to be controvertible except by the unenlightened. They are taken for granted as self-evident, socially necessary, and beneficent—the foundations of "a free enterprise economy." Any further justification is left to ethicists, philosophers, and churchmen, who, in turn, tend to presuppose or justify private property in the abstract and remain generally silent on the discussion of money. In the main, labour right is forgotten, and those left with no property by the operations of the market are dismissed, made "invisible," and assumed to deserve their condition.

If public interest rights or individual human needs impinge on the principle of the right to private property with no limit of inequality, they are designated as being outside the market doctrine, and are opposed.

The doctrine's most basic tenets also rule out the position that limits in principle can be set as to what money can rightfully buy. Believers in the doctrine may accept limits imposed by law—for example, laws against street prostitution or non-prescription drugs—but they do not accept any limit in principle. "In a competitive society, almost everything can be had at a price," Friedrich Hayek says in his famous market monograph, *The Road to Serfdom*. Hayek regards this freedom of exchange as bearing an "importance which can hardly be overrated," and he attacks critics of the "cash nexus" as demanding to impose their choices on "the freedom of the individual."[2] In principle, then, the position is that nothing should be ruled out from money purchase and sale. Exceptions can only be particular, contingent, and relative. For example, Marx's position that people's working lives should in principle not be bought and sold is in absolute contradiction to the free market doctrine.

In summary, the unstated implications of the market's theory of property from Locke on are:

1. Private property right need not be earned by one's own work or production.

2. Private property on the earth, including its resources and its products, is an overriding and inviolable right.

3. Private property can always, and in all things, be rightfully bought and sold by the medium of money exchanges between property-owners (with certain non-defined exceptions, but

never the exception of human labour or any commodity not prohibited by law).

4. Private property can be accumulated by the medium of money exchanges with no limit to its rightful hoarding and global extent, its rightful inequality, or its rightful dispossession of others by exchanges between lawful owners.

These principles are hidden implications; they have not been openly asserted by Locke or market doctrine adherents. They have remained unquestioned in the doctrine for three centuries. One would be hard-pressed to find any exception to their social regulation today. Locke's original grounding principles of private property right—the right of labour to what it has mixed its labour with, non-wastage of the earth's resources and property by those who appropriate them, and "enough left over for others" to work and live from—have been completely discarded. They were expunged—first by the implications of Locke's arguments, and then by explicit market doctrine. The value program retains Locke's final, self-contradictory conclusions as sound, while using their justifying grounds, as pleasing rhetoric for the credulous.

The Problem of Private Property In Slaves

Even the most dogmatic of current marketeers no longer defend one form of private property, though they have made no theoretical adjustment to their doctrine on this account. This form of private property and market exchange—property in other human beings, in slaves—is perhaps the most historically dominant ever: the centrepiece of market transactions for over two thousand years, from classical Athens to the antebellum United States. Innumerable invasions and wars were fought to secure and to protect the right to enslave. Commentators from Plato and Aristotle through to Locke, and long after, have made various justifications of the right to own slaves.[3]

The right to private property necessarily entails the right to exclude others from what is owned. If I own you as a slave I therefore have the right to exclude you from the use of yourself and your body, because I own these things as private property and no one may interfere with my free use of that property—including you.

That governments now generally prohibit slavery by law in market societies represents a great step forward in human civilization. But this means also that government has "interfered with the market" in a fundamental way: it has drawn a line against the right of private property. The doctrine does not usually acknowledge this line. None of the promulgations of private property as the foundation of individual freedom include any explicit line against the rights of slavery.

The issue then arises: if the principles of this doctrine do not rule out slavery as a form of private property, so long as slaves are obtained by the voluntary transaction of slave-seller and slave-buyer, how can such an unqualified doctrine be advanced except by the morally vicious? Conversely, if the right of private property in slaves has indeed been abolished, the implications in principle for the doctrine are profound and as yet uncomprehended.

How Do We Distinguish Buying Slaves from Buying Labour?

From its beginnings the capitalist market system thrived and grew based on free and profitable buying and selling of human slaves in the market. Indeed, this free global market in slaves was the principal basis of the success and spread of market capitalism across the world. Slaves were the primary commodity of world trade, the dominant means of production across the Americas and Asia, and the basic producers of surplus wealth. The capitalist market owes its historical success to human slavery.

But if we accept a principle to limit the free market that prohibits slaves as a form of private property, we thereby reject the historical foundations and genesis of the free market system itself. A consequence that throws the doctrine into contradiction with its own foundations is not one that its adherents will admit to. Free market doctrine continues to draw no line in principle against the right to private property in slaves. Like other unpleasant realities, it is removed from view.

The line, as all such lines protecting life, was drawn by what we call the civil commons.

The state thereby commands the agents of the free market as to what they can and cannot do, "coercively interfering" in the market's "voluntary transactions of purchase and sale." It even "confiscates" their legally acquired property in the process. Market theory now confronts the conundrum of how to distinguish in principle between buying and selling human lives as instruments of labour (slaves) and buying and selling most of the vital waking hours of human lives as instruments of labour (the labour factor of production). On the face of it the distinction seems obvious. But is it sustainable when the human is owned and used as a mere instrument of production?

Karl Marx argued that if a buyer of one's labour owns one's labour as private property, one is a "wage-slave." If a civilized norm exists to rule out humans as proper objects of private property because they ought not to be articles of purchase and sale in the market, this implies that "wage-slavery," too, should be prevented, for example, by guaranteeing effective human and labour rights in the global market. Such a human rights norm would pose an insuperable difficulty for the doctrine. The global market would be transformed if some international agreement ruled out the buying and selling of human lives as commodities. The commodity of labour is the primary "factor of production," and it is not distinguished in economic theory from any other factor of production used as an instrument of its purchaser. The global market buys and uses human labour as a commodity in continuous flows of billions of people's lives across the globe. It is now called "the global labour market," and practitioners of this market increasingly reject obstacles to this free purchase as "inflexible barriers" to the free circulation of capital investment and market exchanges.

Adam Smith, David Ricardo, and classical economics held it as axiomatic that labour was the source of all economic value: "the labour theory of value." Without human labour available for purchase and use on the master's terms, they implied, there would be no source of market value. Contemporary economists reject the labour theory of value as "nonsense," even though it is a foundation of their discipline.

But all market theory presupposes human labour as a basic commodity. Buying humans in their vital waking hours as an article of commerce is a foundational requirement of the capitalist market system.

According to the market doctrine, the difference in principle between the slave proper and the wage-slave is that wage-slaves privately own their labour-power and voluntarily sell this labour-power in the market to buyers at whatever price they can bargain for. Slaves proper have no such private-property and exchange rights. The doctrine can thereby argue a limit exists on what can be bought and sold as private property, and that limit is drawn here. The entire life of the labour commodity cannot be bought or sold, but only what is voluntarily transacted.

Adam Smith said, "I believe that the work done by freemen comes cheaper in the end than that performed by slaves."[4] He recognized the cost-saving nature of wage-labour over slavery. The freedom of the labourer does not draw the line against slavery, this reply could then conclude, but rather the slave's higher business costs. The costs of maintaining twenty-four-hour slaves and families far exceed the payment of a market-set wage, especially in times of an oversupply of labour. The wage-system is just a less costly form of keeping subjugated labour; it is not different in principle from slavery.

The capitalist does not buy all of the living labourer to use as private property, it is argued, but only, say, three-quarters of the worker's vital waking hours. This condition places a limit in contemporary free market doctrine on what can be owned, bought, and sold as private property (even if the limit is only accepted because it is cost-reducing to the market buyer of labour). This argument may be correct, but it still remains consistent with the enslavement of the worker.

Does the free market doctrine now accept other limits on what can be freely owned, bought, and sold? In the example of human labour, a number of limits seem to exist on its sale, purchase, and ownership as private property, at least in more "developed" societies. These limits include, for example, shorter working hours. But this kind of limitation normally depends on labour union protection, which market doctrine does not support. On the contrary, international market co-ordinating bodies such as the World Bank, the International Monetary Fund, and the Organization for Economic Co-operation and Development (OECD) typically criticize labour protections, seeing the union protection of workers as a "distorting influence on the labour market."[5] Moreover, even with union protection, limits on the working day can normally be overruled by compulsory overtime, with or without "deregulation of the labour market." In non-union factories, which employ the vast majority of the world's industrial workers, a typical working week is ten hours a day, six or seven days a week—rivalling the work week of a plantation slave in the U.S. South prior to the Civil War. Life under such conditions would seem to be less than significantly "free."[6]

A responding counterargument suggests that other limitations exist on the use of purchased human labour that do not compare with slave labour. For example, numerous industrialized societies occupational health and safety regulations limit employers' free use of their labour in toxic and dangerous working conditions. Yet here as well, increasing deregulation permits employers to evade enforceable standards protecting the lives and safety of workers, even in the wealthiest nations. Advocates of the free market approach argue that such standards are "anti-competitive" and represent "government interference in the marketplace." They also maintain that actual as opposed to merely pretended contractual agreements between unionized labour and employers limit the slave-like conditions of the buying, selling, and use of human labour; examples are job-security agreements, health and pension benefits, grievance procedures, seniority rights, and job specifications. But these limits on free market transactions and property in human labour are also being cut back and eliminated. Current market doctrine perceives them as "inflexible," as embodying "the excessive powers of big unions," and as "unaffordable restrictions on management." They are limits that are conceived as being "barriers" to the sale of labour that market policy and practice are unwilling to accept. In First World states, accordingly, corporations now avoid standards protecting workers' well-being and contractual equality simply by relocating from regulated or unionized workplaces to workplaces in which few or no such restrictions "fetter private investment" and "employer competitiveness." Child labour and forced labour have returned to the market in forms as brutal as ever.[7] Market policy and practice have once again accepted them, this time to achieve "competitive prices for consumers."

The global market ideal of the free circulation of goods and capital across borders does not rule out child labour or slave labour. The doctrine deplores only "interference in the free market." Bonded labour, forced labour, and child labour are thus rampant in the "booming free markets" of East Asia, with hundreds of millions of workers and children held in subjection. Global market doctrine remains consistent with enslaved labour in all its forms, and transnational trade agreements aggressively seek to remove regulatory barriers that protect labour from the market's inherent drive to reduce the costs of its purchase and control.

The Free Contract Solution

Free marketeers such as Friedrich Hayek and Milton Friedman put overriding emphasis on "voluntary contractual agreement," arguing that it is all up to the independent agents freely agreeing to the conditions of their transactions in an open market of buyers and sellers. Wage-workers, they contend, are just like other sellers of commodities seeking the best price they can get for the goods they are dealing.[8]

The problem with this argument is that the freedom of a market agent does not truly exist if that agent has no choice other than starvation or destitution. To use a familiar business expression, this is not a genuine choice, but "an offer that can't be refused."[9] Yet this is the very situation now faced by the propertyless seller of living labour, with government assistance cut back or eliminated and a vast over-supply of labour for sale in the global market.

Smith and Ricardo were relatively frank about the resolution of such oversupplies of labour in the free market: those who could not sell their labour died, with their children dying first. This system of regulating labour supply to labour demand continued until the labour supply declined to the point at which the demand for it was sufficient to buy it again and keep it alive. Then the labour that had survived to be hired would be paid wages to feed its reproduction until it was no longer needed again. Smith wrote, in a principle that anticipates Darwinian theory:

> The demand for men, like that for any other commodity, necessarily regulates the production of men; quickens it when it goes too slowly, and stops it when it goes too fast. ... Every species of animals naturally multiplies in proportion to the means of their subsistence ... among the inferior ranks of people the scantiness of subsistence sets limits ... [which] it can do in no other way than by destroying a great part of the children.[10]

These words of Adam Smith, the revered founder of the market doctrine, overtly endorse the mass death of children by "free market" operations. Surely only a heinous value system would serenely justify the death by mass starvation and disease of children and their families; but market theory and proclamation never repudiate this position. It is a consequence that follows from the self-regulating operations of the labour market and the laws of supply and demand, and the founder of the market doctrine himself explicitly recognizes this result. So it cannot be denied. We must conclude from their continued adherence to the principles from which these effects follow that "free market" advocates indeed accept the mass death of children and families as an operation of "the invisible hand." It would be difficult to find a more ready embrace of such a homicidal sacrifice of humankind, but market logic assumes this holocaust as "necessary."

Ricardo's "iron law of wages" states that in the normal condition of the labour market, labour's wages for those who were employed could never rise above subsistence level. Ricardo saw this too as a law of the market and had no qualms about it either. The survival of labourers would invariably produce children whose continued life would increase the labour supply and so force down the price of labour again, until the labourers' families died off once more to approximate "an equilibrium of supply and demand."[11]

These conditions, which exist in many societies, are now returning to the First World. "Private property" in the form of labour does not provide much to its owner and leaves little to bargain with in the open market. Yet as excess capacity and oversupply of labour in the global market increase, and as the alternative of government support in unemployment is rapidly eliminated so as not to "encourage bonds of dependency" in working families, market fundamentalists and libertarians exhibit undiminished faith in market laws. Rights of private property, free contract, and the sale of labour at whatever price obtainable in the open market are, indeed, held aloft as the proper and inviolable laws of the Free World. Again, we see a reversion to an "unfettered market" with no limits to the harsh consequences for those caught in the social conditions of an oversupply of labour. Could this be a deliberate form of planning death and destitution for others?

The principles of classical market theory remain basic and defining in the received doctrine. Civilized sensibility may be shocked that such argument could be acceptable and object that it is inhuman, that it treats people as disposable, and that it supports people starving to death if they are not hired for profitable use in an oversupplied labour market. Market doctrine adherents do not seem troubled by these problems. On the contrary, they call for the abolition of welfare support systems for the unemployed, as in the Republican Congressional leaders' 1994 Contract with America.[12] Market doctrine enthusiasts herald the conditions in which workers of the eighteenth and nineteenth centuries struggled to stay alive, and which most of the world's workers still face, as "the tough new international marketplace." Employers seek these conditions of an undeveloped world to "reduce costs." In the guise of the "tough new marketplace" in which First World workers now "learn to compete," "market-reform" governments steadily deprive employees of the legislated protection of their rights and safety and bargaining power.[13]

Despite these conditions, current free market advocates find no reason to revise "free contract" concepts, because, again, mainstream economic theory and balance sheets do not take into account life-insecurity, destitution, malnutrition, and occupational disease. "Free contract" remains "the basis of a free society," even if and when certain conditions prevail:

1. Employers do not negotiate the terms of a contract. Companies offer a job at such-and-such a price per hour or day of labour on a take-it-or-leave-it basis.

2. Employers do not produce, or sign, a contract. The worker accepts the job to survive and, if selected, obeys the employer's orders, including the orders to perform work in hazardous and disease-causing conditions that are in violation of law.

3. Workers have no leverage to better the accept-or-reject agreement that stands in for the contract and can be dismissed at will at any time for seeking terms to protect their lives, security, or well-being.

4. The alternative to accepting these terms of employment is to be without a job and, thereby, stigmatized and without means of life.

Many of us experience these conditions at first hand.[14] Yet still free marketeers insist on the "free contract" basis of the market, although in this regard they have shown their propensity to turn facts on their head by repeating slogans.

Unionized workers are generally not subject to these one-sided terms of free contract in labour sale and purchase. They benefit from collectively negotiated terms, signed documents, means of enforcement, the right to strike, and even severance payment provisions. But the percentage of workers in unions is rapidly declining in the First World (plunging to 10 per cent in the U.S. private sector in the 1990s). In the rest of the world, where the greater part of the labour supply lives, independent unions are relatively rare,[15] with the exception of Europe. Labour unions were prohibited by law for centuries in the developed world as "unlawful combinations in restraint of trade," and independent unions are still effectively prohibited in the most of the world today, with frequent murders, extrajudicial executions, tortures, or a continuing persecution of union and community organizers.[16] Unions provide authentic conditions of free contractual negotiation in the labour market for a small and decreasing percentage of the global labour pool, but the terms of contract invariably rule out any right of workers to determine the organization of their labour. Under the most privileged conditions of contractual negotiation, human labour remains a purchased commodity owned by its employer once the price of its sale has been negotiated. Even this right is not ensured under the coercive conditions that apply.

The "free contract solution," then, is not a solution that speaks to the reality of the labour market. It is, rather, an ideological reversal of facts concealing the captive nature of human labour's purchase and sale. Although a self-evidently specious rhetoric of negotiation and choice, it continues to be repeated at the highest levels of theory and argument.

The Problem of the Propertyless Unemployed

The free market contains two kinds of propertyless private-property owners. The first group encompasses those able to sell their labouring abilities on the open market for a price sufficient to live on. The second group comprises those unable to sell their labour on the open market to the extent that would provide a living wage. What happens to the majority who have no private property but their own bodies if there is not enough market demand to purchase their living labour? According to the market doctrine, this profound problem has only one solution: to lower the price of labour with no floor to its reduction—quite possibly to under a dollar a day in most non-unionized labour markets in the world.[17]

Starvation and destitution are not hypothetical conditions for most workers in the "rapidly more prosperous" global economy. Labour-replacing machineries, in particular electronic technologies, have displaced increasing numbers of full-time jobs. At the same time the global labour market available to transnational firms seeking low labour costs is increasingly oversupplied with labour. Tax-relieved U.S. corporations have not created "jobs, jobs, jobs" as repeatedly promised, but have erased over forty million U.S. jobs since the tax giveaways began in 1981.[18] The consequences of labour supply exceeding labour demand are increasingly insecure employment conditions and workers facing insufficient demand for the only private property they have to sell, their labour. This process has, for example, "impoverished half the population of Mexico over the last 13 years of market-restructuring policies."[19]

It is a mark of the free marketeers' faith in "the invisible hand" that their doctrine manages to ignore such problems. Instead, the various authorities propose shibboleth remedies, including lowering wages, abolition or radical reduction of welfare payments to poor families, and more training for jobs that do not exist. It is thus difficult to avoid the conclusion that the doctrine still accepts, as did its classical founders, the mass starvation of children and families by the free operations of the market's laws of supply and demand. Adherents to the doctrine lead and support political attacks across the world on government welfare and unemployment support for propertyless, jobless, labour sellers, even if these people outnumber the jobs available by a ratio of fifty to one.[20]

The free marketeer's system of private property, money exchange, and unlimited inequality of ownership is hardly better than feudal bonds, or even slavery—because slave-owners at least had, as Adam Smith pointed out, a self-interest in preserving their private property from disease and death. Buyers of labour in a buyer's market have no such rational interest in preserving the lives of the workers they hire, because they can replace them at no cost. The market doctrine presupposes strictly self-interested buyers and sellers, which is its definition of "rationality." Without intervention to protect workers who can find no buyers for their labour, market doctrine can only accept the destitution, malnourishment, or eventual starvation of people when unemployment and underemployment go on the increase.[21]

The value system's insistence on no state intervention in the pricing of commodities entails that unsold labour receives nothing. Ignorant of the necessary implications of their principles, free marketeers are united, whether they are concerned about providing assistance to the propertyless unemployed or not. The doctrine of free exchange of private property for money with no interference from the state in the market's prices of commodities cannot be wrong. This is the inner logic of the system and the invisible hand of its adjustment of supply to demand.

Justifications for Private Property in Money without Limit

The basic value of private property is that it provides its owners with a secure personal possession within which they can live in freedom from external interference. It is not that owners have earned their private property by "mixing their labour" with it. Locke began with this justification of private property title, but left it behind once money was "tacitly consented to" as a way of acquiring property. This was a necessary modification in the private property doctrine if it were to retain credible connection with reality. In Locke's day those unquestioned private property accumulations were very obviously not earned by their owner's own labour. Private property was typically inherited or bought with no justifying labour required. Adam Smith himself made it clear that profit was in no way connected with the skill or difficulty of managing one's capital investment.[22] To these earlier modes of unearned private property, there is now an even more important form of mainstream property acquisition: speculation in the short-term prices of land, stocks, currencies, and market derivatives.

Free market doctrine does not, however, depend on only one justification for the unlimited right to accumulate private property through money transactions. It has many layers of justification to defend unlimited money-property acquisition, some leaving aside the issue of merit altogether. One justification is that as long as the private-property or money acquisition has achieved its hoard "within the law" and by "voluntary exchange," it is an offence against legal entitlement, individual right, and natural liberty to limit it or redistribute it. The state has no right as a matter of principle to interfere with such private wealth accumulation—even on behalf of saving people from starvation. Money-property without limit is, for this "libertarian" view, a sacred right in itself that cannot be moderated for "end-state" purposes without undermining law, justice, and freedom.

"Risk" is another more commonplace justification of unlimited money wealth not earned by one's own work. This justification displays the money investor or speculator as daring and entrepreneurial, ready to meet life's challenges and thus entitled to all gains by way of this motivation. The doctrine says that capital investors and speculators deserve the money profits they receive as "risk-takers" because they are exposed to the possible loss of the private capital they have invested. But there is no correlation whatever between profits gained and investment risks to establish that money gained corresponds to risk undertaken. On the contrary, corporations and investors are systematically concerned about minimizing risk, and they invest accordingly. To "reduce the risk of investment" is the mantra of the investment community, at least until someone raises the issue of justifying their profits. Then investors declare "risk-taking" to be fundamental.

Those who defend the unearned income they receive for their risks of investment are militantly insistent that government's first priority is to protect their investments against risk—a priority they place, in perfect accordance with the doctrine's first principles, far before the education, nutrition, and lives of their society's citizens. The response of "the investment community" to the barest hint that a government will not provide this special assurance to their security before the well-being of all else in the society is normally sufficient to stampede all "risk-taking" investors from the country concerned. The repudiation of any social policy that might conceivably increase "risk to investors," the reluctance of banks to lend to small-business enterprises while receiving record profits, and the reliance of successful corporations and stock investors on minimizing all possible risk by highly predictive information accessible only to them reveal the value system's true commitment.

Profitable investment increasingly does, indeed, require real risks of life and possession from others. Workers, for example, increasingly risk losing their livelihoods at any time in the global labour market, whatever their life-investment in a family, home, and community within the workplace. With no profit in recompense they are also injured, killed, diseased, and variously exposed to serious occupational hazards at an incomparably higher level than those who work at investing money.

The Trickle-Down Theory

A recent justification for the rich holding ever more private property in the form of money no longer pretends that the rich have some meritorious characteristic to justify their unearned money-wealth—"abstinence from luxury," "initiative," "willingness to take risks," "entrepreneurial talent," or "rightful title." It claims that for the rich to become still richer is good for the non-rich. The idea of unearned money-property at the top being good for everybody is a standard stock-in-trade of the market value system. The "trickle-down" theory claims that certain beneficial outcomes follow from more money-property in the hands of the rich.

A contemporary twist on Adam Smith's idea that profit-seeking by producers promotes the social good, this theory is based on the perhaps aptly named "Laffer Curve." The Laffer curve purports to show, with all the econometric trappings of high market theory, a counterintuitive fact. Its graph represents an "optimal tax rate" for the rich, much lower than the then existing tax rate, above which the government will get less tax revenue from the rich. More simply expressed, higher taxes on the wealthy net less tax revenues from the wealthy.

The Laffer curve, impressive for visually oriented audiences, shows taxable revenues declining with higher taxes. That is, when their taxes get too high, the rich invest less in job-creating enterprises. Therefore, lowering their taxes will benefit them and everybody else.[23]

The logic of giving more to the better-off is underwritten by one of the most distinguished social and political philosophers of our time, John Rawls. His famous "difference principle," advanced in the now-classic tome *A Theory of Justice*, promotes the idea that inequality of income is good and just "when it benefits the least advantaged." Rawls sets no limit on how far this unequal income flow to the privileged for the benefit of the poor can be pushed by "rational decision-procedures." He takes it as axiomatic that the "pursuit of self-interest" or "wanting more for oneself" is what the norm of "rationality" means. Therefore, it follows, we must "want more for ourselves" in choosing principles of justice.[24]

Rawls's idea is that giving incentives to the advantaged to produce a larger social pie for all justifies awarding some more than others in a just society. He thinks that all would "rationally" be obliged to choose this sort of society from behind "a veil of ignorance" where none knew where they would end up. But this is an idealized version of the rewards of profit. Rawls's justification has, nevertheless, a peculiar advantage. Unlike other justifications for profit, Rawls's reasoning occupies an abstract theoretical realm with no connection to the actual world. Discussion need never deal with rebuttal by facts, evidence, or how the world actually works. With no connection with the real world, his argument can disregard the charge of subtle evasion or even excuse-making for the rich.

With the Laffer curve leading the way and philosophy providing idealized rationalizations, U.S. presidential policy soon provided many hundreds of billions in tax cuts to the rich in 1981. All were assured that this was to benefit everybody, including the poor. The predicted outcome of higher tax revenues to pay for public goods, however, did not materialize. Government revenues fell precipitously, inequalities of wealth rose dramatically, and 80 per cent of American people came to owe more taxes than before.[25] These results made no difference to the popularity of the "trickle-down" theory among the wealthy, government planners, "neo-liberal" and "neo-conservative" thinkers, mass media, and economists.

The advocates of the free market doctrine do not, as a matter of course, consider it necessary or desirable to produce factual confirmation of the "trickle-down" theory's claims. They have judged the mere repetition of such claims, like other justifications, to be sufficient to prove their truth and reliability. The outcomes emerge into accepted reality by an act of faith, the market's perfect design.

"Trickle-down" theory declares confidently that investment in productive enterprises will increase, jobs will be gained, government revenues will rise, and the least well-off will benefit from tax cuts to wealthy individuals and corporations. Why not, then, make these predicted outcomes an audited condition for receiving the tax reductions?

Where the Rich Refuse Contract

Nothing more quickly exposes a fallacious argument than to demand that its justifying reasons be fulfilled. Governments, professional economists, and certainly the rich themselves never conceive of the possibility of ensuring social-benefit outcomes to justify tax reductions for corporations and the wealthy. Here is a predictable, perfectly circular argument to justify money-wealth accumulation: that private property is private property, and no one but its owner has in the end any right to determine what is done with it.[26]

Surely, there must be a justifying reason for a special group of society to hold unearned money-property without limit, or their right is unjustified. The justifications keep coming; one is no sooner refuted than another leaps in to take its place. Do the claims of positive social benefits for all by means of ever more money-property for the rich have any grounding in fact and outcome?

The market theory's basis of civil legitimacy, negotiation, and reliable expectation of what is promised in exchanges of goods or benefits is contractual. Otherwise it is empty in content, a mere con-game. But these promised benefits are never conceived to be binding on one side, that of the rich, although the tax reductions and other tax-supported incentives they receive are immediately binding on everyone else. States grant hundreds of billions of money-property to one side of the bargain—over $300 billion in one U.S. tax cut alone in 1981—but require nothing in return. This is an agreement rather like Big Jule's blank dice in *Guys and Dolls*. Big Jule called the numbers, and collected his money accordingly. The numbers he said went as true, and no one in the game, in which all consented to play, dared doubt the results. At least Big Jule's game came to an end. "Incentive programs" and other transfers of public wealth to wealthy corporate and private agents continue as instruments of "democratic market societies." Rich corporations and private beneficiaries of tax cuts never have to sign contracts with the rest of society to make good on their promises of social benefits to all. When contract and contract theory are the theoretical core of a doctrine and of its concepts of moral obligation and of justice, but are suspended from all application, the society reveals a deep-structural contradiction in its value bearings.

The rich's money-property increases from tax reductions come with no ties. The money-property will be invested where it is "rational," where it maximizes money returns. It will assuredly not trickle-down to the poor of the society. To project this beneficial outcome is a form of wishful thinking, whose source is market theology.

The outcomes of this approach have been quite the opposite. Between 1980 and 1990, for example, the richest 1 per cent of U.S. citizens benefiting from 30 per cent tax cuts experienced a 60 per cent growth in income, while the income of the bottom 40 per cent of U.S. citizens dropped.[27] At the same time, decreased taxes on investors in the U.S. Fortune 500 resulted in a net total gain of zero jobs.[28] Meanwhile the public debt almost tripled over the next seven years. Yet "trickle-down prosperity," "increased government financial resources," and "getting people off the unemployment rolls" were tirelessly proclaimed as assured benefits to the public good in return for sharply reduced tax rates on the wealthy and corporate stockholders during this entire period.

Politicians across North America continue to repeat the same proclamations almost word for word. The phenomenon expresses a theological value program that is no longer related to reality. The record demonstrates that investors quickly place their "job-creating tax cuts" in cheap-labour, no-tax, and environmentally unregulated manufacturing zones and in leveraged buy-outs or bond, currency, and derivatives markets with no productive commitment. These moves follow from the value program's first principles. Because the "investment community" does not have to contract with society to deliver the promised goods of "jobs, jobs, jobs" or "increased public fiscal resources," or anything else, the consequences are predictable. Society's tacit consent to the market value program as its final ruler has already signed the covenant for redistributing public wealth to the rich and the private sector.

Private Property for and against Life-Interests

"A man's home is his castle," is the motto, tellingly gender-specific, expressing the universal claim to private property right, with the state acting as protector.

The basic, consensual justification of private property, of its protection, and of its right of accumulation and sale is, then, to provide a personal space for people's individual use and enjoyment of their means of life—their dwelling, private possessions, and articles of life-support—in secure freedom from external interference. If we understand private property as a right to be enjoyed by all free individuals in a democratic society, private property is a universal right and not just that of a privileged sect to acquire ever more money-property for themselves. If private property is to protect society as a whole, it cannot be ordered to protect only the few. If so, private property right ceases to be a democratic right and becomes instead a sectarian privilege.

The principal justification for the long war of "free societies" against "communism" was to protect the "individual's right to his own private property," which was continuously proclaimed to be a "sacred right of all citizens." Yet if fewer and fewer citizens come to enjoy the right to have security in their private property, this proclaimed right is not real, but rather a propaganda slogan for the special and unlimited demands of the few to possess more and more for their particular social sect. In this connection even Adam Smith bluntly warns us: the "vile and selfish maxim of all for ourselves and nothing for other people" has been followed by "the masters of mankind in every age."[29]

Defenders of private property right, such as Gary Madison in *The Logic of Liberty*, argue that people can have a right without the means to exercise it.[30] To argue that people have, for example, the right to a roof over their head even if they are homeless exceeds the frivolity of Marie Antoinette, who at least recognized that people without food still had to have something to eat. Market fundamentalism manages to maintain a realm of rights and freedoms in words, but not in reality. In the global market, private property as a right is increasingly non-existent for billions of people throughout the "developed" and "developing" world. At the same time, protection of private property right in money and corporate assets, a costly process involving tax-supported armies, police, and court systems, is increasingly a special-interest operation on behalf of redistributing wealth from the poor to the rich. In Africa and Latin America, for example, the primary role of government fiscal policy is to transfer public wealth to First World banks to pay off loans whose principal has been repaid many times over.[31]

A very small group within societies—sometimes a few oligarchical families—owns or controls most of the wealth and resources as private fiefdoms, while the majority in those same societies steadily lose ground and face malnutrition, homelessness, and starvation. Countries formerly in the orbit of state socialism now display a like pattern of ever more extravagantly rich minorities and increasingly propertyless majorities as they transform into U.S.-advised market systems. In the United States itself, since "the Reagan revolution" a six-fold increase in annual millionaire household incomes has occurred side by side with a steep decrease of real incomes for the working majority.[32] More strikingly, sharply accumulated money-property wealth circulating for speculative investment alone is now many times greater than the dollar turnover for all production and distribution of goods and services. The overall emerging pattern is a process of ever more transfer of money-property from the unrich to the rich, with no commitment by the rich to any socially useful function (a globally erupting pattern to which we will return).

As these disproportions of private property and money-exchange accumulations become more extreme, two distinguishing transformations of private-property structure arise: first, rapidly increasing money accumulations at one end of society's membership, and increasing propertylessness for the rest; and, second, speculative money investment with no commitment to the production of goods or services as a growing, ruling pattern of money investment. Although each problem threatens in a different way the life-base of human society, neither has stirred any doubt in the free market fundamentalists' article of creed. Private-property in money acquisition remains a sacred and unbounded right.

Abstraction as Disguise for Special Interest

At the bottom of people's cross-class support and acceptance of private property rights in goods and in money is a shared grounding reason:

1. assured and unobstructed access of the property-holder to the life-goods needed to continue in a state of healthy well-being;

2. allowance of the property-owner to use and improve the content of his or her private property with no external interference or deprivation of the enjoyment of daily life benefits;

3. prevention of social conflict and uncaring use, which may be consequences of undifferentiated, common ownership.

The great problem of the market doctrine's conception of private property is that it has never been governed in its theory or practice by any of these underlying, shared grounds of private property right. These lived consensual grounds have been appealed to, on the contrary, to attack any position that advocates common property that might interfere with profit maximization. The market doctrine's absolutist principle of money-property acquisition is in rising contradiction with the socially accepted, grounding reason for private property. From the beginnings of the doctrine, one form of private property right has in practice overridden all others: the right to money-property acquisition without limit of need or work contribution.

But since only a very small part of society receives its income through acquisition of money-property by investment rather than work, those who must work for a living—the vast majority—have been essentially left out of the market doctrine's concern for the right of private property. They figure in this right only insofar as they are paid producers or paying consumers within the system of maximizing money-profit. Over the years, this instrumental majority has been seen as "the race of labourers" (Smith), "the servant class" (Ricardo), or "the labour factor of production" (the current economic category). But in all cases, most people in society have been viewed as economic agents only in their function as means for others' profit. It was for this reason that Adam Smith himself, for example, explicitly acknowledged the hard fact that civil authority is "in reality instituted for the defense of the rich against the poor, or of those who have some property against those who have none at all."[33]

Society is now, especially with the disappearance of self-employed farmers and producers, even more clearly divided between those who live from private money-property investment and those who are hired or not hired to produce profit for them. Adam Smith was equally frank about the conflict between the interest of these money-investors and the interests of society's members as a whole. He observed of those who live from the money-to-more-money circuit:

> The interest of the dealers, however, in any particular branch of trade or manufacture is always in some respects different from, and *even opposite to, that of the public*. It comes from an order of men whose interest is never exactly the same with the public, who have generally an interest to deceive and even to oppress the public, and who accordingly have upon many occasions, both deceived and oppressed it.[34]

Significantly, the founder of the theory himself long ago recognized the problems and contradictions, special-interest pleadings, and dispossessions of others we are now seeing in market doctrine and implementation.

Do Property Rights Have Property Obligations?

Across the world, free market politicians increasingly urge those not selling their labour on the market to strive harder, even if no buyers are there to employ them. They therefore legislate drastic reductions to public assistance of unemployed workers, single mothers, the homeless, and other groups without sufficient private income to invest, rather than work for a living. A neomarket ideologue like David

Frum says that the propertyless have a "greedy sense of entitlement" for desiring to maintain a historic right to minimum means of life secured by centuries of democratic social struggle.[35] Frum, interestingly, is a beneficiary and heir to parental fortunes.

The right of the poor to secure protection of individual domains of dwelling, food, medical, educational, and other basic requirements of life is, in accordance with such doctrine, abolished as rapidly as "the free market revolution" can manage to redistribute their small holdings to the wealthy in the form of reduced tax obligations. The poor are dispossessed of their life-entitlements because they are unable to sell their labour in an oversupplied labour market. Their sin is that they do not work for those with money-property to buy them, and they do not themselves have money-property to invest.

In this way, private property rights become rights to the increase of the unearned wealth of the already wealthy. No protection of individual liberty or security is sacred or inviolable to proponents of the market creed, except that of capital gain. People's human rights to life and well-being are repudiated and overridden in principle as soon as they cease to perform a demonstrable function in the money-profit maximization of investors.

The right to remain with one's family in the family home if one is disemployed through no fault of one's own, the right to be secure in service to the public weal at a non-profit job, or the right to be governed by a democratically elected government if it endangers corporate profit-maximization are not entitlements that free market advocates or mainstream economists defend or accept. Rather, they seek to eliminate them. The theory and practice of the doctrine impose the rule of one special interest, private property in money profit, a narrow absolutism overriding and extinguishing other property interests wherever they conflict.

When we understand this more exact determination of the meaning of "the right to private property" in the theory and practice of the free market, we appreciate more fully what the "free" in "free market" ultimately denotes: the freedom to possess ever more money from money-investment. Market ideologues constantly remind the poor that rights carry responsibilities. What are the responsibilities owed by money-property in investment, which seeks as its overriding goal maximally more money-property for its owner? We are frequently assured that this principle of rational self-maximization creates not only private wealth but also more government wealth when government reduces taxes ("supply-side economics"). We are also assured that it "protects old-age pensioners with retirement incomes," although most pensioners have little or no such retirement incomes and market leaders seek to reduce whatever public pensions they have. We are further assured that it "creates jobs for the unemployed" by the investments that increased money-profits bring to any society that ensures the freedom to maximize money-profits, although the evidence demonstrates the opposite. These assurances, again, are never backed by any requirement to make good on their promises.

No social obligation or responsibility is required of rich, individuals or corporate persons who appropriate ever more unearned money-property for themselves from societies across the world, even when they receive it straight from governments in return for promised benefits to society.[36] Here, revealingly, the demand that people "deliver value" to society for what they receive is suspended. Yet market advocates become ever more insistent on such performance from everyone else, in particular, the poor or those in public service. There seems no limit to this double standard. As international trade agreements provide barrier-free access to markets and assets across regional and national boundaries to transnational corporations, this problem of "all for ourselves and nothing for others"—recalling Smith's "vile maxim of the masters of mankind"—becomes totalitarian in its reach. All that is required is that corporate agents agree among themselves through mechanisms of government co-ordination to a system of self-protective rules so as not to infringe on each other's blanket rights to "free trade" access.

Unconditional access to what is owned and exchanged in society has enormous costs, borne by its citizens' past, present, and future taxes and government deficits. Under trade agreements foreign corporations receive the benefits of these domestically tax-supported goods free of charge. These corporations buy and sell across markets without having to contribute proportionately to the immense costs of infrastructures, protection, and public services in any one country. If the corporations' goods are produced elsewhere, and provide no jobs in the markets in which they are sold, that is only a matter of their "competitive" rights under "free trade." "To compete" against other societies the host society is expected to provide armed force and police protection, introduce laws to protect corporate agents and goods, and provide, at public expense, large-truck arteries, low-cost utilities, no cost water supplies and effluent exits, and many other highly expensive protections and infrastructures. The state must now also undertake the added major public costs of protecting transnational corporations' patents (for example, in medicines) and of enforcing intellectual property rights (for example, over farmers' seeds and authors' texts, even against the interests of the host society's own growers and writers).

Corporations paying little or no taxes for these publicly financed supports and services are, thus, free-riders on public expenditures, paid for by increasingly disemployed people. Tax-freed investors and corporations are nicely served by this free-rider status. If they have any tax-obligations at all, they demand still "more competitive tax-rates." This explains the extraordinary unanimity of private corporations' support for free global trade agreements. As free-riders on public purses and deficits, they clearly see that it is in their self-interest to institute free trade regimes that grant them this common corporate right. Consequently, societies must compete against one another in granting these corporations ever more free-riding rights to keep them from taking capital produced in host societies and investing it elsewhere. To pay for the investors and corporations' competitive freedom from obligation, societies must, with reduced revenues, cut back their social spending for public needs. The whole process sets in motion a spiral of bankrupting public sectors to subsidize corporate investors.

Corporate representatives are the first to insist there is "no free lunch" for others. But the right to cost-free access to expensive market infrastructures and services in foreign societies' markets and, increasingly, domestic markets, is a basic contradicting premise of corporate investors—and it is one that has been repressed. The focus has been on the propertyless—students, the disemployed, and the old—to "be responsible for their burdens on society" and "learn to pay their own way."

A society's environmental resources may be polluted, degraded, and exhausted by private corporate exploitation, with no requirement to pay damages or to ensure the prevention of these problems. Those who seek to stop environmental degradation are themselves prosecuted by the state.[37] Whole communities may be deprived of their livelihoods and security by rootless corporations or investors who profit from the local labour and resources and then abandon them at will. This destructive process is neither recognized nor deterred by current law or regulation, and the assumption of current market doctrine that corporations have no responsibility or liability for damage they inflict on the environment by their actions is deemed to be necessary to "attract investors."

The world's multiplying Free Trade Zones, particularly the Maquiladora zones on the border of Mexico and the United States, make explicit this absolute refusal of responsibility. These zones grant private foreign corporations the freedom not to pay taxes, not to reinvest capital, not to allow labour unions, not to be subject to national pollution laws, not to pay minimum wages, not to have maximum work days or weeks, not to obey health and occupational safety laws and, in general, not to be bound by any rule to pay for what they receive in public infrastructure and services, or to be held responsible for the environmental, health, and social damage their regime inflicts.[38] The North American Free Trade Agreement (NAFTA) provides for the perpetuation of this Free Trade Zone structure in Mexico, and the World Trade Organization and the Multilateral Agreement on Investments (MAI) now generalize the principles of "free investment."

Money Investment and Community Fetters

Social struggle, workers' collective organization, civil activism, and economic reform have long confronted the wretchedness of slave labour, sixteen-hour days, starvation, child labour, and other capitalist conditions. But the "self-regulating market" and "free and responsible agents" operating on their own have never achieved social responsibility in such matters.

On the contrary, progress in social responsibility, from the abolition of slavery to laws protecting the air we breathe (so far as it has been protected), has been imposed on the market only in the face of fierce resistance from profit-seeking investors. Governments have had to pass laws to prohibit profitable businesses from production and sales processes that are systematically destructive.

Conventional market doctrine does not in principle rule out any form of free-market profit. It is perfectly consistent with this doctrine that humans are sold as slaves, lethal narcotics and toxins are sold for mass consumption, and lethal weapons are marketed across the world. Slavery was defended for centuries as the very core of private property and right and free market profit. Two very profitable free market activities continue today as central forms of money-property maximization in the global economy: cigarettes and armaments. No preventative limit is normally set to any market activity without external interference by the state. These "community fetters," which throughout history civilization has to some extent managed to impose on money-profit seekers, almost always stem from community resistance.

That which is owned as private property, sold as private property, and profited from as private property has proper ethical limits. These limits, however, require interference with the market, but such constraints are rejected because, ever since Adam Smith, it has been assumed that "employment of capital for the sake of profit alone promotes the public interest."[39] Unconditional greed is thereby justified as the providential working of the invisible hand. Sustained by the idea that ever more greed entails ever more service to the public good, market doctrine and practice have since presided over an increasingly destructive organization of global life.

Market orthodoxy is in principle militantly opposed to state intervention, because the doctrine presupposes that the inherent design of the market transfigures all private-profit pursuit into the well-being of the community through the laws of supply and demand. Market doctrine remains in a closed circle, with all that is harmed by the implementation of its principles excluded from view as external to the costs of the system's transactions.

Milton Friedman, the advisor of successive U.S. Republican presidents, is clear on how any self-imposed obligation or responsibility to any interest beyond money-profit maximization by a corporate agent is to be deplored as a "subversion" of the free market. He argues that "business as a whole cannot be said to have responsibilities." More specifically, he maintains that self-regulation by corporate agents is unjust because in the "free enterprise, private property systems" the sole responsibility of corporate agents is "to make as much money as possible for stockholders."[40]

The New Crusade for Freedom

From Locke to Friedman, only one effective limit has been placed on the demand for ever more money-property by market exchange: the limit of enforced public law. But the market doctrine defends only the right of private property in money profits as sovereign or overriding and views any interference in its freedom as an attack on "the basis of a free society."

What we see over the three centuries' career of this value system is a refusal to internalize any effective obligation to serve any interest other than the maximization of money possession. Only the external action of public government or, within the market, consumer boycotts at the demand end of the investment circuit have effectively reigned in this otherwise absolute right. External constraint by public and state intervention is the only known effective limit to market ideology's imperative of more money for money investors. But the doctrine conceptualizes such interventions as a violation of market laws and now seeks to reduce and abolish any state interference in its operations.

Consequently the doctrine must rely on a fundamentalist theology, a worship of the market's ruling interests as God, to give it the power to command, to punish, and to override all other life-interests.

The doctrine of divine right thus re-enters secular society by another door. Adherents to the doctrine must increasingly retreat to a non-factual realm to sustain their faith, because self-regulating market investment now increasingly fails to deliver the goods.

The more numerous the dispossessed people of the world grow, and the more that the following generations are without the prospects of employment or resources to live, the more the ruling principles of the unfettered market are heralded as the one and only way to achieve "global prosperity and human freedom."[41]

Outspoken U.S. Republican House Leader and Speaker Newt Gingrich exemplifies the ordering principle of this new world order. He declares a holy war against all unbelievers—or, in his own words, "a fight for the future of the country, a fight to the death."[42] This line of attack wars against the traditional rights and social entitlements—the right of the poor to receive medical care in illness or the unemployed to have social assistance—as the enemy of the state, the great Satan to slay in this historic "battle for America's soul." The conversion of private property right in Locke from "what one mixes one's labour with" to the unrestrained accumulation of money by the wealthy and the dispossession of the poor promises America the final solution. The future yearns for the new value vision. No obstacle of reality will stand in its way--not the rights of the unemployed to their subsistence, not the environmental base of life whose thin protection by government regulation is being dismantled, not the reality principle in this "fantastic new world of market opportunities."[43] These are not merely the fantasies of a pre-millennial U.S. leadership, but symptoms of a deep paradigm disorder of the global market itself.

Notes

1. This argument comes in *The Second Treatise of Government*, chapter V. The excerpts here are identified by section numbers, which can be found in most versions of the treatise. The text used is Thomas P. Reardon, ed., *The Second Treatise of Government* (New York: Liberal Arts Press, 1956), pp.16-30.
2. Hayek, *Road to Serfdom*, pp.96-97.
3. Plato's Socrates, for example, presupposes slaves and slavery as a necessary part of even an ideal state; see Plato, *The Republic*, 4,33d. Aristotle states the classic view more explicitly: "For that which can foresee by the exercise of mind is by nature intended to be lord and master,

and that which can with its body give effect to such foresight is a subject, and by nature a slave." *Politics*, 1252a4.

4. Smith, "The Wages of Labour," book I, chapter III, *Inquiry*, p.85.

5. The OECD has prescribed that labour costs and conditions be "more flexible" and free of "restrictions" on lay-offs, wages, and other collectively bargained protections of workers to ensure "the efficient functioning of labour markets." These policies, calling for wholesale structural reforms and deregulation of the labour market, are now prevalent and have been adopted by even moderate political parties such as the Liberal Party of Canada. See OECD, "Progress in Structural Reform," 1990, and "Jobs Study," 1994, reported in Andrew Jackson, *The Liberals' Labour Strategy* (Ottawa: The Canadian Centre for Policy Alternatives, 1995), pp.5-7.

6. For example, in Asia and Latin America child labourers who are as elsewhere still legally constituted as the possessions of their parents (see my "The Case for Children's Liberation," *Interchange*, vol. X, no. 3 (1979-80), pp.10-28), are standardly sold to employers for as little as twenty cents a day for twelve to sixteen hours of labour. See "Children Pay High Price for World's Cheap Labour," *CCPA Monitor* (Canadian Centre for Policy Alternatives, Ottawa), October 1995, p.11. Lest this be thought an exception in the global free market, the *CCPA Monitor*'s source in this matter, UNICEF, also reports: "340 million children in India under the age of 16 are estimated to fall under the definition of child labour. In Africa, over 20 percent of children are thought to be economically active. In Latin America, the proportion is estimated at between 10 percent and 25 percent." Ibid., p.11. However, international trade law such as the World Trade Organization (formerly GATT), or the North American Free Trade Agreement (NAFTA), have no prohibitions against child labour.

7. UNESCO reports the labour of children numbering in the hundreds of millions in the 1990s; see *CCPA Monitor*, October 1995, p.11. But forced adult labour is also widespread in the global market as unpaid prison or captive labour in such rising economic superpowers as China and Indonesia. Here again, no international trade regulation effectively prohibits the sale of goods made by slave labour. It is condoned by trade law. Richard Elgin, director of the trade and environment division of the WTO in Geneva, explains the policy priority of these international trade agreements: "The primary role of the WTO is to avoid trade disputes, not to encourage them." "Conference Debates Human Rights, Global Trade," *The Globe and Mail*, Feb. 23, 1996, p.A14.

8. Friedman and Friedman, *Freedom to Choose*, pp.19-20, 228-47; Hayek, *Road to Serfdom*, p.37.

9. This may help to explain why even U.S. parents under thirty years of age were compelled to accept a 32 per cent cut in their real wages between 1973 and 1991, a median figure that has since declined. U.S. Bureau of the Census, 1992, reported in World Health Organization Commission Health and the Environment, *Our Planet, Our Health* (New York: World Health Organization, 1992).

10. Smith, "Wages of Labour," *Inquiry*, p.85.

11. David Ricardo, "On Wages," chapter V, *The Principles of Political Economy and Taxation* (London: Dent Publishers, 1965), pp.56-57.

12. Ed Gillespie and Bob Schellhas, eds., *Contract with America: The Bold Plan by Rep. Newt Gingrich, Rep. Dick Armey and the House Republicans to Change the Nation* (New York: Times Books, Random House, 1993) pp.65-69.

13. In *Prisoners of the American Dream: Politics and Economics of the U.S. Working Class* (London: Verso, 1986), Mike Davis reports that the Reagan presidency's attack on regulations protecting labour included deregulation of labour relations and transportation, reduction of health and occupational standards, exemptions from minimum wage laws, removal of seventy-year-old restrictions on child labour, ending U.S. Bureau of Labour statistical reporting of

strikes, and repealing National Labour Relations Board provisions on collective rights.

14. In Ontario, formerly one of the world's most advanced jurisdictions in protection of workers, the Conservative government after its election in 1995 deprived farm workers of the right to organize, abolished the individual's right to refuse unsafe work, withdrew the option of declining overtime hours, and largely dismantled the enforcement staff of the Ministry of Labour, although "study after study documented the lack of enforcement of basic legislated rights in non-union workplaces." Buzz Hargrove, "The Fight over Ontario's Labour Law Has Just Begun," *The Globe and Mail*, Feb. 6, 1995, p.A17.

15. Friedman would eliminate labour unions altogether as "a throwback to the feudal period" and, before that, to "the medical men of Greece." Friedman and Friedman, *Freedom to Choose*, p.229. In this repudiation of unions, he is in agreement with those governments that prohibit independent trade unions in the labour market in Indonesia, China, and other burgeoning "miracle economies" in the global market. Adam Smith, significantly, was far more evenhanded than his "free market" heirs in his conception of unions. "Masters are everywhere and always," he said, "in a sort of tacit, but constant and uniform combination, not to raise the wages of labour--[but] the law authorizes, or at least does not prohibit their combinations, while it prohibits those of workmen." Adam Smith, "Wages of Labour," *Inquiry*, p.70.

16. See, for example, Noam Chomsky and Edward S. Herman, *The Washington Connection and Third World Fascism: The Political Economy of Human Rights* (Montreal: Black Rose Books, 1979). For police intimidation and goon killing of union organizers in the contemporary United States, see Michael Parenti, *Democracy for the Few* (New York: St. Martin's Press, 1988), pp.135-38, 207-8.

17. The World Bank estimates that over a billion workers live on an income of under a dollar a day, a sum it considers, without evidence, to be "a vastly better standard of living than their parents had." "Workers in an Integrating World," *World Bank Development Report 1995* (Oxford: Oxford University Press, 1995), p.1.

18. Louis Uchitelle and N.R. Kleinfield. "On the Battlefields of Business Millions of Casualties," *The New York Times*, March 3, 1996, p.28.

19. Canadian Centre for Policy Alternatives and Choices Coalition for Social Justice, "Alternative Federal Budget 1996: Framework Document," Ottawa, 1996, p.42.

20. "Daily bloodletting in the foreign exchange arena now exceeds trade in goods and services by an astounding fifty to one." "Power of Financial Capital Overrides Governments," *CCPA Monitor*, April 1995, p.8.

21. The standard laissez-faire position is that assistance to the starving unemployed or anyone else should be entirely "voluntary," not "coercive." Where this position is moderated by the idea of a "negative income tax" by Milton Friedman, in *Capitalism and Freedom* (Chicago: University of Chicago Press, 1969), the only tax-subsidy figure he mentions is $300 (p.192). Even the idea of a "negative income tax" is no longer proposed in market doctrine and practice, because the global market has increasingly released investment capital from problems of local destitution and uprisings.

22. Adam Smith, "Of the Component Parts of the Price of Commodities," book I, chapter VI, *Inquiry*, p. 51; and "Of Wages and Profit in the Different Employments of Labour and Stock," book I, chapter 10, *Inquiry*, p.109.

23. Thus, between 1981 and 1988, the top rate of income tax fell by 60 per cent in the United States, 51.8 per cent in the United Kingdom, 44.5 per cent in New Zealand, and 27.7 per cent in Canada. "The Politics of Greed--The Facts," *New Internationalist*, October 1988, p.17. Further major cuts of between 30 and 50 per cent for the richest income bracket are currently being proposed by market-driven governments in these countries.

24. John Rawls, *A Theory of Justice* (Cambridge Mass.: Harvard University Press, 1971), pp.141-43. Rawls's presupposition here is an indicator of the pervasive powers of market

system indoctrination.

25. William Greider, *Secrets of the Temple: How the Federal Reserve Runs the Country* (New York: Simon and Schuster), pp.577-78. Michael Lind, "To Have and Have Not," *Harpers*, June 1995, p.38.

26. Robert Nozick, *Anarchy, State and Utopia* (New York: Pantheon, 1974). This is the last recourse of the certitude of money-property's absolute rights, made popular by John Rawls's Harvard colleague Robert Nozick. Nozick, typical of market ideologists, justifies inequality of wealth without limit by avoiding the real world of profit from ownership of more capital rather than superior input. Like Rawls and others in the philosophers' game of norm-gazing in the abstract, he builds on the just-so story that more money is received from the discharge of superior ability or talent, ignoring the issue of getting more money from having more money, and no other reason. In his justifying model of market-derived riches, a black basketballer, Wilt Chamberlain, demands 25 cents from every fan who chooses to watch him play, and collects $250,000 for doing so (Ibid., pp.161-62). This example stands in for the capital investor receiving profit for no work of his own, or it does not stand in for the capital investor. If the former, the example is fraudulent. If the latter, the example is irrelevant. In neither case does it justify money profit from investment of money capital. In this way, philosophers sidestep the issues of the actual market order by inventing worlds more amenable to justification.

27. C. Cobb, T. Hastead, and J. Rowe, "If the G.D.P. Is Up, Why Is America Down?" *Atlantic Monthly*, October 1995, p.72.

28. *Money Matters*, Newsletter of Working Assets Money Fund, Winter 1991-92, p.2.

29. Robert Brank Fulton, *Adam Smith Speaks to Our Times* (Boston: Christopher House, 1963), pp.388-89.

30. Gary Madison, *The Logic of Liberty* (New York: Greenwood Press, 1986).

31. *Economic Justice Report* (Ecumenical Coalition for Economic Justice, Toronto), vol. 5, no. 2 (1994), p.7.

32. Edward N. Luttwak, "The Poor Get Poorer," *Times Literary Supplement*, June 10, 1994, p.10.

33. Quoted by Michael Parenti, *Land of Idols* (New York: Alfred A. Knopf, 1991), p.85.

34. Smith, "Of the Rent of Land," book I, chapter XI, *Inquiry*, pp.219-20; emphasis added.

35. Quoted in *The Toronto Star*, Aug. 24, 1995, p.A17.

36. The U.S. Department of Energy spends $4.2 billion a year merely paying for unsuccessful disposal of the U.S. nuclear industry's wastes (with General Electric Corporation the industry leader in that regard). The government will spend at least $230 billion more, it is estimated, in this subsidizing activity. See "Botched Nuclear Report," *U.S.A. Today*, Feb. 16, 1996, p.10A.

37. A revealing example of this use of the state by wealthy corporations to attack those who seek to prevent the corporation's destruction of public property occurred in Clayoquot Sound, British Columbia, in the summer of 1993. Over three hundred citizens who sought to block the clear-cutting of remaining ancient coastal rainforests in British Columbia by MacMillan Bloedel Ltd. were arrested and imprisoned by a private court order issued to the corporation by the B.C. government years earlier to prevent anyone from interfering with its private logging operations. At the same time, MacMillan Bloedel was a fifty-times convicted violator over the previous thirty months of provincial and federal laws protecting the environment. I am indebted to Ontario and B.C. environmental lawyer Douglas Chapman for this information.

38. "The North American Commission for Environmental Protection (NACEC) which was established by the NAFTA's Environmental Side Agreement [provides a] review process [which is] complicated, lengthy and secretive--permits only NAFTA Parties (not provincial

governments or citizens or environmental groups) to participate. It is to be conducted in the absence of proper legal procedures and without adequate opportunities to collect evidence or call expert witnesses. The evidentiary requirements which must be met in order to penalize a government [not private corporations who inflict the damage] for not enforcing its environmental laws appear to be insurmountable. The resource exclusion [in the agreement] embraces an untenable definition of environmental law. The environmental side deal will not redress NAFTA's erosion of environmental standards and resource conservation. In many ways, it represents a significant step backwards." *The Development GAP*, Nafta thoughts, vol. 4, pp.3-4.

39. Smith, "Restraints of Particular Imports," *Inquiry*, p.351.

40. Milton Friedman, "The Social Responsibility of Business Is to Increase Its Profits," *New York Times Magazine*, Sept. 13, 1970.

41. See, for example, Geoffrey Hawthorne, "Capitalism without Capital," *London Review of Books*, May 26, 1994, p.12; and Edward N. Wolff, *Top Heavy: A Study of the Increasing Inequality of Wealth in America* (New York: Twentieth Century Fund, 1995).

42. Unless otherwise stated, the attributions of this section are based on *Contract with America*; Kevin Phillips, "The Right Stuff," *The Guardian Weekly*, Aug. 13, 1995, p.20; Newt Gingrich, *To Renew America* (New York: Harper Collins, 1995); Martin Walker, "Capitol Braced for Head-on Collision," *The Guardian Weekly*, Sept. 17, 1995, p.6; and Newt Gingrich, Foreword to Alvin and Heidi Toffler, *Creating a New Civilization* (Atlanta: Turner Publishing, 1994).

43. To have a sense of the degeneration of civil responsibility under the rule of the "new order" market doctrine since the days of Franklin Delano Roosevelt, when there was recognition of the need for social intervention to respond to the market's one-sided operations, it is worthwhile pondering President Roosevelt's words in his 1944 State of the Union Address:

We cannot be content, no matter how high that general standard of living may be, if some fraction of our people—whether it be one-third or one-fifth or one-tenth—is ill-fed, ill-clothed, ill-housed, and insecure.

This Republic had its beginning, and grew to its present strength, under the protection of certain inalienable rights—among them the right of free speech, free press, free worship, trial by jury, freedom from unreasonable searches and seizures. They were our rights to life and liberty.

As our Nation has grown in size and stature, however—as our industrial economy expanded—these political rights proved inadequate to assure us equality in the pursuit of happiness. We have come to a clear realization of the fact that true individual freedom cannot exist without economic security and independence. "Necessitous men are not free men ..."

In our day these economic truths have become accepted as self-evident. We have accepted, so to speak, a second Bill of Rights under which a new basis of security and prosperity can be established for all—regardless of station, race, or creed.

Among these are:

1. The right to a useful and remunerative job in the industries or shops or farms or mines of the nation;

2. The right to earn enough to provide adequate food and clothing and recreation;

3. The right of every farmer to raise and sell his products at a return which will give him and his family a decent living;

4. The right of every business man, large and small, to trade in an atmosphere of freedom from unfair competition and domination by monopolies at home and abroad;

5. The right of every family to a decent home;

6. The right to adequate medical care and the opportunity to achieve and enjoy good health;

7. The right to adequate protection from the economic fears of old age, sickness, accident, and unemployment;

8. The right to a good education.

America's rightful place in the world depends in large part upon how fully these and similar rights have been carried into practice for our citizens. For unless there is security here at home there cannot be lasting peace in the world.... [There are] grave dangers of rightist reaction in this Nation.... If such reaction should develop--then it is certain that, even though we shall have conquered our enemies abroad, we shall have yielded to the spirit of fascism here at home.

Private Profit, Competition, and the Social Good

Adam Smith's Moral Revolution

Adam Smith began this moral revolution with a few lines of theoretical text within his master work, *An Inquiry into the Nature and Causes of the Wealth of Nations*, published in 1776, the same year as the American Revolution. His statement of general principle was thin, but the impact of his defining core concept was epochal:

> Every individual is continually exerting himself to find out the most advantageous employment for whatever capital he can command. It is his own advantage, indeed, and not that of the society, which he has in view. But the study of his own advantage naturally, or rather necessarily leads him to prefer that employment which is most advantageous to the society... He generally, indeed, neither intends to promote the public interest, nor knows how much he is promoting it...[But] by directing that industry in such a manner as its produce may be of the greatest value, he intends only his own gain, and in this, as in many other cases, led by an invisible hand to promote an end which was no part of his intention.[1]

Thus, one of the most important revolutions in Western thought occurred with an idea that in previous periods of history was unthinkable, the idea that the exclusive pursuit of one's own private advantage in production and commerce promoted the social good.

Smith's principle struck a mighty chord in the rising capitalist society, relieving self-maximizing investors of the burden of thinking beyond rewards to themselves.

The social organicist Georg Wilhelm Hegel dismissed "atomic individualism" and the idea of the individual person being independent and prior to society, an idea that has prevailed in "the free world" from John Locke to the heirs of Thatcher and Reagan. Hegel argued that this idea of the individual was an "absurd abstraction" and conceived of individuals as embedded in their historical social relations, apart from which they were "an unreality." Nonetheless, Hegel's theory echoed Adam Smith's idea that being selfish in the direction of ordering reality for one's gains was also good for others, a principle, "the cunning of Reason," whereby selfishness is transmuted into its opposite, the good of the whole. He argued that "world-historical individuals" bring about great social advances in "the institutionalization of right and law on earth" through the militant pursuit of their own interests imposed on others, thereby organizing them into larger nation-state unities of ruling purpose and will.[2]

Smith's, and subsequently Hegel's, general idea is now part of the canon of "great man" narratives of Western history. It was an idea that enabled rationalization of power and the powerful. The underlying, connective idea here is that the leadership of society is properly left in the hands of those who rule over large numbers of people and powerful technologies and impose an organizing will on them that is more efficient and larger-scaled than any competitor's. We can see a vast concatenation of theorists and theories clustering around and growing from this seminal idea introduced by Smith, such as Darwin's struggle for existence yielding ever more developed individuals and species by its life-and-death contest for survival and genetic self-reproduction; the Nietzschean *Übermensch*, whose will to power imposes its noble ruling forms on the "natural" slaves and lower beings moulded to the higher will; and Marx's idea that history moves forward through the ruthless self-interest of capitalists and the revolutionary self-interest of proletarians seizing power for themselves.

Behind all of these different and opposing theories, atomist and organicist, Nietzschean and capitalist, Marxian and Darwinian, was the seminal idea that exclusively self-seeking action in competition against others is good for society overall. Marx alone drew the line against these theoretical rationalizations for the moral high ground of self-serving, although those who ruled in his name did not.

This was hardly an idea that could be generalized without qualification. If it were true that sometimes exclusive pursuit of one's own interest by the advantaged might work for the benefit of society, it was also true that often it did not. Smith confined his principle to the production and purchase of commodities for sale in the marketplace. Here, he perceived a special serendipity of outcome: that investors seeking profit in competition for buyers have to provide lower-priced or better goods in order to succeed. Even here, as we shall see, the production of goodness by selfishness, Smith's "the work of an invisible hand," was not nearly so beneficial in consequence as was supposed.

I Am Rational, Therefore I Self-Maximize

Integral to economic theory, Smith's idea of the pursuit of self-interest and profit as the servant of the social good became canonical. Three principles crystallized from the "invisible hand," leading selfish economic agents to promote the common interest:

1. The self-seeking pursuit of profit automatically equilibrated supply to demand because the incentive of private gain motivated investors to invest their capital in the production of goods or services in short supply. Producers of goods in short supply could then sell them at a higher price on account of their unavailability elsewhere.

2. The pursuit of profit for oneself also maximized economic efficiency because it motivated the self-interested investor to

produce goods and services at the lowest possible cost so as to draw buyers from competitors by lower prices.

3. The self-maximizing pursuit of profit also promoted individual welfare by providing an incentive to producers to offer improved or new products to buyers, who would otherwise not purchase. This outcome was again advantageous to both buyer and seller because it ensured progressively superior goods and services that producers competed amongst one another to provide in the market.

These favourable consequences were singled out over many other social outcomes that were ignored, but their inner logic, simplicity, and appeal have captivated theoretical and applied consciousness ever since, giving rise to a mind-set that has become the established way of comprehending reality for an epoch. Smith's proposed principle soon came to be treated as a self-evident axiom revealing the omniscience of the "invisible hand."

An even more general principle has consequently become entrenched in market theory and practice, and within social science and philosophy as a whole: the idea of self-maximization as a universal principle of rationality. This view supposes that to be rational is to consistently seek to gain as much for oneself as possible. Any choice or decision that is not "self-maximizing" in its pursuit is, therefore, not rational. Consequently, for corporations to reduce their money profits before laying off workers or releasing their effluents into the environment is irrational. Behaviour that is not self-seeking is excluded a priori from economic models, and from decision-making models in general, even treatises on the nature and meaning of justice.

John Rawls's influential work in social and political philosophy, *A Theory of Justice*, assumes the principle of self-maximizing rationality as a given. Although his architectonic account of the ultimate norms of justice places "the least advantaged" of society at the centre of its concern, the premise of rationality as self-maximization governs his argument throughout. Rawls writes:

I have assumed throughout that the persons in the original position [of seeking the general principles of social justice] are
rational. In choosing between principles, each tries as best he
can to advance his interests.... *It is rational for the parties to
suppose that they do want a larger share.... The concept of rationality invoked here ... is the standard one familiar in social
theory.*[3]

That one of the most widely respected philosophers of justice
in this century adopts without question the market theory axiom that
rationality means self-maximization is a measure of the doctrine's
grip on the contemporary mind. Critical examination of first premises
is suspended. Philosophers yield to market dogma on the nature of
reasoning itself. Rawls's case demonstrates to us how hardened into
a priori bias Adam Smith's principle of calculated self-serving has
become. Like Smith, Rawls seeks to show how the principle of maximum gain for oneself is the ultimate ground of the social good's
achievement, although he shows this optimal consequence by a "veil
of ignorance" rather than by an "invisible hand."

That rationality could mean anything other than consistently
seeking more for oneself is no longer a thought that seriously occurs
to the market-acculturated mind-set, even within a study of first principles. Individuals are confined to the *homo economicus* of one ruling, homogenous goal, to maximize one's own holdings. If the individual does not maximize money income for the self, he or she is not
"rational." The market is conceived as a game, with but one objective,
to have and accumulate as much money for oneself as possible.

The idea of rationality as "the pursuit of one's self-interest" and
"self-maximization" is now almost universal in social thought. It is
standard, for example, not only in social and political theory, but also in
moral philosophy itself.[4] But it is a counterintuitive assumption, for
normally we think of someone as rational precisely because they think
beyond their own self-seeking and count others' interests as important as their own. In the market doctrine, however, rigorously consistent self-seeking is cemented in the mind as the regulating norm of reason. From Smith on, self-serving is assumed to promote the public

good, and alternative strategies that seek to maximize the interests of all by other routes are denounced.

Abstraction enables deductions that would otherwise be bogged down in shifting empirical phenomena. The following principles are part of the regulating framework of market analysis, the underlying metaphysic of its calculus. They have been manifested in game theory as the market system's highest forms of strategic thinking. The dehumanization evident in this doctrine's mind-set is taken as given at the highest levels of its theoretical analysis. Contrary to normal sensibility, it is assumed that:

1. all agents seek only to maximize their own preferences;

2. each agent's preference-object is fixed;

3. one's competitors in the game are not subject to choice;

4. one can appeal to no standard of justice or right external to the game-structure;

5. each player's position is preordained, independent of moral acceptability or deserving;

6. all choices and outcomes are in known terms of money or money-equivalents;

7. the preference order of payoffs or losses is prescribed in advance and inalterable;

8. no concern for the opponent's interests can influence a decision save by its impact on one's own payoffs or losses;

9. no outcome is related to any relationship or tie of the players beyond the game, or to any consequences to anybody or anything that is not included in (6);

10. no payoff received by the players in their game of competitive self-maximization need be deserved by any productive contribution.

The deepest assumption in this value system, the ruling goal of self-maximization, is never rationally explained or accounted for. All further presuppositions follow from this first major premise, which remains unexamined. All are taken for granted as givens from which to proceed. People are thereby transformed into homogenous, self-maximizing calculators who seek only the very most for themselves, independent of all other considerations. Payoffs and losses to self alone regulate all decision-making. Rationality thus becomes the mechanical operations of atomic greed in a social machine of like atoms.

This standard of rationality fails to recognize that reason requires impartiality before consistency. Consistency is reason's means. Non-partiality to one's own interests is reason's standpoint. Thinking must remain open to others' interests as much as one's own to be truly rational in nature. Reason overcomes partiality as the law of its movement. The more thinking is confined by the partiality of pure selfishness, the more irrational it is. Thus we properly judge someone who cannot or will not consider anything beyond getting more for himself as an irrational person, perhaps insane. Is not the market's regulating norm of pursuing one's own moneyed interests to the exclusion of all other life-interests a form of insanity?

John Ralston Saul, in *Voltaire's Bastards,*[5] and other thinkers have come to be suspicious of "reason" and "rationality" as such. They have wrongly supposed that rationality is its insane reduction. This is merely the mirror image of the error. For this view, rationality is a closed, systemized thinking that can indeed remain rational when disconnected from the world of living beings. But it is not reason or rationality as such that is deranged, but rather the perversion of reason. In the case of the market rationality, the reasonable overcoming of partiality in thought and judgement has been usurped by rigorously consistent selfishness, foolishly assumed to constitute the nature of reasoning itself.

If we understand reason or rationality in its non-deformed sense, as requiring us precisely to think beyond the calculus of self-seeking, then we can see that rationality is the opposite of what the market value program prescribes. Systematic self-serving is not rationality. It is greed pursued with mechanical consistency. That such an ideal could become our ruling norm of "reason" is testimony to the incarceration of established thought within market dogma.

Dehumanizing Adam Smith

To this day, "the invisible hand" is the foundational idea of economic theory in general. It is worth citing Smith's own original text here because of its continuing profound influence.

> The produce of industry is what it adds to the subjects or materials upon which it is employed. In proportion, as the value of this produce is great or small, so likewise will the profits of the employer. But it is only for the sake of the profit that any man employs a capital in support of industry. By directing an industry so that its produce may be of the greatest value, he intends only his own gain, and he is in this, as in many other cases, led by an invisible hand to promote an end which was no part of his intention.... What is the species of domestic industry which his capital can employ, and of which the produce is likely to be of the greatest value, every individual, it is evident, can, in his local situation judge much better than any statesman or lawgiver can do for him.[6]

Smith's concept of acquisitive self-seeking in capital investment is limited in at least three ways in which the current market doctrine of self-maximization is not.

First, he is referring to self-interested investment of money-capital only, not of other types of self-maximizing behaviour, such as seeking "a larger share" of what's already there.

Second, he is referring to self-interested investment in domestic production, not to "flight capital" investment in foreign countries.

Third, he is referring to capital investment in the long-term employment of productive labour, not speculation in land currencies, bonds, or any other investment or capital expenditure that "diminishes the funds destined for the employment of productive labour."[7]

Smith's original principle of the pursuit of self-interest to promote the public interest has been so stripped of its limiting conditions as to now imply the opposite. The principle of self-serving for money accumulation in all conditions, with no constraining obligation to one's own society or to use-value production, has become the overriding, abstract imperative of market doctrine. The promotion of the public interest, on the other hand, has become a token mantra with no demonstrated connection to money self-maximization.

In his different historical context, Smith could not conceive of such deformations. In the 1990s, over fifty times more dollars in stockmarket trade turnover are devoted to currency speculation than to the real economy's production of use-values (that is, goods and services).[8] Only a very small fraction of the volume of investment in the current global marketplace can still be justified by Smith's criterion of "the real wealth and revenue of a country—the value of its annual produce."[9]

Second, even profit-seeking investment in real wealth can now conveniently and securely flow to the other side of the world in a nano-second by computer via satellite. It does not remain at home to increase domestic wealth, but moves to wherever it can maximize money-returns, to lower-cost conditions of wages, worker safety, environmental protection, or taxes. Thus Smith's expectation that capital investment would stay in the society where it was earned no longer holds. Smith assumed that the inconvenience, the inaccessibility to surveillance, the lack of long-distance communications, the insecurities of a foreign society, and the loyalty to one's own country would together discourage the flight of capital from its home society as long as returns were "ordinary or not a great deal less than the ordinary profits of stock."[10] Smith's assumed conditions for the pursuit of profit no longer apply.

Third, Smith's principle of self-interested profit-seeking by "capital investment in productive enterprises" is much more limited than the principle of pure self- or profit-maximization as such. For one can self-interestedly seek a money profit in one's investment without seeking to maximize it.[11]

Self-maximization is a radically more sweeping principle than the pursuit of profit. For example, one can pursue profit, but not avoid taxes to pay for public services, as a self-maximizing free-rider does. One can pursue profit through investment in productive enterprises, not in enterprises that produce nothing at all (for example, currency or land speculation) or produce harmful goods (for example, addictive narcotics like cigarettes or mass-homicidal weapons). Yet again, one can seek profit, but not by means that destroy the life environment by pollution or that cause injury and disease to workers.

What alone remains of Smith's doctrine here is the superstition that maximization of profits promotes the social good. According to Milton Friedman, a leader of the "Chicago School" of current market fundamentalism, no other objective is needed to manage society's means of existence. He argues that business has "no social responsibilities" and that "the one and only responsibility of business" is "to make as much money as possible." This is the basic meaning of "a free society" for Friedman, and he declares that the "doctrine of social responsibility" for business is "a fundamentally subversive doctrine in a free society."[12]

Friedman, like all marketeers, claims Smith as a forebear. But he, too, is blind to Smith's limiting conditions. He remains certain that the unconstrained principle of pursuing money-profit by itself must still promote a free society and social well-being.

Friedman is not an exception. He is an articulate spokesman for a ruling value program. His policies and views, such as those on high-interest monetarism, have been instituted by violence and state law, from 1970s Chile to the 1990s Republican programs of the U.S. presidency. Their incoherence does not deter their influence. Their success is grounded on the inviolate assumption that unlimited private-profit enrichment providentially promotes the social good, the generative principle of the aptly named "American Dream." Thus, Adam Smith's moral revolution has transformed into a licence to overrun every life-interest except that of money making more money in the name of "a free and democratic society."

The Corporate Person

The institutional systems seeking to maximize money profits, which we know as "multinationals," are not recognized as such in "classical" or "neoclassical" economic models. The logical spaces of "freely transacting market agents" are occupied by self-maximizing functions that might as well all be "Mom-and-Pop" stores. This is one of the advantages of mathematical abstractions. They make no real-world distinctions between transnational conglomerates and market agents with none of their distinguishing powers in the market. Adam Smith himself ruled joint-stock corporations out of his analysis. He thought of them as retarded mechanisms with no place in a free market.[13] But none of this has made any difference to the general assumption of market theory that the market consists only of "free, independent, and responsible individuals" as producers, sellers, and buyers in a contractual paradise of "voluntary negotiations and transactions."[14]

This individuated market model assumes as given a central myth of the doctrine: that the market system is composed of individual owners, producers, exchangers, vying against each other in an open competition of equal opportunity in which none can dominate supply or demand or prices. But it is manifestly false that the contemporary world market is individualist, open to all on equal terms, and undeformed by oligarchical control.

Milton Friedman, for instance, presupposes in his writing that independent individuals are the only responsible agents of the market. He explicitly asserts the metaphysical dictum that "nothing over and above individuals exists."[15] But multinationals are certainly not individuals; and they, not individuals, are the responsible agents under law for what is owned and exchanged in the market. They hire and fire people, invest money, own assets, and they, not individuals, legally bear responsibility for incurred debts and liabilities. Are they then precisely not "responsible individual agents"?

Friedman declares not only that the "social responsibility of business" not only does not exist, but also that people who claim that it should represent "intellectual forces that have been undermining the basis of a free society."[16] It is important for Friedman and market interests to preserve the myth of independent individual responsibility—so important that they attack those who disagree as traitors against "individual freedom." But even in the boardrooms of corporations and courts of corporate law adjudication, corporations are everywhere recognized as "separate legal persons."[17] In the real world of the market outside the ideological models economists and others erect for us, the legal entity of the corporate person explicitly exempts individuals from responsibility for what they do on behalf of the corporations from which they profit. Directors, managers, and investors are free of accountability for the actions of the corporation they direct, manage, and invest in. The meaning of "Ltd." is "limited liability."

The corporation was historically created to exempt investors and their agents from responsibility for the debts or wrongdoings of the collective vehicle, the corporation. Liability for civil or criminal offence or debt, in other words, is thereby assumed by the legal agent by whose authority it is incurred—the fictitious corporate person. "The company may become insolvent, while its members remain rich."[18] In this way, the corporation that replaces the individual responsibility of market agents assumes the liability of violated obligations, wrongs, and criminal offences instead. It, not individuals, is the "separate legal person" that is normally accountable for whatever civil or criminal wrongdoings and liabilities profit-maximizing investors and executives may perpetrate and incur in their market choices and preferences.

Friedman's blanket assertion of "individual responsibility" as the sole agency of the market contradicts the facts, but it is considered a self-evident given in market doctrine. He writes that the "great virtue of private competitive enterprise" is that "it forces people to be responsible for their own actions."[19] Here we are not confronting a deliberate lie so much as an acculturated metaphysic that has lost touch with the real world outside of its value program. Pervasive repetition is hypnotic.

> The incorporation of a firm—that process whereby an ordinary partnership is transmuted into a company—effects a fundamental change in the legal relations of its members. It is nothing less than the birth of a new being... a being without soul or body,

not visible to the eye of the law, but of a kind whose power, importance, wealth and activity are already great and grow greater every day.[20]

Over nearly a century after the eminent jurist Salmond wrote these words the corporation has become "greater every day" in its "power, importance, wealth and activity." Moreover, while individual money-property owners profit without legal accountability as individual persons, the corporation itself as "a separate person" is guaranteed individual rights—to "freedom of speech," "the right to remain silent," "freedom of association," "freedom from regulatory discrimination," and most of the rights and freedoms once thought to belong solely to individuals. Transnational corporations are now protected with all the force of the law not available to human individuals in their individual rights and freedoms. Droves of lawyers and public relations consultants can, for example, override municipal zoning regulations, which may rule out 40,000-square-foot, cement-block stores like Walmart from a small-scale city environment. They might protect corporate-financed individuals from having to pay union dues and saturate public communications with corporate propaganda in defiance of would-be government restrictions on dangerous-drug commercials or limits on electoral spending. Workers' unions, unlike corporations, do not qualify for any of these protections of "individual rights" because they are not recognized as legal persons.

The market value program thus biases constitutional law itself towards for-profit corporations, protecting them with individual rights legislation couched in the language of safeguarding real human persons from excessively empowered governments. The law to protect society and individuals from corporations is thereby systemically weakened, for bills and charters of rights normally apply only against governments, not against multinational corporate "persons." The market value program subjugates even the rule of law to its ideological constructions.[21]

The myth of the "corporate person" not only nullifies individual responsibility for harms done to others, but also receives protections of individual freedom in pursuing its non-individual interests of maximizing money profits. Its special legal and economic status resembles that of a medieval sovereign. It owns and claims such rights as it finds convenient to protect its ruling interests, however these may contradict themselves or others' life and security. These special rights further include the right to pay increasingly lower taxes than individuals (a single bank teller may pay more taxes than a major bank),[22] the right to assert the property rights of national citizenship of other countries as well as one's own at will (a central prescription of such "free trade" documents as NAFTA), and the right to exploit and damage human and environmental life with effective immunity from liability for such harms (a "deregulated environment for investors").

As the real world of governing corporate law and right makes clear to us, it is certainly not human individuals or individual responsibility that are the self-determining agencies of the contemporary market and its freedoms. It is unions of investors constituted as corporations. It is predominantly transnational or global corporations, within whose armour of nation-size financial assets, strict liability limits, borderless property and investment rights, multiple subsidiary identities, and tax-exemption privileges the market's most dominant players hold extensive powers undreamed of by medieval kings. Within the corporate oligopoly of the world market, individuals are precisely not independent or responsible market agents, but retainers and beneficiaries of another kind of being altogether—a Leviathan of money accumulation seeking to be maximally more money accumulation with every circuit of its investment.

Once the free and independent individual is no longer perceived as the market's sovereign player, but rather the corporate system in which individuals are, as workers, replaceable cogs or, as stockholders, non-responsible beneficiaries of its gains, the value appeal of the doctrine collapses at its core. It is no longer a real-world ethic of "individual freedom," but an ideology masking an underlying reality of an all-embracing corporate global oligarchy.[23] Yet "realistic" market advocates remain indifferent to this extreme contradiction between their metaphysical assumption and prevailing fact. They do not, and they cannot, solve the contradiction, however, because its admission undermines the doctrine at its ethical base.

Smith's economic model, in contrast, presupposes individual producers and merchants in open competition with none in any position of influence on supply, demand, or prices. Smith also argues that a corporate agent in the market—"the joint stock company" as he calls it—is a lamentable exception in a free market system. Smith legitimated pools of private capital as the outward and visible mover of the inward and invisible design he deified as "the invisible hand." Yet the market doctrine's founder glimpsed the profoundly anti-individual nature of the corporation as a market agent. In Smith's judgement, the joint stock company or corporation is fit solely for "uniformity of method ... of little or no variation."[24] We are unlikely to be exposed in economics classes to Adam Smith's declaration that corporate control requires a method of "uniformity," the opposite of the "individual independence and freedom" that market theory proponents claim as their foundational value.

The New Global Market Sovereign

In the real world individuals have been replaced by corporations as the effective agents of the global market. Global corporations of increasingly large size and concentration control increasingly large sections of market supply. The lion's share of international trade involves corporate conglomerates buying and selling to themselves. At the same time a few hundred corporations control 80 per cent of all land cultivated for the export of the world's food and, even more strikingly, 98 per cent of all foreign direct investment.[25]

For example, one of these corporate conglomerates, General Electric, discloses a deep pattern in its many-levelled connectedness across the political and economic life of the world. Besides being a global producer and seller of electrical appliances, General Electric was at the top of the U.S. military industrial complex, a dominant recipient of Pentagon contracts for nuclear armaments. It was also the long-term employer of Ronald Reagan as host of *General Electric Theatre*, years before he became U.S. president. During this period it was the leading toxic polluter in the United States. The corporation also became the majority owner of NBC Television and Cable NBC, which report "the news." From these manifestations of economic power General Electric could exert special influence over government policy and contracts (market demand), over production within a semimonopoly manufacturing sector (market supply), and over public opinion by the mass media.

General Electric Corporation is hardly unique. Two competitors in the oligopolist media business, Walt Disney and Time Warner, acquired control in 1995 over Capital Cities, ABC Television, Sports Network, and Turner/CNN Broadcasting. A major electrical appliance corporation, Westinghouse, took control in the same year of the remaining national U.S. television network, CBS. The U.S. "infotainment" industry controlled by these corporations has grown to nearly 30 per cent of the nation's Gross National Product.

Some three hundred global corporations control about 70 per cent of all international trade and 98 per cent of all foreign direct investment. Given their ability to confer or withdraw investment from national economies in free movement across boundaries, regulatory standards, tax regimes, natural resource sites, and labour forces, they have no accountability to nation-states and their electorates. On the contrary, nations and societies have become accountable to them. Societies are reminded daily that they must do this or do that "to attract" or "to compete for investment," which corporations must control "if the country is to survive."

For example, NAFTA, whose 2,400 articles specify rights of businesses to trade freely across national boundaries, was an "executive agreement passed against public opposition in which a majority (two to one) of Americans opposed it."[26] According to the U.S. Labour Advisory Council, established by the American Trade Act of 1974, this trade agreement has "the effect of prohibiting democratically elected bodies at all levels of government from enacting measures deemed inconsistent with the provisions of the Agreement." The agreement specifies no other rights but those of business corporations selling across borders, which explicitly override democratically elected governments laws "deemed inconsistent." In this way the binding law of such trade agreements themselves entails the sovereignty of the rights of international corporations over national governments and their electorates. This dominance complements the de facto sovereign power of corporations to withdraw investment from any nation or region that dares to tax, regulate, or otherwise impose limits deemed "uncompetitive."

There remain scattered markets around the world in which independent and individual producers of foods and crafts offer their goods for sale to local buyers in open local marketplaces, where no special advantage or influence over supply, demand, or prices is held by any market player. But this order of affairs in a world of mass production, mass distribution, mass advertising, corporate-financed politicians, and servant governments is rapidly disappearing. The new global market is not a negotiating site through which independent, individual producers and buyers can exercise their free choices and wills to each other's mutual advantage in an equal-opportunity framework of supply and demand.

On the level of market supply and demand, the supply of the global market is increasingly controlled by large supranational corporations, while the demand of the global market is simultaneously generated by pervasive communication systems operating as vehicles of these same corporations' advertising messages. On the level of elected governments, the once-sovereign state increasingly becomes a compliant promoter of these corporate interests. On the level of civil society, peoples across the world now compete to lower their established standards of wages, taxes, working conditions, and environmental protections to the cost levels demanded by global corporate investors. That is, they compete against each other to serve corporations.

Finally, citizens obliged to work rather than invest for a living must compete against one another to sell their working lives to corporate and business buyers in order to subsist. They do so, moreover, within market conditions of ever greater labour oversupply and increasing shutdowns of public-service occupations and social assistance to the unemployed. This pattern of rule is justified by the slogan

"There is no alternative." But there is another term to describe this system: "terrorist." To terrorize is to threaten people with loss of their lives or means of life if they do not submit, and to clearly demonstrate that this threat is real. In what way is this system of rule not terrorist to most people?

Exempt from the laws of mortality that afflict individual market agents, stretching its limbs across the compass of the globe, exerting powers of life and death over the survival and growth of peoples, societies and environments across national borders, and unaccountable to any government, the global corporation rules across the bounds of time and space as a world sovereign of money–command. By comparison, the absolute monarchs of the past are parochial despots. In this new medium of money seeking to be more money through the instituted bodies of ever larger, non-responsible conglomerates, the life-organizations of the individual, society, and host planet itself are all transformed into subordinate functions of its system.

The Money Ground of Value

This value program dictates an underlying, totalitarian principle of rule: The ultimate vehicle of value is the corporate person, and the ultimate measure of value is money profitability. It follows from this ultimate system of non-human value that what increases corporate revenues and profits, on the one hand, is good and to be approved; on the other hand, what decreases corporate revenues and profits is bad and to be condemned. This prescriptive duality of Good and Bad is no less absolute and binding than religious commandments, and the implications of the market value system are well confirmed in practice. For example, government regulations for environmental protection are vigorously fought against by corporations and their political representatives as "a threat to jobs and investment." Because they are "a regulatory burden on business" and increase the "costs of production," they are "bad for the economy." In the meantime, unregulated environmental destruction—by clear-cut rainforests, paved green spaces, and factory-ship scraping of the ocean bottoms—increases revenues and profits for corporations. Therefore it is "good for the economy."

How could such a value program come to rule society when its effects are so destructive to life-organization? One normative source of the problem is that the very framework of evaluation accepted by societies, governments, and international organizations to judge social progress is conceived in these very terms: namely, that whatever increases money revenues within a society is good, and whatever decreases money revenues is bad. This value metric for nations is known as the Gross Domestic Product (or the Gross National Product before 1991).

The value system of the GNP/GDP is simple. It is governed by the money principle of value, as are all market values. Good means more money-demand. Bad means less money-demand. The GNP/GDP is: the gross sum of national or domestic money-revenues derived from all sales of goods and services by or within a society. The GNP refers to the total sum of money for such sales received by residents of a nation (including money income retained from sales abroad by residents). The GDP refers to the total sum of money received for such sales by both residents and non-residents of a nation. The difference between these metrics of value lies only in the citizenship of the recipients of money-revenues, not in the measure itself. Money-revenues from sales of goods and services remain the single measure of all value.

Nothing else but money derived from the sale of goods and services counts as a value—not the quality of a society's conditions of life of air, water, earth, and forests, not the health or freedoms of the people living in that society, nothing except what increases money revenues from sales of goods and services.

This final measure of social value refers to gross money-revenues from sales of goods and services in a society. Thus, the distribution of this money-wealth is ruled out of view. The GDP of a society may climb while the majority of citizens grow poorer, and a quarter or more fall into absolute poverty (a pattern that has occurred across the world in the last decade).

If an environmental disaster occurs, such as a major oil spill or a hole in the ozone layer or some other "externality" caused by the activities of corporations, these environmental disasters are great strides forward for the GNP. They generate billions of dollars in sales of commodities and services. According to the only metric that market culture uses, the value and progress of these societies have risen in absolute terms, even though the environment and the health of society are devastated.

There is no limit to how far losses of human and environmental life can precipitate market value gains. If a nation's ecosystems are irreversibly damaged, then the societies so despoiled are assessed as better off by the market's value system, assuming no direct money costs are imposed on the corporations exploiting them and increased revenues and profits are derived. Thus, millions of acres of rainforest habitat are destroyed for market products across Canada, Central America, the Amazon, Borneo, Indonesia, the Cameroons, and so on, and these societies are rated by the market value system as achieving great value gains. If they limit or curtail this life-destruction, they are, conversely, judged to be opposed to production of market value, and therefore "uncompetitive." This is the "limitless future of opportunity and prosperity" to which the global market beckons us, while threatening "loss of jobs" and "economic downturn" if any society is so "inflexible" as to limit the looting of its life-grounds and natural heritage.[27]

The fate of regions and countries across the world are now determined by this business calculus. GNPs or GDPs rise or soar as life-systems are stripped. The pattern advances rapidly across the globe's rainforests, ocean bottoms, soils, and atmospheres. Even when profits are exported to other zones, the societies suffering the loss are considered to have registered absolute economic gains.

The 1991 Gulf War against Iraq killed hundreds of thousands of children through infrastructural damage and destroyed the ocean environment by exploding oil wells, but it counts in the market value system as a windfall GNP gain.[28] Hundreds of billions of dollars of revenues in corporate sales of goods and services were added to the U.S. GNP by weapons sold and marketed and by the multibillion-dollar engineering and construction contracts after the war (which also serendipitously increased the GDP of one victim society, Kuwait).[29]

As for the hundreds of thousands of children who die from the infrastructural damage to "the Enemy," they are an "externality" to a highly prosperous market of military and engineering sales. All that counts in this market measure of value is the increase or decrease in money revenues for goods and services, even if the vast majority of people in the societies in question never see or spend it.

In short, value is determined by the single criterion of monetary sum of goods and services sold. This is the global value ground for judgement of social well-being from Toronto to Ho Chi Minh City. Social conception and policy, which more or less universally presuppose the GNP/GDP as society's measure of prosperity, is so presupposed as a ruling benchmark that perceived competition with its social value metric is not tolerated, even if it is to keep stock of society's long-term supply of natural resources available for market exploitation.[30]

A typical inference inside the market value system is that it is necessary to sacrifice certain life-interests such as environmental sustainability in order to lift the poor or the unemployed up to a higher standard of living through an increased GDP. But this is a non-sequitur, for neither the GNP or GDP growth measure takes any account of how the gross gains in money-spent aggregates are distributed among society's members. The general pattern of Third World societies in the last twenty years is a stark indicator. After the aggregate growth of Third World money economies in recent decades, by 1997 447 billionaires had more wealth than the total annual income of half of the world's population. It is not difficult to understand how a value system with these outcomes may have a vested interest in ignoring potential disaster, even as it looms in the sun we walk in or the air we breathe.[31]

The more that human or environmental life imposes tax costs on business, the more that societies turn to non-commercial alternatives of public goods and services, the worse it is by the judgement of the market value system. Thus, if education that is not useful to business costs business taxes, it is bad by the corporate measure of GDP/GNP So is providing nutritional food to the poor, ensuring safe working conditions, and prohibiting toxic effluents and resource deple-tion. Therefore, all such unprofitable costs are eliminated as fast as market governments can manage "to eliminate the waste" and make governments "accountable to market discipline."

Such axings and shock treatments, market society's policy leaders argue, purge "wasteful" and "unaffordable" social spending, while fashioning "miracle growths" in GDP/GNP. Whatever must be sacrificed is "the price of survival in the tough new international mar-ketplace." Gross money-product, not life, is the ruling goal of this sys-tem.

The Logic of Comparative Advantage

The market system is conventionally considered to be more efficient in its production of goods and services than any system ever known to humanity. A basic reason given for this claimed superior efficiency is the principle of comparative advantage, whereby socie-ties produce those goods and services in which they have a lower re-source input cost than other countries. The principle holds that it is to the mutual advantage of all if societies produce what they are most cost-efficient at producing, and trade among each other those goods and services that they produce at the lowest comparative costs. For example, it is best that Costa Rica produces coffee and bananas, Canada pulp and wheat, the United States automobiles and entertain-ment, and so on—all trading with one another at mutually advanta-geous prices. Societies best seek their own advantage by producing goods for which their cost/output ratio is comparatively lowest and by exporting these goods to each other. Through the self-maximizing pursuit of competitive advantage, producers and sellers in the market are impelled to invest wherever costs are relatively lower. Thus the market's outcome is always to allocate resources in a maximally ra-tional and cost-effective way.

Adam Smith first introduces the principle of comparative ad-vantage in his *Wealth of Nations*, observing that it is to the "mutual advantage" of everyone in the market "to buy as cheap and to sell as dear as possible."[32] Smith writes:

The taylor does not attempt to make his own shoes but buys them of the shoemaker. The shoemaker does not attempt to make his own clothes, but employs a taylor. The farmer attempts to make neither the one nor the other, but employs those different artificers. All of them find it for their individual interest to employ their whole industry in a way which they have some advantage over their neighbours, and to purchase with a part of its produce, or what is the same thing, with the price of a part of it, whatever else they have the occasion for.[33]

Smith writes the same principle large in the trade among nations to which the principle of comparative advantage has come to be conventionally applied.

What is prudence in the conduct of every private family can scarce be folly in that of a great kingdom. If a foreign country can supply us with a commodity cheaper than we ourselves can make it, better buy it of them with some part of the produce of our own industry, employed in a way in which we have some advantage. The general industry of the country, being always in proportion to the capital that employs, will not thereby be diminished, no more than that of the above-mentioned artificers.... As long as the one country has those advantages, and the other wants them, it will always be more advantageous for the latter rather to buy of the former than to make.[34]

Smith claimed that for nations, the act of producing what is most cost-effective for them to produce and importing the rest was always advantageous. Since Smith's canonical *Wealth of Nations* was published over two hundred years ago, this has remained the basis of the "free trade" doctrine, and the practical core of market fundamentalism everywhere.

But we should consider the matter more carefully. Comparative advantage does not distinguish between goods and services that promote life-welfare and those that destroy it. For example, it was the overall comparative advantage of India's geography combined with

England's imperial rule in the East that made the mass production of opium to sell in China a profitable trade for Britain, in preference to devoting these resources to the production of other commodities. The "opportunity cost" of foregoing this dynamically lucrative trade would, in the judgement of the market's value system, be irrational. Similarly, it is now better by this principle of comparative advantage for regions of Southeast Asia and South America to produce opium and cocaine, when the overall cost-output ratio and value-added margin are favourable in international market competition. In the latter case, the state forbids it. In the former case, it prescribes it. But in both cases the free circulation of goods in international trade is a good to the market's value system, and the achievement of comparative advantage in such trade is a victory for the good of "international competitiveness." Only state interference makes it illegal.

Again, it was a comparative advantage for certain national empires and Arab traders to have armed access to Africa's communities in order to sell slaves in burgeoning world markets. They could bring slaves to market more cheaply and more efficiently than anyone else. Today, it is a comparative advantage for a nation's agricultural businesses in regions of appropriate climate and soil composition to grow tobacco, rather than other farm products, to sell to U.S. global corporations. These corporations, in turn, have comparative advantages of production scale, market access, brand loyalty, and demand stimulation better suited to the mass production and sale of cigarettes as opposed to dedicating these resources to non-lethal products.

It follows from the principle of comparative advantage that the United States, France, the Czech Republic, Israel, and other industrialized nations are better positioned to produce mass-homicidal weapons for sale in the international marketplace at high value-added prices than to locate their resources to alternative forms of production in which other nations have a lower input cost.

The principle of comparative advantage leads to a situation of "mutual advantage," "efficient resource allocation," and "reduced costs," which can be ruinous to the well-being of societies. But this problem has been overlooked by market theory and practice. "International market competitiveness" has become an end in itself, an end to which non-market values must be sacrificed.

A nation can gain an advantage over its competitors in the costs of production it offers to investors if it maintains wages at subsistence levels in a labour-glutted market (say, below one dollar a day, now considered "a competitive price"), prevents any union organization and suppresses public advocacy for better work and safety conditions. It is also a further comparative advantage for a government to ensure that no environmental protections are instituted to increase business costs. Nations endorse "open to business" conditions in order to offer global investors the lowest possible ratios of production costs to production outputs or "comparative advantage."

According to this principle of competitive advantage, First World nations benefit both by the low cost of consumer products bought from these lower-end countries and the "favourable climates for investment" these poorer societies offer. At the same time, buyers in these poorer countries are able to buy goods and services (such as planes, banking services, luxury cars, and electronic goods) from their richer trading partners at prices lower than these goods could be produced domestically. This is considered a "win-win game" for the value system of the free market doctrine.

The more the principle of comparative advantage is successfully achieved, the more it can lead to the intensifying oppression of labour, environmental despoliation, and exploitation of the poor. No internal principle of the market doctrine rules against any one of these outcomes. Massive worldwide increases in environmental degradation, an increasing movement of people into part-time or starvation wages, and the murder and torture of resisting oppositions, human rights activists, and union organizers may all occur in direct correlation with global market penetration of societies.[35]

The logic of market competition ensures by its wholly different starting points of assets and productive development that there will be more non-starters and losers than winners in this competition amongst nations for investment dollars, market shares, and jobs. Each nation, by the market's criterion of rationality, seeks only its own competitive advantage in this game, and thus this defective collective outcome of the competition cannot be discerned; for the only value calculus at work is to maximize the comparative advantage of individual nations. Only an analysis that looks beyond self-maximizing strategies to the collective outcome of such a calculus can uncover destructive patterns of international trade beyond market "rationality."

The starting condition for less developed societies is confined to natural resource exports, low-wage production, and a narrow base of internationally marketable commodities. Being so dependent and restricted in initial "comparative advantage" options, these undeveloped societies will leave other production to more "efficient" and developed societies, whose finished products will be imported at more cost-effective rates and higher quality standards. These more developed societies will for this reason attract international capital investment in their more highly skilled labour forces and technological infrastructures. By the same logic of comparative advantage, the less developed societies will become specialized in producing much the same sort of goods for exports in which they have a "comparative advantage"—for example, raw logs, coffee, sugar, and other primary commodities, as well as low-cost labour and environmental conditions. Their necessary specialization in a narrow range of comparative advantages will in turn expose their economies to price fluctuations more than more rounded and developed economies that are less dependent on any one good or set of goods for export. At the same time, the prices of the less developed societies' goods will fall as international competition amongst them increases to supply these primary commodities and low-cost conditions. They will in this framework of global competition require international loans or investment capital to develop beyond their confined state. If protectionism and government assembling of capital are ruled out, which they are by the nature of a free trade regime, less developed societies are made dependent on external loans and capital investment. But loans of international capital will require these societies to transfer their earnings to compound interest payments to money-lenders. Yet at the same time foreign investment will yield the ownership of domestic productive resources and profits to foreign investors.

As long as the principle of comparative advantage in free market conditions regulates production and distribution decisions, less developed societies will therefore be held hostage to foreign moneylenders and investors. This pattern has resulted across Third World societies from Latin America to Africa as the logic of "development" has been applied. The sole exceptions are societies that have successfully pursued an independent growth strategy of protecting domestic industries against foreign competition until they have developed and have systematically intervened in the market with government creation and direction of domestic capital pools. This has been the universal pattern of the successful East Asian economies.[36]

The Homogenization of Nations in the World Market

Since a comparative advantage means a lower cost to output ratio in producing a good or service, it entails that the input of resource costs and the output of product can be quantified in uniform units of money-measurement. It also entails by the requirement of competitive comparison that the products produced are of uniform kinds (for example, standard automobiles, standard-time television program units, standard fresh vegetable or fruit sizes and appearances). As in other forms of competition, the contesting candidates must be alike in their nature and their conditions of operation to compete. While some products will be new in type, market competition requires that there will soon be similar, vying alternatives for buyers. Competition thus entails resemblance or uniformity of product among competitors. It follows that the more global the competition is, the more uniformity across national and cultural boundaries there must be.

Because it does not fit well with the revered values of "individuality," "diversity," and "independence" that the market claims as its own, this consequence is blinkered out from view. In the real world, however, this pattern of uniformity has become increasingly pervasive—from cultural entertainments and automobile design to body-shape sizes and daily consumables. More deeply, human aspiration itself has been reduced to the lingua franca of more money for oneself. No decision can be made within this value system, which does not seek to maximize pay-offs to self, for this is the regulating rule of the game. The observant may recognize this as a debilitating law of life, but market ideology so pervasively trumpets this as "individualism" that even critics accept this inverted designation, imagining that individualism is the problem.

Mass production cannot by its nature individuate its products or its processes, however much advertising assures us that it is only by purchasing such products that we can prove our individuality. A handful of transnational corporate producers, with interlocked production and distribution processes, manufacture more or less identical commodities for billions of consumers. Diversity of peoples and ways of life are increasingly ruled out by the requirements of world product mandates, and transnational economies of scale are instituted for the global production and distribution of goods.

The global pattern of increasing uniformity grows as more fields of human life are penetrated by the manufacture of commercial products to substitute for autonomous activities—for example, mass-audience television programs in the home and the community centre instead of independent, local cultural activities.

Thus, as well, the world's system of food supply is dominated by a few corporately owned product-lines in a narrow range of artificially cultivated environmental conditions. Of seventy-five types of vegetables available at the beginning of the twentieth century, about 97 per cent of the varieties of each type are now extinct.[37] At the same time thousands of local varieties of rice, wheat, and maize—along with the potato, the basis of 50 per cent of humanity's total calorific intake—have been eliminated. In India, for example, thirty thousand different varieties of rice have been replaced by ten varieties across three-quarters of this diverse country.[38]

In this corporate food production regime, the local farmers' right to save the seeds of their own crops has also been removed by international patent conventions. The life-forms of animals as well as plants are now subject to global "intellectual property rights." These property rights, even when originally derived from indigenous knowledge of Third World farmers and herbalists, and even if only a product of simply shuffling genes in existing varieties, are, in turn, owned by transnational corporations. The corporate patent-holders, in consequence, charge local growers a royalty on the mass-produced life-forms, which increasingly become the only breed-lines available on the market. This pattern, which is now advancing rapidly under new World Trade Organization law, homogenizes the life-world, and by doing so reduces its capacities to adapt and reproduce in changing biological conditions.[39] Biological conditions, in still further turn, are undergoing rapid transformation due to climatic and other environmental changes induced by fossil fuel and other chemical emissions, toxins, and pollutants distributed across the world by global market methods and commodities.

Cultural interrelations, farms, crops, and foods, the evolved genetic structures of life-forms themselves, are increasingly reduced to the uniform mass products of global corporations. Organic life is undergoing a sea change of mutation towards homogeneity and unevolved forms. This pattern of "competitive cost reduction for consumers" is celebrated as a triumph of "global free trade," "cost-reduction," and "international development." This artificial homogenization of life-processes has no limits in market theory or practice. A society that resists risks being marked for embargo, destabilization, and armed invasion until it succumbs.[40]

This restructuring of the planetary life diversity into corporately programmed entropy is not a product of failures in the global market system. It is advanced by the successful operations of "global market competition" and "cost efficiency." Cost efficiency in production by the pursuit of comparative advantage can certainly be an instrumental good. But, the question must arise for those who think beyond means only, good for what? In the market doctrine the final good is maximization of profits for investors, combined with more goods at lower prices for consumers. But what are these goods for? Are they final, self-justifying goods, ultimate ends in themselves?

Market theory and practice never pose these questions. Both assume that the instrumental good of money-cost reduction advances "individual freedom" by necessity—a causal law presupposed as given, along with its fellow articles of creed of "lower prices" and "more for consumers." But this is systematically contradicted by the logic and facts of actual global market competition. The internal necessity of the system to subordinate human and natural life to mass-scale methods of production and distribution at every level cannot coherently be described as "an increase of individual freedom." On the contrary, it is a monoculture that liquidates differentiation by its nature.[41]

The most fundamental problem of this uniformity pattern of global market competition is its life-destructive consequences. Biodiversity is well recognized as a basic law of life survival and development. This is because variation of capacity confers abilities to adapt to diverse circumstances. Such circumstances always change, now more than ever by industrial assaults on the atmosphere and the basic elements of the biosphere in general. At the same time uniformity of capacity cannot adapt to new circumstances that are bound to arise. At the level of a food seed, for example, reducing the biodiversity of the genetic codes of these seeds, as the system of multinational control of seed production and distribution now systematically prescribes, militates against these seeds' chances of survival in new circumstances induced by changing climate, soil composition, and insect or pest infestations. The genetic variety of seeds, in contrast, which has developed over millennia of evolution, enables a versatile and diverse adaptability in circumstances of new blights, weather changes, or other altering environmental conditions. Such diversity-based adaptability may indeed be the difference between the starvation or the survival of hundreds of millions of people—the majority of humanity in the case of rice and maize seeds, which carry the Third World.

As for human creativity and self-expression, diversity of form is needed even more to provide people with the variety of activities and life-possibilities they require to be healthy, vital, and self-reliant, both as individual persons and as communities. But the more there is uniformity of life-aspirations, of work purposes, of products, of life-means, and of methods of production, the less variety of activity and individuation there can be for both persons and societies. People feel their differentiation melting into the air, but all are exhorted to compete harder or they will not survive. Atavistic movements to recover ethnic roots now sweep across the globe in desperate, cornered protests at the loss of security in life-grounds, and for a human identity that is not mass-produced.

In the global competition for minimum costs and maximum money returns to investors, the law of survival is to fit without variance into the assigned function. People become in this way repetitive operations and working parts within a structure of vertical command, replaceable functionaries in corporate machines to maximize shareholder revenues and profits. There is no longer a choice. Individuals or societies, as we are continuously reminded, "either adapt to the new order, or are punished harshly by the market."

Beyond the eventually biocidal consequences of this logic of "global market competition," there remains the value of enjoying the rich beauty of the planet's diverse miracle of life itself. Uniformity of separate products with no connective place in their environment is perfectly antithetical to this value. We recognize this brutal fact when we refer to these mass-production items as "trash" or "junk." By "junk," we mean any mass-produced commodity that does not contribute to, but reduces, vital life-capacity. Since market doctrine assumes as axiomatic that human desires are limitless, and that there is no end to the wants that can be created by "demand stimulation," commodities for sale proliferate in ever more regions of our lives--and always with more motor noise in the world, more effluents, more pervasive commercials and signs for mass products, more occupancy of life-space by manufactured commodities and their excreta, and fewer jobs for the young, except as selling agents of this system.

The fossil-fuel motor is, we might say, the drive-piston and engine of the global market system—moving all its wheels to transform life into money, making all that is diverse uniform, flat, and insentient.

Here as elsewhere, only a wider standpoint that finds life as a value in itself, and not a means, is capable of protecting life from this global market program.

Notes

1. Smith's text on the promotion of the public good by the pursuit of private profit occurs in "Of Restraints upon the Importation from Foreign Countries of Such Goods As Can Be Produced at Home," book IV, chapter II, *Inquiry*, pp.351-52; emphasis added.
2. These arguments are made in Hegel's *Philosophy of History* and, to a lesser extent, his *Philosophy of Right* (or *Philosophy of Law*). Representative selections from these works can be found in the standard anthology, J. Loewenberg, *Hegel: Selections* (New York: The Modern Student's Library of Philosophy, 1929).
3. John Rawls, *A Theory of Justice* (Cambridge, Mass.: Harvard University Press, 1968), pp.142-43; emphasis added.
4. David Gauthier, *Morals By Agreement* (New York: Oxford University Press, 1986), p.7. Gauthier hedges the extremism of the self-maximization conception of reason by a logical dodge. He says that it is "interests of the self" that are to be maximized, not interests *in* the self. His distinction between prepositions is, presumably, to make pure selfishness of interest more palatable as the rational ground of moral theory.
5. John Ralston Saul. *Voltaire's Bastards: The Dictatorship of Reason in the West.* Toronto: Penguin, 1992.
6. Smith, *Inquiry*, pp.351-52.
7. Milton Friedman, "The Social Responsibility of Business Is to Increase Its Profits," *The New York Times Magazine*, Sept. 13, 1970.
8. "Power of Financial Capital Overrides Governments," *CCPA Monitor*, April 1995, p.8.
9. Smith, "Of the Different Employment of Capitals," book II, chapter V, *Inquiry*, p.304.
10. Smith, "Of Restraints," p.349.
11. For example, Fairtrade Foundation in Britain and Max Havelaar in Europe offer a guaranteed market price for coffee produced in accordance with decent social and environmental standards, thereby forfeiting potential profits. Interestingly, the demand for such coffee and other products from developing countries is growing because consumers too are willing to forfeit additional costs to purchase fair-trade products. John Vidal, "Harvesting Hope in the Banfields," *The Guardian Weekly*, March 17, 1992, p.23. Although such decisions are supposed to be expressions of the free choices of market agents, they contradict the market doctrine at a deeper level: its very principle of self-serving rational choice upon which all its policies and practices are based.
12. Friedman, "Social Responsibility of Business."
13. Smith, *Inquiry*, pp.480-82.
14. See, for example, Friedman, *Capitalism and Freedom*, p.27; and Hayek, *Road to Serfdom*, p.37, and *Law, Legislation and Liberty* (London: Routledge and Kegan Paul), p.82.
15. Friedman pervasively refers to "the individual," "individual liberty," "individual freedom in the market," the "free man," "the free person," "a society of free individuals," "individual responsibility," "the individual citizen," "protection of the individual," and "the private and voluntary contracts of individuals" throughout his books and articles. These phrases of individualist metaphysics are taken to be self-evident in meaning.
16. Friedman, "Social Responsibility of Business."
17. P.J. Fitzgerald, ed., *Salmond on Jurisprudence* (London: Sweet and Maxwell), 1996, p.306.
18. Ibid., p.309.

19. Friedman, "Social Responsibility of Business."

20. Fitzgerald, *Salmond*, p.310.

21. For a detailed critique of the courts' application of individual rights to protect corporations from public legislation and the bargaining strength of workers' unions, see H.J. Glasbeek, "A No-Frills Look at the Charter of Rights and Freedoms or How Politicians and Lawyers Hide Reality," in *The Windsor Yearbook of Access to Justice*, vol. IX (1989), pp.293-352. For the role of judges in biasing the law towards protecting the interests of corporations against democratic interests, see Joel Bakan, "Constitutional Arguments: Interpretation and Legitimacy in Canadian Constitutional Theory," *Osgoode Hall Law Journal*, vol. 27 (1989), pp.123ff.

22. In 1992, for example, the Royal Bank of Canada paid no taxes on profits of $63 million while one of its tellers paid $5,732 on a $25,000 salary. "Tax Facts," *Canadian Perspectives*, September 1993, p.2.

23. See chapter 7 for the empirical substantiation of this general fact.

24. Adam Smith, "Of the Expenses of the Sovereign or Commonwealth," book V, chapter 1, *Inquiry*, p.482.

25. Ibid.

26. Noam Chomsky, "Notes on NAFTA," *The Nation*, March 14, 1993, p.412.

27. It is sometimes supposed that the threat to the world's forests is not corporations felling them for money gains, but Third World peoples cutting them for fuel, which is not converted into money or profit. Alternative Energy Development Inc., though, reports that more than 95 per cent of deforestation is caused by land-use changes. Keith Openshaw, "Fuelling the Third World's Energy Crisis," *The Guardian Weekly*, Oct. 13, 1996, p.2.

28. David Israelson, "1 Million Iraqui Kids Starving," *The Toronto Star*, Oct. 22, 1991.

29. As an estimated $100 billion was spent on the U.S.-led Gulf War, stock markets climbed and U.S. Treasury Secretary Nicholas Brady enthused: "It looks as though things are going according to plan [in the Gulf War] and I expect that to release significant energy into the economy." Jack Cahill, "Does the U.S. Economy Need Wars?" *The Toronto Star*, Jan. 26, 1991, p.D1.

30. In 1994 Chile's Central Bank set up an environmental accounting unit to build up a balance sheet of the country's resources. It would register the damages caused by corporate tree-cutting, mining, and fishing to the air, water, and soil, incorporating these now ignored costs into the conventional GNP/GDP. When the evidence indicated there might not be any forests left within twenty-five to thirty years at the forestry corporations' present rate of wholesale cutting and burning, the forestry corporations assailed the central bank for "meddling in matters beyond its sphere," challenged the credentials of the economists, rejected the principles of accounting, and declared the figures as false. The economist leading the resources accounting unit was suspended and later resigned. The assessments were effectively discontinued. Associated Press, "Chile Wrangles over Resources," *The Globe and Mail*, Feb. 6, 1996, p.A6. Note that the corporate press describes the private corporate prohibition of government collecting facts of large-scale destruction to society's natural resources by corporations' operating on public property as "Chile wrangling."

31. Thus, in "If the G.D.P. Is Up, Why Is America Down?" *The Atlantic*, October 95, 1995, pp.59-78, Cobb, Halstead, and Rowe write: "The more the nation depletes its natural resources, the more the G.D.P. increases.... The Oklahoma bombing becomes an uptick by the share prices of forms making anti-crime devices.... Medical bills arising from dirty air show up as a growth in the G.D.P.... The United States fishes its cod down to remnants [and] this counts as an economic boom.... The G.D.P. treats air and water as having no value at all.... The O.J. Simpson trial [produces] a total of about $200 million in new G.D.P.... The sale of non-renewable resources [is treated] entirely as income.--Family breakdown and crime, the destruction of farmland and entire species, underemployment and the loss of free time, count for nothing in the economic balance."

32. Smith, "Of Restraints," p.360.

33. Ibid., p.352.

34. Ibid., p.353-54; emphasis added.

35. For these outcomes, see, for example, William D. Perdue, *Terrorism and the State: A Critique of Domination through Fear* (New York: Praeger, 1988); and Franz J. Hinkelammert, "Our Project for the New Society in Latin America: The Regulating Role of the State and Problems of Self-Regulation in the Market," *Social Justice*, vol. 19, no.4 (Winter 1992), pp.9-24.

36. A telling example is the case of Japan. In 1939 Japan passed legislation that resulted in U.S. automakers removing their investments from the country. Japan developed a domestic automotive industry, which produced only 32,000 motor vehicles a year in 1950, much less than Canada produced. The approach was criticized by the president of the Bank of Japan, who was certain that such efforts were doomed because they violated the received principle of comparative advantage. "It is meaningless," he said, "to try to build an automotive industry in Japan. This is the age of the international division of labor and Japan would best rely on the United States for motor vehicles." Quoted in David Orchard, "National Party Ideas Not Its Undoing," *The Star-Phoenix* (Saskatoon), Oct. 14, 1994. Such examples do not compute to the global market mind-set because they are "protectionist," and this is bad in principle whatever the facts may mislead us to believe.

37. *The New Internationalist*, March 1991, p.17.

38. *The Toronto Star*, Oct. 23, 1993, p.B6.

39. See, for example, Jane F. Rissler and Margaret G. Mellon, *The Ecological Risks of Engineered Crops* (Cambridge Mass.: MIT Press, 1996).

40. Consider, for example, Nicaragua. After the U.S. Reagan government had covertly supported Contra armed forces to overthrow the Sandinista government and performed other crimes under international law (and was so convicted by the International Court at the Hague in 1986, a decision the U.S. government said did not apply to it) the newly liberated country experienced a destruction of half of its agricultural co-operatives, a 60 per cent unemployment rate, a 40 per cent increase of the absolute poverty rate to 70 per cent of the population, and an IMF-imposed debt regime that appropriated 60 per cent of its GDP for foreign money-lenders. *Tools for Peace*, June 27, 1994; *The Guardian Weekly*, March 4, 1996, p.23.

41. Vandana Shiva, "The Monoculture of the Mind, Understanding Threats to Biological and Cultural Diversity." Inaugural Hopper Lecture, University of Guelph, Sept. 21, 1992.

The Free Market and Democracy

Parties in the market should be free to buy and sell at any price at which they can find a partner to the transaction— free to produce, buy and sell anything that can be produced or sold at all.

Friedrich A. Hayek, *The Road to Serfdom*[1]

Hayek's formula emphasizes that the principal argument for the free market is the freedom it grants producers, buyers, and sellers from any external control in the production and exchange of goods. Because this freedom applies to people's lives—what they eat, where they live, and so on—it is the most important and fundamental realm of freedom there is. Or so it seems.

Freedom of the Consumer—If You Can Pay

If consumers do not have the money required to pay for the goods (such as food or shelter) that they need or desire, the consumers cannot buy those goods and thus cannot possess or consume them. Those who do not have enough money in the free market to pay for what they require to live therefore have no right to food or shelter or any other required means of life that is produced and sold. To call this freedom is self-contradictory, because freedom cannot exist for those with no means to act freely.

We can put this matter another way. Under the rules of the free market, need without effective demand (that is, the purchasing power of money) is not recognized. It counts for nothing. Need with no money to back it has no reality or value for the market.

The "freedom of the consumer" in the free market is really only the freedom of those who have enough money to demand what they need or want. For all those do not possess this money, there is no freedom of the consumer, even to eat. It follows that people without the money to purchase the goods they need—about 20 per cent of the world's population and increasing—do not have the right to live under the rules of the free market.[2]

What then happens to the jobless when real unemployment rates are between 10 and 20 per cent across the developed world, and as high as 60 per cent in poorer countries such as Nicaragua?[3] People who are unemployed or partly employed are caught in a tightening vice, increasingly without social programs to provide them with even subsistence allowances, as governments across the world undergo "structural readjustment programs" and "social service cutbacks" in the new global order of "liberating civil society from the state."

An increasing number of the world's population are not "free" as consumers and may increasingly lack the means to go on living. That those without money to buy what they need have no right in the market to live follows straightforwardly from market premises. But instead of reflecting on such doctrinal consequences, believers prefer to hold the poor responsible for their poverty. It is not easy for a value system, even the market value system, to rule out people's right to live, so its implications are blocked out of view. Political parties in rich countries such as the United States and Canada have, accordingly, drastically reduced welfare allowances—recently by 21.6 per cent in Ontario (Canada's richest province) and by 10 per cent in the case of food stamps for the poor in the United States. Such assistance is commonly called "handouts" to those "who should be working for a living." The destitution, disease, and even death the indigent face as "consumers" without money to buy anything to consume are then easy to accept. The poor deserve their fate for being "wilfully unemployed," for being "too dependent," for "lack of initiative." This viewpoint does not accept that those who do have jobs may lose them as rapidly as companies and governments can "downsize" and "shed workers" and that banks do not lend start-up capital to those without money in the first place.

The market doctrine's ethic of life is that all value is based on what people with money are willing to pay. That is the positive principle of value on which the freedom of the consumer is based. But if one does not have the money, one has no value, only "dependent" want, the opposite of "effective demand." There is nothing to be gained from such beings in the market, only trouble from their attempts to go on living in some other way—by demands for welfare, scrounging in garbage, panhandling, or other impecunious efforts to survive. Therefore, the poor are pronounced bad. They offer nothing in the market to buy or to profit from, and they seek only to get money from those who have it. Poverty is the one sin that market theory and practice cannot forgive. The state of being without enough money is beyond the pale.

In the ethical world of the market there is no fault, no more grievous wrong, than for a citizen to be without effective demand. This is a principle of badness that admits of degrees. As the world turns, ever more people have less money, even in the world's richest market, where the bottom 40 per cent of workers have seen their real wages fall by more than 20 per cent in the last two decades.[4] People learn in such a value system to be ashamed of not having enough, or even as much, money as others. They show it on their faces and in their body movements, and they are gnawed by it within. The less money one has, the less worthy of respect and more blameworthy one is. That is why people are terrified of losing their source of income, and that is why they count money loss as always bad and money gain as always good.

But another wrong is still greater than having no money, and that is to take money from those who have it. The global market's prisons bulge with the perpetrators of this double, unforgivable sin. White-collar criminals are not such a problem to the ideology because they still fit into the market ethic as people with money wanting more money, and willing to buy from others. But those who have no money and take it from others who have it have no redeeming trait in the market morality. Such miscreants are duly incarcerated and, if need be, killed.[5]

The poor suffer by far the greatest discrimination, with race, gender, and ethnic exclusions rising and falling in direct proportion to the lack of money of the victims. As the rising majority of people in the world are increasingly pushed off the land or out of their jobs to make way for the global market, this discrimination across race and gender becomes a single systemic war against the poor that is the undeclared agenda of the corporate-market program.

The Question of Need

We might wonder here why market theory and practice, with their highly developed lexicon of concepts and principles, have no idea of the meaning of need. The burning issue of what people need, as distinguished from their "effective demand," is never raised in market analysis. Although the market system of value has been constructed to speak to the issue of societies' allocation of scarce resources in a maximally efficient way, it excludes all reference to what humans require to reproduce their lives. This astonishing fact is almost never mentioned. Indeed, one can look through the entire canon from John Locke and Adam Smith to any mainstream contemporary economist and not once see the category of "need" occur. The doctrine's sole concern is with what people with money demand. Need without money-demand does not compute. Desire or appetite with no need, however, is served as long as it is backed by cash. If I want weapons to kill, or people to buy, and I have money to pay, no desire I may have is hindered. This, as Hayek puts it, is the "freedom to buy and sell anything as long as one can find a partner to the transaction." The value system of the market doctrine, therefore, comes down in the end to a ruling principle:

> *x is of value if and only if, and to the extent that, those with money are willing to pay for it.*

Thus it follows from the market value system that a gold-plated toilet priced at $100,000, to be installed in a currency speculator's plane, is a thousand times more valuable than a source of clean water for a rural village that can pay $100 for the resources to locate and dig the well. The market allocates society's scarce resources solely in accordance with money-demand and distributes those resources in accordance with how much money stands behind the demand. This is its sole criterion of efficient distribution of society's resources. If the villagers do not have the $100 to pay for what is required to make the well, even with the lives of the whole village depending on it, their needs draw no allocation of society's resources to them. In contrast, the gold toilet or the private jet appropriates as much of society's resources as its buyer wants so long as there is the moneyed demand for it. This remains true even if fewer and fewer resources are left for other people whose "effective demand" cannot compete. It is worth recalling here that market doctrine is triumphal in its claim that it "allocates scarce resources among competing demands more efficiently than any system yet known to man." Given that a few hundred billionaires own more in money demand or its equivalent than the total income of the majority of the world's population, we can indeed see where this market system of resource allocation leads to.[6] In the market realm of distributive justice, it follows that those who have more money have more rights, while those who have less money have fewer rights.

Since market theory and practice recognize only "effective demand," need without the money to back it has no right at all. At the same time, market ethics endorse any money-backed desire at all— even if it is for, say, weapons of mass destruction or cancer-causing consumables. "Effective demand" in the market is in this way both too narrow and too broad a criterion of distribution to properly serve humanity. Although some healthy people may remain more concerned with meeting human needs in the market by their personal choices, this criterion for allocating society's scarce resources is ruled out by the market's principles of production and distribution. To think that individual choices in aggregate are the same as society's choices, as the doctrine assumes, is, in turn, to commit the elementary logical error of the "fallacy of composition." In the face of this deformation of value bearings, a convenient and widely propagated belief has arisen: the view that no reliable criterion of human need can be found. "One man's meat is another man's poison," or "What is a need to some is a want to others," and so on.

A more grounded connection with the real world, however, will soon reveal a rebuttal, for it is demonstrable that all of us need oxygen-bearing and non-toxic air, food nourishment (a need acted on by need-sceptics every few hours), and habitation (another need the market subjectivist will be sure to ensure for himself every night). When we consult reality rather than market ideology, we recognize that there are vital life-needs common to us all across language and culture and taste divisions. Indeed, we can without exception exactly define what a need is by a principle that distinguishes every need from every mere want:

> *N is a need if and only if, and to the extent that, deprivation of N always leads to a reduction of organic capability.*

By "organic capability," I mean the agent's organic abilities to move, think, and feel. Reduction of one or the other of these abilities occurs to the extent that the normal range of movement of any part of the body, of conceptual or perceptual thought, or of sentient and emotional life, is reduced in the range of operations it can perform. Thus, deprive a human of breathable air for a period of minutes, and all of these life-powers will soon be reduced to none. Deprive a child of all clean water or protein, and the child will invariably suffer rapid degeneration of life-powers.[7] Deprive a person of habitation in most climates, and that person will soon experience a very reduced range of thought, feeling, and movement and, perhaps, in a number of hours, death from exposure.

The final limit of basic need deprivation is death of the organism. But prior to this limit of life-range, there are degrees of morbidity or, what is the same thing, loss of life-power in some degree. This loss of life can be a marginal reduction (for example, respiratory diseases that afflict city-dwellers) or a cumulatively disabling organic breakdown from starvation or disease (caused, for example, by the malnutrition now faced by at least one-quarter of the earth's population).

The world is now an ongoing site of increasing need deprivations for the many and rising desire service for the few, with correspondingly serious reductions of life-range for the many. There is at
the same time the felt pain and suffering that accompany these systematic deprivations or assaults on the organism. These internal
correlatives of need deprivation we know as the "pangs of hunger" or
the "sufferings of want." Market doctrine, however, is in principle
indifferent to the feelings as well as the disablements of unsatisfied
need, even if demonstrable. Whatever it is these consumers want and
however much they want that will leave countless others without the
resources to live are not problems for the doctrine, for it is theoretically blind to it. But this blindness is not recognized. On the contrary
it is called "rigorous economics" and "market discipline." The measure of all market "efficiency" is how swiftly and cheaply goods are
delivered to money-demand. However pathological these demands
might be and however many people may be left in a state of morbidity or disease in consequence of its allocations of scarce resources are
matters of indifference to the market paradigm of value. The "freedom to do with our money what we want," if we have money, is the
final court of appeal in evaluating the claims of desire.

Common sense recognizes, nevertheless, that there are life-
needs that a society's economy should be geared to meet—for example, the needs of its children and next generations to reproduce in a
healthy state. The global market has no measure for these needs.
Thus it follows from its value system that staggering growths of child
poverty, as profits and stock-market values simultaneously sky-
rocket, pose no problem.[8] They only pose a problem to the value system's parameters of judgement to the extent that more and more children without the means to live may cause "instability for investors."
For this, there is the remedy of "getting tougher on juvenile crime."

A theoretical dodge becomes indispensable to the doctrine to
counter the insistence of practical reason that attention must still be
paid to starving and malnourished children. This dodge is that needs
cannot be distinguished from wants. Mere wants and the "authoritarian" notion of needs, says the doctrine, must be set aside in the name
of "letting people decide for themselves."[9] The appeal to human

needs is a pretext, it is said, to tell people what they must have, while "consumer choice" and "consumer sovereignty" leave the decision to the individual buyers who instruct the market what to invest in by their aggregate demand. In this way, the market doctrine circumvents the problem of allocation of society's scarce resources for gold toilets or nuclear submarines instead of clean air or food and shelter for children, and it claims the moral high ground of "democratic individualism" and "free choice."

It is clear what true need is for all of us, and what it is not. Not only can we tell need from mere want, but we can also tell the precise degrees of need by the extent of disablement that its deprivation regularly causes. All life-needs and their degree of necessity can be identified by testable criterion. Medical science is the history of these tests. There is no more an "authoritarian" judgement here than in preventing and treating the transmission of disease or other bodily breakdown. Mere wants, conversely, can be told by the same measure. The conflation of the market doctrine's "utilities" and the human life-needs is, in the end, an ideological smokescreen to release the market doctrine from any distinction between what money-owners demand and what people's lives require for their vital function.

Consumer Sovereignty or Infantile Demand?

The idea of "consumer sovereignty" is most appealing to those privileged people of the world who have more than enough money to buy what they need. The global market operates to provide such consumers with goods and services of all kinds from across the world. For these fortunate people, still a minority, their effective demands direct the market to produce whatever they desire. "Demand" is a term that deserves our reflection. This measure of consumer freedom entails an unlimited inequality of freedom. The more money one has, the more freedom one is entitled to, from none at all to limitless rights to consume. This is the ground of individual freedom the doctrine declares, never reconciling this vastly unequal freedom of citizens with its strong claims of equality of opportunity for all at the same time. These contradictions do not detain market believers, for they know that the market confers on them the unlimited freedom to choose, to have, and to enjoy consumer goods the more money they have.

Advocates of the "global free market" have a special interest in supporting the market ideology, because it favours them above the greater part of humanity. This market principle explains the devotion of the better-off to the global market doctrine, as they are free to effectively demand whatever they want and what others produce. But this unequal freedom raises a question as to the nature of the "sovereignty" it confers on the minority.

It is a question that is seldom asked, even by those who oppose the resulting patterns of inequality. But, when we reflect on people getting whatever they want by other people producing it for them, delivering it to them, serving them throughout its consumption, and generally doing everything for them from one day's end to the next with no respite, the concept of "freedom" or "sovereignty" applies less and less intelligibly to their condition. On the contrary, what we might term their demanding dependency resembles the condition of a helpless child. To put the matter another way, insofar as consumers wholly depend upon and demand from others what they want with no required responsibility for the production, preparation, delivery, and service of any of it, they approach an infantile state.

This helpless dependency may sometimes be unavoidable, but to say this is to miss the point. The point is that this demanding dependency is not a disvalue for the doctrine, as long as it borne by the rich and not the poor. Rather, it is celebrated as "consumer freedom," and there is no limit in the doctrine to how far this consumer demand for others' work and service can extend. A primary assumption of the doctrine is, indeed, that consumer wants are unlimited and are to be served to any extent backed by the money to pay.[10] Those consumers who have the money to pay for others to do everything for them, therefore, become ever more dependent in their consumer demands on others. The conventional term for their consumer position, "*effective demand*," implies a common meaning with the "demand feeding" of the helpless infant. The difference is that the infantile demand of the consumer with money has no relationship to actual need.

The concept of "freedom" or "sovereignty" for the limitless, non-productive demand on others' work to serve one's desires is, therefore, in principle the opposite of what we normally mean by "freedom." Freedom implies self-determination, self-government, and accepting responsibility for one's own life, until recently a notion agreed upon by philosophers of all centuries. Consequently, market ideology is vociferous in proclaiming the value of "responsibility" and "non-dependency" when it comes to poor people. In the case of those requiring social assistance, for example, market devotees, outraged at welfare recipients' "dependency" and "lack of responsibility," deprive them and their children of their food and homes to "teach them self-reliance." At the same time they assert the "freedom" of "sovereign consumers" to demand commodities and services to move them physically from place to place, to prepare and deliver all their meals ready-made, to clean up after them everywhere they go, to perform continuous activities to please and entertain them around the clock, and in general do everything whatever that can be done to fulfil their desires. Such behaviour is not considered "dependency on others." On the contrary, the media lionize it as "jet set," "high-flying," and "reaping the rewards of success."

The cultivation of the infantile maw of consumer demand for others' services is not confined to the rich, but can occur wherever there is more money than need. Obviously certain market goods enable the consumer's life and are of value to the extent that they maintain and increase its vitality and scope. Any means whereby thought, feeling, or action can grow and become more comprehensive is a good from a human-value standpoint. But the very concept of "consumer"—a term denoting a passive using up of the ready-made—does not refer to the human agency of the purchaser at all, but only to the moment of the buying of others' products, and their extinction by consumption to reproduce the demand once again. This money-demand for others' work or product when it does not enable one's own greater capacities to think or to do for oneself is corrupting to one's own life-powers.

By the market measure, the more the consumer can demand from others, the more "sovereign" the consumer is. This freedom to depend is, in the name of freedom, proclaimed as a market ideal. Thus, at the end of the rainbow of market value the shining goal beckons, the goal which only the special few can ever attain. It is the final joy of never "making do," but being able to consume anything, all the time. The market's infantile dream of paradise is to regress to a state of unconditional, horizonless desire that is always satisfied by others' compliance with serving it. This is hardly sovereignty or freedom. It is the very ultimate of the insatiable dependency on others' work that the rich project upon the poor.

The Truth of Consumer Choice

The market theory's concept and practice of "consumer freedom" are the opposite of freedom as self-reliance or autonomy. But we should consider the nature of the consumer's choice. Where consumer demand exceeds life-need, what makes it want the goods it chooses to buy? The world's multibillion-dollar advertising business "stimulates demand," ensuring consumer wants are conditioned to demand to buy the products that are on the market for sale.

What is common to this conditioning advertising is that a behaviourial objective (to buy product x) is set for the consumer by a set of stimulations, which reinforce the desire for the product until there is sufficient demand to buy it at a price that nets maximum revenues and sales. A scientifically tested schedule of reinforcements (the advertisement) is programmed at a cost of up to a million dollars a minute into a media vehicle (television, billboard, newspaper) to condition a target audience into desiring the product. Trial market surveys are conducted until the maximum efficiency of conditioning paying consumers into desiring the designated product has been achieved. The goal of the advertisement is "to make everyone want it"—whether they need it or not.[11] The targeted consumers normally purchase enough of the product being sold to generate an expected sum of money profits, proving the indoctrination's success. This successful method is now used to sell elected politicians in "market democracies."

Is the consumer truly "free" in this process of alleged choice? The decision to purchase, the sole choice of the consumer, is itself programmed by others. Advertising firms only attract clients by achieving successfully conditioned response. Corporations do not invest unless they can count on multibillion-dollar advertising conditioning customers to select their products.

So much for the "individual consumer sovereign" that market theory asserts as its democratic foundation. Individuals are either without money-demand to pay for this freedom or, at the other extreme, become infantile demanders of others' labour to get what they want. In the great range between these extremes, the individual is conceived and treated as an operantly conditioned potential to respond in mass-predictable ways to an advertiser's program to induce a biased selection. When the slogans have been cleared away from the facts, little evidence remains of "free" and "sovereign" consumer choice. However, consumers with the money to pay do have a choice in three important respects:

1. the choice between products they need, but have limited means to purchase, the choice of the "best buy" to secure freedom from want (such as nutritious food in volume rather than food and nutrition at the same price from other venues);

2. the choice between products that do or do not enable their own more vital range of life—a choice between what advances or diminishes their freedom of human agency (such as "quality programming" versus "trash" TV);

3. the choice between products that do or do not harm other life-interests than their own—that is, the choice of product endorsement or boycott (for example, local products of environmentally responsible producers versus exploitative products of transnational corporations).

Even in an advertising-saturated environment, these choices retain remain radical potential. Even when significant alternatives seem not to exist, for example in buying a fossil-fuel-powered automobile, the option remains to reduce or eliminate the demand for the automobile itself. This choice is largely proportional to the consumer's voting income, but it is a pivotal realm of choice within the global market system. Enough consumers choosing not to buy a product can alter the behaviour of the most powerful world corporation.

Corporations know this very well. Products must pass through the gates of buyer choice before they convert into money-profit, and a bad "image" or reputation, at worst a collective boycott, can bring disaster. They "protect their image" not only by making immense expenditures on positive reinforcers prepared by psychologists, public relations experts, and entertainers, but also by a pervasive propagation across the media to reach the maximum number of buyers with maximum indoctrination effect. Behind the scenes they sue boycotters, intimidate them with court costs and damages, and threaten media with withdrawing advertising if they carry any criticism that might tarnish their images. More effectively, they purchase major media outlets in order to directly control public communications systems.[12]

Corporations also construct an invisible wall against any public criticism that might reduce their sales or market control. They manage this through a myriad of channels, lucrative contracts of purchase, interlocking directorates, arts and science sponsorships and programs, political action committees, public relations agents, and watchful editors in the media. The result is hardly a democratic marketplace of consumer choice, but it follows from the value program of seeking to maximize sales and profits by any legal means. The law itself is then rolled back from interfering with this process, through the weakening of antimonopoly or antifalsehood regulation.

Corporate producers and sellers are, as extensively documented, also disposed to criminal and other violations of law.[13] Why then are corporations and their leaderships so seldom exposed or challenged in the mass media compared to, say, politicians, bureaucrats, or unions? Certainly their self-serving, environmentally destructive, and democratically unaccountable behaviours are far more systemic. They are not publicly criticized as a group, however, because they succeed in blocking criticism of their behaviour in the media and in most other public forums, such as classrooms. The consumer's informed choice to vote against specific corporations for, say, their co-operation with murderous military dictatorships, their ecocidal production methods, or their violations of employees' human rights is restricted in many unseen ways, obstructing and reducing the individual consumer's ability to choose not to buy from them.

Precisely because the consumer's choice is so important and necessary a moment to the market's production and distribution cycles, corporations seek to contain consumers' options within conditioned bounds, hedged around by walls to foreclose this very choice. The structure of sale and purchase is already controlled within strict parameters. Armed-force protection guarantees market and corporate ownership domains on both sides of any market transaction. Those without money to spend are not admitted into any exchange or access to market good. The process of market production and exchange is ruled by an oligopoly in which a small percentage of firms control most of the manufacture and distribution of goods. Finally, those with the most money are entitled to cast thousands of times more votes for products and services than their fellow "consumer sovereigns" in the global market's "democratic" process.

If consumers are so locked into a predetermined structure of walls and doorways, conditioned beneath the processes of conscious deliberation and choice by operations in which they have no voice, how is there any actual freedom left in this consumer moment of market choice? To paraphrase Noam Chomsky, "Propaganda is to the market what violence is to dictatorship." So how can we be free even in the narrow space left to us, that of choosing to buy or not to buy a product?

To buy or not to buy—is that the question? Even if we assume that we have the money to buy, that alternative products are available, and that the time to recognize and exercise our options exists—all major and unexamined assumptions—are we left with a significant choice?

A propaganda system cannot succeed on those who see through it. Alternative sources of information remain available outside the mainstream. We should keep in mind that buyers alone complete every circuit of money-returns by which corporations are able to reproduce themselves. Without this choice to buy its commodity, the corporation has no money-supply to go on living.

Every time we cast "a dollar vote," we are voting for the corporation whose product or service we buy. With buyers acting as a group that can grow to any size, individual market agents moving beyond market doctrine to social purpose can move to redirect the most powerful oligopolist corporation towards life-responsible ends. Corporations are very sensitive to this possibility and will go to any length to prevent its critical mass forming. Examples are the response to consumer boycotts of California grape-growers, Nestlé Limited's deadly marketing of baby formula to Third World mothers, and MacMillan Bloedel's clear-cut logging of ancient rainforests in British Columbia.

Of course, the "buy or boycott" option only has effect insofar as it moves beyond the market doctrine's assumptions and goals. This point is usually lost on market crusaders. To boycott a market product chooses from an ethical ground of life-responsible behaviour and not the self-maximization principle of more consumer utility or money revenue for oneself. The boycott option seeks to serve interests lacking private money-demand, rather than serving money-demand. Finally, it operates in conjunction with others, rather than in isolation, with individual consumers having no wider goal than their individual satisfaction. In these three ways, this "freedom of the consumer" is opposite in nature to the freedom of the market value system. But this higher freedom works from a space for such freedom that is basic to the market system, the only basis that may still remain for market agents as a whole.

The movement of non-market agency into the choice spaces of the market can be organized beyond boycotts. It can join organizations together to promote the public interest and negotiate with large retailers and producers to be socially responsible in their methods of production in return for consumer patronage. Two major grocery chains in Britain, for example, agreed with the Fairtrade Foundation, a non-governmental organization (NGO), to develop codes of labour rights based on international norms as a marketing strategy to increase market share.[14] The method may be a form of bribing harm-doers, but it is a practical one. Yet even this form of regulating global corporations is under attack by corporate self-maximizers. World trade law makes a legal distinction between "traded products" and "processing and production methods." By this distinction, major corporations are succeeding, with the support of the World Trade Organization and collaborating governments, in outlawing the labelling of products to show whether or not their processes of production comply with international or life-protective law.[15]

Freedom of the Producer or the Non-Producer?

In his classic testament to free market ideology, *The Road to Serfdom*, Friedrich Hayek strongly affirms "the freedom to produce" in the market, regarding socially planned production as "totalitarian."[16]

Hayek's claim has obvious truth-value. So long as the market has independent producers vying to attract buyers, to this extent the market permits a freedom to compete not available in an economy with monopoly conditions of production, such as the former Soviet economy. Although this freedom of producers to compete in the world has increasingly diminished with the oligopolist control of supply and demand in the major sectors of production, let us examine the market claim of the "freedom of the producer" in principle, setting aside these oligopolist conditions.

First of all, who is the producer? In the peculiar language and logic of global market theory and practice, "producers" are not those who produce. Rather, owners of private capital purchase the labour of those who produce, including that of white-collar managerial and technical workers. In many firms investing owners may also be producers, paying themselves as managers on top of remuneration as owners. Generally, though, the private capital investors constituting corporate "producers" do not produce at all. Owners of the factors of production are typically constituted as fictitious legal entities, "corporate persons," which have organizations of employees under chief-executive command seeking to maximize their profits and assets. The owners, in turn, typically have no role whatever in production, even as spectators. They are free only as money investors in others' production, free to invest as they please to secure more money from the sale of others' work products for private profit. Meanwhile those who do produce the goods and services do not count in market theory as "the producers." Instead, they are conceived, as one of the "factors of production," along with "capital," "natural resources," and an undefined factor called "enterprise." Workers are employed by the owners of capital, renamed the "producers." These agents of "enterprise" do not normally participate in any step of the good's production.

What freedom under this doctrine remains for the actual producers, those who produce the goods and services that others buy? According to market theory, they are instruments, a "factor" of production, which owners of capital "employ." But if they are instruments of another, they cannot, then, be free. One cannot be free and an instrument of another's will at the same time. Since the producer's service or labour has been purchased by another, this service or labour, whatever its level of skill, belongs to the employer. As another's property, the person can no longer make or control the decisions governing his or her working life. The term "company time" makes this point very clear. From the work of those who plan the company's product to that of those who materialize these plans as saleable products, the "producers" are precisely not free, but belong as "a factor of production" to the firm that has bought their service or labour.

The employer, having paid or, rather, agreed to pay for the work, owns it and has therefore the right to receive prescribed performances in return. That is to say, the employer has the right as the private owner of the factors of production to exercise an owner's control over everything these factors do. This right, in turn, is exercised by management employees, whose hours of work have been purchased as well, through a hierarchy of command ending with the chief executive officer. To ensure his identification with the non-producing owners, a CEO is also a stockholder, typically receiving far more in stock options than in salary. Along with other senior executives who own stocks, CEOs are normally the only owners involved in production at all. The only freedom or self-government that seems to exist for the actual producers is at the top levels of management, where there is some freedom to design and implement alternative structures, but only so far as it conforms to the ruling command of maximizing profitability for stockholders and owners.

As the scale of productive enterprises increases, the actual producers in this corporate Leviathan are organized as substitutable insert-operations in a system directed from a centre they do not see, fearful that they may not continue even as cogs in the machine in a world in which capitals compete to shed workers. Where disemployment means destitution, their "freedom" as productive beings exists only as a reiterated doctrinal slogan, which is as opposite of free as one could imagine.

The sixty-five-hour-a-week job of the Nike running-shoe producer in a sweatshop of the new "free labour zones" of the East or South, with a wage of less than $40 a week, is arguably less free than the work of a nineteenth-century field-slave.[17] But here, too, the ideology stays the course against the evidence, closing out the real world by incantations of "freedom." As far as corporate shareholders and executives go, even their freedom is dubious, for according to market doctrine they have no choice but to seek to maximize their profits to compete. So who is left free if even they cannot choose to do otherwise?

Perhaps "free" here means only that corporate producers can access factors of production cost; free, with society paying the input charges. Consider "labour" and "natural resources." They arrive ready-made and at no cost of production for private investors' use. But these pre-market costs of producing people and life-forms are not costs according to market theory and practice, because business has not had to pay for them. People and the life-world as a whole are selected as ready-at-hand resources to be used to transform materials into commodities for profitable sale. But these life-environments and humans come to be "factors of production" only through extremely complex processes of creation. They are then appropriated ready-formed by corporations for profit. Still, they do not drop from the sky ready-made for exploitation. They must first be produced, often at great cost to society.

The two main producers of "labour" and "natural resource" factors of production are nature itself, which has taken about two billion years of reproductive life-organization to create every resource that money investors presuppose as given for their use, and unpaid human labour, primarily that of women, who produce by childbirth and child-rearing those who eventually come to sell their labour. Along with rainforests or oceans, profit-seeking enterprises select already produced workers free of charge. Therefore, when we hear economic theory's concern with the "costs of production and distribution," and with the "factors of production" required, we should keep in mind that, typically, none of the time, work, or costs of producing these foundational inputs of production themselves are paid for by those who profit from their use and exploitation. The great costs of labour and time that enter first into their production, and the costs of reproducing them subsequently, do not enter into market theory or practice as a cost at all. That is why market doctrine invariably opposes money investment in child care or environmental preservation. Such expenditures are deemed to "waste money" on what does not cost money for business in the first place.

Ralph Nader describes this freedom from costs bestowed on private corporations in the case of natural resources. He writes:

> The public *owns* one third of the United States ... [but] companies, most multinationals, *control* these rich resources of timber, oil, gas, copper, iron, zinc, etc., through leaseholds. And taxpayers put up the money ... to facilitate cutting [and extraction] ... in virgin timberlands, for example, more than ten times what they get back in royalties.[18]

Those who actually produce within the market, then, are not free in any intelligible sense of the term, because they are instruments of production whose hours of work belong to the control and direction of those who have bought them. On the other hand, according to the doctrine, human beings and natural resources, which are produced for the market free of cost to business prior to their offering ready-made for profitable exploitation, do not exist for the market until they are appropriated. In either case the life paid for or not paid for is solely as *means* of others' projects and, as such, unfree by definition.

In this overall system, what alone seems to remain as "free" (if by free we mean *self-governing*) is the owner of productive investment capital. He can choose or not choose to hire others to produce goods and services for sale in the market at the highest price that buyers in the market are willing to pay for them. But the employer's position requires a prescribed form of decision and action at every step: *that is, to maximize profits and assets for shareholders*. Because this position rules out all options other than selfish monetary gain, the employer or capital investor is also unfree by his subjugation to this ruling program of decision. He thinks and acts only for one system-prescribed end, not a self-determined, human goal. This is not freedom or self-government, but a structure of moral slavery.

Freedom is not simply a slogan, but requires an option to do other than what is prescribed. Few agents of the market system are in truth free, even those at the top. In the end, then, only the "free market" itself is free or self-regulating. As in other fundamentalist creeds, however, obedience to this god is conceived as the acme of personal freedom and self-realization.

The Knowledge-Based Economy

To affirm its epistemic credentials, a new value of the global market has recently come to be prized. Known as "the knowledge revolution," it is propagated across the global marketplace. All who can read, hear, or see have been declared to live in a new and higher order of human understanding, the "knowledge-based economy."

Market enthusiasts are so propelled by the lustrous categories of this vision of the "the knowledge revolution," "the information age," "the post-industrial era," or "the rule of symbolic analysts" that the whole of past history is considered a preparation for the transfiguration of the world by the microchip. New World Order guru Alvin Toffler heralds this configuration as "The Third Wave" and the "New Civilization," transforming social relations, democracy, the workplace, and civic responsibility. Anything in its way is an "old line," "smoke-stack," and "rearguard" reaction against the new progress-line of history.[19]

It is commonplace to conceive the "knowledge revolution" and the "information economy" as the scaffolding of a new and higher intelligence bearing the world to an age of universal knowledge and connectiveness. But there is one fatal flaw to this global vision. The distinction between truth and falsehood is overlooked.

What do this knowledge and this information actually mean? If it is knowledge, we can tell it apart from non-knowledge, or ignorance. If it is information, we can tell it apart from disinformation, or drivel. But such basic lines of distinction do not arise in this "knowledge-based economy." In the new "knowledge economy," knowledge is not an issue.

Thus no criterion of truth has ever emerged in the new knowledge order. It is enough to declare "knowledge" and "information" as self-certifying slogans. It requires *thinking* to tell these apart from what they are not, but that is now "left to the software." It requires a commitment to meaning to understand that knowledge and information are not simply any symbolic sequence. But these requirements of sense are time-wasting stopovers on the "information superhighway." As with ritual hypnotics, it is sufficient to repeat the words. The utterance of the syllables, repeated often and pervasively, inscribe neural pathways of accepted order and well-being and compel the experience of self-evidence.

One may have expected some critical response from the academic world, which stewards the evolved knowledge and information of millennia, but there has been silent acquiescence or, more conspicuously, enthusiastic collaboration. University administrators and education bureaucrats have rushed to invoke "the rule of the knowledge-based economy," with no questions asked as to what "knowledge" or "information" is. In the rush to agree to any terms set by the "new global market reality," the academy no longer insists on telling apart the assertions of truth and propaganda. Instead its leadership tirelessly conceptualizes education as "necessary to get on board the new knowledge economy." We face an unseen crisis. It heralds a new dark age not recognized by those within it, in which the distinction between truth and falsehood collapses and commercial advantage rules as the final arbiter of knowledge.

Dr. Keith Bezanson, president of the International Development Research Centre (IDRC), explains the new doctrine's necessity:

"Researchers are faced with a new reality.... We have to accept the new reality is everywhere.... Researchers can't expect to receive funds to do research just because it's good research. We have to relate research to the marketplace." In other words, even within universities, the market's values are overriding. Our good is not truth or knowledge, but to serve corporate advantage. Corporate advantage in maximizing profits is, in turn, the sole object of market research. The explanation here is not an issue. It follows straightforwardly from market principles and the claim that universities must serve market needs. All that is missing is the recognition. We must, concludes the instruction, transform higher learning to become one with "the most dramatic and most rapid change the world has ever known."[20]

Such old-time thinking as the pursuit of truth as an end in itself, or critical understanding without deference to special interest, is no longer education's vocation. Knowledge instead comes to mean whatever idea advances the business profitability of the sponsoring corporations that own and use it. There is no corporation, or collaborating university, that does not follow this principle of thought and action as its law. This is not denied. It is selected out of mind. It has a deep consequence, which, in turn, is not seen. True, justified belief is no longer required in this epistemology, nor is openness to learned debate. These are values that do not figure in "the new global reality." As such, they are "out of date."

U.S. Xerox chairman David Kearns is plainspoken about who is in the position of master and ruler in this "new knowledge economy." He says, "Business will have to set the agenda ... a complete restructure [sic] driven by competition and market discipline, unfamiliar ground for educators."[21] Dr. Tom Brzustowski, former vice-president academic and provost of the University of Waterloo and Ontario deputy minister of colleges and universities, agrees. He demands that all public education be subordinated to one absolute aim, success in producing money-wealth and profit: "I contend that the one global object of education must be for a greater capability of the people of Ontario to create wealth ... [to] export products in which our knowledge and skills provide the value added ... to develop new services which we can offer in trade in the world market."[22]

Everyone, it seems, from academic leaderships and business executives to best-selling authors and editorialists, presupposes this sequence of thought as self-evident in the "new knowledge-driven era." Yet the most fundamental requirement of knowledge and truth—to overcome the biases of special interest and partiality—is reversed. Now special interest and partiality reign as the determiners of truth-value.

"Knowledge" and "information" in this new order are subjugated to the final goal of the market: "value-added wealth creation" in a "competitive international economy." What value-added means is the difference between a firm's annual sales revenues and its costs: that is, its money profits. It follows, then, that if the ruling goal of a "knowledge industry" is to maximize "valued-added" or private money profits, any knowledge or information that does not contribute to this goal has no right to existence. This is the market's principle of selection and what is meant by "market discipline."

This market criterion excludes more than any state censors could imagine. Any knowledge or information is ruled out that is not able to be owned and used for money profit. What does not serve it is of no value, by definition. To make a special interest in the final touchstone of truth requires another "adjustment," however. Propaganda is the repetition and selection of a special-interest claim that is not open to rebuttal or debate. To subserve thought to a special-interest demand that cannot itself be questioned is, therefore, a rule of propaganda, which must be adjusted to truth. In this way, knowledge comes to be accepted by the academy itself as subjugation to a ruling dogma. This is where we see the closure of this value program at its most absurd, for it proclaims as its ultimate achievement what it in principle abolishes.

Six Ways in which the Knowledge-Based Economy Is Structured against Knowing the Truth

The first canon of the "knowledge economy" is that what does not sell corporate products is refused communication. Knowledge or information not geared to entertain is, therefore, excluded, as well as any truth that, even if entertaining, is not approved by corporate sponsors.

In a 1992 survey of newspaper editors by Marquette University, for example, 90 per cent of editors said they received "interference from advertisers," 90 per cent said corporate sponsors had "acted on" their threats, and 40 per cent admitted that the contents of stories that were published had been "influenced by advertisers."[23] This information itself was originally produced by a non-profit, public organization of higher learning, was subsequently published by a non-profit, non-advertising magazine, and was not reproduced on the "information superhighway."

It might be argued that the "knowledge-based economy" may not communicate much information, but it does deploy scientific knowledge in its commercial products. This is true, but if there is knowledge, for example, that a product is unsafe—whether it be an automobile, a tobacco product with 4,000 additives, or a carcinogenic substance in foodstuffs—this knowledge will be excluded from the market's information system.[24] Hundreds of thousands, in some cases millions, of innocent people have died tortuous deaths as a result of these hazardous or lethal products and processes—for example, from exposure to the chemicals of cigarette smoke, which the *American Journal of Public Health* has reported is "by far the largest single preventable cause of premature mortality in the United States."[25] Such knowledge will be denied and, wherever possible, erased by any affected corporate producer by invoking the constitutional right to "freedom of speech" in order to misrepresent facts. Information regarding dangers to human or environmental life is, in this manner, standardly repudiated, decried, kept from publication, falsified, or otherwise prevented from being known on the "information superhighway." Only knowledge or information that promotes producers' profits is selected for production and distribution.

According to Edward Hochstedler's classic study *Corporate Criminality*, over 600,000 people a year in the world's wealthiest market economy die from hazardous processes and products of corporate manufacture, a finding that is kept concealed from workers and buyers.[26] This is one variation on the theme of the "knowledge economy" systematically blocking the advancement and dissemination of knowledge in its operations in order to fulfil "market obligations to maximize the money gains of stockholders." Mass media managements will, in compliance with this value program, continue to exclude whatever is not entertaining to mass audiences and suppress whatever is unacceptable to the corporate advertising sponsors who purchase their programs. "Corporate image" is an overruling concern in marketing, and corporately employed protectors predictably select against whatever information or knowledge is known about the dangers to human or environmental life, even if such knowledge and information is a life-and-death matter affecting the futures of millions of people. This behaviour is not repelled by the market ethic, but is perfectly in accord with market principles of maximizing shareholder value.

Some kinds of information, however, can be embodied in a commercial product, which can be useful and healthy to consumers. These kinds of information would seem to suit the "knowledge-based economy." But even here the profitability criterion excludes them from the market. For example, many natural substances have been long known for their medicinal properties and absence of harmful side effects but are nevertheless rejected by the market's "research-intensive" corporations, for two reasons. First, the natural substances cannot be patented, and thus the genetic codes they bear cannot be owned as private property. Second, since knowledge patents on pharmaceutical products now extend to twenty years by GATT/World Trade Organization law—up from eight or zero years—patented, artificial substances now confer a global monopoly of production and distribution of these substances for two decades. Since the new regime of twenty-year patent monopolies in pharmaceutical products renders natural substances with medicinal properties undesirable as knowledge-products, corporations will not pursue the safety tests of their properties to pass government regulations. The safety-proved, natural product cannot be owned as a monopoly for twenty years, unlike artificial drugs contrived by corporate laboratories. If governments pursued safety tests of these natural products as a form of public-health service (justified by millennia of successful natural remedies) we can infer that those governments would be attacked by market corporations for "interfering in the free market."

In this way, knowledge of natural substances with curative powers is ruled out by the "knowledge-driven economy." As a Canada Department of Health official has stated, "Pharmaceutical firms will not be interested in going through the safety approval process [for any natural curative agent] because it is a natural substance and cannot be patented."[27]

Only a patent granting a long-term monopoly of production and distribution, which allows, in turn, a monopoly price to be extracted from users, is judged worthwhile by "knowledge producers." In such market conditions corporations carry a clear advantage if they can prevent this natural, medicinal substance from being recognized or coming onto the market. In the current market context, the trade category of "natural substance" is a demand-intensifying reinforcer of compelling power to educated consumers averse to the addictive consequences of artificial drugs, stimulants, and pills. A "natural substance" that truly cures is thus a competitor for market share that pharmaceutical corporations would have every reason to discredit and exclude from the "new knowledge order." The medical-industrial complex opposes natural-substance cures as "fads," and transnational "health maintenance organizations" rapidly convert medical treatment to programmed procedures dependent on pharmaceutical drugs. Added to this, monopolized patent medicines keep rising in price, tripling, for example, in the last ten years in Canada under international trade agreements that exclusively protect corporate rights. The Canadian government's Bill C-7 would have deprived Canadians of legal access to even the most common medicinal herbs such as camomile, echinacea, and over fifty other natural plant substances.[28] These connected patterns of phenomena may deeply disquiet our sense of fair play and concern for public health, but they are all in strict accord with the overriding market value goal of maximizing sales and profits for corporations and their shareholders.

The private-profit criterion of "knowledge industries" is now universal in the current global market order, which leads to a paradox. The "knowledge-based economy" rules out the production and circulation of knowledge. Another level of this contradiction follows from corporate ownership rights over "intellectual property." An "information" or "knowledge" commodity states that an owner's copyright is held on it, and the "violation" of this copyright "is an offence against and punishable by law." This is the condition of its publication as knowledge or information both in cases in which it is genuine knowledge or information and in cases in which it is not. Normally a private corporation appropriates this copyright, usually without paying for it. With most knowledge and information, such as that found in scholarly journals and texts, authors must typically seek permission from corporations to reproduce their own work, even though it has been independently created without recompense from the appropriating corporation. Thus the work is both created by others and paid for by others: individual scholars, universities, and tax-paying citizens. But a corporation gains copyright over the information and knowledge to sell in the market for profit, without paying for the cost of its creation. Universities then enforce this unpaid for corporate copyright across international boundaries, and it is a mark of the subjugation of the academic community to this regime that its administrators comply without question.

If an author does not sign over ownership of the knowledge or information commodity to the publishing corporation, the work will not normally be published at all. Where the creator or author retains copyright, the knowledge or information product must still fulfil the condition of private profit for it to be produced in the market. The profit criterion rules here as well as elsewhere, whether by long-term monopoly right or other avenue of selection and control. Knowledge or information that does not meet the criterion, true or not, will thus be ruled out of existence. For example, in Canada, where over 85 per cent of all college and university textbooks sold are produced by foreign multinational corporations, this profit criterion of knowledge eliminates Canadian content itself as an impediment to an international scale of sales and distribution, applying it usually as an "add-on" to the homogeneous product whenever domestic market share is considered profitable. We should not be surprised that the principles of private-profit maximization and the requirements of knowledge within this interlocking system of bias against knowledge production and distribution in the "new information order" are fundamentally opposed. But the validity of the "knowledge" of the "knowledge economy" or of the "information" of the "information order" is not an issue in the public or scholarly realms. The truth is what can be made to sell.

Let us keep in mind here that the only international system of information exchange that qualifies as being not biased by special-interest ownership and control is the Internet and its subsystem, the World Wide Web. The Internet's information content, however, has from the beginning been produced and circulated by professors and students from public-sector learning institutions. This is why this medium of communication has not yet been systematically distorted by special-interest biases. This enabling condition of knowledge and information transmission, however, is now being displaced as corporations are moving onto the Internet as a global, low-cost marketing site to display their advertising billboards.

More generally, we need to be aware of another, more elementary distinction, the distinction between the means whereby information and knowledge can be stored and communicated, and the content of this system of message storage and communication. However advanced in velocity, volume, and global range the instruments of electronic communications become, nothing in these technologies distinguishes between information and misinformation, or between knowledge and propaganda. To hail the arrival of "new information technologies" and "knowledge transmission systems" is, therefore, a perfectly false claim enabling these commodities to be aggressively marketed to schools and universities. A "dumbing-down" process is thus prescribed across education systems by educationists who fail to acknowledge the most fundamental non-sequiturs of thought. Marketing slogans are not questioned, but prescribed as given truth by education administrations, who are thereby empowered with new leverages of rule over "the delivery of education." Machines do not talk back or concern themselves with requirements of critical understanding. Once we confuse the means of conveying computer contents with the wholly different process of seeking truth, education it-self becomes indistinguishable from indoctrination.

Here again we see the themal limitation of the global market's "knowledge economy". The primary movement and obligation of all knowledge are to *overcome partiality towards a more comprehensive taking account.* But this requirement of all truth-seeking is in systematic conflict with seeking above all to maximize profits for corporate shareholders. Partiality here rules in its blind form—the partiality of maximizing money acquisition above and beyond money contribution. Whatever claim opposes this ruling bias of objective is ignored, or it is attacked as "socialist." Whatever promotes the goal of monetary self-seeking, in contrast, is selected for affirmation as "value-adding," however it may damage the planet's life-forms or harm innocent people. "Rationality" in this game, as we have seen, means self-maximization, so it is irrational to expect that any market agent would do otherwise.

In this way, the concepts of "rationality" and "knowledge" come to be absurd expressions. What knowledge requires, the "knowledge-based economy" rules out. What wider comprehension and impartiality demand, the "rationality" of profit-maximization blinkers from view. When we examine the assertion of the "new knowledge-based economy" more closely, we come to realize that it selects against whatever does not conform to its demand structures. It is, in this way, more properly designated as "an ignorance-based economy."

Education and the Market Model

As the principles of the global market are applied to public education, contradictions between the two systems of value are ignored. The ideology has become pervasive and unquestioned, carried along like a religious crusade, with educationists and bureaucrats leaping to join the corporate propaganda apparatus, urging students, teachers, and professors to "adapt to the new reality." Computers are more amenable to the bureaucratic mind-set than teachers, and much cheaper to reproduce. The "management perspective" crosses the lines between public and private sector, and "partnership" between the public education process and the corporate sector is thus declared an "inevitable trend." The education system at all levels must, administrators agree, "restructure" itself to fit "the needs of the economy."

This reduction of public education to "the needs of the economy," that is, of profit-maximizing corporations, has not been perceived as a problem even by most teachers. The new order has succeeded so well in its indoctrination that the language of education itself has undergone a sea-shift into business terminology and the mechanistic discourse of corporate culture: "resource units" for what used to be subject disciplines and their professors; educational "consumers" for what used to be students and learners; "uniform standards" for what used to be the search for quality, depth, and originality; "program packages" for what used to be curriculum; "products" for what used to be graduates; "competing in the international economy" for what used to be the search for truth.

Concept structures have been so successfully re-engineered that it is difficult not to conclude that the educational process has been so pervasively subordinated to business aims that its agents can no longer comprehend their vocation in any other terms. Since Plato, educators have traditionally resisted the reduction of education to the demands of appetite and social conditioning. What is lacking today is any clear understanding of the oppositions in principle between the market and education. Without such understanding, we are unable to comprehend, let alone resist, the assimilation of goals and methods of learning to those of commodity production and sale. Members of the academy themselves, lost in the shadows of the corporate media cave, can only see the global marketplace and its demands as the ultimate framework of human freedom and value.[29]

The following table of oppositions shows the underlying contradictions between the guiding principles of the capitalist market and of education, allowing us to see past the slogans of "the knowledge-based economy."

Goals

The overriding goal of corporate agents in the marketplace is to maximize private money-profits.

The overriding goal of educational agents in schools, colleges, and universities is to advance and disseminate shared knowledge.

Motivations

The determining motivation of the market is to satisfy any want at all of anyone who has the money to purchase what is wanted.

The determining motivation of education is to satisfy the desire for knowledge of anyone who seeks it, whether they have the money to pay for it or not.

Methods

The method of the market is to buy or to sell ready-made products at whatever price one can get.

The method of education is never to buy or to sell its good to anyone, but to require of all who would have it that they fulfil its requirements autonomously.

Standards of Excellence

The measures of excellence in the market are:

a. how one-sidedly its own product-line is made to sell;

b. how problem-free the product is and remains for its buyer.

The measures of excellence in education are

a. how inclusively it takes into account others' interests and avoids one-sided biases.

b. how deep and broad the problems it poses are to one who has it.

At the bottom of these contradictions between standards of excellence in the market and in education is an ultimate contradiction between logics of achievement. The one accomplishes development of a person's own capacities for autonomous use. The other achieves the production of external conveniences for others to depend upon. The better the education, the more its bearers become independent to think and do on their own. The better the market, the more its agents depend on the products and services of others to provide their thinking and doing for them.

This fundamental contradiction in standards of development leads, in turn, to opposite ethics of interaction. The best way to treat a buyer, to agree that the customer "is always right," makes teaching a learner impossible. The accepted way in which to gain market favour, to offend no one and no vested interest, is the most certain way to block critical inquiry and the search for truth. The principles of co-operation here are contradictory, increasingly so the more faithfully each is pursued.

These oppositions between the nature of the market and of education mean that the subordination of one to the other is a form of liquidation for the subordinated value system. But, as elsewhere, the market's destruction of what is not itself is seen as "increased efficiency."

One counterargument to the systematic contradiction found between the principles of the market and of education is that formal education has been the training ground for business and labour positions since at least the late nineteenth century. With increasing global competition, the imperative of educating for the marketplace has simply become more demanding. The change here does not consist in a takeover of education by external corporate control, but rather in updated requirements of what has long determined modern formal education, society's economic system.

This argument raises the stakes of our problem. If society's education system is ineluctably determined by economic requirements, and these are the requirements of the global market, it follows that we face the prospect of an inevitable transformation of our educational process into an organ of the corporate market. Since, as we have seen, the logics of the market and of education are opposed, this economic determination of education must then entail the systematic negation of educational goals and standards.

With education thus subserved to a universalized corporate circuit of producing consumer goods for profitable sale, what can remain of mental life outside this circuit? A society's educational process bears, as Matthew Arnold once put it, "the best that humanity has thought and said" to its next generations. Therefore its absorption into the oppositely disposed process of commodity manufacture and sale must leave society in a very real sense without its historically achieved capacity to think. Society becomes a kind of mass creature, a collective system of gratifying present desires for profit and consumption with no movement beyond itself towards understanding and consciousness as a human end in itself.

A counterargument might claim that the contradictions between the principles of education and of the market cannot be wholly true, because corporations increasingly recruit employees who can think autonomously, critically, and dialogically.

However, these educative virtues will only be permitted to the extent that they contribute to the firm's goal of profitable marketing of its products. Such thinking, then, is not truly autonomous, critical, or dialogical. It is, rather, extrinsically motivated, subordinate to non-cognitive demand, and pre-emptive of any alternative not judged to advance the employer's interests. The only self-direction, critical assessment, or alternative viewpoint valued is that which promotes an overriding end, the employer's special interest of commercial advantage. What does not further this end will, by the market's accepted principles of employer-employee relations, be rejected. If it continues, the critically questioning employee will almost certainly be dismissed "in the interests of the firm."

The second part of the counterargument presupposes that independent institutions of education exist from which profit-seeking enterprises can draw their expertise (for example, scientists for scientific texts), and to which they can market their educational products (for example, literary classics to academic courses). But would corporations ever invest in scientifically impartial or cognitively challenging texts without non-market learning institutions to sell them to? We know that corporate control of content and economies of international scale now regulate market production, and that this control rules out what contradicts it and typically produces for the lowest common denominator of human intelligence in order to maximize sales.[30] Given these hard facts of "mass-marketing reality," it is not clear how anything that appeals beyond consumer pleasure or contradicts corporate interests could ever be produced for profit. It is only non-profit educational institutions that provide the effective demand for these goods, thus ensuring the profitability of their production. Without non-profit, public institutions of learning, there is nothing in the market to ensure that these forms of human thought survive.

Therefore, as public education is increasingly stripped of its resources and bent to the demands of the global market, the only remaining institutional ground of human intelligence and reason is undercut. A new form of barbarism enters the gates, one quite as hostile to advanced thought and understanding as any barbarian invasion of the past. As the global market crusade rides through schools and universities cutting and axing, we see that the "marketplace of ideas" that it is the vocation of education to nurture is being destroyed by the market system itself.[31] The corporate market, whilst claiming the contesting of ideas as its justification, is structured to seek out any value or assertion that does not serve it.

Freedom of the Press—For Those Who Own One

Does the "free press" provide the freedom to criticize this system? We have certainly long been told that the "freedom of the press" is the most cherished expression of our great democratic tradition, the open competition of opinions in which the common weal and the truth will eventually prevail. In the venerable ideal of "a marketplace of ideas," the "freedom of the press" is the jewel in the crown. It promises a vital congress of contesting voices and views, a debate of the public good in which all who come to the meeting place of fellow citizens can be heard by and argue with their peers.

It is not clear whether these ideals were ever fulfilled, but certain conditions for a free press were more in evidence in North America in the second half of the nineteenth century. Typically cities had rival, independent newspapers, and corporate advertisers had not yet bought up most of the daily papers' reading space. The views of workers and perspectives critical of business were carried in a non-corporate daily press. This changed forever when the mass press became a vehicle for advertising, without whose growing revenues no publisher could continue to compete. As James Curran and Jean Seaton report in *Power without Responsibility*: "Advertisers ... acquired a de facto licensing authority since, without their support, newspapers ceased to be economically viable."[32] Edward Herman and Noam Chomsky point out in *Manufacturing Consent* that even until the mid-1960s, a social-democratic press flourished in Britain with an average daily readership of 9.3 million, until it was absorbed by larger newspaper chains, or undercut in prices by ever-rising ad revenues financing rival pro-business dailies.[33] In the long term, throughout a century of advancing exclusion of any opposition press, business-owned and business-financed newspapers came to be the only mass-circulation newspapers around. Today, an increasing number of cities in the world are served by only one newspaper, which almost always belongs to a corporate chain and is financed almost entirely by corporate advertisers. The free press has become, in the words of one former major publisher, "first and foremost a vehicle for advertising messages." He said this not in criticism, but in recognition of the nature of the press in the contemporary world.

Television, radio, film, video, and book media are no less concentrated in the hands of profit-maximizing private corporations than newspapers. Sometimes this concentration of ownership spans all the mass media at once. For example, Italy's former and still aspiring prime minister, Silvio Berlusconi, owns three television channels, taking in 45 per cent of the national audience, along with a daily newspaper, weekly magazine, publishing house, advertising firm, and Italy's top soccer club (the sports-entertainment industry is as much a mass medium as the others).[34] Seagram Distillers, owned by the Bronfman family, is more diversified in its market shares. It purchased the Hollywood Studio MCA from Japan's Matsushita Electric in 1995, and is now Time Warner's largest shareholder. Time Warner, which also bought CNN in 1995, is, in turn, the world's largest or next-to-largest entertainment corporation.[35] Time Warner is now rivalled by Disney Corporation, which in 1995 bought Capital

Cities/ABC Television for $19 billion. These global media conglomerates, however, are more specialized than other corporate owners of the "free press," such as General Electric, which is not only one of the world's major producers of electric appliances but has also long been a major Pentagon armaments contractor, specializing in nuclear weapons. Thus its ownership of the NBC Television Network, which includes Cable NBC with 56 million subscribers, has the complementary function of public relations, conferring upon it the power to ensure that the daily content of network television does not criticize its operations. *Deadly Deceptions*, a long-researched documentary about GE's nation-leading environmental violations of pollution laws, was banned from the U.S. airwaves, including the PBS Television Network.[36] CBS Television, the United States' remaining major television network, was purchased in 1995 by another electric appliance corporation, Westinghouse Electric.

Rupert Murdoch's News Corp. Ltd. now controls mass media in forty-six countries, including five national newspapers (such as *The Times* of London, its blue-chip voice), the Fox television network, and various magazines, book publishers, and film studios. Murdoch's media empire directly owns and controls channels of communication to an estimated 700 million people across the world, and in 1995 linked with MCI Communications Corp. for more extended corporate alliance to control the global production and distribution of communications.[37]

Other major controllers of public communications systems are more specialized. Kenneth Thomson, Canada's richest man, has specialized in owning hundreds of daily and weekly newspapers across North America. His junior in the business, Conrad Black, owned 162 dailies and 474 non-dailies across four continents by 1995.[38] In 1996 Black became owner of 58 of Canada's 104 dailies, controlling over half the nation's newspapers. This was deemed by the federal government's supine Competition Bureau "not to be unduly restrictive of competition."[39]

These are all symptoms of a general, globalizing pattern in which the corporate oligopoly occupies human consciousness itself, using the media to reach the roots of unconscious wishes and desires.

"The free press" does not refer to reality, except as the freedom of media owners to condition the conscious and unconscious lives of masses across the globe. However, because of its resonance as a social ideal, "the free press" is still expounded as a sacred value, indeed, as the ultimate expression of the "free market." This, in turn, is conceived as synonymous to "a free society" or to "the Free World." Anyone who ever doubts the freedom of "the free press" risks being condemned as hostile to society's most basic liberties.

We thus face a dilemma. How can we be free if the ultimate expression of our freedom of communication to one another, the media, is owned and controlled across the globe by a few multinational corporations and wealthy men?

Nevertheless, the logic of the corporate market is to extend this monopoly control of public communication still further. As Ted Turner put it, before his CNN network itself was sold to Disney for $8 billion (not long after Disney also bought the public image of the Royal Canadian Mounted Police from the RCMP), "We are going to end up with four or five mega companies that control everything we see *[sic]* on radio and television." Turner added, in the spirit of our time, "I would like to own everything."[40]

This pattern of reducing the world's mass public communications to a one-party monologue has been growing rapidly for years. As the eminent journalist and author of *The Media Monopoly*, Ben Bagdikian, points out, U.S. President Ronald Reagan and major market trusts such as General Electric made a tacit agreement to exchange favours in the early 1980s. Reagan was a former General Electric employee. In exchange for the U.S. government's "help in accelerating the concentration of ownership through changes in anti-trust laws, the mass media owned by these trusts would put on kid gloves in dealing with the Reagan administration, and back away from investigative political stories altogether."[41] Those who wonder how a president who argued that trees caused acid rain and presided over criminal invasions of neighbouring Nicaragua financed by drug-running[42] could be so fondly treated by the media may now understand why.

Although not much of a free press is left when its ownership, control, editorial policy, and pay-master management are in the hands of the chief executives of a few major corporations, any notice of this undeniable pattern is dismissed as a "media conspiracy theory." However, the facts are less easy to discount.

In 1988, when I published the following note in the journal *Informal Logic*, the pattern was already well advanced. But the pattern was no less denied by U.S. referees and respondents to the paper than by employees of the corporate media.

Four new agencies, Reuters, Agence France Presse (AFB), Associated Press (AP) and United Press International (UPI), "provide 90% of the entire foreign news output of the world's newspapers and radio and television stations".[43] The authors also point out that two-thirds of the school text market in North America is controlled by eight multinationals[44] (a control that has escalated since to over 85% of the Canadian college and university textbook market by 1991).[45] Twenty-seven corporations control most of the American mass-media, according to the recently revised edition of Ben Bagdikian's *The Media Monopoly*,[46] a figure that has dropped by almost 50% from the 1983 first edition. "Ten business and financial corporations control the three major television and radio networks (NBC, CBC, ABC), 34 subsidiary television stations, 201 cable T.V. stations, 62 radio stations, 20 record companies, 59 magazines including *Time* and *Newsweek*, 58 newspapers including *The New York Times*, the *Washington Post*, the *Wall Street Journal* and the *Los Angeles Times*, 41 book publishers and Twentieth Century Fox."[47] Parenti also points out that "a 1975 Senate intelligence committee found that the C.I.A. owned outright 'more than 200 wire services, newspapers, magazines and book publishing complexes' and subsidized many more," an ownership to which he proceeds to show 50 further media outlets and over 12 book publishing houses have since been discovered.[48] According to Canada's Royal Commission on Newspapers: "Three chains control nine-tenths of French-language daily newspaper circulation. Three other chains control two-thirds of English-language circulation ... under concentrated [chain] ownership, three-quarters of the total. In seven provinces ... two-thirds or more of provincial circulation is controlled by a single chain."[49]

This overall system of monopoly is made internally consistent by the common interests of its chain-owners and corporate sponsors and by corresponding unstated editorial policy to keep news reports consistent with each other. In the words of Peter Raymont's documentary *The World is Watching*, about the news production process at ABC National News headquarters in New York:[50] "Above all, reporters must match what their rivals file from the field. Any variation makes editors nervous. So although the news business is driven by competition, everyone's story looks and sounds the same."[51]

Why is further management of "the free press" by the central security apparatus of the U.S. government necessary when concentrated corporate ownership seems already sufficient? The Central Intelligence Agency's presence adds a transglobal, military perspective, with all the resources of the world's most powerful state-security apparatus to inform it and to facilitate foreign intervention. This transnational, unseen, and militarily backed assistance from the world's most powerful state makes the control of the press and the stories its mass audiences read, see, or hear more widely secure from hostile criticism. The CIA and U.S. armed forces one-sidedly operate on behalf of private corporate interests and provide the back-up of direct coercion to neutralize worker, community, and other organizations opposing transnational control of local labour and resources.[52]

The question persists: How can we be free if the media are owned, controlled, and content-managed by corporations that demonstrably rule out criticism of the system of power and possession by which they prosper? Are we not approaching the controlled press we deplore in other regimes, which overtly suppress criticism of their ruling order?

We are informed that owners of media conglomerates "do not interfere with the editorial independence of their newspapers." However false, this claim is seldom made of radio or television stations or other non-print media. Is this because it is important to maintain public belief in the freedom of the printed word, as distinguished from other less traditional communications systems that seem less important in communicating facts, opinions, and arguments? The U.S. public's apparent acceptance since the Vietnam War of blanket military censorship of television coverage of U.S. war zones (in Grenada, Panama, and Iraq, for example) seems not to have aroused the same concern as direct censorship of the printed word.

The very movement of public communications into managed images instead of words is a sea-change in the dominant mode of public communications. Critical understanding is ruled out by the nature of the medium itself. The television format of rapid, non-sequential sound-bites and changing "shadows" makes active thought on the part of the audience impossible or unlikely, its censorship unnecessary. This kind of thought-control operates at the level of the brain's neural processes, which, when preconceptual, do not admit of alternatives of meaning. An image medium bypasses critical response by the very nature of its format, and the medium has little need for censorship intervention. It puts the brain into a passive, somnambulist state.[53] The print media is a somewhat different matter. Here monopoly control and payroll management of the medium's content may need to be invoked to ensure that active thinking beyond corporate slogans and formats does not occur. Hence the reassuring ideal of "non-interference with editorial independence" and "leaving journalists free to freely investigate and report the facts" is very widely cultivated, not an easy myth to expose because critics of the media are regarded as "conspiracy theorists."

I was once commissioned to write a feature article on the Olympics for a major magazine, and the editor wanted to cut the word "corporate" or "corporation" from every context in which it might appear critical. The article raised the issue of the Olympics being a publicly subsidized marketing-site for private corporate sponsors and businesses, a subsidy that governments could ill afford when basic social and environmental needs were not being met. The Canadian investigative journalist Linda McQuaig has reported that a Toronto *Globe and Mail* editor objected to her using the term "rich" when she was writing an article for the newspaper on generous exemptions to upper-bracket taxpayers in the Canadian tax system. The term "Irangate" was simply banned from the pages of Britain's *Daily Telegraph* during Ronald Reagan's U.S. presidency.[54] In general, one will never see or hear the words "U.S. violations of international law" for its invasions of smaller countries, or the term "government overspending" for multibillion tax subsidies to major private corporations by national governments. The "free press" is very selective in the words it allows to be freely used.

Most tellingly, global press "barons" openly declare their right to control what their newspapers print. Here is what newspaper-owner Conrad Black's chief executive officer once said on his right to compel the editors of six hundred newspapers to his owner's views on the news:

> If editors disagree with us, they should disagree with us when they're no longer in our employ. The buck stops with the ownership I am responsible for meeting the payroll. Therefore, I will ultimately determine what the papers say, and how they're going to be run.[55]

Black later added to this forthright disclosure: "If the small guy's guardian is the media, then the small guy is in bigger trouble than I thought."[56]

"Freedom of the press" certainly belongs to those who own one. This "freedom" narrows down, as Ted Turner prophesied, to a monopoly of "four or five megacompanies" controlling all we see, hear, and read in the world's major public communications systems.

If a market-critical statement is ever published or broadcast, it is an exception that indicates the rule. It will not be widely reproduced. We regularly hear or read about "the need to compete," "the need to reassure international investors," "the need to adapt to the global market," and the "necessity to reject the forces of protectionism." But nowhere in "the free press" do we find any sustained challenge or doubt expressed about these social dictates, even when they demand a "revolution" in the way all societies of the world must live. All of this is symptomatic of a closed value program regulating the global market's mass media.

The Invisible Curtain of the Media

Propaganda and indoctrination are identifiable by repetition of a one-sided view that is not open to counterevidence or argument, by closure to opposing voices and facts, and by incessant repetition of a received doctrine. With the media as with other capitalist enterprises, private owners and their advertiser patrons have the legal right to select and exclude as they choose, unless there is an external norm of public responsibility to oblige them to be balanced (as with, for example, community radio stations). Media proprietors "pay the bills" of the media's operations, and so they assert their entitlement to choose who will produce and convey their messages, and what these messages will be, a right conferred on them by the "self-regulating" structure of market exchange. Anyone who disagrees with any vendor of a media product, the defence of this free market right asserts, has the choice to transact with someone else for the desired product or to establish their own media vehicle.

All this is plain to the market doctrinaire, and there is no faulting the case from within the confines of the doctrine. The "sanctimonious nonsense," as Conrad Black describes the defence of "editorial and journalist independence from owner and advertiser interference," contradicts the rights of the media's private owners. As private proprietors and employers, they have the right to manage their property and direct their employees as they choose. Media production systems and the services of media employees are no exception.

"Freedom of the press" belongs, by the rules of market itself, only to those who own one. Thus the market's traditional claim of a "free press" is at odds with its ownership structure. But "freedom" and "control" of the mass media admit of degrees, which we need to be able to identify. Members of the Communist Party used to insist that the Soviet press was free and independent because, first, its organs were owned by the people in the public interest; and, second, because they could point to many cases in which members of the ruling Communist Party were exposed and criticized in the mass media.

Despite such reassurances an underlying grammar of censorship is now at work in most media systems in the world. Sometimes such a system of one-sided bias and distortion is quite overt in promulgating a ruling view, as when a committee to protect "public morality" or "religious faith" prohibits the publication of anything that contradicts the received doctrine prescribed by the state's rulers (a situation we find in force not only in all contemporary Islamic societies, but also in more secular societies such as China and Indonesia.) The matter is more subtle when we come to societies in which the censorship of the mass media is not by state intervention or decree, but by the private-property rights of mass media owners, their designated managements, and their advertisers, who together establish a range of what can be said or represented in the media of public communication they control. This is "the invisible curtain" of censorship in developed market societies. To understand it we need to go beyond the particular examples that are exposed by the "alternative" media to look at the *underlying structure* of censorship. We need a general framework of analysis that exposes the invisible curtain across media censorship in all its forms, however it may be manifested in this or that censored story.

The Grammar of Censorship

Basic Social Structural Fact (B.S.S.F.)

Principle I: Large capitalist corporations (as in the global market) or a state party (as in the former Soviet Union) control production and distribution of social goods so as to maximize capital/social command owned by these corporations or state party.

What Can Be Said

Principle II: This B.S.S.F. sets the limits of the range of possibility of what will be produced in the mass media of this society.

What Cannot Be Said

Principle III: Nothing is produced in a society's mass media that contradicts the necessity or value of the B.S.S.F.

Operations of Exclusion from the Range

Principle IV: The degree of exclusion is in proportion to the extent to which B.S.S.F. is overtly contradicted. Operations of exclusion are:

1. ruled out as unspeakable

2. omitted

3. selected out

4. marginalized.

Operations of Selection within the Range

Principle V: Publications normally select for reproduction only what validates B.S.S.F. as necessary/moral and what invalidates opposition to B.S.S.F. as impractical/immoral. Operations of selection are:

1. selection of point of view

2. selection of events/issues

3. selection of descriptive terms.

Principle I defines the social basis upon which a controlled press operates. Canada, the United States, Britain, and Germany are examples of countries in which "large capitalist corporations control production and distribution of social goods so as to maximize capital owned by these corporations." So are all other countries in the global market, from the Philippines to Argentina. This control over the manufacture and distribution of society's goods, however, admits of degrees. The more social goods that private corporations control in the global market and the less this control is externally regulated by any electorally responsible public authority, the more total is the corporate control of social goods. Thus, increasing privatization, deregulation, and commodification of social goods extend this control to increasing degrees.

Principle II follows on the basis of Principle I. It means that the extent of control over a society's production and distribution of goods by capitalist corporations or a state party sets the limits of possibility within which published communication will be produced. If there is more or less total control over society's production and distribution of goods, this control will be reflected in the society's public communications. That is, the bounds of what can be communicated in the print and other media will be correspondingly narrow, ruling out whatever does not reproduce the ruling orthodoxy in all respects. Islamic and Soviet regimes have exhibited this totalitarian control of public thought. Capitalist societies vary in the totality of corporate ownership control of society's production and distribution of social goods, and so also vary in the extent to which the range of public thought is narrowed to a single, pervasive ideology.

Principle III states that nothing in such a society's media will contradict the value or the necessity of this extending system of private corporate control of social goods. To contradict the value of this rule, on one hand, would be to assert that this rule is in some way "exploitative," "against society's interests," "undemocratic," or in some other way bad for the wider community. To contradict this system's necessity, on the other hand, would be to represent its pattern of control as "unnatural," "inefficient," or even "impermanent" as the regulating order of society's life. For example, in a capitalist society, prior to the exclusions of any such out-of-bounds representations, this pattern of corporate control of society's life is ruled out from arising as an issue. Such a pattern of social control is obscured or idealized by representing it, not as a pattern of control, but as what everybody "chooses" to live within, as if by a kind of universal agreement or "social contract."

Principle III, in other words, operates on two levels at once. It not only rules out arguments, evidence, and images from public reproduction that question, criticize, or challenge the Basic Social Structural Fact, but also rules out the exposure of the underlying system itself. This fits well with the grammar of censorship, because what cannot be seen cannot be criticized. For example, any conflicts of interest between those who work and those who invest money for a living are taboo topics in the media, just as it was taboo in the former Soviet Union to hold that the interests of the Communist Party and of the workers were not one and the same.

We can test this principle, as we can also test the other principles here, by observation. If anything in a market society's mass media does contradict the value or necessity of the control of the production and distribution of social goods by private capital owners and corporations, or exposes it to critical consideration, Principle III is disconfirmed. If few or no such disconfirming cases can be found in the round-the-clock operations of all the mass media in market societies, Principle III is strongly confirmed.

Principle IV states that the degree of exclusion of oppositional representations and views in a market (or other) society is proportionate to how clearly such representations or views contradict its pattern of rule or B.S.S.F. For example, in a capitalist society, the claim "the profit-maximizing imperative of market society is a law of greed" is in contradiction with the value system of market society. It represents the market society's ruling principle of social conduct as immoral. Thus, no privately owned medium will publish such an explicit statement unless greed is made to look good and necessary. This finding is predictable based on our selection/exclusion model. Such words are unspeakable in the market mass media. Even a moderate statement, such as "to always want to take out more than you put in, as in money profits, is a morally dubious code to live by," will not be published. The chances of publication of such a statement in the market media are better, because it does not so clearly contradict the value of the market order. But in all likelihood it would be kept out. On the other hand, if a public figure criticizes higher profits at the expense of people's jobs and well-being, the statement may be published to retain the credibility of the media, but the position would be subject to well-publicized attacks as being "nonsense," "out of touch with reality," or "a disservice."[57]

Some positions or facts are not unspeakable in a contemporary market society, but are nevertheless omitted. That global market society is founded on centuries of mass genocide of first peoples around the globe, numbering tens of millions of victims, is, for example, a basic and provocative fact. But it is predictably omitted from any mention in the mass media of any market society. It is not, however, an unspeakable fact. One can know this fact and still accept contemporary market society: "It's all in the past." It is not as contradictory to the market order as a critical phrase such as, say, "parasitic greed" to describe the logic of profit-maximization. If we were to accept the truth of this latter claim, or even to think about it, it would make the market's ruling principle difficult to accept. On the other hand, past genocides of indigenous societies in establishing a market order remain consistent with acceptance of market capitalism today. The fact is speakable, but reference to it is rare or in general omitted.

Many plausible or true claims or facts are neither unspeakable in the market mass media nor omitted, but do emerge in a brief media space before being selected out. Homicidal actions, practices, or criminal violations of law by large corporations, or by state security apparatuses representing their ownership and profit interests, are on occasion acknowledged in the corporate media. But usually such reports are short, isolated, and disclosed after the story has already broken in smaller, non-profit publications (for example, Ford's known exploding gas tank in the Pinto automobile, or U.S.-trained death-squads in Latin America, where "backyard" resources and markets are relied on by U.S. agribusiness and other corporations). These stories may appear in very condensed form—for example, the World Court's $12.2 billion judgment against the U.S. government's criminal violations of international law in its bombing of Nicaragua's main harbour during the Reagan presidency.[58] But such stories quickly disappear, "selected out" because they cast a bad light on market society's leader of the Free World. They must be put "down the memory hole," as George Orwell puts it, if such facts are connected to the interests of transnational corporations with ownership stakes in the societies in question.

Another kind of exclusion is involved in the fourth and final operation of unseen media censorship. Some voices and views clearly conflict with the value system of the market order. Those voices cannot simply be ignored or isolated to a once-only report; they are too long-standing to "write out of the script." Perhaps an established union with a mass membership, an alliance of community organizations or leaders, or a highly respected individual or group of individuals asserts a position or policy that clearly conflicts with the dominant market ideology and practice. One such example would be a widely supported call for public ownership of a vital resource or service, or popular opposition to "free trade." To exclude this position completely from the press and media would disclose a bias too important to have publicly recognized. In these cases, the operation of exclusion is to marginalize the known critical position, to consider it not worth taking seriously, or as socially irresponsible. The voices whose facts or arguments contradict the desirability or necessity of the market prescription are described as "uninformed," "leftist," "divisive," "driven by dogma," "fearful," or in some way unworthy of attention or deserving of indignant rejection. These responses may seem contradictory, but they all serve to place the position at the fringes of society, where it can be rejected and dismissed as beyond the pale of the "moderate middle ground."[59]

All of the above operations of covert censorship of the mass media's products are modalities of silencing. But there are also operations within the range of what is reproduced in the market media that are no less important. On the positive side, they systemically select for approval those events, images, or stories that confirm the market order as a beneficent system: a system that provides golden opportunities for individuals to become rich in business or play, and a system that "liberates" and "democratizes" societies everywhere from the former "communist bloc" to the "miracle economies" of the emerging Third World.

There are three main operations of selecting events and issues that validate the market order as desirable and necessary for all peoples. First of all, the mass media adopt the point of view of market leaders, representatives, and allies, but not their opponents. Thus it is "CEOs," not "union bosses," whose pictures, words, and advice are canvassed, reported, and approvingly represented on a daily basis across the globe. There are "business sections" and "business reports," but not "workers sections" or "workers' reports" in daily newspapers, magazines, and television broadcasts. In all cases of conflict between "free world societies" and opposing societies or cultural formations, it is the point of view of leaders, soldiers, civilians, or representatives of the "free world" that are selected for elaboration. Those that stand against their advance are, in contrast, perceived as external faceless enemies or old-line militants who refuse to adapt. Insofar as the "other side" is reported, its people are generally shown in pathetic or mob-like scenes, and its leaders and governments are described as being involved in cynical "manoeuvres" or "power-grabs." People cannot identify with or comprehend a point of view they do not see. The media's selection of point of view may for this reason be the most importantly biasing operation of all, for it makes one side of a conflict "us" and the other side "them." The other side is external, alien.

Secondly, corporation-controlled media select for representation events and issues that show the market system in a favourable light, and, in contrast, its opponents and critics as the basic cause of the world's problems. For example, the murder, starvation, dispossession, imprisonment, persecution, misery, and class divisions of non-market societies have been invariably covered in a sensationalist way. Similar problems, or worse, in market societies will seldom be thought events or issues worth reporting. We are told, for example, of the 55,000 U.S. soldiers who tragically died at the hands of the communist "V.C." in the Vietnam War, but not that over three million Vietnamese, mostly civilians, were killed within their own country by U.S. soldiers. Over a seventy-year period, we have heard countless times about the "crimes of the Soviet Union" and its "communist dictatorship," and the endless state killings, starvations, persecutions, and exploitations imposed on innocent people—a non-stop stream of invalidating events, stories, and images. But the corporate market media never report the current collapse of market capitalism in the same societies, which has been by every measure far more destructive of people's daily and long-term security and well-being than any Communist Party policy since the Second World War, as a failure of the market system.[60] Is there an exception here? Could a major issue of the second half of the twentieth century be unspeakable? Even in the face of market-reform failures of world-historic proportions, selective validation of the global market order and invalidation of any alternative to it proceed apace. Herein may lie the most fateful flaw of this order's public communication system. It is blocked to the value of any alternative approach to social relations, and similarly blocked to the limits of market relations themselves, a dogmatic block of social consciousness that seriously imperils the capacity of society to resolve its most serious problems.

The final operation of bias in the "grammar of censorship" is the use of selective descriptive terms for the actions, motives, personalities, and practices of social leaders and groups. These descriptive terms validate or invalidate depending on whether the entity they describe is for or against the market system's ruling interests. Government transfers of public revenues to private corporations and capital investors in the form of tax-reductions, write-offs, export subsidies, and allowances, for example, are always "incentives." In contrast, far lower tax expenditures on those out of work or pursuing non-profit research and artistic activities are characterized as "government handouts." Military dictators imposing market "restructural adjustments" or "anti-communist measures" on their societies, sometimes with tens of thousands of deaths, are "firm-handed," "austere," "no-nonsense," or "pragmatic." Social leaderships or groups resisting these reforms, on the other hand, are "doctrinaire," "extremist," "resistant to change," or "leftist." Yet again, rapid profit escalations are celebrated as "breakthroughs," "good news for the economy," "confidence-building," and "spectacular." Wage rises or social security upgrades of a fraction the increase of profits, in contrast, are "cause for concern," "inflationary," "bad for the economy," "non-competitive,"or "alarming."

The market media's vocabulary and images of approval or disapproval are more or less perfectly predictable. If the reported event or gain is for owners of private capital, the predicate selected for description will invariably be positive, upbeat. If the reported event or gain is for anyone else, then the term of attribution will be cautionary and often indignant at the additional "strain on the economy." If the gain is at the expense of private capital, as in a "wage-hike demand" or, worse, a rise in public ownership, the terms of description will range from stern warnings to threats of "economic meltdown."

Notes

1. Hayek, *Road to Serfdom*, p.37.
2. The World Health Organization reports that more than one-fifth of the 5.6 billion people of the world live in extreme poverty and that almost one-third of the world's children are malnourished. "Poverty Is World's Greatest Killer," *The Guardian Weekly*, May 21, 1995, p.1.
3. "Nearly one-third of the world's 2.2 billion workers are unemployed." Ed Finn, "Don't Count on Its Collapse or Its Restraint as long as Corporate Rule Goes Unchallenged," *CCCP Monitor*, November 1996, p.10.
4. Larry Elliott, "Straws in the Wind for Change," *The Guardian Weekly*, citing Ravi Batra, *The Great American Deception* (London: John Wiley and Sons, 1996).
5. In California, where penitentiary guards are paid 25 per cent more than teachers, the so-called three-strikes legislation has resulted in state expenditures on prisons larger than the total bill for postsecondary education. On the national level, the U.S. Justice Department reports that if the current rate of increase of imprisoning people continues, in a decade more Americans will be behind bars than live in New York City, and more than are enrolled in U.S. colleges and universities. "Canadians Appear Far Less Likely to Be Imprisoned," and "Statistics on Violent Crime Need to Be Seen in Perspective," *The Globe and Mail*, March 17, 1995.
6. Melissa McLean, "Neo-liberalism," *Americas Update*, vol. xvi, no. 3 (1995), p.15.
7. See chapter 8, "The Mutations of the Profit System and Their Cure." See also *Social Justice*, vol. 22, no. 4 (1995), pp.1-25.
8. In Canada, for example, by 1995 the real rate of return on capital in the business sector had risen to its highest level in twenty years. Andrew Jackson, "Corporate Profits," *The Globe and Mail*, Dec. 1, 1995, p.A20. At the same time Statistics Canada reported the rise in child poverty at 34 per cent higher than six years earlier. "Rights Violated, UN Advisor Says," *The Globe and Mail*, Nov. 25, 1995, p.A10.
9. When Herbert Marcuse's famous book *One Dimensional Man* (Boston: Beacon Press, 1965) was an international best-seller in 1968, an oft-repeated criticism of his analysis was that its central distinction between "true" and "false needs" was "authoritarian." It was widely argued that Marcuse prescribed to people what they should and should not want. Because Marcuse's book made the distinction (for example, pp.4-12), but did not provide a principle whereby we can impartially judge what is a "true" versus a "false" need, his argument was open to such objection. The testable criterion of need offered in this section meets such counterarguments.
10. As a definition of "economics" in C.P.Pass, B. Lowes, L. Davies, and S.J. Konish, *The Harper-Collins Dictionary for Economics* (New York: 1991), for example, the text reads: "Economics is the study of the problem of using available factors of production as efficiently as possible to attain

maximum fulfilment of society's [sic] *unlimited demand* for goods and services." P.154, emphasis added.

11. Sometimes at a total cost of $1,000 million of advertising in a few weeks, as with the software, "Windows 95," owned by the world's richest man, Bill Gates.

12. Antonio Gerbisias, "Newsfun Inc: Do Not Adjust Your Set," *The Toronto Star*, Aug. 27, 1995, p.C2.

13. "One of the most staggering statistics to be revealed in modern times," writes a noted U.S. trial lawyer who represented the (later murdered) anti-nuclear activist Karen Silkwood, "is that every year the dollar cost of corporate crime in America, as estimated by the Bureau of National Affairs, is over ten times greater than the combined larcenies, robberies, burglaries, and auto thefts committed by individuals." Gerry Spence, *With Justice for None* (New York: Times Books, Random House, 1989), p.198.

14. Roger Cove, "Retailers Back Code For Third World," *The Guardian Weekly*, October 13, 1996, p 19.

15. This issue is examined in chapter 9, "The Economics of Life and Death." Corporations that have demanded an end to such "discrimination" are the U.S. Paper Manufacturers Association (over labelling how forests are cut for their products) and Monsanto Ltd. (over the labelling of milk products as products of bovine growth hormones). See Kevin Watkins, "Goods for Some Are Bads for Others," *The Guardian Weekly*, Dec. 15, 1996.

16. Hayek, *Road to Serfdom*, pp.56, 90, 134-36, 88-100.

17. Jeffrey Ballinger, "Nike's Profits Jump on the Backs of Asian Workers," *Harper's*, August 1992, p.47.

18. Ralph Nader, "Nader's Nineties," *Mother Jones*, July-August 1990, p.25.

19. Alvin and Heidi Toffler, *Creating a New Civilization* (Atlanta: Turner Publishing, 1994).

20. At Guelph, Nov. 30, 1994, p.5.

21. David T. Kearns and Denis P. Doyle, *Winning the Brain Race: A Bold Plan to Make Our Schools Competitive* (San Francisco: FCS Press Institute for Contemporary Studies, 1989), p.42.

22. William Graham, "From the President," *Ontario Confederation of University Faculty Associations Bulletin*, vol. 6, no. 15 (1989), pp.2-3.

23. Andrew Carothers, "Who Runs the Media?," *The New Internationalist*, August 1992, p.16.

24. See, for example, N. Campbell, M. Lawrence, J. Reese, *Biological Concepts and Connections* (San Francisco: Benjamin Publishing Company, 1994).

25. "Cancer Deaths Soar among Women Smokers," *The Globe and Mail*, Sept. 16, 1995, p.D8.

26. Ronald Kramer, "Corporate Criminality," in *Corporations as Criminals*, ed. E. Hochstedler (Beverly Hills, Cal.: Sage Publications, 1984), p.19.

27. "Canadian Clamour for Illegal Cure-All," *The Globe and Mail*, Nov. 18, 1995, p.A13.

28. Dr. Zoltan Rona, "Have You Heard about Bill C-?" *Chrysalis*, Fall 1995, p.5.

29. See, for example, Maude Barlow and Heather-Jane Robertson, *Class Warfare: The Corporate Takeover of Our Schools* (Toronto: Stoddart, 1995). On the university level, in September 1996 a national conference of the Canadian Association of University, business officers distributed the following text as an assertion of corporate management rights over the academy: "CAUT (the Canadian Association of University Teachers) has executed a brilliant campaign over the last two decades or so. CAUT formulated a *strong ideological agenda*, centrally co-ordinated, internally coherent and managed to have this package installed in the collective agreements or faculty agreements of just about all Canadian universities. *Severe curtailments of management rights* were achieved in this fashion—CAUT, in fact, while posing as a mere professional organization, has a truly amazing record as a union, unmatched we think by the likes of the CAW *or the Teamsters*." In "Conference Had No Place For Faculty," *CAUT Bulletin*, November 1996, p.3; emphasis added. As the italicized phrases show, the business officers of the public universities have managed to confuse the protection of academic freedom, which is the essence of the university's mission, with "an ideological agenda," its faculty association body with "Teamsters," and themselves with

corporate-executive "management" presiding over privately owned stock. Such reductionist confusions of mind are now so endemic that higher education itself is assaulted by them from within. These "business officers" do not recognize that they have no such rights under law or practice, nor any competence in the enterprise for which they are ancillary functionaries. Their usurpacious conceits, however, stimulated no reproofs from academic administrators.

30. It might be objected that magazines like *The Atlantic Monthly*, *Harper's*, and *The New Yorker* show that a profit-seeking firm can publish material for an educationally advanced audience and still succeed in the market. However, the editor of one of these magazines, Lewis Lapham, points out that all of these quality publications continuously lose money. See *The Globe and Mail*, March 15, 1996, p.E6. They are, he argues, sustained by the non-market principle of producing thoughtful analysis for the sake of a goal other than profit. It follows, then, that it is only by proceeding against the principle of profit—that is, by continuously losing money for their owners—that these educative magazines survive.

31. The destruction of public education resources via continuous reductions of real funding by "radical market reforms" has now circled the globe. By 1989, 60 per cent of U.S. universities were eliminating academic departments (Leonard Minsky and David Noble, "The Corporate Takeover on Campus," *The Nation*, 1989, p.496), while the British government had, among other major cuts, already eliminated 30 to 40 per cent of all university philosophy positions (Graham, "From the President," p.2). By 1996 in Ontario, per-student real funding had dropped by over 27 per cent before another 15.7 per cent was slashed by the new Conservative Ontario government. As thousands of teachers were dismissed, however, the market-reform government continued to assert that it was implementing its election promise that "the classroom would not be affected by cuts," thereby exemplifying the current doctrine's mastery of self-contradictory statements as true. Meanwhile, the federal Liberal government was cutting all transfer payments for higher education to provinces by 50 per cent, with budgetary plans to reduce them to zero in the near future. In Africa, World Bank and International Monetary Fund "structural reforms" left countries such as Tanzania and Zambia with, according to an Oxfam International study, primary school budgets at one-sixth of their level a decade earlier. Victoria Britain, "Debt Repayments Imperil 21 Million Children,'" *The Guardian Weekly*, March 3, 1996, p.12.

32. James Curran and Jean Seaton, *Power without Responsibility* (London: Methuen and Co., 1985), p.31.

33. Edward S. Herman and Noam Chomsky, *Manufacturing Consent: The Political Economy of the Mass Media* (New York: Pantheon, 1988), pp.14-15.

34. *The Guardian Weekly*, April 29, 1994, p.11.

35. *The Globe and Mail*, Sept. 2, 1995, p.B1.

36. John Turner, "Public Television," *The Ontarion*, Jan. 31-Feb. 6, 1995, p.15.

37. *The Globe and Mail*, Sept. 2, 1995, p.B1.

38. *The Globe and Mail*, Dec. 29, 1995, p.B4.

39. See James Winter, *Democracy's Oxygen: How Corporations Control the News* (Montreal: Black Rose Books, 1996).

40. *The Guardian Weekly*, Sept. 10, 1995, p.15.

41. *Georgia Strait*, April 15-22, 1994, p.7.

42. Alan Moore and Bill Sienkiewicz, *Brought to Light* (Forestville, Cal.: 1989), p.24.

43. Quoted in Rowland Lorimer and Jean McNulty, *Mass Communication in Canada* (Toronto: McClelland and Stewart), 1987, p.232.

44. Ibid., p.108.

45. Statscan 87-210, 1991-92.

46. Ben Bagdikian, *The Media Monopoly* (New York: Beaverbrooks, 1987).

47. Michael Parenti, *Inventing Reality: The Politics of the Mass Media* (New York: St. Martin's Press, 1986), p.27.

48. Ibid., p.233.

49. Minister of Supply and Services Canada, 1981, p.1.

50. Peter Raymont, *The World Is Watching*, Toronto Investigative Productions, 1988.

51. John McMurtry, "Understanding the System of Fallacy in the Mass Media," *Informal Logic*, vol. 10, no. 3 (1988), pp.133-50.

52. See, for example, Thomas Bodenheimer and Robert Gould, *Rollback: Right Wing Power in U.S. Foreign Policy* (Boston: South End Press, 1989), pp.5-7, 25-34, 54-55, 65-79, 84-84, 89-99.

53. Herbert E. Krugman, "Brain-Wave Measures of Media Involvement," *Journal of Advertising Research*, February 1971, pp.3-9.

54. *The Globe and Mail*, Nov. 18, 1995, p.C23.

55. Quoted in James Winter, "Black's Plans," *The Globe and Mail*, March 12, 1994, p.D7.

56. Richard Siklos, *Shades of Black* (Toronto: Reed Books Canada, 1995), p.14.

57. Precisely this pattern of discrediting mass media attack occurred in 1983 when the Canadian Conference of Catholic Bishops published a statement, "Ethical Reflections on the Economic Crisis," which criticized, among other things, "abandoned one-industry towns, depleting unemployment insurance benefits, cut-backs in health and social services and line-ups at local soup kitchens." Despite much more severe occurrences of this sort in Canada since 1983, no such statement has been made by the Conference of Bishops since. The Bishops had, unwittingly, crossed the line of market tolerance by linking these deteriorations in human welfare to "a structural crisis in the international system of capitalism." Such critical comment was attacked from all sides in the mass media as "uninformed," "meddling," and "politicizing the church," including by the bishops' own primate, Emmett Cardinal Carter. Such words were not even to be tolerated in university textbooks, or at least not in Deborah Poff's and Wil Waluchow's *Business Ethics in Canada* (Toronto: Prentice-Hall, 1987), which expunged the statement and other articles in a section entitled "Ethical Challenges to Capitalism" from the second edition of the book.

58. I am grateful to Miguel d'Escoto, former foreign minister of Nicaragua, for pointing out the amount of the International Court's judgment, and how it was arrived at (by UN economic consultants from Oxford University and Harvard University subsequent to the Court's decision against the United States). The U.S. government, however, refused to accept the jurisdiction of the International Court of Justice, preferring instead to declare Nicaragua an "aggressor" and to identify the impoverished army of the tiny nation "a clear and present danger to the security of the United States" (words it also used in 1996 regarding Cuba). The U.S. government repudiated its own signature on a 1946 international treaty accepting the compulsory jurisdiction of the International Court, on the extraordinary grounds that the 1946 declaration must "exclude disputes with any Central American states, or arising out of or relating to events in South America." Julius Lobel, "Memorandum of the National Emergency Civil Liberties Committee on the United States, Nicaragua and the World Court," University of Pittsburgh School of Law, April 13, 1984, cited in Noam Chomsky, *Turning the Tide* (Montreal: Black Rose Books, 1986), pp.90-1.

59. While I was writing this book, *The Globe and Mail* published a letter I wrote concerning Canada's national debt (March 6, 1996). The letter pointed out that 93 per cent of Canada's federal debt was due to compounding high interest rates, a fact reported in February 1995 by the Dominion Bond Rating Service and a matter of concern to many critics of the debt-driven destruction of Canada's social infrastructure. The letter also pointed out that the Bank of Canada was mandated to hold Canada's bonds and receive the interest on behalf of the government and taxpayers, rather than to privatize the high-interest debt to bond dealers at insupportable costs to the Canadian public and its social programs. Within three days, *The Globe* published three letters of reply, denouncing the position I advocated as "frenzied rhetoric," as "peddling a crank notion," as being penned by a writer who puts one "in a mood to rip the wings off flies," and as one more "letter that serves only to obscure the issues" whose publication the "Globe should stop". In this way the operation of marginalization puts the position beyond the pale, as one of the letter writers put it, of "the solid,

commonsense views of more thoughtful Canadians." At the same time, in hallmark exemplification of current market ideology, this operation of marginalization discredits the opposing position by ignoring the evidence it reports and by declining to refer to any counterevidence.

60. Since the "market reform" policies in Russia were introduced, "industrial production has dropped by 50 percent, investment has dropped to one-third its previous level, and living standards have fallen by 28 percent." In Larry Elliott, "Russian Woe," *The Guardian Weekly*, Feb. 25, 1996, p.19. But, boasts market reformer and Russian Prime Minister Viktor Chernomyrdin, "We were one of the few countries to meet a whole series of International Monetary Fund requirements." Francoise Lazare and Sophie Shihab, "No One Can Calculate the Cost of Change," *The Guardian Weekly*, March 10, 1996, p.19. The relationship between catastrophic economic decline and compliance with free market prescriptions is not noted in the article or elsewhere.

The Market
Metaphysic:
Rallying Cries and
True Meanings

Getting the State off Our Backs

One of the strongest moral appeals to true believers in the global market is that its individual liberties and open competition ensure "freedom from government interference." But is the market, even in its most laissez-faire modes, in truth "self-regulating" or "free from state interference"? The "free market," in practice, requires expensive government intervention to provide continuous protection and services for its operations. These permanent and increasingly costly government assistances include extensive police forces and legal systems guarding capital assets and exchanges; armed forces to protect private investments abroad (in the U.S. case the cost of those forces exceeds all other federal government expenditures); and state diplomatic offices and personnel to promote private business interests abroad. The corporate market also requires continuous government financing and construction of truck corridors to transport private business goods to production and exchange sites, as well as cost-free training and subsidized natural resource infrastructures to supply business with the human and resource capital required to produce commodities.

Using public resources, governments provide these massive financings, protections, services, and goods free of user charges to capital investors and business. For these reasons the idea of the "self-regulating market" being "free of government intervention" is one of the more preposterous myths of the doctrine.

Free market proponents seldom criticize state expenditures that directly benefit business—for example, more police, prisons, armies, highways, free employee training, and giveaways of increasingly valuable natural resources owned by the public. Free marketeers only criticize government interventions that they consider do not directly benefit business operations and profitability, such as social security or workplace and environmental regulations.

At the same time as publicly paid-for government services to business are not challenged so long as they benefit the private-profit sector, government tax loopholes, deferments, and subsidies to business and the wealthy are increasingly demanded and received, even though they contribute to the very government deficits that business attacks.[1]

Government's collective functions have been won over many decades of social struggle against continuous criticism from market advocates to the effect that these functions are "wasteful," "unaffordable," or "interferences in the free market." For example, elected governments throughout the world have passed legislation to limit the hours of the working day and week; to establish safety standards and environmental regulations for factories and businesses; to permit employees to organize in workers' unions; to provide unemployment insurance and income security for those without jobs; to institute programs of health care available to all independent of their ability to pay; to provide universal public education and subsidized university education; and to construct publicly accessible transit systems, parks, and cultural centres free of cost or at below-cost prices.

None of these social goods can be provided by the market free from "government intervention." Every one of them has required "government interference in the free market." These "government interferences" have been achieved through public democratic process, not through private business. None are privately owned or run for profit. All require not only government intervention, but also government enforcement and taxation, and all have been, at one time or another, militantly opposed by business, often violently (for example, the killing of labour and community organizers, which goes on in many market societies today). Freedom from government interference in the free market, therefore, entails loss of all these public goods. The call to "get the state off our backs" is, we might say, a code for dispossessing the public of most of what we know as civilization.

We should ask who benefits from the campaigns to "reduce government regulations," "privatize" public-sector goods, and "cut social programs"? Market ideologues argue that taxpayers can no longer pay for these "excessive and costly programs" and "unnecessary regulations on business." Yet if the free market is really so "efficient," why is it that most of society becomes increasingly insecure and unprotected the "freer" the market becomes?

The global marketeer is apt to change the subject at this point, turning to a discussion of how superior the market system is to "socialism" or "communism." Freedom has come to mean the negation of any alternative to the market system. This justification is a diversion that changes the topic from analysis of "government interference in the market" to the issue of an alien economic order that is conventionally repudiated as wicked. This stock-in-trade move in market ideology succeeds in deterring critics by putting them on the side of a traditional social enemy. Those who continue to support "government interference in the market" for social programs, or regulations on business pollution and hazardous working conditions, are associated with the social enemy, a red-herring tactic that I analyse elsewhere as "the *ad adversarium* fallacy."[2] In this case it merely changes the issue from government's role in the economy to ritual denunciation of an accepted "Great Satan," to borrow Noam Chomsky's apt phrase.

As in any fundamentalist doctrine, market theology bifurcates the world into two great opposing camps: a Manichaean world of the Good and the Free versus the Bad and the Communist (or Socialist). Advocates of more public-sector ownership or regulation of market forces, even those who merely recommend "a mixed economy," are, to use Milton Friedman's words, "subverters of a free society" who, it is hinted, are secretly communists and thus enemies of those who love liberty.

In market societies, to be a "socialist" is conventionally perceived to be *wrong in principle*. Socialism, it is assumed, backs the state against "personal freedom." But to be a "Marxist" or a "Communist" is abhorrent by definition, for to be either is to seek to destroy the market and therefore to be pledged to the destruction of freedom itself, a conclusion that does not follow but is also built into this value program. Anyone identified with the proscribed view is therefore perceived as a supporter of "tyranny" and "dictatorship," which are believed to follow naturally from such a position.

The metaphysic at work here begins from the assumption that the individual is free in the market, which, as Smith put it, is "the natural course of things," whereas government interferes with this "natural freedom" to the extent that it regulates or provides alternatives to the market. If not curtailed by market forces, this doctrine holds, government inexorably becomes dictatorial and the owner of the individual's own personal being. In this dualistic view, the market is freedom and the state, which interferes with the market, is the opposite of freedom, so the end result of government regulating or displacing market operations is inevitably slavery to the state. The logic may be bizarre—for how can universal access to public health care, old-age pensions, or higher education be "slavery"?—but it has become ingrained as a social mind-set, especially among economists. "Libertarians" are the pure-type expressers of this metaphysical program, but it is an increasingly hardening dogma from Adam Smith through Friedrich Hayek to contemporary market ideology.

In market societies, therefore, those who are perceived to recommend "government control" of anything are stigmatized as potential enemies of freedom, in particular of money property. Reputations and life-prospects can be destroyed for holding such heresies. Often, as in the McCarthyite phenomenon of the 1950s, but also by normal processes of state-security operations, the advocate of "government interference" becomes identified as an enemy of free society itself.

The conditions of armed force intimidation and imprisonment do not bother free marketeers' sensitivity to state powers, as long as these means are used to "protect private property" or "national interests abroad." Heavy-handed interventions of the state are not questioned, but accepted as necessary protective walls for the market, whose primacy is presupposed as ultimate and inviolable. The interventions are not "state interferences" at all. The metaphysic of what is necessary and good here reaches into what is *real*. The state does not interfere here, because it is only protecting what is natural and necessary. Even the shedding of thousands' blood in such state functions is not really interference, because it maintains what is and must be as a matter of the "real world's" necessity. For market theory and practice, the slippery slope of the true enemy of freedom only begins with government intervention against these necessary operations of the free market, such as new regulations or taxes on corporations or investors that reduce profit maximization. Here begins the Gulag. For this all-or-nothing market view, "socialism" or "communism" begins its subversion with "socialized medicine" or an "environmentalist Gestapo" regulating business. The underlying assumption of this line of thought is that a society is only democratic to the extent that its state protects private property and the market's self-regulating mechanisms. Yet this assumption that democracy depends on and flows from the market is false. For it ignores a basic requirement of a right: that an individual who exercises this right must have the means to do so. But if I do not own any money in the global market where all access to its goods has the condition of a price I cannot pay, how can I exercise my rights to freedom in it? If many people lack the means to exercise their freedom, this freedom becomes a slogan of empty ideology. "Freedoms" and "rights" cease to exist in a society to the extent that their enjoyments are inaccessible to its citizens.

The financing of U.S. elections provides an example of the market's relationship to the state and of the possibility that the more the market regulates society's life-organization, the less democratic the state becomes. In 99 per cent of all U.S. election campaigns, the candidate who spends the most money wins.[3] As with other unregulated freedoms asserted by advocates of the free market, the freedom of democratic elections can turn out to be antidemocratic. Less than 10 per cent of the U.S. population makes political donations at all. Over one-third of all political-support donations come from a mere 1 per cent of the eligible electorate. The Republican Party, as it promised the "end of the welfare state," "lower taxes" for the wealthy and corporations, and the "bringing to heel" of the U.S. Environmental Protection Agency, received donations at the rate of $123,121 per day in the first two months of 1995.[4] The ruling project of this market-led politics was "getting the government off our backs."

A small minority of citizens can thus dominate the means of election and the politicians elected. The successful politicians are in turn sold as commodities in the market by the conditioning devices of mass media commercial campaigns. As the current quip goes, "It's the best Congress that money can buy." The "revolutionary" movement of the U.S. Republican Party and its recent imitators in Canada and elsewhere "to get the state off our backs" has had, thus far, a very special meaning. It has meant putting those who represent the rich into office and then redistributing wealth from the public sector and the less affluent to them. The only people who have been relieved from the burden of paying taxes are those in the top income brackets.[5]

In light of this tendency, ever more "deregulation," "privatization," and "public-sector cutbacks" to "get the state off our backs" cannot truthfully be called a move towards "more freedom and democracy." The more that public goods and regulations accountable to electorates and open to public criticism are transferred to "the private sector," the more democratic accountability is abolished, and the more control is transferred to those accountable to no one but private investors. According to U.S. Congressional statistics, the top 1 per cent of the U.S. population controls more private wealth than the bottom 90 per cent, and the gap is widening.[6] This transfer of responsibility to the private sector is essentially a transfer of power to a tiny minority that already holds the most power: the wealthiest 1 per cent of the population. In such conditions, the movement to "get the state off our backs" reduces people's democratic rights and freedoms the more it takes over resources and regulation from an electorally accountable public sector and transfers them to the rule of the private sector.

"Getting the state off our backs" can be spurred by privatization of "inefficient government sectors" and may seem a clear and plausible way to lower taxes and improve services. But this market article of creed is contradicted, for example, by the cost of the U.S. private health-care system, which is $1,000 per capita more expensive than the Canadian government-funded system. The U.S. health-care system fails to provide any health care to 48 million Americans, grossly underinsures another 30 million, and costs over twice as much in administrative bureaucracy.[7]

The private, for-profit health insurance industry is one of the world's fastest-growing businesses, displacing more efficient public health-care systems. Yet because it is an article of creed that "the market is far more efficient than government," evidence to the contrary cannot compute in the market value program. Such evidence is not reported in the corporate media, and so the public does not have access to the facts. To acknowledge the reality that government can run a skill-intensive system with greater efficiency than private enterprise is not possible in this metaphysic. The paradigm we are dealing with here is as impervious to counterevidence as past theologies, and just as habituated to denial in the face of facts that contradict it.

"Getting the state off our backs" has a coded meaning. It does not mean more freedom for citizens, more freedom of speech, or more accountable government. Tracking its consequences reveals that its inner program is to redistribute wealth and effective rights from the public sector and the less well-off to the market and its dominant corporate and investment players. This pattern of redistribution is deducible from the reiterated operation of this system's principles and becomes increasingly more biased the less hedged in it is by the powers of the common interest that only public authority can bring to bear.

Such a pattern of increasingly unaccountable, special-interest rule and social restructuring requires a rationale to provide citizens with a sense of empowerment as they are being disempowered. Many emancipatory exhortations are ceaselessly reaffirmed to assist in the required reprogramming of public consciousness: "freedom from state interference," "lower tax burdens," "more incentives to create jobs," "cutting government bureaucracy," "encouraging independence and initiative," "greater market efficiency," "less red-tape and regulations," "reducing government waste," "becoming free from big brother,"and, above all in recent years, "cutting government deficits." Behind these slogans, more political power, social protection, and after-tax income are redistributed to the market and its dominant special-interest groups; and less real income, public voice, social security, health, and educational opportunity remain for everyone else.

We can directly observe this pattern in action. "Big brother government" and "intrusive government" are militantly criticized by market ideology. But market advocates do not demand "slashing" of government spending for the state's instruments of violence and terror used to protect market property from movements of local populations to regain control over the resources involved. Lavish expenditures on protecting corporate investments abroad, typically far in excess of the costs of any social program, are, therefore, not cut back as "unaffordable expenditures." These publicly financed protections of foreign off-shore investments may directly deprive the home society of jobs and domestically earned capital, but it is assumed to be in the "national interest" for governments to protect them. Spending on the security of citizens at home, in contrast, is "spending beyond our means."

Thus, taxes to pay for these lavish expenditures on protecting private interests in other countries fall mainly on those who have no investment interests abroad, while those who own these investments are granted ever lower taxes so that they have "an incentive to invest" (even in competing economies). Thus export subsidies, tax abatements, capital gains reductions, tax preferences, grants, and emergency bank and corporate debt payments are granted more or less exclusively to those corporations and investors whose investments are protected by the public treasury. Market critics do not target these obvious "big government" intrusions into private-sector "global" enterprises as government waste or "government on the people's backs," even as they claim that the government's inability to pay its debts is a "crisis" and an "emergency." The more we look at the actual expenditure patterns, the more the rallying cries of emancipation from the state indicate government at public expense for dominant corporate and private investors, and less government for society as a whole by way of social security, health, learning, the environment, and non-commercial life and culture. Thus, the meaning of "getting the government off our backs" becomes more explicit.

To comprehend the full sense of this market slogan we can deconstruct its more specific expression, *"freedom from government regulations."* Laws, inspectors, police, bureaucracies, records, forms, limits, employee rights, and no end of red-tape and obstacles have, we are told, burdened business with "mountains of regulations." This phrase strikes a chord with citizens who have to put up with everyday bureaucratic rituals and offices. But on closer examination we find that it is *life-protective* regulations that the free marketeers seek to eliminate. "Environmental fanatics," "tree-huggers," "union bureaucrats," "complaining workers," and "do-gooders," they say, "have climbed all over the companies and entrepreneurs who are creating wealth and jobs." Government interference in the market economy has "reached crisis proportions," and "It is time to call a halt to the red-tape and meddling that is choking the engine of market prosperity." Behind all these market battle cries an unseen pattern builds. "Deregulation" has come to mean an attack on the rule of law itself, in particular laws preserving human and environmental life.

In recent decades government regulations have developed in two central areas: occupational health and safety and the environment. As far back as 1984, more than 100,000 annual deaths in the United States were "attributed to occupationally related diseases," and the majority of them were "caused by knowing and wilful violation of occupational health and safety laws by corporations."[8] At the same time, "at least one in five of America's 500 largest corporations has been convicted of at least one major crime."[9] An estimated

240,000 people will die over thirty years from work exposure to a single industrial substance, asbestos. Although corporations were fully aware of the research findings, they neither disclosed nor acted upon this evidence. U.S. trial lawyer Gerry Spence, who has acted for victims of such corporate crimes, observes, "It is still not a crime to knowingly market an unsafe product or to conceal a hazard in the workplace."[10] In this context of corporate criminality, which results in the real world in the painful deaths of hundreds of thousands of workers, government health and occupational research safety regulations and inspections are attacked as "a nuisance," a "bureaucratic nightmare," and "claws in the backs of business". Consequently, they have been increasingly dismantled across North America, as "costly regulations" that have to be eliminated "to reduce government deficits."

In Ontario, one decision of the newly elected Conservative government in September 1995 removed one-third of the Ministry of Labour's safety inspectors, over half of its physicians, half of its hygienists, all of its air-quality technicians, all of its nurses, all of its ergonomists, half of its engineers, and over half of its health and occupational research laboratories. This "pro-market government" was elected with 22 per cent of eligible voter support.[11] This new government of the "Common Sense Revolution" also passed laws to prohibit farm workers from joining unions, to cut truck-safety examinations, and to abolish the right of workers to refuse unsafe work.[12]

A few months earlier the Republican Congressional Whip had dramatically attacked the U.S. Environmental Protection Agency as "the Gestapo" and "one of the major clawholds that the government has maintained on the backs of our constituents." These remarks came after a coalition of 115 corporate and industrial lobby groups called "Project Relief" had contributed a gift of $10.3 million to Republican congressional campaigns.[13] "Project Relief" was dedicated to the goal of "getting government off our backs," and the new Republican-controlled Congress quickly proceeded to institute legislation to abolish the EPA. Congressional committees charged with drafting the laws invited lawyers from major petrochemical, power, and hydro corporations to chair the meetings, excluding all the EPA's own environmental experts. The corporation-chaired committees then placed a moratorium on all new federal environmental regulations, barring the courts from enforcing new requirements on auto exhausts and prohibiting the EPA from setting water-quality guidelines in the Great Lakes, limiting raw sewage dumped into rivers, and protecting wetlands. In addition, regulations requiring chemical corporations to have contingency plans in the event of an accident were prohibited. The requirements of the Clean Water Act, the Endangered Species Act, and the Safe Drinking Water Act were revoked or put into moratorium. The Arctic National Wildlife Refuge was opened to offshore oil drilling, companies were exempted from responsibility to clean up hazardous waste dumps, and emission standards for oil refineries and pesticide controls were banned. Controls on mining, oil-drilling, and timber-cutting were dismantled.[14] Legislation regulating 170 million acres of public land focused entirely on management for private livestock production.[15] The EPA's budget was cut by 30 per cent, and new procedural requirements were initiated to forbid any environmental legislation whose costs to corporations is not first established and compared to the money benefits of the law's enforcement, a prescription described by environmental experts as "next to impossible to fulfill."[16]

In these ways government is made "to get off the people's backs." The protection of citizens' lives and the preservation of their life environment are simply ruled out of view. The function of government is to assist corporations and their stockholders to maximize profit. This is the freedom from government interference to which the self-regulating market logically leads. Followed through to its unseen implications, it means abolishing the right of government agencies to protect the lives of citizens and natural environments against destruction in competitive, global market conditions. This is not a consequence that registers on the doctrine.

Where the state could truthfully be said to "climb all over the backs of the people," market ideologues aggressively call for more. Debt-driving armament build-ups, prisons for the poor, military invasions and threats against smaller countries, and tax systems and state subsidies benefiting the rich are justified as "making the country great," "encouraging investment," "creating jobs," "punishing lawbreakers," and "promoting leading-edge technology." On the other hand, government assistance to the poor, public health, and enforced regulations against life-destroying work conditions and toxic effluents (social needs that can only be provided by a non-profit public sector) are attacked without pause. There is a deeper, pathological pattern than ideological incoherence at work here, and it threatens the life-organization of society itself.

Removing Barriers to Trade

The international regime of competitive production and distribution of commodities across boundaries has a long history. The global market began its modern phase with the European wool trade. Britain became the world leader in that trade, and subsequently all trade, by "enclosing" village commons across the isle and expropriating small farmers from their land to make room for large-scale sheep farms. This clearing of the land of people to make way for "more efficient production" is perhaps the international market's most enduring tradition, and it continues today across sub-Saharan Africa, Brazil, Northern Canada, China, the Indonesia archipelago—indeed, most places in which subsistence agriculture or hunting still exists. Britain's leading-edge process of privatizing people's shared land continued for almost three hundred years, from the fifteenth to the eighteenth century. Countless small farmers were expelled from their lands and livelihoods, and communities by the thousands were dispossessed of their commons to make way for livestock grazing and natural resource access.

This large-scale expulsion of the people from their land was serendipitous for the "competitive international market" because it not only gave over the land for world-class sheep flocks instead of villages and people, but it also provided the source of propertyless labour for masters to employ for wages. Workshops and eventually factories flourished, with bountiful supplies of "free labour" after the penalties of mutilation and capital punishment for unemployment had discouraged alternatives such as "vagabondry."[17]

This progress in the advancement of market restructuring brought Britain to the forefront of the great modern adventure of international trade. The next great historic leap forward in the long epic of the global market came with the "discovery" of America, then occupied by an estimated 20 to 50 million indigenous people. This continental treasure-house soon provided vast new natural resources and markets based on which transnational trade could flourish at even higher levels of productivity and transboundary exchange. Some tens of millions of indigenous people were killed or forcibly removed from their ancestral lands to make room for the new freedom of the global market. The extinctions of peoples were not reckoned as costs or violations of their rights, because then (as well as now) only market rights were recognized as legitimate in practice. In the matter of expropriating the resources of the original peoples, the first communisms were fair game as an "inferior" order of being. The same arguably holds true today—for example, in the oil-rich territories of Canada's Lubicon Indians, Guatemala's highland Mayans, and the island of East Timor.[18]

More dramatically perhaps, before Somalia disintegrated in civil war, the indigenous people's traditional agricultural lands there were taken over for agribusiness, turned to monoculture cash-crops for export, exhausted by single-crop and chemical farming, and, as across Africa, set into a cycle of desertification.[19]

If people within the world's leading trade nations and millions more outside it were and still are dispossessed against their wills and their interests by "development" and "free trade," how can these concepts still coherently represent such continuous mass compulsion and deprivation as "freedom"? Is this "removal of barriers for trade across borders" really the removal of people from their lands and resources to be replaced by corporate systems of commodity production for consumers with money-demand? Is it in the end dictated expropriation that is preceded and protected by armed force and followed by destitution and destruction of the home peoples on whom it is imposed?

Britain's imposition of the international opium trade on China by used of armed forces and gunboats of Britain is an example of the protection of "the free circulation of goods and capital," which continued for over a century down to 1917. Britain's armed occupation of India provided, among other resources, the production base for this lucrative transnational trade. When we examine history, we find that what has for centuries been called "prosperous international trade" or "free trade" has been, in truth, anything but prosperous or free for the peoples upon whom it has been forced. The great cotton and market system exports of England during the nineteenth century, for example, brought "consumers cheaper goods," but in India village people and local cotton weavers died by the tens of millions through starvation, caused by loss of livelihood brought on by the opening up of their country's borders to floods of mass-produced imports from Britain, and by cutting off the thumbs of the master-weavers.[20] Like the Chinese who bought opium, Indians were free to buy food and cotton goods in individually voluntary transactions, but this did not save them from mass starvation if they had no jobs or money to pay for these goods. The peoples of India, like most of us, were not permitted a choice as to whether or not this movement to a borderless corporate market would be decided for them as "free trade."

The rubber trade between 1890 and 1910 in the French and Belgian Congos is a less well-known case of dynamically value-adding global trade, but may have been more life-destructive even than opium. In 1890 the population of the Belgian Congo was estimated at between 20 and 40 million. In 1911 the official census showed eight and a half million.[21] That is, between 40 and 80 per cent of the population disappeared within twenty-one years of the Congo becoming "open for business" to the rubber trade. In the whole of the Congo, as many as 50 million people were uprooted and finally destroyed in the efforts to produce rubber. In the market value system, international trade is by definition good if it introduces new commodities and lowers prices for consumers in the competitive production of goods that buyers choose to buy, and that is an end to it. The millions of people killed by it are not computed, any more than the trader Kurtz in Conrad's *Heart of Darkness* counted bodies in the Belgian Congo. Kurtz eventually saw "the horror," but not by application of market values.

One might argue that today's advanced international trading system "lowers barriers to the free circulation of goods and capital" and is different from years past, as it is agreed to by elected governments in postcolonial conditions. But we should consider the recently instituted North American Free Trade Agreement (NAFTA) as a principal example. Its basic rationale is that nations should not erect tariff or other barriers to the free flow of goods across borders when these goods can be produced more cost-effectively by others. This is the rationale of "the logic of comparative advantage," but even today the doctrine still does not rule out lethal goods or substances in cross-border trade, does not discriminate against goods produced by murderous or massively life-destructive processes, and possesses no principle whereby systematic obliteration or violation of life can be recognized as wrong.

There are still no life-protective standards in international trade agreements to this day, including the newly minted Multilateral Agreement on Investment (MAI). Since no rights of life are protected, anything goes as long as it can find buyers and sellers. Labour can be without any human-rights protections or be paid starvation wages. Safety conditions may not exist or be unenforced. Environments may be systematically plundered without regulatory restraint. Millions may be disemployed by the new corporate multinational regime. Countless people may become destitute or die from the free trade system that uproots their traditional ways of life. All of these consequences have already occurred. The thick treaties have no articles prohibiting or monitoring any of these systematic attacks on life.[22]

The Mayan Indians of the south of Mexico in the Chiapas region, like many others, were alarmed by the prospects of the "lower barriers to trade" as they unfolded in the 1992 North American Free Trade Agreement. They were especially alarmed because the agreement had been preceded by the Mexican government's preparatory abolition of their constitutional communal land rights. This was done by the Mexican government, in line with established international trading practice, so that the people would not be a barrier to large-scale corporate agribusiness using the land "more efficiently" with the "competitive cost advantage" of machine-tilled and people-free lands. Corn and beans, which the Mayans grew for themselves as well as for local sale, could not be produced and marketed at the price at which huge and industrialized U.S. farms could sell them, so they would be undersold by foreign competition. In other words, the Mayans were, as countless peoples around the world before them, to be forced off their ancestral lands and deprived of traditional markets so that "free trade" for transnational business interests could be implemented. As usual, the justification was that all would have lower priced goods, albeit many without the money to pay for them or any longer the means to produce for themselves. This is the value logic of "global market development."

Such "necessary sacrifices," however, applied not only to Mexico's indigenous people, but also to farmers across Canada, as established tariff and marketing board systems of secure prices and sales were to be progressively dismantled by NAFTA. The problem also applied to the estimated 500,000 manufacturing workers who, according to the Canadian Labour Congress, lost their jobs within three years of the original U.S.-Canada free trade agreement, because goods could be produced elsewhere at lower wages (for example, at sixty-three cents an hour paid out by U.S. corporations operating in Mexico) and in lower-cost conditions of production (for example, with lower corporate taxes and few or no safety or pollution regulations protecting workers or the environment). The problem was also applicable to Mexican workers. Their life-wages eventually collapsed by 60 per cent, and unemployment rates sky-rocketed as transnationally mobile capital left the Mexican economy in massive splurges of speculative currency ventures, quick-profit investments, and capital flights.[23]

The Mayans of Chiapas who anticipated the destruction of their lives by this system of "lower barriers to trade" declared their concern on the inception of NAFTA on January 1, 1994. They called it "The Death Sentence of NAFTA." An indigenous movement called the Zapatistas, after Mexico's revolutionary leader, Emiliano Zapata, took up arms against the trade regime's imposition. Disturbed by the "lack of confidence" for international bankers and investors that the rebellion in Chiapas was fomenting, the Rockefeller-owned Chase Manhattan Bank published an analysis of the Mexican crisis. It sought immediate compliance with the new market order and the elimination of the resisters. "While Chiapas, in our opinion, does not pose a fundamental threat to Mexican political stability," the Bank intoned, "it is perceived to be so by many in the investment community. The government will need to eliminate the Zapatistas."[24]

The essential "barrier to trade" here is human beings. They will not accept its necessity, are willing to resist it with their own bodies, and so they must be removed. The Mexican people were not given an opportunity to accept or reject NAFTA. The election over the issue was fraudulently "won" by the long-ruling Institutional Revolutionary Party (PRI). The United States and Canada also elected governments that instituted NAFTA. We might think, in line with market understanding, that the "free trade agreement" was agreed to by the peoples of the affected societies, but the story is more complex than that.

In the Canadian federal election of 1988, fought largely on the issue, a majority of the electorate voted against the party that went on to sign the original U.S.-Canada Free Trade Agreement (FTA). This election was won by Brian Mulroney's Progressive Conservative Party with 43 per cent of the vote; 57 per cent of the electorate voted against Mulroney, and 53 per cent voted for parties whose explicit policy was to oppose the FTA. This is worth bearing in mind, because the figures have rarely been mentioned. Mulroney's minority victory was preceded by a sustained and unprecedented blitz by corporate media-chains promoting the deal on the promise of "Jobs! Jobs! Jobs!" At the same time, the opposing Liberal and New Democratic parties were attacked on a daily basis. In the words of Canada's chief negotiator, they were "traitors" or, more moderately, "timid protectionists." To oppose the agreement was a "betrayal of the national interest." The Liberals' unlikely business-leader opponent, John Turner, long a favourite of the commercial media, was now reviled. Toronto's *Globe and Mail*, Canada's national newspaper, published a front-page photo of Turner with horns out of his head in silhouette behind him. A similarly prominent photograph of NDP leader Ed Broadbent showed him looking like a gargoyle with a dead fish in his hand. Mulroney was repeatedly portrayed as a strong-jawed idealist, once on a cover-page of the *Globe*'s *Report on Business Magazine* with a halo of light over his head. Nevertheless, 53.6 per cent of the population voted for parties opposed to the trade agreement, but the vote was split between the parties. By the time the later NAFTA agreement was signed, an astonishing 91 per cent of the Canadian population disapproved of Brian Mulroney, the lowest public support for a Canadian prime minister ever recorded. But once such barriers to the transnational trade regime were overcome, they dissolved into the memory hole as non-existent. Barriers to trade that are merely the people's will or common interest only compute to the doctrine as obstructions. Since the removal of barriers to trade is by definition good for consumers, democratic opposition to it by even the majority is necessarily misguided.

All the terms of the original FTA and its successor, NAFTA, were for this reason negotiated behind closed doors. There was no participation by Parliament in the historic rewriting of Canadian law. There was not, indeed, any scrutiny or debate until after the over 2,400-article deal had been negotiated by appointed government representatives from the corporate sector. The chief U.S. trade representative, Clayton Yeulter, stated after the Canada-U.S. trade agreement was signed: "The Canadians don't know what they've signed."[25] Head of state Mulroney, who had promised in 1983 that "Free Trade affects Canadian sovereignty and we will have none of it," was euphoric about the deal, promising again after it was signed that it would not be extended to Mexico. In the next election, an aroused population reduced the Conservative government, a party that had been either the government or the official opposition since Confederation, but that had signed the two deals, to a rump of two seats in Parliament. Liberal leader Jean Chrétien's successful campaign against the Conservatives featured denunciations of "bad Tory trade deals" and promised, "If we can't renegotiate, you know we'll abrogate." Still, the deals remained law after he became prime minister. "Side agreement" additions changed no requirement of FTA or its successor, NAFTA, and were not enforceable. Even if an election had been won by promising refusal, it was, we might say, a deal that could not be refused.

The majority opposition of the Canadian people, the most one-sided defeat in Canadian history of the party that had signed the transnational trade deals, and the public promises of successive prime ministers to reject them made no difference to the program. The new trade regime was to be law for the country whether the people supported it or not. Nor was there any recourse to the country's established law-making capacities to qualify the no-amendment agreement. The relevant articles of the new trade regime law were, by the agreement, to override all past, present, or future laws passed by any elected legislature or government—municipal, provincial, or national, in all matters on which the executive treaty prescribed. Here big government could be as intrusive, dictatorial, and secretively bureaucratic as it chose, so long as it was signing and protecting an agreement whose terms were entirely devoted to overriding law to protect transnational corporate access to foreign societies' markets and resources. In such ways are the "barriers to trade" overcome.

Among the prescriptions of the new transnational trade regime was the prohibition of any government policy at any level requiring foreign corporations operating in Canada to contribute to the employment of Canadians or to purchase any Canadian product. The now-standard prescriptions also included prohibition of any government right:

1. to reduce or to regulate foreign ownership of the economy;

2. to preserve non-renewable natural resources for Canadian use;

3. to buy Canadian products in preference to foreign ones; and

4. to in any way differentiate between Canadian and U.S. business interests in Canada.[26]

The democratically opposed transnational trade law rewrote the law of Canada. The sovereign legislative powers of the country could no longer lawfully regulate in the interests of the people if this constituted any "barrier to trade" by transnational corporations. Since "trade" here includes ownership and control of the societies' respective resources and markets, there seemed no barrier left to remove. Democratic sovereignty itself could no longer erect impediments to the rights of transnationals to own and control national and regional economies. In keeping with this new arrangement of societies to be open to transnational corporate control of their economies, the new trade regime prohibited any measure taken in Canada that might reduce "any benefit" that U.S. corporations might "reasonably expect" to receive "directly or indirectly" from Canada's economy. For example, it was now illegal for any elected government in Canada to introduce public ownership in any area in which U.S. corporations had an expected business stake, such as energy reserves, public auto insurance, or industrial infrastructure.[27]

This new trade regime set up a higher, unelected authority to prescribe to societies what their economies must henceforth do and conform to, whatever their elected governments might decide, or what their electorates might support or vote for. The new transnational sovereign was not accountable to electorates or to any law that conflicted with it. Under NAFTA, its unelected officials, and its corporate participants, this higher prescriptive authority now reposed in business-specified, transnational laws whose articles overrode all existing or future Canadian legislation or government policies. This pattern of relocating control of national and regional economies in the hands of bodies no longer accountable to electorates is, indeed, worldwide and not confined to Canada, Mexico, and the United States.[28]

The terms of this transnational trade regime are, with few exceptions, the same for all North American peoples. They have come under a new form of government against the will of the majority and without their participation or their elected representatives' participation in the prescriptions of transnational law to which they are now bound. They are powerless to override by means of elected governments, public policy, or legislation any of the terms of these trade agreements imposed on them. These steps are ruled out by the requirements of the new regime, by internal processes answerable to nobody but themselves, and by mechanisms of dispute resolution open to no public participation.

George Bush signed NAFTA after he had been voted out of office in the United States and with no prior electoral vote on the issue. Bill Clinton (like Chrétien in Canada) campaigned against the deal, calling it "George Bush's NAFTA" and indirectly assisting a third candidate, Ross Perot, who split the Republican vote by opposing NAFTA more strongly still (putting a decisive majority of Americans in opposition to the trade regime). Once in the presidency, Clinton quickly changed his position and became a militant convert to NAFTA, using hundreds of millions of taxpayers' dollars to lure Congressional representatives onto the side of the transnational regime. This was a telling subordination of the U.S. government to the transnational corporate agenda, an agenda opposed by the U.S. electorate itself.

If we wonder how politicians can reverse their positions so transparently once in office, this is because we underestimate the extent to which they have internalized the mind-set of those who finance and publicize them. The achievement of sovereign transnational power over formerly independent economies accountable to sovereign peoples was declared "necessary," and even democracy itself was not permitted to obstruct it. The moves had been planned for many years by such bodies as the transnational Trilateral Commission, and the corporate oligopoly was understandably unanimous in its support. No elected government or interest stood against the diktat, and the stated purpose of the trade regime was to ensure against any elected government holding to or passing laws that might impede transnational corporations in their push to gain open access to domestic markets and resources.[29]

A clear indicator of the lengths to which executive government power was willing to go to impose the entirety of this transnational value regime was the non-involvement of any other interest in the formation of the new system of rule. By the requirements of the American Trade Act of 1974, the U.S. Labour Advisory Council, representing under Congressional law all the workers of the United States, must advise the executive branch of government on any trade agreement that it undertakes. How was this barrier to open borders to corporations to be overcome? The remedy was blunt. The text of NAFTA was given to the Labour Advisory Council one day before the deadline for receiving its report. The Council was thus effectively excluded from the process. Established U.S. law itself did not assist the Council's voice. Along with all other constituencies of the U.S. public, its position was not of interest because it might represent "a barrier" that would impede the program's implementation. The Labour Council observed in its response, nevertheless, "NAFTA will have the effect of prohibiting democratically elected bodies at all levels of government from enacting measures deemed inconsistent with the provisions of the Agreement."[30]

The subordination of the Mexican people to the free trade program was more overtly imposed. The 1988 election was, as virtually all external observers agreed, won in the ballot box by the anti-free trade coalition led by Cuauhtémoc Cárdenas. But the Institutional Revolutionary Party advocated NAFTA as Mexico's "salvation." Despite a resounding defeat at the polls, the IRP retained power. This became an internationally acknowledged national election fraud, not surprisingly because the IRP had effectively installed an increasingly corrupt one-party state in Mexico in 1929. The IRP, however, was not inhibited from retaining power by its electoral defeat or the largest mass demonstrations in Mexico's history, and the party continued to impose NAFTA on the resistant Mexican people amidst hosannas across North America of a "new economic miracle." President Carlos Salinas de Gortari reputedly joined Mexico's rash of new billionaires, but the vast majority of the Mexican people were less fortunate. They were quickly deprived of almost half their incomes by a series of crises led by the hit-and-run speculations of foreign and domestic investors. These capital crises resulted in ever higher unemployment, a loss of two million jobs between December 1994 and August 1995, a 40 per cent fall of the national minimum wage, and a 45 per cent fall in the average wage in the same period, accompanied by an inflation rate of over 50 per cent.[31]

The concept of free trade seems an Orwellian use of the word "free," applied to a closed and undemocratically imposed system of transnational rule. Since the "forced trade" NAFTA government of Mexico was elected in 1988, over 260 opponents of the regime have been murdered. The country's largest independent union has been liquidated, and a number of union leaders have been killed. Employees of multinationals such as Pentagon-contractors General Electric Company and Honeywell have been threatened with death. However, there has been no response from NAFTA's appointed labour committee to any of this rule of terror to sustain the new trade regime.[32]

NAFTA has not been imposed in an overtly violent way on Canada and the United States, but it is hardly more accountable to democratic process and the legislative sovereignty of the people. It overrides both, usurps the rights of government at all levels to form economic policy in the common interest, and is responsible to no authority but itself. The World Trade Organization, in turn, seeks to dictate these terms for all countries through such instruments as the Multilateral Agreement on Investment. John Locke wrote many years ago that, at a certain point, people have the right to rebel. His words bear a special poignancy:

> All the slips of human frailty will be borne by the people without mutiny or murmur. But if a long train of abuses, prevarications and artifices, all tending the same way, make the design visible to people, and they cannot but feel what they lie under and see whether they are going, it is not to be wondered that they should then rouse themselves and endeavour to put the rule into such hands which may secure to them the ends for which government was first erected.[33]

Subsequent to the FTA and NAFTA, economic bureaucrats and corporate advisers began secretly negotiating the MAI under the auspices of the WTO. The MAI expanded the terms of the NAFTA across the developed world. The MAI was first leaked in 1997— some two years after the plan had begun to be put in place. Here too the evident design was to replace responsible government by a borderless corporate regime whose rules few knew or voted on.

No Free Lunches

A "government handout" or so-called "free lunch" in the generic sense is *a transfer of money value from public ownership to private possession and use by human or corporate persons*. According to this definition, welfare assistance is a "government handout" and so too is a government expenditure of tax revenues on a subsidy, credit, or write-off to wealthy individuals and corporations. An anomaly thus arises. Government is declared to be in "a debt crisis" and "too lavish" in its "handouts" and "giveaways" to citizens or "special interests" who have not earned the money. At the same time there is no word of criticism from market quarters about most of the public wealth being redistributed in this other way—that is, to wealthy corporations and individuals in the form of tax exemptions, reductions, write-offs, subsidies, export credits, resource giveaways, airwave privatizations, and inflated contracts. A double standard is thereby instituted. "Free lunch" applies only to the poor.

Free market ideology has from its beginnings placed primary emphasis on poor people "working for their living." Until legal limits began to be placed on the working day in the mid-nineteenth century, children and women (as well as men) were required to work twelve to sixteen hours a day, six days a week, for the wages they required to stay alive (for example, fifteen hours of labour a day for a child seven years old, as documented in the first report of England's Children's Employment Commission of 1863). The Factory Acts from 1833 to 1864 gradually shortened the sixteen-hour working day, one of the first acts of government "on the backs of business." This was widely decried as a coercive "theft of profit hours" from industry. This market pattern of overriding any barrier of life was first interfered with by "meddling government" with the limiting of child labour to twelve hours a day in 1833, an "interference in the free market" that was also adamantly opposed by employers and economists.[34]

Employers have long insisted that people without investment income must earn their bread by continuous productive labour "to make their lives useful." One of the favourite criticisms of legislation limiting the working day for children and others was that shorter working hours would leave the workers with excessive free time in which to indulge in sinful diversions. The market war cry of "no free lunches" has a long moral history of concern for the way people are corrupted by not working hard enough for their masters.

For example, from the late fifteenth century in England, hundreds of thousands of people were forcibly dispossessed and evicted from their small land tenures by enclosures of farmlands and dissolution of Church manors to make room for sheep and the wool trade. By law these people had to sell their labour to new masters hiring by the day for wages, or they were punished severely. Such laws to enforce people's willingness to work rather than to beg for "free lunches" continued as legally binding statutes until the early years of the eighteenth century.[35]

From the eighteenth century on, labour was left "free" to work for wages, or to starve. Labour was now a commodity for sale like any other. This condition was not hidden, and it remains today a major premise of market theory, terminology, and practice. Workers must either adapt to selling their labour to masters willing to buy it, or they and their families are to be without lunches and all the other means of living. This work-or-death ultimatum was built into the "free labour market" from the beginning, and the work was always for others. The market was thought to be a "self-regulating" order of beneficent "efficiency" in which "the laws of supply and demand" continuously ensured that labour oversupplies were corrected by starvation. The unfreedom of this arrangement never occurred as a problem to investors or their economist apologists. In this way, the "equilibrium" of supply and demand was always established. Adam Smith described this felicitous design of worker supply to labour for lunches in the free market:

> It is in this way that the demand for men, like any other commodity, necessarily regulates the production of men; quickens when it goes on too slowly, and stops it when it advances too fast. It is this demand which regulates and determines the state of propagation in all the different countries of the world.... The

wear and tear of a slave, it has been said, is at the expense of the master, but that of a free servant is at his own expense.[36]

Smith's combination of religious faith in the perfect design of the market and scientific impartiality to those made destitute by its operations has remained serenely intact over centuries. Workers are "a factor of production," and their price, as any other commodity, "must be set by the market." To conceive the labour factor in any less rigorous sense—for example, by understanding working people and their children as values in themselves—is not a point of view that market theory has ever permitted. To ensure that the labour factor of production has enough food to eat when it is not paying for itself and profit by labour is a contradiction in market terms. Life as such has no value in this ethical system. Questions about starving people and malnourished children belong to the clergy, the moralist, and the politician and must be kept from interfering in the market's laws of supply and demand.

It is by this logic of moral reasoning that the market ideology claims a supreme authority in matters of food to eat. Economists ignore matters of moral choice by the nature of their discipline, but they have never doubted their qualifications to prescribe the destiny of life or death for others. This authority is seen to derive from "scientific laws" akin to the law of gravitation. Transgressions such as handouts, welfare schemes, or "free lunches" of any kind must end in "market punishments" or "shock treatments" for exceeding the strict requirements of "market discipline."

Voluntary gifts outside the market's immutable laws of supply and demand are permitted by the doctrine, but as a matter of principle these must be restricted to those who choose to give. "Choice" is a precious heritage to those who have enough money to give or not to give. This liberty is violated if potential givers are "coerced" by the state's tax system to have their money redistributed to the needy without voluntarily deciding to give it. This is called by high theory an "expropriation," tantamount to "confiscation" or, even, "subjugation to state tyranny" and "enslavement."

The commandment of "no free lunches" is more than a mean-spirited slogan. It is based on an article of creed reaching back into the private-property basis of market theory and its first principle of voluntary transaction between self-maximizing agents. It is the wall of doctrine by which those who have much more wealth than they need are protected with rectitude against the needs of those who do not. In this supreme partiality of market metaphysics, democratic government has one ultimate goal—to serve and protect those who have property, in particular those with money property, and their voluntary transactions with its demand. While current believers inveigh with righteous indignation against taxing the rich to give "handouts" to the poor or the unemployed, countless more government tax expenditures are conferred on the wealthy and private corporations.

Handouts by government to rich market agents are not called "handouts" or "corporate welfare payments." These terms are reserved for those who need the money to live, not to acquire more money. Having money is virtuous in the market moral code, whereas having little or none is blameworthy. Thus receiving handouts from governments is an incentive for those with money to be more virtuous, and have still more. This is the American, now the Global Dream. One's virtue is ranked by how much money one has, and corresponding rights to society's goods flow from this underlying moral order. In contrast, receiving money from government when one has little or no money cannot lead to virtue because it will be spent on food or a roof over one's head, on merely reproducing life. That is a bad entitlement, because it does not lead to more money in the hands of the market moral agent, but is wasted on life that is not making money.

Government is assumed to be fulfilling its proper purpose by serving and protecting the market and its sequences of money increase for those investing money. Dire warnings of "government indebtedness" and of "dependency on government" do not apply here. Owners of capital must be "encouraged to save and invest," "relieved from tax burdens," and "provided market infrastructures." Systematic state subsidization and tax-transfers are corollaries of global market doctrine.[37] There is no limit to affordable subsidies if they are "necessary to compete in the international market" and are held to "contribute to prosperity," even if the majority of taxpaying populations grow more insecure and reduced in their circumstances by this transfer of wealth from social security to private investment sequences. "National security" and "self-defence" here do not mean protection and enablement of the citizen body, but the protection and facilitation of the sequences of turning money into more money for those investing money.

The pattern of government "free lunches" at work in the global market's leading North America sector is revealing. The Reagan 1981 tax reforms began by removing over $500 billion in tax obligations from the wealthiest 5 per cent of the taxable population, and the poorest 80 per cent of U.S. taxpayers ended up owing more taxes than before by these "tax cuts to the American people."[38] This redistribution of wealth began the greatest rise in government debt in U.S. peacetime history, with the U.S. federal debt tripling in eight years. This tripling was caused not only by hundreds of billions of dollars of government expenditures on those with most money, but also by government expenditures on the semimonopoly, highly subsidized armaments business, which escalated to almost $1 billion a day. Stronger armies ensured that the global market order "prevailed over the forces of evil," over any society seeking a non-global market way, whether indigenous peoples called "communists" or the "superpower" Soviet Union.[39]

But the pattern of "free lunches" did not end with tax giveaways to those with most money or with hundreds of millions of dollars a day of public contracts guaranteeing profits to armaments manufacturers. In 1986 government revenue giveaways to U.S. corporations in general reached such a height of "incentives" that tax grants to industry "exceeded the federal government's entire receipts from personal income tax."[40]

In Canada, reflecting this pattern a few years later, new tax handout programs redistributed $105 billion of public money from the government's rapidly shrinking fiscal base to private market corporations and individuals with private capital gains or high incomes.[41] This was in addition to the $40 billion in interest-free, deferred tax obligations not collected as "depreciation allowances." In one of those years, 1991, seventy-two corporations with over $25 million in profits paid no tax at all.[42] In striking contrast, between 1984 and 1991, total taxes paid by the working poor increased by 44 per cent.[43] In the "public servant" realm itself, Paul Martin's private corporation, the CSL Group Inc., paid no income tax on a profit of $19,700,000. Subsequently, as Canadian finance minister, Martin went on to represent this program of competitive avoidance of tax obligation in government.[44]

In both the United States and Canada, huge government debts accumulated to pay for the redistribution of wealth to the market and its sequences of turning money into more money for those with money. "The spending binge," as it was called by its beneficiaries, was, however, always attributed to social programs and "free lunches" to others. But the government's still functioning statistics branch calculated that 94 per cent of the escalating deficit in Canada between 1979 and 1991 was due to tax reductions for corporations and upper-income taxpayers and increased compound interest rates paid to private banks and money-lenders.[45] Such facts did not get published in the market media, and the rising debt and deficits continued to be blamed on "free lunches" for those with less money-demand.

Government expenditures on the poor, the unemployed, social programs, higher education, and public broadcasting were subjected to increasing attack. These expenditures of public revenues were seen as "irresponsible" and "spending beyond our means." To end "the spending binge" and its ever heavier "millstone around the neck of our children," all such programs for the citizen body as a whole were steadily decreased towards zero, including assistance to poor children, while the redistribution of government revenues to those positioned within the market's money-sequences continued unabated.

The examples of this underlying pattern of government handouts reveal a disturbing paradigm shift. Where government had come with democratic gains to represent the life-interests of the less well-off in society, a movement towards serving "the common interest" and not only the privileged, the deep trend was now in the opposite direction. All the transfers of wealth through government back to society were now moving away from the interests of *life*'s security and growth towards the security and growth of money-demand accumulations. If the rhetoric of the new order was "no free lunches" and "an end to government handouts," the reality was an increase of both in one direction—towards money circuits and away from the needs of society's citizens.

Thus in the "market friendly" province of Alberta, a 20 per cent reduction across the board of the government's health, education, and social security programs in 1992 went soon after to a $2.3 billion gift of royalties to wealthy oil companies extracting oil from the province's publicly owned oil reserves.[46] On the national level a 1993 federal Ministry of Finance report disclosed that $90 billion was spent in "tax expenditures" on tax credits, deferrals, deductions, and exemptions, which was one and a half times the total federal government expenditures on old-age security, health, unemployment insurance, social assistance, education, and the rest of Canada's social infrastructure.[47]

In the United States, Congress proposed a still further reduction of $270 billion in government expenditures on Medicare to "pay down the government debt." It simultaneously promised an equivalent tax giveaway of $245 billion, whose benefits would again go preponderantly to citizens with the highest incomes.[48] The problem of the "ever deepening debt crisis" in this paradigm shift of government comes and goes in predictable outbursts and silences. If the direction of revenue is towards the public's needs, it is a "crisis of overspending." If the direction of revenue is towards wealth transfers to corporations and investors, it is a "job-creating strategy," even as the ranks of the jobless swell from continuous and planned downsizings of workforces.

Financial institutions and banks, in general, have done especially well out of these government programs of redistributing public revenues to the market and its most privileged positions of money reproduction and gain (see, for instance, chapter 4, note 22). Banks have benefited from generic corporate welfare programs of ever lower taxes on higher profits, as corporate taxes declined in Canada from the lion's share of government revenues in 1961 to 7.29 per cent in 1993.[49] More significantly, banks have continuously received extraordinary bonanzas in government-set minimum interest rates on privately created debt-loans, which have multiplied their profits to historic highs year after year since 1993. In Canada, for example, the cost of compounding high interest payments to banks and private lenders was estimated by the Dominion Bond Rating Service to have accounted for 93 per cent of Canada's skyrocketing debt growth since 1984.[50] In the United States, which started the trend with an escalating series of interest-rate increases by the Federal Reserve Board from 1979 on, a similar vast transfer of wealth from the public sector to banks and other money-lenders occurred by the same mode of redistribution. As government indebtedness increased, market advocates predictably remained silent on these causes of government deficits, instead attacking "unaffordable social programs" and anyone who exposed the facts.[51]

The underlying law of the global market program is to redistribute society's wealth from the protection of citizens' lives to the protection of the market's money accumulations. This internal law is expressed in many ways, which are hidden from view. Consistent with the market code's defining repudiation of those without money, only those with much money are to be permitted the largesse of the public purse.

Across the border, government channels hundreds of billions of taxpayers' dollars to various corporations and capital investors in subsidies, investment incentives, grants, and free public services: for example, 40 per cent of all research money spent at large U.S. corporations, as well as the extension of corporate patent rights over the higher research done at public universities.[52] These transfers also include up to $500 billion in a single U.S. program to bail out deregulated "savings and loan" corporations and their financial speculations.[53] Elsewhere they include billions of dollars of state subsidies to U.S., French, British, Canadian, Israeli, and other corporations producing armaments.[54] None of these government handouts is seen as a problem to free market crusaders, and none is targeted as an "unaffordable handout." Abuse is reserved for social programs, such as education, health, and income security. In the market value program, "government handouts" and "waste" refer exclusively to expenditures on public enterprises serving non-profit interests of life as an end in itself.

The public owns one-third of the United States and over four-fifths of Canada, but corporations control the rich mineral resources such as timber, oil, and gas for their exclusive profit, which may be removed from the host society and invested elsewhere at will. In addition, taxpayers provide the money for roads and other infrastructure to enable these corporations to clear-cut, extract, and deplete publicly owned resources for "a fraction of their market worth," as corporations themselves recognize.[55] The public also owns the airwaves used to transmit television, radio, and other communications. But private corporations control these as well, with little or no accountability to the public interest. As market doctrine makes clear, the right of the private communications industry to "freedom of expression" is not exercised to serve the public interest, but to maximize private profits for shareholders. Despite this handover of public airwaves at a fraction of market worth to media conglomerates, what little remains of public broadcasting is hunted down as an enemy to "market accountability" by business representatives and corporate-financed politicians. Once again, what is handed out by governments to private corporate interests at great cost to the public is "essential," but what is left for the life and culture of the public is "living beyond our means," however much evidence may refute both claims.[56]

A small number of multinational corporations also control the production and distribution of health goods. Governments provide, free of charge, state-enforced monopolies over the production and distribution of these corporate products—monopolies recently extended to twenty years by worldwide NAFTA and GATT/WTO trade regulations. Under these long-term prohibitions of competition, a transnational monopoly has been instituted that protects the multinational pharmaceutical corporations at public expense. After this patent monopoly was introduced, prices to consumers rose to ever higher levels: for example, by over 93 per cent in Canada from 1987 to 1993.[57]

In defence of these government-protected market monopolies, pharmaceutical transnationals argue that they must have these long-term restrictions of competition "to pay for their research costs." In fact these corporations spend about twice as much on advertising for their products as they spend on all research.[58] Meanwhile, governments cut drug-benefit plans for seniors, the unemployed, and children, because these social programs have "become too costly."

The banking system is at the core of the entire system of transfers of public wealth, resources, and privileges to private market corporations. Government offers an ongoing and increasing menu of giveaways that seldom surface to view, so effectively secretive and internalized is their modus operandi. There can be no pretence of "increased productivity" to justify this system of government transfers of wealth, because banks produce nothing. Their revenues derive not from producing goods, but from lending and investing money with no productive function involved. Government provides banks with an effective licence to print money free of public charge. Once the exclusive reserve of sovereign governments, this right has been unofficially transferred to private banking institutions by the modern device of credit entered into account books as money owed. Along with this right, government has granted the right to extract compound rates of interest with no upper limit. On the foundation of other people's money stocks and credit-created money, the banks are then in a position in the market to receive ever more money back to lend and invest in an ad infinitum circuit of money multiplication and gain.

Government grants these rights by charter to banks and private depository institutions. Recent estimates show that 96 per cent of all new money that enters the U.S. and Canadian markets is created and controlled by private money-lending corporations. In 1982, when the market frenzy of "deregulation" began in the United States, the eminent economist Lester Thurow observed, "The Federal Reserve Board announced that it was giving up on its attempts to control the U.S. money supply on the grounds that [banks and other leading institutions] ... had essentially *taken over the government's nominal role as the printer of money.*"[59] Banks and other institutional lenders have thus become "private mints" controlling and adding to society's money supply as they please to maximize their profits, all with free government protection and assistance, with no obligation to share the proceeds with the public at even a nominal rate and with no requirement to lend the money to productive investments or to enterprises in the public interest. The money can be kept from small accounts, such as local business, and lent to foreign interests to turn the country's ownership over to foreign nationals. Both these decision-patterns have been pursued by private banks as standard profit-maximizing strategies, which are only possible on the basis of their carte blanche entitlements from government.[60] The largesse of market governments is here effectively without bounds, making banks the greatest of all beneficiaries of the government-catered free lunch.

All that is needed to create money privately to loan to others at interest rates as high as can be extracted is a government-granted charter, the stock of other people's money deposits to cover demands for cash, and instant debt-accounts entered in books for interest-paying debtors. This process of creating money, and then charging more money for its use in the form of interest, can be as leveraged or multiplied as the bank chooses for maximum profits to itself, moving past seventy times its cash base in the current global financial regime.

The former money-reserve requirement of approximately 4 per cent to cover depositors' demands and to restrain inflation was quietly abolished by the Canadian government in 1991, so quietly that even an ex-minister and president of a major stock exchange did not know of it.[61] The giveaway of money-creating powers to private banks is a long historical practice of governments dominated by money-lenders, dating from the founding of the private Bank of England in 1694. In the case of Canada's abolition of reserves, the "deregulation," or licence to manufacture money and demand cumulative interest payments from debtors, permitted profit-maximizing bank corporations to lend any amount of money they chose for compounding interest payments to governments, individuals, students, and the rest of society, far beyond the original twenty-five-times limit formerly imposed. The already whittled-down limit of 4 per cent reserve was condemned by the banks as "inflexible regulations" and a "hidden tax." The governor of the Bank of Canada thereafter repeated the private banks' justification for no money collateral on money lent as a self-evident banking necessity.[62]

Governments' giveaway of limitless entitlements to private financial institutions to control society's money creation and supply includes the right to extract very high minimum rates of usury from all debtors. These rates have gone as high as 22.5 per cent prime in Canada, loan-shark levels that destroyed households, businesses, jobs, and government solvency itself in a runaway fashion.[63] With the inner logic of compound interest geometrically multiplying debts, banks and other institutional money-lenders have been able to dip deeper into people's and governments' pockets to accelerate the redistribution of public and individual wealth to private banking operations. Individual citizens are now in historically unprecedented debt to banks and corporate money-lenders. U.S. and Canadian household debt, for example, has risen to a new record level of over 90 per cent of after-tax income, with ever more interest payments to pay for these rising debts from declining wages and salaries.[64]

Interestingly, government's role of prescribing compulsory and minimum rates of interest has never been publicly criticized by free market crusaders as "an interference in the price system of the market." Critics of "government meddling in the economy" prefer to focus their moral concern about compulsory minimum prices on such issues as a minimum wage protecting the working poor from destitution.

Private banks have thus come to lend ever more money to people and governments in ever deeper debt, while speculating ever more grandly abroad with domestic savings in non-productive transactions, such as buying foreign banks. In the process of benefiting from government's unstinting special privileges, they have increased their overall extractions of interest money from debtors by twenty-five times in constant dollars between 1957 and 1991.[65] This geometrically rising flow of money to banks is said to have the serendipitous effect of "keeping down inflation." But, rather, the banks' creation of money, and their further compound interest rates on it, represent an uncontrolled inflationary force, by constituting an ever greater pool of new money-demand for no good produced, the very recipe of inflation. Because the inflationary force comes from the owners of money, not those who work for it, it does not register in the market mind-set. Inflation, or money rise without product rise, is only a problem in this value program when it is the requirements of life, not money itself, which are generating more money-demand without productive gains, as, for example, in workers' benefits beyond productivity increase. We understand what is initially anomalous in market logic if we understand that it is gain in money-demand over life, not gain in life, that drives this system of value. This will be our major critical concern ahead.

Since the right of banks to create money and to lend it at historically high interest rates impacts heavily on governments themselves as debtors, we might wonder why governments do nothing to forestall the bankrupting of their public sectors by such giveaways to the private banking system. The Bank of Canada, for example, is a publicly owned bank, and it is constitutionally authorized to lend to the government at low rates. Government, however, has handed away these rights to private banks and, increasingly, to foreign money-lenders. Instead of the Canadian federal government owing money to the central bank at low interest rates, it now owes principal and high compounding interest charges to private banks and foreign bond-holders. As the government cuts ever more of its social expenditures towards zero on such values as public education, health, and welfare, the money it "saves" goes out the other door to the compounding demands of private banks and bond dealers, to whom it has transferred the right to extract high debt-service payments it could be paying to itself. Taxpayers increasingly pay taxes to enrich banks and financiers, while their elected governments dismantle their social rights and the productive economy.

Between 1989 and 1994 (the latter a record-setting year for bank profits in Canada), the government giveaway to banks was increased. The Bank of Canada radically reduced its own purchase of government bonds, which would leave interest payments in government possession. Instead of holding the public bonds at minimal interest costs to the public, the Bank of Canada transferred these bonds to private banks as risk-free capital. The banks collected compound interest with no service necessary or risk of loss. This latest free lunch bailed out the banks from major losses in speculative financial adventures abroad, while further running up the government's debt to the banks. Self-maximizing banks predictably loaded up on high-interest government bonds by a 700 per cent rise in holdings to provide "risk-free" assets to back up more created loans and financial speculations. The 38 per cent drop in the Bank of Canada's own holdings of government bonds thereby provided further room for the private banks to create new debt money and interest-demands for themselves, an estimated $31.5 billions. This massive transfer of debt money to the private banks left the public now paying high interest rates to private banks instead of low interest costs to the publicly owned Bank of Canada. But increases of money gain to the market are always good in its value program, while losses to public accounts are celebrated as "downsizing government."

In this way, the government gave away the interest rates that would have gone to the Bank of Canada's sole shareholder, the Government of Canada, to the coffers of private banks. The private banks were handed, free of charge, another $3 billion per year of taxpayers' interest payments "for storing the public debt in their private vaults."[66] This new government scheme provided almost three-quarters of the banks' total record profits of 1994, while one social program after another was slashed to "pay down the deficit." Underneath a public discourse of "no free lunches," "the welfare disaster," and "the public debt crisis," the greatest redistribution of wealth in history had silently occurred—taking from the life of people and society and giving to the money-investment sequences of the global market.

Across the Atlantic, the British government has handed over control of monetary policy to the Bank of England, while the European Union is set to do the same for a European Central Bank under the current plans of monetary union.

There is doubtless individual fault in collaborating with and carrying out such a value program, which turns the economic lifelines of society over to bankers and their parasitic money extractions.

But the disorder runs much deeper. It permeates the decision structures of government itself through pliant functionaries and officials into the very structure of social organization and thought. It is regulated by mutating elaborations of unexamined market principles, whereby the market is no longer a means to enrich life, but life is a means to enrich the rich.

Notes

1. For example, at the height of corporate attacks on public debt in Canada and calls for ever more reduction of the country's social infrastructure, over sixty thousand corporations paid no income tax at all, and over $40 billion in taxes owed by the country's major corporations remained deferred as interest-free loans with no requirement to repay. "Index on Taxes," (*CCCP Monitor*, February 1995, p.2; and *Infoglobe Report on Business Corporate Database*, Dec. 19, 1994, cited in "Unfair Shares: Corporations and Taxation in Canada," Ontario Federation of Labour and the Ontario Coalition for Social Justice, February 1995, p.3.

2. John McMurtry, "The Argumentum Ad Adversarium," *Informal Logic*, vol. 8, no. 1 (1986), pp.29-37.

3. Speech by Noam Chomsky, Vancouver, March 5, 1996. Robert Dole, the U.S. Republican leader, acknowledged that money wins elections. After he lost the Arizona primary to business magazine mogul Steve Forbes, he explained: "I lost because he spent over four million [on the Arizona primary], and I spent only $640,000." CNN, Feb. 27, 1996.

4. *Harper's Index*, June 1995, p.43.

5. After the Reagan government's 30 per cent tax cut in 1981, 80 per cent of the population ended up losing in their after-tax household incomes, while the top 5 per cent received most of the benefits. Greider, *Secrets of the Temple*, p.578. A similar outcome seemed likely to occur with the same promised 30 per cent reduction in Ontario in 1996, a Reagan program being recycled fifteen years later as "the common sense revolution."

6. This was a figure I first saw in *The Hindustani Times* in Tamil Nadu, India, in October 1992 in an article prior to the presidential elections of that year. The article was authored by Bill Clinton, but was not published in North America. The figure is also cited by Geoffrey Hawthorne, "Capitalism without Limits," *London Review of Books*, May 26, 1994, p.12.

7. Ralph Nader, "Stop Americanizing Medicare," *CCPA Monitor*, February 1996, p.17. The markedly superior efficiency of government over private-enterprise organization of production of public goods is not confined to health care. The Canadian Pension Plan costs less than 1 per cent of benefits to operate. For-profit plans, in contrast, cost on average five times that amount. "Five Reasons to Keep It Public," *Canadian Perspectives*, Spring 1996, p.5. With the public good of education, the market is in principle opposed to its defining principles. See chapter 5, "The Knowledge-Based Economy," and "Education and the Market Model."

8. Kramer, "Corporate Criminality," p.19.

9. Spence, *With Justice for None*, p.98.

10. Ibid., pp.200, 213.

11. *The Globe and Mail*, Sept. 23, 1995, p.A8.

12. These changes were not enough for *Globe and Mail* editorialists, who called also for cuts in the minimum wage. "A Frontal Assault on Unemployment," *The Globe and Mail*, Sept. 10, 1997, p.A6.

13. Unless otherwise stated, the facts and figures cited in this and the following paragraph are drawn from Martin Walker, "Green Enforcers Face Ambush in U.S.," *The Guardian Weekly*, Sept. 24, 1995, p.32; and Carol Goar, "The De-Greening of America," *The Toronto Star*, Aug. 6, 1995, p.F6.

14. *The Sunday Star* (Toronto), Dec. 17, 1995, p.F3.

15. *The Globe and Mail*, July 18, 1995, p.A7.

16. *Contrast with America: The Bold Plan by Rep. Newt Gingrich, Rep. Dick Armey and the House Republicans to Change the Nation*, ed. Ed Gillespie and Bob Schellas (New York: Times Books, Random House, 1993), pp.131-32.

17. Karl Marx, "The Secret of Primitive Accumulation," "Expropriation of the Agricultural Population from the Land," and "Bloody Legislation against the Expropriated from the End of the 15th Century," vol. I, chapters XXVII-XXIX, *Capital* (New York: Progress Publishers, 1967), pp.717-44.

18. See, for example, Carmel Budiardjo and Liem Soei Liong, *The War against East Timor* (London: Zed Books, 1984); and for the Canadian government's support of this and its own genocidal expropriation of indigenous people's resources for international trade, Sharon Scharfe, *Complicity, Human Rights and Canadian Foreign Policy* (Montreal: Black Rose Books, 1996), and Bruce Cockburn, "Greed, Betrayal and Deceit," The Lubicon Legal Defence Fund, Toronto, March 1995.

19. Kristin Dawkins, *NAFTA, GATT and the World Trade Organization: The Emerging New World Order* (Westfield, N.J.: Open Magazine Pamphlet Series, 1993), pp.3-7. See also Terisa Turner, ed., *Arise Ye People: Gender, Class and Race in Popular Struggles* (Trenton, N.J.: Africa World Press, 1994).

20. See Polanyi, *Great Transformation*, pp.159-60.

21. I am indebted to Robert Good's unpublished manuscript, "Free Trade, Forced Trade and the Market: An Overview" for these figures on the Belgian Congo.

22. Even the lonely "Agriculture and Sanitary and Phytosanitary Measures" Articles 701-724, *North American Free Trade Agreement*, 1992, pp.143-175 do not require minimum standards. For an informative discussion of the openness of NAFTA to environmental abuse, see Michelle Swenarchuk, "The Environmental Implications of NAFTA: A Legal Analysis," in *Growth, Trade and Environmental Values*, ed. Ted Schrecker and Jean Dagleish (London: Westminster Institute for Ethics and Human Values, 1994), pp.83-112.

23. David Orchard, *The Fight for Canada* (Toronto: Stoddart, 1994), pp.224-31; "Mexican People Speak Out: Reject Government Policies," *Economic Justice Report*, vol. 6, no. 3 (November 1995).

24. John McMurtry, "A Day in the Life of the New World Order," *The Globe and Mail*, April 1, 1995, p.A7.

25. Orchard, *Fight for Canada*, p.176.

26. These "national treatment" requirements for foreign multinational corporations and business agents are prescribed in *inter alia*, the original Canada-U.S. FTA, articles 105 and 502, 1989; and NAFTA, articles 301 and 1102. It is interesting to note in this connection that these articles conferred greater rights on foreign corporations and business agents than permitted to Canadian corporations and business agents from out of province.

27. NAFTA, articles 502, 1402, 2010, 2011. See Orchard, *Fight for Canada*, pp.169-71.

28. Once governments sign these transnational trade laws, such as the overarching GATT, which puts their economies under the regulation of the World Trade Organization, they are obliged to be governed by its overriding regulations, however these might harm their populations--for example, by massive unemployment, loss of their resources and infrastructures to foreign corporate control, or even the right of their subsistence farmers to plant home-grown seeds for which transnational corporations have achieved a patent. Under the terms of the Maastricht Treaty of the European Union, the fiscal policy of all governments is prescribed by a central formula--for example, a deficit-to-GDP ratio that requires governments to reduce their social spending. Moreover, the control of

society's money and credit policies is now presided over by a European Central Bank and a European System of Central Banks, which under Article 107 is accountable to no electoral or other body but itself.

29. A confidential 1987 memorandum prepared for the U.S. treasury secretary James Baker and the chief U.S. trade negotiator, Clayton Yeutter, prior to the agreement said: "Canadian governments must be prevented from retrogressing to the highly unsatisfactory policy regime from just a few years ago." The reference was to Canada's National Energy Policy, supported by 84 per cent of the Canadian electorate in 1984 in a poll commissioned by U.S. oil corporations themselves. In Mexico, U.S. Ambassador John Negroponte declared in another leaked document: "The F.T.A. negotiations themselves will be a useful lever in prying open the Mexican economy even further [and] we can reasonably expect the foreign investment law to change." This referred to a law also supported by the great majority of the Mexican people. See Orchard, *Fight For Canada*, pp.129,231. As the ever-deferring Fraser Institute rationalized in the wake of this effective usurpation of democratically supported government authority and legislation by transnational corporation rule, "A trade deal simply limits the extent to which the U.S. or other signatory government may respond to pressure from their citizens." Calvert and Krehm, *Pandora's Box*, p.158.

30. Noam Chomsky, "Notes on NAFTA," *The Nation*, March 14, 1993, p.414.

31. Linda Diebel, "NAFTA: Where Did the Jobs Go?" *Sunday Star*, Sept. 24, 1995, p.F7.

32. Ibid.

33. Locke, *Second Treatise on Government*, p.126.

34. Marx, "The Working Day," *Capital*, part III, chapter X, p.271.

35. Marx, "Expropriation of the Agricultural Population from the Land," part VIII, chapter XXVII, *Capital*, pp.717-33.

36. Smith, "The Wages of Labour," book I, chapter III, *Inquiry*, p.85.

37. When questioned at a local press conference about the $87 million interest-free, non-recallable "loan" of shrinking government revenues to one of the nation's richest corporations during a "crisis of government indebtedness," Canada's finance minister, Paul Martin, was unapologetic. He justified the handout to Bombardier Inc., a major transnational corporation, by stating that this practice was now standard. "Boeing in the U.S. could not survive without the U.S. government," he observed. He then asserted the handouts as necessary to playing the global market game: "You're either going to be in that game and recognize the nature of it, which is a partnership between government and the private sector, or you don't want to be in that game." *Guelph Tribune*, Nov. 16, 1996, p.7.

38. See note 5.

39. See, for example, chapter 3, notes 28, 29, 43, and 49.

40. *The Economist*, Feb. 4, 1993.

41. *CCPA Monitor*, February 1995, p.2.

42. For the general causal mechanism behind the fall of corporate taxation, see pp.272-73.

43. *Canadian Perspectives*, Winter 1994, p.21.

44. *Canadian Perspectives*, Autumn 1994, p.24; Frances Russell, "A View of Taxes and Debt from Another Angle," *The Winnipeg Free Press*, Sept. 24, 1994, p.A18.

45. H. Mimoto and P.Cross, "The Growth of the Federal Debt," *The Canadian Economic Observer*, vol.3, no.1 (June 1991), p.3; Bruce Campbell, "Stats Can Study on Our Debt/Deficit Crises," *CCPA Monitor*, April 1995, pp.14-15.

46. Linda Goyette, "We Don't Want Cheeky Professors Questioning Our Oil Barons, Do We?" *Canadian Association of University Teachers Bulletin*, March 1996, p.9.

47. Goyette, "We Don't Want Cheeky Professors," p.18.

48. *The Guardian Weekly*, Oct. 15, 1995, p.6.

49. *CCPA Monitor*, February 1995, p.2.

50. Duncan Cameron and Ed Finn, *10 Deficit Myths* (Ottawa: Canadian Centre for Policy Alternatives, 1996), p.15.

51. A Statistics Canada study showing that less than 10 percent of federal debt growth was due to social spending was suppressed by the Ministry of Finance, although over twenty well-qualified economists had vetted its findings beforehand. See Linda McQuaig, *Shooting the Hippo: Death by Deficit and Other Canadian Myths* (Toronto: Penguin Books, 1994), pp. 53-62.

52. Nader, "Stop Americanizing Medicare"; Calvert and Krehm, *Pandora's Box*, p.125.

53. David Ransom, "Smokescreen: CIA Involvement in Savings Bank Scandal," *The New Internationalist*, September 1990, p.27.

54. See John McMurtry, "The Political Economy of Militarism," in *Understanding War* (Toronto: Science for Peace and Samuel Stevens, 1989), pp.35-44, 62.

55. Nader, "Stop Americanizing Medicare"; Drew Fagan, "Quebec, Washington Nearing Softwood Deal," *The Globe and Mail*, Jan. 15, 1996, p.B1.

56. See, for example, this chapter, note 7.

57. *CCPA Monitor*, March 1995, p.9.

58. Roxanne Snyder, "Patents and Profits," *The New Internationalist*, August 1993, pp.20-21.

59. William Henry Pope, "The Re-Nationalization of Money," *Options Politiques*, February 1992, p.33; emphasis added.

60. While banks are, as any small businessman will tell you, reluctant to lend money to domestic small business, they are very keen to lend domestic savings to foreign corporations to buy out domestic corporations and to enter speculative adventures abroad. For example, Canadian banks have long provided an estimated 60 per cent of the financing of U.S. takeovers of Canadian corporations and now seek to purchase failed Mexican banks by an export of almost $1 billion from the Canadian economy. See William Krehm, "The Anatomy of Deceit," *Economic Reform*, March 1996, p.2.

61. William Krehm, "Publisher's Mail-Box," *Economic Reform*, August 1995, p.2.

62. When, for example, the Governor of the Bank of Canada, Gordon Thiessen, was questioned by the Standing Committee on Public Accounts about the need for reserve requirements, he replied (in a manner suitable to a public-relations representative for the private banks) that "reserve require-ments are a form of tax." "Time for Thiessen to Go?" *Economic Reform*, February 1996, p.3. Thiessen did not think it necessary to support this claim with any argument, even though having money on hand to pay for the money you lend is no more a tax than is loan collateral. His exchange discloses how in our current period even the chief officer of a public central bank conceives of his role as a representative of the interests of private banks against the interests of the public that employs him. The private bank reserve is under law deposited in the central bank and operates as its reserve to, for example, buy national bonds, a function enabling the bank to reduce public debt at low or no interest. But such a function is now abolished to allow private banks to be free of reserve requirements to extract more usury from privatized government bonds, and to hold these bonds as risk-free collateral under new international banking regulations set by the Swiss-based Bank of International Settlements (made up of private bankers). In this way, the banks use national and international regulatory institutions to enrich themselves at public expense. All of this activity is in accord with the ruling logic of the "new global market order."

63. Usury costs on Canada's national debt, for example, are now 37 cents on every dollar. *The Globe and Mail*, March 1, 1996, p.A6.

64. *The Guardian Weekly*, Dec. 24, p.7. The rise of individual debt in Canada, for example, has been almost 40 per cent since 1985. *The Globe and Mail*, Nov. 18, 1995.

65. Krehm, "Publisher's Mail-Box," August 1995, p.7.

66. William Krehm, "Why Banks Rate as Number One Corporate Bums," *CCPA Monitor*, March 1995, p.6.

Part III

Planetary Health,
the Global Market,
and the Civil Commons

The Decoupling of Capital from Civil and Environmental Life

Like any moral doctrine, the global market ethic implies a prescriptive set that designates and determines its exclusions and choices and backs its commands and prohibitions with rewards and deprivations. We have seen the underlying ethic of the market program operating across cultural and national boundaries, determining all outcomes it can control by a system of financial allocations and withdrawals that have all tended to manifest a unifying pattern. The details are complex, diverse, and many-levelled, but together they reveal an unmistakable and mutant value code that is increasingly confirmed. The master program of this value code is to take from the social commons, and those it protects and enables, and to give to market transactions of private capital owners to do with as they please. The worldwide "public debt crisis" has been one prime instrument for imposition of this underlying global market program. But pincers need two edges to cut. The second severing cut of society from the requirements of its internal life was to be the simultaneous policy instrument of "free trade."

Freeing Capital from Society: The Function of Free Trade

There has been a covert side to the "market restructuring" of societies, a movement that has swept across the globe since the holy war against "world communism" was won. This hidden side has been the war against "socialism within." It is a war waged, first, with the weapon of policy-created "debt crises" to reduce social spending and, second, with the age-old panacea of "international free trade" to make social spending "too expensive to compete." But unlike the days of Adam Smith, when free trade was a way of breaking royal monopolies, these monopolist forces of the past no longer existed. On the contrary, what now existed as monopolizing power in world production and distribution was transnational corporate empires. As we have seen, the annual gross revenues of the top forty-seven corporations exceed those of 130 states, and their merely intracompany dealings manage an increasing lion's share of international trade.[1] "Free trade" is now not the breaker of economic monopolies, as in the days of Adam Smith, but their maker.

The key to understanding the new "free trade" is that it really means free transnational capital. The freedom it designates is not that of people to exchange, but of private capital and corporations to own and sell across national boundaries with no limits to their access and control of other societies' means of existence. All former "obstructions" and "barriers" to "the free movement of goods and capital across borders" have been increasingly phased out as "protectionism."

The right of a society to self-protection against the "race to the bottom" might have seemed something worth saving in this context. Importing into a society goods manufactured by labourers for under a dollar a day over seventy-hour weeks—in conditions that ruled out workers' independent organization, enforced no health and safety regulations, required no restrictions on industrial pollution, and demanded few or no taxes from corporations to pay for their share of government social costs—would seem to be a recipe for civil suicide. How could domestic workers and producers compete against the low costs of such conditions of labour and production if minimum standards no longer protected them? How could governments continue to provide public benefits to their citizens if their corporate tax levels had to compete with the low or zero tax levels granted to corporations elsewhere to "attract capital investment"? How could the atmospheric and air quality, the waters and the oceans, the forest covers, the fish stocks, the environment in general be safeguarded from ever more toxins, destructive pollution loads, overextractions and depletions if competing firms from other jurisdictions were required to provide no such cost-adding protections? How could people feel any longer secure in their societies or jobs if it was much cheaper for corporations and employers to offer them part-time, temporary, and no-benefits work or replace them altogether with low-cost labour elsewhere? Or, more and more the case, what if labour itself became increasingly dispensable in the worldwide campaign to "shed work forces"? How, in short, could an ever-faster and widening "race to the bottom" to "cut costs of production" be prevented if the "new international competition" introduced by transnational trade regimes removed society's only sovereign powers to protect its citizens against it?

What defined the new transnational trade agreements, from the U.S.-Canada FTA and NAFTA to the emerging Multinational Agreement on Investment (MAI), was a single master principle: Remove any and all restrictions on the access of transnational corporations to ownership of the economies of the world. Private corporations and capital were indeed "free" from old "barriers." But their freedom permitted them, among other things, to slash costs on evolved social, labour, and environmental standards and protections. In consequence, every life-form other than the corporation was now decidedly less free because no effective rights or protections for them were instituted in these transnational trade regulations. These new rule-books for societies prescribed thousands of pages of detailed articles for the unfettered mobility and rights of capital to own, exit, and sell across borders—a new regime of regulations overriding all local and national laws conflicting with them. This new transnational regime was, indeed, by its own description, accountable to no body or norms beyond itself.[2] There were no corresponding international electorates or international laws to protect humans and environments from the "restructurings" and hit-and-run movements of speculative capital that could now strip societies of their domestic capital, the value of their currency, and the price of their labour overnight (as, for example, Mexico in 1995 and the "miracle economies" of Southeast Asia in 1997). The new regulatory regime to govern international production and distribution served no interests other than those of transnational businesses. No social and environmental right, indeed, was effectively protected at all, despite non-binding cosmetic "side agreements" in NAFTA to satisfy popular discontent.

In consequence of their one-sided conferral of rights and freedoms, these trade instruments enabled corporations to bid down national and regional standards of life-protection to lower cost-levels, with no bottom to the reduction. Wages could now be driven below subsistence level in increasing marginal workforces by ever more part-time workers and low-pay zones. Shedding workforces by the tens of thousands could proceed with no limit imposed by governments.[3] Environments could be polluted and plundered more widely in the new freedom of movement of money seeking to be more with no inhibition of life-protective standards. Work and safety regulations could be downgraded and abolished to "keep costs competitive." Unions could be prohibited or effectively driven out of the market with little effective recourse of work stoppage. There were no articles to rule out child-labour, seventy-five-hour working weeks, or human rights violations of any kind. Corporate free-riding on social infrastructures was now encouraged, as societies had to keep reducing their taxes and offering borderless capital incentives of free infrastructure and subsidies to "attract investors." There was no limit of these trade agreements to this transnational ratcheting down of social employment, standards, and costs to ever lower levels—which, as we have seen, can go to inhuman levels "to add value."

As the policy-driven "debt crisis" began to take hold in the United States, Canada, and New Zealand and other nations across the world, countries whose debts were compounded to unmanageable levels by U.S.-led high interest rates, the second great pincer for reducing government social spending went into effect. This second, historic line of attack against the enemy of socialism within, the "welfare state," was sold as "freedom and prosperity." While "painful cuts" were the bad cop in the new order, visions of tariff-free cars, more jobs, and global liberty were the good cop, more than enough to make up for the loss of social programs.

Just as the policy-manufactured "debt crisis" had mounted ever increasing pressure on government social spending and standards, so too did the simultaneously occurring transnational trade agreements. Government standards and budgets devoted to such common interests as public health, universal education, old-age pensions, unemployment insurance, social and family assistance, environmental protection, and public transit and communications were now under a two-sided attack. Transnational trade was not a guiding idea that its proponents and sponsors cared to balance with other factors of concern. National independence, self-sufficiency, protection of undeveloped domestic industries, or even maintenance of society's employment levels were, on the contrary, morally condemned as "narrowly nationalist," "protectionist," and "failing to adjust to international competition."

In an interesting double-talk of this period, people's jobs and social programs were said to be threatened if nations did not enter these new, borderless trade arrangements. So, too, it was warned, were "domestic productivity," "standards of living," and "the ability to survive as an independent nation." All that was to be lost by these bills of rights for transnational corporations was, at the same time, said to be at risk if they were not signed. No one dared call this campaign a reign of terror, but there were incessant threats about people losing their jobs, their futures, their standards of living, and their very survival as a society if they did not "compete in the new international market."

A major "free trade" advocate and economic guru, Peter Drucker, justified the moral goal of this new campaign of the Market Crusades as a battle to "defang the nationalist monster." The problem with this justification was that no state armed force or repressive mechanism was to be "defanged" by the new trade arrangements— only governments' capacities to regulate corporations.[4] Indeed, the freedoms of transnational corporations to destabilize the lives of tens of millions of people, and to sell arms to keep them in line, significantly increased the conditions of terror to which most people were now subject.

Freeing Corporations from Workers' Demands

Criticism of the new order was dismissed as "defeatist," "scaremongering," and "fear of competition." Global market leaders were in a triumphal mood, for if private capital and corporations could be free to enter and exit from national markets and economies at will, they would be released from two historic millstones around their necks. The first millstone—and this point seemed overlooked even by the many critics of free trade—was the requirement for domestic demand to remain high if corporations were to be able to sell their goods. The long-ruling Keynesian strategy of government spending to stimulate the economy was, indeed, founded on this basic need for sufficient aggregate demand in the domestic economy to keep the wheels of private production and profits turning from business cycle to cycle. The Great Depression, after all, only ended with the initiation of the Second World War, during which massive infusions of government-created demand set the seized-up wheels of the private sector into motion again.

This dependency on government intervention in the market economy to sustain its aggregate demand seemed a fatal flaw in the system. It meant that, against all doctrine, the market required massive external expenditures by government to intervene in its operations to keep it from self-destructing. Marxian economists claimed that this was why capitalist economies had to maintain a state of actual or threatened war, in order to keep domestic demand high for capitalism's products, which would otherwise lack demand in periodic crises of "overproduction."

Economists and devotees to market doctrine have typically denied the existence of this requirement, even as private corporations have continuously called for government-created demand in the form of ever more costly military budgets, subsidies to foreign and domestic purchasers of high-tech products, and guaranteed markets for excess production. But none of the lavish government interventions on behalf of corporations made private enterprise less dependent on the effective demand of workers for their products, which in turn depended on the workers having jobs and money to buy the products. This was the age-old dilemma. If unemployment grew and/or wages fell, this was, on the one hand, a boon for private capital and employers. It reduced the price of labour and thus the costs of production. On the other hand, and with more serious long-term consequences, it meant a corresponding fall in aggregate demand. Business would, therefore, inevitably suffer in sales and profits, which could be ruinous, as the Great Depression had made clear. High employment and good wages might increase the cost of labour and even make it independent in negotiations. But this was the price that had to be paid to keep the business cycle turning and profitable, and it was paid for decades after the Second World War in what Eric Hobsbawm has called the "Golden Age."[5]

Borderless trade liberated transnational business from these ties to the domestic demand of domestic workers. Its new "freedom" quickly transformed the previously interdependent fabric of society's workers and employers. For if transnational capital and corporations could now enter and exit national markets at will, to go on selling their products and making profits they no longer needed to depend on their home society's domestic demand remaining high. If demand was falling off in one society due to increasing unemployment and lower wages—as in Mexico in 1995, when the jobless rate skyrocketed to 40 per cent of the total workforce while the wages of those left working plunged by 30 per cent—this would not be a problem for transnational private capital and corporations.[6] Under borderless trade regimes, with no final dependency on domestic demand for their sales and business profits, they could pull up stakes or export to other societies.

In such conditions, the "free flow of goods and capital across borders" would face no "impediments" and "barriers." It could, increasingly, move quickly in and out of societies at will. Even if only 40 per cent of the head-office society itself still had secure employment—as is the case today in First World societies such as Britain, the United States and Canada—there would still be enough secure income consumers across NAFTA, the European Union, and World Trade Organization countries organized under free trade agreements to sustain effective demand for any competitively priced product.[7] Corporations were freed from the pinch of any society's economic problems, even though they might have caused these problems themselves by underinvestment, capital flight, or resource exhaustion. They no longer needed the full domestic demand of any one society or region, but could carry on profitably with ever more "global market opportunities" offered by other societies' now open markets. Keynesian "pump-prime" methods and other government interventions to sustain high employment in this or that society become obsolete in such conditions, at least for transnational business, which was freed from the requirements of the people formerly depended upon for purchasing power. This is a central, but unacknowledged, consequence of the new borderless trade.

The implications of such a decoupling of transnational corporations from local societies were shattering for the life-security of ordinary people, but were ideal for maximizing the revenues of private corporations. All the old arguments to employers, such as "you must pay your workers well enough so that their demand remains high enough to buy your products" or "government employees and income-security plans create consumers in the market" or "government intervention is required here to stimulate demand" or "what will come of our society if you do not invest in it as you increase your profits?" are no longer plausible constraints on corporate market rationality. Revenue-maximizing corporations can exit and enter national markets at will. Millions of consumers around the world could still bear sufficient aggregate demand to buy lower-priced products, even though more and more people in more and more societies might no longer have steady, well-paying employment, and even though countless millions might be homeless and starving. What in the market value system would require a corporation to spend its privately earned capital on resolving these external misfortunes? What in the market's moral ordering would not affirm this new, borderless freedom from social costs and responsibilities as still a "limitless business opportunity"?

Freeing Corporations from Governments

The other ancient millstone around the neck of transnational business enterprises was political. The political problem was that corporations were continuously being "held hostage" by "government regulations" and "big unions," which were allowed to "dictate their terms to business." "Big Government" and "Big Unions" were favoured code-words for these great obstacles to "market flexibility," but there were many variations on the theme: "government interferences in the market" and "union bosses," of course, but also "crushing tax burdens for business," "undisciplined political leaderships," "barriers against competition," "rigid labour costs," "narrow nationalism," "distortions of the market," "costly social programs," and "protectionist barriers," among others. The culture of complaint knows no more energetic and strident bearers than dominant market agents. This is why they are so hostile to others' complaining. It creates a glut, and thus a lower exchange value.

There seemed to be no end of barriers and impediments to business performing its moral vocation of "value-adding" and "creating wealth for society." The new free trade agreements in one swoop overcame this gauntlet of obstructions. No government big brother or union bosses could stand in the way once the deals were in place. If those opponents resisted, investment could move elsewhere with no problem, and the markets of the world were open for the taking. That was why a new phrase now entered the corporate vocabulary: "inevitable adjustment."

All government activities that "get in the way of business" require three bases of leverage. First, governments must have the legal jurisdiction to regulate or to enter into agreements with private corporations. Governments cannot, for example, normally regulate private corporations in other countries (although, in a rare exception, the U.S. government imposes laws on branch-plants to restrict foreign trade with resistant societies, such as Cuba). Governments must be empowered by law, for example, to govern or to regulate or to impose contractual requirements on foreign corporations operating in their countries. As sovereign states they have traditionally always had this legal capacity. This power cannot be "left to the marketplace" if societies are to have any effective representation of their common interests, for which the market has no buyers. Lacking any other enduring mechanism whereby to protect the public interest against the very different, private interests of transnational corporations, societies are dependent on public authority. Governments alone possess the institutional base to represent the common interest in an organized, sustained way, whether or not they actually do this. Postmodern slogans like "liberating civil society from the state" or "no more government interference" merely promote the corporate agenda of replacing public authority in a masked way.

If, then, a democratic government's powers to negotiate conditions of market access and resource ownership with transnational corporations is abolished by a free trade regime, something very important has been lost to that society: its ability to govern itself in the common interest of its people against powerful special interests not linked to that society. A society becomes to that extent "open to business" in a way it had not counted on. Its government no longer has the powers or the jurisdiction to impose democratic or life-requirements on transnational businesses. The corporations, in turn, are obliged to seek lower costs and standards of wages, lower working conditions, and lower environmental protection as a matter of "market competitiveness."

Transnational trade agreements in this manner provided transnational corporations with freedom from accountability to societies and elected governments. That was, indeed, the central point of the agreements, as business-funded organs such as the Fraser Institute publicly declared. The Institute's CEO assured us: *"A trade deal simply limits the extent to which government may respond to its citizens."* That is, "free trade" frees corporations and investment capital from the "limits" of democratic process. Accordingly, the FTA and NAFTA specify in great detail the ways in which society was no longer permitted to require of internationally mobile corporations anything in return for their access to resources and markets.[8] Whatever the citizens of a society or their government might decide in the way of proper returns for their natural resources, infrastructures and markets were now overridden by the new transnational trade agreements.

For instance, it was formerly the case that a government could require a foreign multinational selling its goods in domestic markets to invest in that country in return for tariff-free access. This was the nature of the Canada-U.S. Auto Pact. Although FTA and NAFTA advocates flagrantly misrepresented this arrangement of job-creating, managed trade as "free trade," it was in practice the opposite: It set terms for foreign corporations selling in the domestic market, namely the creation of jobs in exchange for access to this home market. The new trade regimes prohibited all such arrangements. After the U.S.-Canada Auto Pact had been grandfathered, corporations were freed by these trade regulations from all "performance requirements" whatever. Right of access to other societies' markets was conferred unconditionally. The condition that they created jobs or invested their profits back into these societies was now illegal.

This revolutionary new arrangement suited all transnationally mobile corporations, wherever their head office might be located. It effectively freed them from society. They were no longer accountable to their workers, their environments, or anything else, but solely to "value-added to their shareholders." Commercial interest was to be free of any social responsibility and, following market self-maximization principles, transnational corporations were understandably pleased with the new global free trade. All this was predictable given the value program of the corporate market. The market's main players were placed above electoral control and could fire workforces, capture domestic markets with cheaper mass products, and mine foreign natural resources as they pleased. The rights of a society's people to count on investment or employment or a stable market were now null and void.

In return for this giveaway of untold billions of domestic market demand and abdication of government responsibility to legislate on behalf of its citizens' interests in employment, the societies involved in these free trade agreements received nothing but more transnational commodities to buy, if they could pay. Indeed, they were prohibited from seeking in the future to negotiate back any of these rights. Only the right of each society's corporations to buy and sell across borders was now recognized as binding; and only the corporations received the unheard of new entitlement: equal rights of citizenship in all societies to own or control everything in them.[9] What formerly belonged to the sovereign rights of a citizen body of a country—its natural resources, assets, built heritage, infrastructures, and markets—was now open, free of any requirement or trade-off, to any foreign business investor or corporation covered under the new trade regimes. They could buy, access, exploit—or abandon—any of these social means of existence at will. This new blanket condition was known as the "right to national treatment." Having secured from the courts and governments the rights of the human person, transnational corporations now received rights of a supercitizenship that crossed borders: the right to buy or sell or remove any society's natural or produced goods with no condition except the price. No foreign army in the past ever won such a blanket entitlement without unconditional surrender. But here domestic political parties funded by corporations instituted these rights of conquest as an act of "necessity" and—note the phrase—"freedom from protectionism." In this way, former sovereign countries could be truthfully said to have become, in effect, occupied societies through the instrument of corporate trade treaties.

In abolishing the jurisdictions of elected governments to protect the economic interests of their peoples, the new transnational trade regimes commanded many concessions, prohibiting governments from preferentially purchasing the goods of their own countries and preventing limits on foreign ownership of the domestic economy. They prohibited public ownership of any business area that might "directly or indirectly" reduce the "reasonably expected" value of a foreign investment. They prohibited society's ownership control over its own natural resources in preference for the needs of its own members.[10] And, finally, they prohibited, as did GATT—later the World Trade Organization—the application to foreign imports of protective standards for workers, health, or the environment, even in cases in which the processes of producing these imported products were criminally unlawful within the home society.[11]

In all of these abdications of former jurisdiction over the economic and life-interests of their own societies, no government or society received any compensating power or right in return—except to buy more commodities from corporations. "Jobs! Jobs! Jobs!" were incessantly proclaimed, but hundreds of thousands of former transnational corporate jobs soon disappeared in every society involved.[12] As we have seen, the promise of "jobs, jobs, jobs" is invariably made at no cost when governments deliver subsidies, tax-cuts, incentives—or here, entire societies—to corporate control. But since the promises of more jobs have no contractual basis, and performance requirements are ruled out, they can be safely ignored once they have served their purpose. Societies in this manner play the rube. Having superseded the authority of national, provincial, and municipal governments on all matters covered by these international trade agreements, the big business sector was now, in effect, society's new sovereign. Free trade regimes removed the barriers with which societies had previously been legally empowered to defend themselves.

This is why this new social sovereignty was so desirable to corporate agents despite the opposition of social majorities. The trade regimes were, with ruling-party comlplicity, a transnational *coup d'état*. Their prescriptions replaced democratically responsible government by a corporation-driven system of regulatory decrees permanently overriding the rights of sovereign governments to protect any portion of domestic markets, home control of natural resources, or national ownership of companies. Also proscribed was the right to make any public investment that would result in a "lost opportunity to profit from a planned investment" for a foreign corporation.[13]

The second basis of leverage that public authority possesses to ensure the accountability of private business is the power to tax profitable business on behalf of the public interest in a manner consistent with the obligations of citizenship. As we have seen, this revenue base to pay for public health, welfare, education, and other areas of the common good has been redistributed to the market by manufactured government debts, which required more and more government revenues to go to paying the high-interest demands of banks, as well to ratchet down taxes for corporations and the rich. This redistribution of wealth to the already wealthy, in turn, more than tripled and quintupled government debts in the United States and Canada respectively, a "debt crisis" that was, again in turn, the reason given to dismantle social infrastructures in these countries. The new instrument of free trade provided the third flank of attack on the civil commons of public education, social assistance to the poor and unemployed, old age pensions, universal health care, and protection of the environment. It did not take much foresight to know in advance that private capital and transnational business operations in a borderless world of free capital movement would no longer be confined to any one national or regional tax jurisdiction. The trade agreements guaranteed this transnational leverage by enforceable law. If taxes were perceived to be "excessive" in one jurisdiction, therefore, it followed that business could move to another society or region where tax rates were "more competitive." This "market discipline" on taxation ensured that taxes on transnational capital would drop over time to lower and lower levels, led by zero tax rates in free trade zones. Indeed, replacing taxes by "incentives to invest" would increasingly be required of societies if they were to "effectively compete to attract capital" in the "tough new international marketplace." This pattern of exchanging taxation for "incentives" to private corporations and capital has occurred across all jurisdictions involved in free trade agreements, with no apparent limit to this redistributive trend. Corporate taxes are globally now a fraction of normal wage-earner rates, and subsidies from taxpayers to "encourage investment" have tended to grow larger. Only a universal, minimum corporate tax standard can prevent this plundering of the civic fabric, but market governments do not discuss such a remedy.

In many places, as we have seen, private capital and corporations pay little or no taxes at all and are, to the contrary, net tax recipients. Here again, free trade or, more accurately stated, free-capital arrangements are "free" in more than one sense. In addition to the freedom to move across borders with no need to negotiate for access to other societies' markets, they have instituted a global pattern of freeing private corporations and investors from tax obligations as well, and giving them, besides, a wide assortment of publicly paid-for subsidies worth countless hundreds of billions of dollars in the United States alone (see chapter 6, "No Free Lunches"). By thus enabling transnational investors and corporations to become free-riders on the public purse, governments reduced themselves to servants to the demands of business—increasingly supplying, at ever lower cost to investors and corporations, road, power, and sewage infrastructures, armed force property protection inside and outside the country, debt-collection services to money-lenders, export subsidies, routes and diplomatic trade offices, and ever new instruments for subsidizing industry's operations. To serve transnational business has in this "new reality" become the overriding function of the state. In symbolic representation of this new service function, heads of state can now be observed, as with Prime Minister Chrétien's "Team Canada," devoting their public offices to soliciting business deals abroad from human-rights violating and genocidal states on behalf of home-office corporations.

The third and final basis of responsible government's power to govern private capital and corporations is familiar enough: the sovereign power to institute regulations and laws to prevent physical harm and damages to domestic citizens and their natural environments. The conflict between the private capital and corporate drive to maximize money profits for themselves, on the one hand, and the larger society's rights to the health and safety of its citizens' lives and their environments, on the other hand, is a profound and market-ignored issue. But this remaining capacity of government to govern on behalf of the common interest has also been ruled out by current trade regimes.

To begin with, the dismantling of government's domestic regulatory powers for the protection of the life of its citizens and environment in the "race to the bottom" of corporate cost-reduction puts increasing pressure on societies to lower their regulatory standards in order to be "cost-competitive." This propensity to drive down life-protective standards to lower denominators by a process of competitive cost-cutting can be observed in even the discount store next door in thousands of North American towns. Walmart Inc. is the world's largest and richest retailer. Its chain of factory-style compounds now reaches across twenty thousand neighbourhoods and cities, and across national borders, and it grows in sales revenues at the rate of 21 per cent per year.[14] It sells to U.S. and Canadian consumers everywhere clothes manufactured at rates as low as five to eight cents an hour by indentured child labourers in Asia.[15] It carries on its free trade business beneath rows of stars-and-stripes signs in its U.S. stores, which are emblazoned with "Made in the U.S.A.!." This commercial freedom from civilized standards is now enshrined in FTA and NAFTA.

This pattern of no-standard trade across borders is now worldwide. "In one Asian factory," which exports its goods under the global trade protection rules of GATT, "children as young as 5 are forced to work from 6 in the morning until 7 at night for less than 20 cents a day."[16] The problem of universalizing life-destructive norms by the "free circulation of goods and capital across borders," with no minimum standards of civilization to govern it, was not, however, altogether unnoted by the architects of these trade agreements. In the case of NAFTA, they included a provision to acknowledge that the problem might exist, but ensured that nothing could be done about it. As the Canadian Centre for Policy Alternatives reports: "The NAFTA provision which prohibits member countries from lowering their standards to attract investment is virtually unenforceable, since complaints about failures to abide by it cannot be taken to the NAFTA dispute resolution mechanism."[17]

The CCPA adds that even with respect to the safety standards of foods crossing borders—the one area in which there is some recognition of norms to protect interests other than those of transnational business activities—NAFTA prescribes no minimum standards, and any established domestic standards higher than what the NAFTA regime allows are prohibited from being applied to imported products. The *Codex Alimentarius* is the new maximum standard of life-protective regulation that is permitted by the new trade sovereign. The *Codex Alimentarius*, not surprisingly, was written by a UN group dominated by corporate food, chemical and agribusiness interests—and currently allows levels of DDT and other long-banned agrochemicals fifty times higher than those permitted in the United States.[18] Any national standard stricter than this is "presumed not to comply." Here again, international market prescriptions operate in a way that downgrades domestic regulatory standards to the lowest common denominator.

The principal way in which this downgrading of social standards is achieved is by the long-term eroding process of cost undercutting. Where government regulations do remain in place over the domestic market operations of private corporations, they are made vulnerable to the price competition of low-cost and low-standard zones, whose products cross borders "free of tariff or non-tariff barriers." In this way, commodities manufactured by forced child labour, by people working seventy hours a week, by a workforce without the protection of human rights or the right to organize, or by methods of production with no health and safety protections can cross borders at "competitive costs for consumers" with "no obstacle to their free circulation," including no labels that designate their method of production. Similarly, products manufactured in jurisdictions and zones with little no environmental protection against damaging emissions, toxic chemicals, ecological degradation, or rapid resource depletion are "unfettered" to move across borders to places in which they can be sold at "advantageous" prices.

In such a system, domestic regulations to protect the rights and living conditions of workers or to preserve the environment from poisoning and destruction become "unaffordable." It is, therefore, rational in this global market regime for private corporations to stop investing in life-protective civil societies. A skill advantage to support such investment may exist for a time in certain developed regions, such as Germany or Canada, but there is no guarantee that this advantage will persist. Life-protective regulations are perceived in market doctrine as "structural rigidities" or "regulatory obstacles." These, say the policy-leaders of the doctrine, "discourage investors" with "a non-competitive investment environment." In this value program, more money for investors is a goal that *a priori* overrules the worth of human or environmental life.

By its predictable sequence of outcomes, irresistible pressure is put on societies and their governments to reduce their standards to the cost denominators of the "tough new international marketplace." There are "harsh realities" in this new competitive order, because "the market will punish higher costs for producers." Governments thus succumb to "the new reality." Indeed, their leaders are handsomely rewarded by election financing, corporate and press support, and directorships for their "deregulation initiatives" and for "getting society on track." In rather rapid succession, society's life-protective regulations are singled out for attack as "preventing business competitiveness." Thus government regulations that protect workers' rights to collective bargaining and union status, to safety-inspected working conditions, to minimum wages and compensation for job-caused diseases and injuries, or to security of basic income in conditions under which workers' jobs have been lost due to no fault of their own—all these "restrictions" on the market are attacked as "a burden on employers" or "a barrier to investment in our economy." Consequently, they are ratcheted down by "legislative reforms," "deregulation," and "restructuring" to make the economy "more cost-efficient." No form of human or environmental life is, therefore, left secure from further "adjustments" to "adapt to rapidly changing global market conditions."

At the same time, demands for business "self-regulation" and "voluntary restraints" become increasingly aggressive. As the dismantling of long-evolved government protection of human and environmental life has been militantly pursued by "market revolutions" across the world, no standard of civilized life not useful to money investors has been deemed to "pay its way." Any people who or social institutions that do not pay their way within the market's money cycles, it follows, do not have the right to exist. If we do not "listen to what the market is telling us" about the need to "re-engineer" and "deregulate" resistant life-substance, private, mobile corporations will obey global-market norms of "more competitive conditions."

One might here ask whether a regime that is undermining the conditions of life itself is really "saving on costs." On the contrary, such cost-reductions for business are costly beyond calculation for both civil and environmental life. But such a question cannot arise within this value program. "Costs" are costs to business in the balance sheet of its profit-ledgers, no more and no less. "Efficiency" is what reduces business input of money to each unit of revenue production, no more and no less. Life and life's requirements do not have a place in this value sequence.

The U.S. Republican-controlled Congress in 1995, for example, launched a full-scale attack on the federal government's national Environmental Protection Agency for "driving up the costs of doing business and endangering American competitiveness in the world." These new freedoms from "Big Government's regulatory nightmare" were unanimously justified by their corporate sponsors as "essential for America to compete in the new market conditions of global free trade."[19]

At the same time in Canada Bill 62, subtitled the "Regulatory Efficiency Act," was before Parliament, proposing to permit corporations to be exempt from established environmental legislation. Corporations were to be encouraged instead to create their own individually tailored schemes to comply with regulatory requirements. In Canada's wealthiest province, Ontario, the attack on environmental regulations was more along the slash-and-burn lines of free marketeers to the south. Just as the 1981 Reaganite policy of a 30 per cent tax cut to reduce the deficit had now worked its way north, so too had the idea of freedom to strip costly environmental protections, though it was now called the "Common Sense Revolution." Omnibus Bill 26 was passed in early 1996 and systematically dismantled twenty-five years of environmental legislation. It eliminated planning act regulations on commercial development of rural land, repealed legislation and support for toxic waste reduction and municipal garbage recycling, and prescribed new cost ceilings on municipal charges on developer corporations for installing infrastructures at public expense. It slashed Conservation Authority budgets by 70 per cent and allowed conservation areas to be sold off by municipalities whose own budgets had been simultaneously reduced by 20 to 60 per cent. The "Common Sense Revolution" also amended the Mining Act to relieve mining corporations from regulations ensuring environmental clean-ups and from the requirement to plan prevention of environmental hazards.[20] These and other blanket abdications of the government's remaining domestic jurisdictions were declared to be "necessary to reduce barriers to competitiveness" and to "cut costs and red tape for business." The job of the "new Common Sense Revolution," proclaimed the province's hotelier premier, was to "unlegislate, to unregulate, and to ungovern."[21] These words express a value program that is nihilist towards any social practice that does not put more money into the market.

By this overall pattern of displacing, definancing, and under-cutting public authority's capacities to serve the common interest, the "new world order" approaches an outcome not before seen. It inexorably uncouples the profit imperative from its obligations to life-requirements in any form—to host societies, to workforces, to peoples, to environments, even to the physical conditions of life upon which all depend.

In the "real world" of ensuring the health of quarterly profit statements, there is always more left in the world market's "limitless opportunities." Rootless, transnationally mobile money-demand can now enter and exit societies at will and with no barriers to its free appropriations and expansions. Life is the medium for turning money into more money with no "impediments" or "restrictions" left to fetter market freedom. The long-term of life does not exist for this value calculus. This is not a polemical point, but a condition of the regulating logic of this value paradigm.

In these new, borderless conditions of investment and trade, even the long-standing recourse of social populations to rebellion and revolt seems no longer to pose a threat, for the freedom of profit-seeking funds and corporations to move in and out of the world's societies provides them with security from social unrest. The global market's twenty-four-hour-a-day circuits of instant information-circulation make any hint of "political instability" an occasion for instant capital flight to "politically stable" investment zones. The problem is a global one, and so will be its solution. Slavery of the individual kind was global, we may recall, and it too came to an end by other than market means.

Rootless Investors and the Age of Disposable Life

In the moral vision of this advanced stage of the global market, the state's overriding purpose is to ensure that no social, political, or environmental impediment blocks "the free circulation of capital and goods." This is the new and universal norm for world civil society, a norm portrayed to all alike as "freedom."

It is a mistake to imagine, as social scientists and analysts have traditionally assumed, that this new order of the market system is amoral or can be understood in a "value-free" way. It is by its nature a moral absolutism. Its rules of prescription and obedience are backed up by armed forces across the world, and every society can soon face the financial threat of ruination by currency speculators for any deviation from the value program's demands. The global market system is a more totalized regime of prescribing how to live than any in history. Its sweeping demands are now imposed on societies around the world on a continuous, twenty-four-hour basis. Its threats and punishments for violations of its laws exceed in their severity the most punitive of theological fundamentalisms. There is no domain or level of existence over which the doctrine does not claim rightful authority. Even the movements of subatomic particles, the genetic codes of germ plasms, the information of human discovery, the unconscious regions of the id, and the reaches of human technology towards the stars are appropriated for money-profit rule. Any opposition to this rule is perceived as heresy and condemned as a threat to freedom.

The known degradation of the planet's air, waters, and soils by market processes and products; the usurpation of the world's climates by the emissions of its "cost-efficient" production; the destitution of rising numbers of children under its distributive rule; the daily extinction of long-evolved species by its resource-extraction methods; the loss of life-functions for ever more people by its unregulated laws of supply and demand: these results are each and all undeniable. But none is related back to the market's principles of value themselves.

Testimonies of belief in the "miracles" of the "invisible hand," on the contrary, proliferate in government and in the media. Prescriptions of "hard sacrifices" for the many are pronounced, justifying another "harsh punishment" of a capital-deserted country, stripping another "entitlement" from the poor, demanding another "breaking of the bonds of dependency" of those without the means to live. How is it possible for such a system to self-correct?

We have seen through history a recurrent tendency of possessing classes to impose regimes that yield them ever more disproportionate concentrations of wealth and power, and we have watched these value orders again and again degenerate into self-idolizing dogma and life-devastation. The difference in this case is that the regime's principles of avarice are universally instituted as received laws of nature and are not hedged in by any socially recognized limit. To say that this regime is "out of control" is merely descriptive. It abhors any alternative to its rule and denies accountability to responsible government itself. Rather, governments are accountable to corporate courts in new corporate trade treaties. The global market formation has come to program its closed-system prescriptions as a final, global solution precisely as its failures become overwhelming. But the "end of history" solution it prescribes escalates the damages caused by its value system. For every problem it faces, it now prescribes more of the same. If a society's life-fabric is unravelled by market prescriptions, as we have seen from Nicaragua and Russia to Zambia and New Zealand, this only means not enough "market solutions" have been tried. Therefore, societies must be more completely "opened to the market." Now corporations are being invited to write school curricula, trade in pollution credits, and manage prisons and hospitals.

The freedom of borderless private capital to become more borderless private capital, ad infinitum, does not, however, resolve any of the problems it causes. As it becomes ever more unfettered from the life-requirements and limits of the societies and environments it uses as temporary instruments for its self-expansion, it is by trade decree unanswerable to any authority but itself. As long as money becomes more money for money investors, all is well. It is a closed value paradigm. Only reiteration of its pattern can register as success, whether what accompanies it is life-depredation or not. One must stay the course through the illusions of life-loss. The victories over social "barriers" and "protectionist walls," over "resistant populations" and "backward economies," over "nationalist rigidities" and "communist expansionism in the Third World" were not easily or quickly won in this grand progress of freedom. It was a war of many battles and obstacles. Franz Hinkelammert graphically describes the process from the standpoint of its negations in his trenchant summary of "the victory of the total market" over resistant Third World peoples in the late 1970s and 1980s.

> National-security dictatorships emerged which were different from the traditional type of military dictatorship in Latin America. The new dictatorships were highly ideological and even metaphysical in comparison to the traditional dictatorships that simply supported the status quo. The national-security dictatorships defined a new relationship with civil society and the state based on military power supported by systematic state terrorism.... Although these dictatorships often operated with a "democratic" facade ... they imposed by force an economic system that abandoned any consensus with the people.

> In the name of anti-statism, the national security dictatorships performed in a double sense. On the one hand, they destroyed civil society as it had emerged in previous decades. They destroyed the popular movements in all their manifestations—trade unions, co-operatives, neighbourhoods. They also destroyed the social organization stemming from the agrarian reforms in the countryside.... On the other hand, they destroyed the activities of the state itself that had accompanied and mediated this civil society i.e. the ability of the state to devise an economic strategy and the health and education systems. All of this was carried out in the name of "dismantling the state" and of "privatizing" its functions...The new state was a state of violent imposition ... inspired by the politics of the total market. The new state was an enemy of civil society, which it reduced to private enterprise operating in terms of market relations.[22]

The total market objective here is clearly similar in the structure of its outcome to what was later applied to the First World. The civil commons, which existed as counterbalance to and refuge from the private-profit demands of the market, was, here as well, rapidly defunded and dismantled to leave only unmediated market relations. The non-profit sector of public health, education, social assistance to the poor, universal old-age pensions, environmental protections, community transit, and public broadcasting and culture was definanced at an escalating rate of financial and program cutbacks and axings. Very little remained intact within just a few years of this "market revolution" across the globe.

Given the conditions of "developed societies," there was no need for domestic death-squads and armed force dictatorship to prevail. The method of government definancing terrorized in another way and was no less effective. Instead of attacking popular movements, it disemployed. Instead of killing, it removed alternative means of life-support. Instead of anticommunist justifications, it attacked "government debts." Free-capital trade regimes did the rest. Nothing that resisted the total market had any leg of financial support to stand on. Only what assisted free and expanded capital circulations and flows was any longer acceptable in "the new reality."

All this "re-engineering" and "restructuring" originated in an underlying value code presupposed as first truth. It was not a massive coincidence that its revolution of "world society" occurred in over one hundred nations at roughly the same time. In the end, none of its socially destructive effects was perceived as undesirable by market crusaders, any more than dead bodies on the fields of battle. The "austerities," "sacrifices," and "shock treatments" were first relentlessly demanded, and then celebrated as "paying for past excesses," all leading to a promised after-paradise of "prosperity and freedom." The destruction of the evolved civil commons across most of the First World was a policy triumph for market doctrine and practice that almost matched in its singlemindedness the victory over external communism. The destruction of social entitlements and alternatives to the cash-nexus was a good in itself. The consequences to people's lives did not matter to the militant triumphalism of the doctrine. It confirmed it with non-market costs. Consequences to people's lives do not matter in this calculus unless they are costs to stockholders. They do not register. The objective is to transform reality into full compliance with the demands of the market, and beyond that this program cannot comprehend.

Once the walls of "socialism within" began as well to be dismantled, the frenzy for ever more "discipline" and "harsh measures" continued into the last years of the millennium. For example, in the relatively evolved civil society of Canada (identified from 1995 to 1997 by the United Nations as the best place in the world to live in), pro-business governments defunded the social infrastructures that had been a basis of this achievement as rapidly as possible. This stampede to dismantle the country's civil commons was incited by the central bank's manufacture of a privatized public debt, along with multibillion-dollar tax redistributions of public wealth to corporations and capital investors. Once the debt was thus set out of control, the transnational corporate sector struck with all the resources at its disposal to ensure that bankrupted governments were made accountable to its agenda.

Directed by transnational corporate lobbies such as the Business Council on National Issues, publicly preached to daily in the media by tax-free think-tanks of market fundamentalists like the corporation-funded Fraser and C.D. Howe institutes, nipped at the heels by small-business ideologues who were unable to distinguish their own interests from those of multinational corporations, and indoctrinated around the clock by the chain media, politicians imagined they were showing how "competitive" they were by an all-fronts stripping of the country's world-leading public sector, which had taken over half a century to build. Within a few years of "market restructuring" and "tough decisions," poverty rates were up one-third and sharply rising, over a million children were eating from food banks, a stunning 41.2 per cent of families with parents under thirty were living in poverty, and all social assistance and higher education financing had been scaled back dramatically by the federal government.[23] All these moments of the market revolution were obscured in public pronouncements and reports concerning how everyone must compete harder against the world.

The key to comprehending this extraordinary corporate revolution by means of proxy governments is to understand that its global uncoupling of private money-demand from life requirements is perfectly in accord with neoclassical market doctrine. It is the freedom of private corporate and investors from accountability to any objective but maximal holdings of share value. This is the global market's ultimate touchstone of truth, and it is enough to ensure that it is happening—whatever else is—to prove success. That people or environments might increasingly be subjugated, devastated, or transformed into waste by this end-game is not an issue that can enter the gates of what is designated as "the real world."

If the world's money-demand is rapidly redistributed by the global market to those who already have the most, some might see a problem of inequality. But for the market value system, this consequence is what the market has rightfully ordained by its voluntary exchanges and invisible hand of adjusting supply to demand. The pattern is thus proclaimed as good. Canada and the world, says Peter Cook to the members of his business audience, who know him as a man of recognized moderation, is "clearly in the transitional business of reapportioning national income so that a larger share goes to corporations and less to wage earners. This is a fundamentally necessary process."[24]

It is "necessary" because it increases accumulations of money-demand to be invested for still more by corporations and shareholders. They, in turn, demand more so that their investment returns are "competitive." The investment returns must be competitive, in further turn, so that the corporations "can continue in business in an ever more cost-conscious global economy." Wages to workers as a share of production costs must, in final turn, decrease "to compete effectively in the new trade environment." Every step of the pressure downwards on people's means of life follows from the value calculus of market freedom. The inevitable outcome is more money in money cycles and less in life-cycles. There is, declares this doctrine of freedom, "no alternative."

The system in this manner turns in a closed circle. Excluding all concerns but its own "value-adding" imperative, it can no longer relate to any other reality than the self-expansion of money circuits. All consequences to global life-organization beyond this value round are ruled out. If increasing numbers of people are paid less than a living wage in this system of redistribution, that is because the "market is only prepared to pay this price to wage-earners in the present conditions of the market." If there are ever increasing numbers of people without any resources or jobs to live on, this is because unions, minimum wages, or other "excessive costs" to capital "are distorting market supply." If none of these "restrictions to the flow of capital investment" exist, workers are without employment because of their "unwillingness to work," "lack of initiative," or "poor training." If they can no longer be blamed for the fall in corporate demand for labour, the gods must be angry and only more "freedom to investors" and "incentives to invest" must be needed to bring in the private capital that societies require to survive. If all this still fails, the society "has not adapted to the market" and "must pay the harsh price for its inability to adjust."

The 1990s program of the U.S. Republican Party's Congressional Majority, its Contract with America, was an exemplar of this pattern of moral deduction. It was soon imitated across the world by "market reform" politicians with the "political will to make the necessary changes." Thus under the Contract's rubric of "The Job Creation and Wage Enhancement Act," the market doctine's predictable solution was to ensure that private capital was given the incentive it needed of lower taxes.[25] The Contract with America did not, however, guarantee a single new job or the rise of a single wage. It did not ensure in any way against the still further decline of both jobs and wages. On the contrary, the past record of "job creation" and "wage enhancement" under previous Republican tax transfers to the rich was followed by opposite consequences. After the Reagan administration's 30 per cent tax cut in the early 1980s, salaries and wages fell by 13 per cent, and 17 million jobs disappeared. Meanwhile, America's poverty rate rose by 28 per cent during the same 1981-88 period.[26] None of these facts deterred market leaders, politicians, or the media from declaring the opposite as certitudes on a daily basis.

The very same program was exported north to Canada fifteen years later, with the same promises of "more economic activities" and "jobs for Ontarios." All that such proposals were geared to ensure was the growth and development of the money cycle, like the 36 per cent rise in the U.S. stock markets the year of the Contract with America. Even when supporters of the other party proclaimed the "social irresponsibility" of Republicans, their own presidential candidate, Bill Clinton, "saved" medical care for the aged by slashing assistance to them by $124 billion rather than by the Republicans' "heartless" $158 billion.[27] In this way, the consensus of the political parties to reduce support for human life to increase it for money profits was demonstrated beneath appearances of political contest.

No national leader in a market economy yet conceives that developments might call for reform to the market's value program. The panacea of all ills remains the "freer circulation of goods and capital," whatever its harms to life-structures might be. Value in this system reposes in a higher and inviolable law: the money price that those with money are willing to pay, and the "value-adding" to money rounds that these paid prices put into effect. Conversely, there is no disvalue except what may interfere with this higher law, and no cost-money that its market players have not spent by market choice.

It follows from this program of social purpose that the best society is the society that is most free in its money exchanges and its capital circulations and flows. Thus, as the Fraser Institute and other institutional crusaders for the final solution advised us before Hong Kong's 1997 crash, the very best society in the world to be alive in was Hong Kong. Here market discipline was exemplary. Social welfare assistance was extended to the poor and disabled at the price of one-quarter of a month's rent for a one-room flat.[28] The destitute lived in box cages. Hong Kong had "the fundamentals right." Society's wherewithal was scrupulously confined to making the market's cycles of money reproduction and growth ever larger. But what such a delinked value program can never see is that decoupled money flows that can leave any society overnight are not what any society needs to renew its life.

Market guru Peter Drucker takes as a given that the structure of behaviour of this new order overrules the requirements of life as its inner *telos*. He prescribes the new order as the law societies must live by: "Every country and every industry will have to learn," he counsels, "that the first question is not *is this measure desirable*? but *what will be the impact on the country's competitive position in the world economy.*"[29] "Competitive position" refers, as we know, to the rate of money profit that can be made from private investment in this vehicle or country in comparison to rival vehicles or countries. Countries rank low or high in "competitive position," therefore, in relation to how much money profit can be extracted from them. In this competition to maximize money returns for borderless private corporations and investors, it is an error to conceive of the arrangement here as an inevitable fact. It is a value system, imposed by absolute commands. It tells us how we must think and act as individuals and societies. Its rules are prescribed to the entire world. Failure to conform to them is, we are daily reminded, subject to the harshest punishments.

The World Bank, for example, has explained that this value system must override all traditional and codified human rights as a higher good. For if we trade and make profits with countries that violate human rights, no matter how grossly, conditional on their respecting human rights in the production of their exports to us, this places limits on "the freedom of capital to invest." This, the Bank is certain, is bad in the market's epistemology of right and wrong. For the same reason, "minimum wages" and "unions" are just as bad as "linkages of human rights to trade." They are all to be repudiated, because they limit the "free transactions of the market" and its "unimpeded circulations of goods and capital," which are the obligatory co-ordinates for regulating the world.[30] International trade agreements now codify this value framework as overriding law.

Traditional moral sensibility may find such narrow economic absolutism repugnant. But to evade moral debate, economists of the market creed have learned to proclaim the "value neutrality" of "science," which makes the doctrine's commands akin to laws of nature. A doctrine becomes a *fanaticism* when it rationalizes away whatever damage it causes as necessary and inevitable.

Traditional professions such as law and medicine might seem to afford us some critical reflection on this structure of value judgement, but its members are by and large too busy at the market game of maximizing revenues for their firms to see beyond it. Lawyers are valued for the billings or bottom-line profits they produce. Health care for profit is amongst the fastest growing corporate oligopolies, replacing more efficient and universally accessible public systems.[31] Even public education is funded for its money returns, as "human capital." Students and societies "invest in training for the market," an investment increasingly paid for by students themselves as the next generation is converted en masse to the effective role of debt-servants to banks. Unions that led the century-old struggle for the civil commons of social security, public health care, old-age pensions, minimum wages, and workplace safety are assailed as "distorters of the labour market" and a "barrier to capital investment." Those who still have secure jobs in the age of "flexible employment" are conditioned to presuppose that their future security is dependent on investing their savings in the global stock market driving the wheels of the system.

"No one else will look after you," the financial managers of the market's private mutual and pension funds now warn, "you must look after yourself." The world is being rapidly transformed into a competition of all against all for enough money to live. But in predictable accord with internal market mechanisms, ever more of the money ends in ever fewer hands.[32] The collective security of a human community in which each supports all and is supported in turn, a community evolved over millennia, is now replaced by the closed reproduction and growth cycles of money. Care is allocated in accordance with how much money one has to demand it.

The planetary environment loses one million acres of rainforest a week. The world's oceans are ploughed until life is depleted or desertified. The air is filled with lung-choking combusted fossil fuels, and earth-surrounding gases accumulate, deforming climates and raising ocean levels. Hundreds of millions of animals replace forests and farmlands, to be slaughtered for meat that increases human disease. The world's creatures and habitats are destroyed for the sake of commercial products that serve no vital life-need. All of these consequences proceed in perfect accord with the value program of the global market. The underlying causal pattern that joins is not recognized, for such connections are ruled out of view.

If there is life that resists the program, it is deemed to be an offence against order and freedom. This was the fate of the Movement for the Survival of the Ogoni People in Nigeria, who rallied against the conversion of their lives, their community, and their ancestral lands into oil-pools, destroyed fields and villages, and profits for Shell Oil. Their non-violent resistance was declared an "inciting of disturbances." Their internationally recognized leader, writer Ken Saro-Wiwa, was hanged with his colleagues, and no country in the world boycotted the flow of oil.[33]

It is sometimes thought that such barbarity is an exception. But this view overlooks the wider circuitry of the system. For in the centre of the global market's most prosperous countries, massive multibillion-dollar government subsidies and contracts finance the corporate armaments industry and its downstream death count of 1,000 soldiers and 5,000 civilians per day, every day, for a total of over two million deaths per year long after the Cold War had ended.[34]

Alongside these direct campaigns against the life-substance, "labour-replacing technologies" and "restructurings" separate people from their livelihoods around the clock—41.7 million jobs in the United States alone since 1980.[35] Because the value of labour is a disvalue for employers insofar as it increases their money costs, it follows that employment should be reduced as rapidly as business and government "downsizing" can manage. The "New Master Class in Radical Change," as *Fortune* magazine enthused in admiration of the new order, can triumphally "shed over 200,000 employees [in a single corporation] while its net income nearly tripled, and its market value increased by $67.6 billion."[36]

A non-government, British research study disclosed in 1995 that 30 per cent of the people in the leading U.K. market economy are now "unemployed or economically inactive," and another 30 per cent work in jobs that are "structurally insecure." That adds up to 60 per cent of the members of the "booming British economy."[37]

Conscious, planned policies of corporate workforce shedding here and elsewhere combine with deliberate central-bank policies to raise interest rates and unemployment to a "natural rate" whenever employment gains are deemed to have "overheated the economy." These policies are, significantly, advocated by the very market crusaders who blame the unemployed for their unemployment.

In Canada at the end of 1995, the moderator of the United Church responded to the sacrificial cult and called on her membership "to stop a growing war against the poor in our society." But the national newspaper had its defenders of doctrine ready to rout any such resistance. The moderator lectures from "The Comfortable Pulpit," rebuked *The Globe and Mail*, owned by Canada's richest man. She should keep, it was suggested, her criticisms of the market's punishments to herself.[38]

The likely outcomes of this release of ever more jobless populations from their bonds of dependency on food and lodging are quite clear. The proven consequences are destitution and breakdown, malnourishment, disease, and permanent mental retardation.[39] But this too is not a problem for those who trust in the solutions of the market. There are well-known laws of supply and demand. Effective demand, or money willing to be spent, is the ultimate arbiter of the world's reproduction of life, and so it must rule in the production and distribution of goods if we are to remain "a free society."

Ronald Reagan advised us when his presidency began of this value's system's final ethical goal: "What I want to see above all else is that this country remains a country where some can always get rich. That is the thing we have and that must be preserved."[40] A few years after his presidency had ended, and after the Cold War had been triumphally won against "the forces of darkness," this is what the secretary-general of Amnesty International, Pierre Sané, had to say as to the progress of humanity since then:

> Four years ago, when the Berlin Wall came tumbling down, we were promised a bright new future. But far from prosperity, we see even more people plunged into poverty and despair and a quarter of the world starving. One in nine people live as refugees.... In every region of the world, it seems that human rights are being rolled back ... fuelled by economic policies which make the rich richer and the poor poorer.[41]

Seeing through the Rich to the Value Program

"The vile maxim of the masters of mankind," remarked Adam Smith, is "all for ourselves and nothing for others."[42] Here, interestingly, both the founder of free market theory and the revolutionary Karl Marx agree. But Marx, following the scientistic bent of post-Smith economics, did not like to acknowledge moral judgements in his scientific work. He did not distinguish between closed value programs and "iron economic laws." He too accepted the internal mechanics of the unregulated capitalism he studied as propelled by "necessity." Thus he declared his project in *Capital* as the quest to uncover "the economic law of motion of modern society."[43] By adopting the necessitarian language of Newtonian physics, the role of chosen values in Marx's explanatory model is downgraded to an element of the "ideological superstructure," which, in turn, is seen as determined by the economic substructure. Marx did not recognize that a social value system is the inherited and developing social decision-structure through which every decision of the market system itself is made. When it rigidifies and totalizes into a closed program of preference-sequences, its internally determining structure is not, as market economists and Marxists suppose, a set of iron laws leading to "inevitable" results. It is a system of sclerotic dogma regulating economic organization, a system that has come to be obeyed as laws of nature.

We see all the symptoms of a closed value program within the global market. Its most striking feature is the limitless inequality it generates in its outcomes. Such effects may seem caused by the rich, who appropriate the most payoffs. But beneath the rich is the social construct that they are creatures of. Certainly, dominant market agents do resort to extraordinary lengths and viciousness to defend and protect this social construct at others' life-expense. This is what Smith himself saw as "vile," and there can be no plausible argument against his moral judgement. But it would be a mistake to conclude that this behaviour explains the value program it *expresses*, or that the liquidation of its vilest standard-bearers will end its hold on society. The problem runs deeper, and it is seated in a deformed structure of motivation.

All normal people are governed by their own life-interests, or they could not survive or flourish as embodied beings. The disorder of "self-interest" only arises when there are "surplus interests" that the self seeks at others' expense, interests that are not enabling to the life-vitality of the self-maximizer. In the market value program, these purely selfish interests have no limit of legitimate aspiration. As we have seen, a few hundred billionaires in the global market now have more money wealth than the total annual life income of almost half the world's population. These billionaires demand still more by the requirement of the market's investment sequence, and there is in this value system no market principle that can regard this as other than successful growth, natural and law-like in its compulsion to multiply further. But the disorder here is far beyond that of an individual agent or agents, however vile their particular character formations. They are "playing by the rules of the game," and it is the structure of this game's purpose that needs correction.

The disorder is now deeper in the fabric of society than either Smith or Marx ever theorized. It is not only the character of Smith's "vile master class" that is dismantling the world's social and environmental life-organization. It is, more deeply, an institutionalized decision-system of value that is at work, within which the temporary occupants of its leading financial and corporate roles are but short-term executive functions, even as they elaborate its pathological sequences of life-invasion. They succeed through their more efficient servitude to the life-blind code of value they effect. Behind them lurks a ruling program of what is and what is not to count as value, in precise degrees of money quantification, a program that now governs every calculation and decision in the global market. The implementation of this disconnected system of value is, in turn, ever more destructively reflected in civil and environmental crises around the globe.

In examining classical and contemporary principles and arguments professed by the market paradigm's advocates, we find an architectonic structure of covert ethical premises, unseen implications, systemic blind-spots, and ruling biases blocked from conscious view. These cognitive blocks of the market paradigm, in turn, have been incorporated into practice, decoupled from connection to their consequences, and rigidified into ruling dogmas that no longer relate to the life-requirements of human or natural beings. With the latest turn of this value system's unconditional "freedom" for money-to-more-money circuits in the world, the system has by force and now finance attacked and expelled whatever seeks to limit, regulate, or obstruct it.

The task here has been to lay bare the destructive effects that follow from the regulating principles of the value program. Once we come to comprehend the inner logic of the program behind the problems, we see that its demands to develop and re-engineer the evolved forms of social and natural life around it are only functions of its self-expansion, converting all life into its disposable means and deploring any rule but its own.

Notes

1. Jeremy Brecker, "Talking Back to the Right," *Z Magazine*, March 1996, p.37; Kimon Valasteakis, "Wanted: A GATT Agreement That Covers Workers, *The Globe and Mail*, April 22, 1994, p.A11.
2. Thus the president of the U.S. Business Council for International Relations advised U.S. trade officials in their negotiation of the MAI: "We will oppose any and all measures to create or even imply binding obligations for government or business relating to the environment or labour." Tony Clarke, *The Corporate Rule Treaty* (Ottawa: Canadian Centre for Policy Alternatives, 1997), p.9.
3. In 1992-96, in the United States alone, for example, AT&T has "shed" 123,000 workers, IBM 122,000, General Motors 99,400, Boeing 61,000, and Sears-Roebuck 50,000. In total 13.5 million

jobs were lost with no new regular jobs created by the disemploying firms. Louis Uchetelle and N.R. Kleinfield, "On the Battlefields of Business, Millions of Casualties," *The New York Times*, March 3, 1996, pp.14-16.

4. Joyce Nelson, "The Trilateral Commission," *Canadian Forum*, December 1993, p.5.

5. Eric Hobsbawm, *The Age of Extremes: The Short Twentieth Century 1914-1991* (London: Abacus, 1994), pp.257-87.

6. For the details on Mexico, see Linda Diebel, "Politics of Poverty," *The Toronto Star*, Nov. 26, 1995, p.F6; Ecumenical Coalition for Social Justice, "The Failure of Neo-Liberalism," November 1995, p.7.

7. Will Hutton, "High Risk Strategy Not Paying Off," *The Guardian Weekly*, Nov. 12, 1995, p.13.

8. See chapter 6, "Removing Barriers to Trade."

9. This right is known as "national treatment." One important exception was foreign ownership of Mexican oil resources or control of over 50 per cent of its sales, both forbidden by the Mexican constitution. Mexico also reserved the right to use 30 per cent of its theatre time for Mexican films. Orchard, *Fight for Canada*, pp.224, 228. Canada's trade representatives, who were more or less entirely ruled by a branch-plant value code and decision structure in the construction of these deals, gained no such exception to foreign ownership of everything in the home-country economy.

10. Orchard, *Fight for Canada*, pp.225-26.

11. NAFTA, chapter 7; GATT, articles XI(1), XX.

12. Members of the transnational corporate lobby Business Council on National Issues, Canada's most aggressive demander of the 1988 FTA, themselves laid off 200,000 workers while increasing their revenues by $32.1 billion. "Jobs, Jobs, Jobs," *Canadian Perspectives*, Summer 1996, p.7.

13. This NAFTA proscription against certain public investments prevented, for example, the New Democratic Party from keeping its election promise of public automobile insurance after winning the Ontario provincial election in 1990. The primary justification of these supraparliamentary trade laws is that domestic economies rely on foreign investment. What is not mentioned is that almost all foreign "investment" is for takeovers of domestic firms (97.5 per cent in the case of Canada in 1997, for example, and over 80 per cent worldwide). These takeovers, in turn, are dominantly financed by domestic banks (65 per cent in the case of Canada between 1985 and 1986) and typically result in lost jobs by downsizings after purchase. Mel Hurtig, "How Much of Canada Do We Want to Sell?" *The Globe and Mail*, Feb. 5, 1998, p.A23.

14. I am indebted for these figures to the 1995-97 campaign of citizens of Guelph to stop the rezoning of the city to serve Walmart.

15. UNICEF, "Children Pay High Price for World's Cheap Labour," *CCPA Bulletin*, October 1995, p.11.

16. Ibid.

17. "NAFTA's 5 Flaws," *CCPA Bulletin*, September 1995, p.18.

18. Wayne Ellwood, "Multinationals and the Subversion of Sovereignty," *The New Internationalist*, August 1993, p.7.

19. Martin Walker, "Green Enforcers Ambush in U.S.," *The Guardian Weekly*, Sept. 24, 1995, p.32.

20. Canadian Environmental Law Association, *Cutting Ontario's Environment*, Toronto, April 1996, pp.1-6.

21. Cited by Harry Glasbeek in "Democracy for Corporations: Corporations against Democracy," Corporations at the Crossroads, Meredith Lectures, Osgoode Hall Law School, York University, May 1995, p.63.

22. Franz J. Hinkelammert, "Our Project for the New Society in Latin America: The Regulating Role of the State and Problems of Self-Regulation in the Market," *Social Justice*, Winter 1992, pp.9-24.

23. Ontario Federation of Labour and Ontario Federation for Social Justice, *Unfair Shares: Corporations and Taxes in Canada*, February 1995; based on InfoGlobe Report on Business

Corporate Database, Dec. 14, 1994, pp.1-2, 42-48.

24. *The Globe and Mail*, Aug. 19, 1994, p.B2.

25. "Job Creation and Wage Enhancement," in *Bold Plan by Rep. Newt Gingrich and Rep. Dick Armey*, ed. Gillespie and Schellas.

26. John Kenneth Galbraith, *The Culture of Containment* (New York: Thomas Allen and Son, 1992), cited by Ramsey Cook, "The Tyranny of the Smug," *The Globe and Mail*, April 19, 1992, p.C16; Uchitelles and Kleinfield, "On the Battlefields of Business," pp.15-16; Julian Beltrane, "Rich Get Richer and the Poor Poorer," Southam News Syndicate, Sept. 2, 1995.

27. These figures and quotations are reported in Drew Fagan, "Clinton and Congress to Take Another Run at Budget Balancing," *The Globe and Mail*, Jan. 3, 1997.

28. Will Hutton and Andrew Higgins, "Tory Fantasy of Far Eastern Promise," *The Guardian Weekly*, Nov. 15, 1995, p.13; Paul Watson, "Waging a Desperate War for Survival in a Land of Plenty," *The Toronto Star*, Nov. 26, 1995, p.F7.

29. Peter Drucker, "The Age of Social Transformation," *The Atlantic Monthly*, September 1994, p.77.

30. Dave Todd, "Wages, Unions Targeted by World Bank," *The Toronto Star*, June 27, p.D3; William Thorsell, "Higher Standards in All Countries Ensue as the Economy Goes Global," *The Globe and Mail*, July 8, 1995, p.A7.

31. Ralph Nader, "Stop Americanizing Medicare," *CCPA Monitor*, February 1995, p.10.

32. According to Noam Chomsky, "60 percent of income growth is going to one percent of the population." Noam Chomsky, speech, Vancouver, March 5, 1996. At the same time, Chomsky reports, entry-level wages have declined by 30 per cent since 1980.

33. See, for example, Deborah Robinson, *Ogonia: The Struggle Continues*, Geneva World Council of Churches, 1996; and Terisa E. Turner, "Oil Workers and Oil Communities in Africa: Nigerian Women and Grassroots Environmentalism," *Labour, Capital and Society*, vol.30, no.1 (April 1997), pp.66-89.

34. John Ralston Saul, *The Unconscious Civilization* (Toronto: House of Anansi Press, 1995), p.11.

35. Uchitelle and Kleinfield, "On the Battlefields of Business," p.14.

36. "The New Master Class," *Fortune*, Dec. 13, 1993, p.82.

37. Judy Jones, "Poverty Is Blamed for Diet Crisis," *The Guardian Weekly*, Nov. 15, 1995, p.10.

38. "The Comfortable Pulpit," *The Globe and Mail*, Dec. 20, 1995, p.A7. A few months earlier, the *Globe*'s editorial team had been egging on the government of China to attack its people with more market discipline, declaring that only by government "taking away their subsidized food" and "laying them off in the millions" could China demonstrate to the new global market its willingness to make sacrifices. "If China fails to make these hard choices, the consequences ... will be much worse," it intoned. "China really has no choice but to go forward." "The Threats to China's 'Miracle,'" Sept. 16, 1995, p.D.6.

39. J. Larry Brown and Ernest Pollitt, "Malnutrition, Poverty and Intellectual Development," *Scientific American*, February 1996, pp.39-41; "Infant Deaths 60% Higher among Poor," *The Globe and Mail*, Dec. 15, 1995, p.A16.

40. *The Globe and Mail*, July 24, 1983, p.A17.

41. Pierre Sané, "Amnesty's Report Card from Hell," *The Globe and Mail*, Dec. 10, 1993, p.A21.

42. Fulton, *Adam Smith Speaks to Our Times*, p.94.

43. Marx deploys all the quoted concepts in his Preface to the first edition of *Capital*. But Marx did not conceive these "economic laws" as inalterable, as Ricardo did with his likening of the market's laws to the law of gravitation. He thought the "laws" in question were limited to a historical epoch. But since they were still "laws" for the "capitalist epoch," their significant modification or limitation was thought to be impossible without social revolution. In this way, Marxist and market economics similarly reify the economic decision-structure regulating the industrial market's production and distribution processes.

The Mutations of the Profit System and Their Cure

Until the control of the issue of currency and credit is restored to government and recognized as its most conspicuous and sacred responsibility, all talk of the sovereignty of Parliament and of democracy is idle and futile.... Once a nation parts with control of its credit, it matters not who makes the nation's laws.... Usury once in control will wreck any nation.

Prime Minister William Lyon Mackenzie King[1]

I believe that banking institutions are more dangerous to our liberties than standing armies. Already they have raised up a monied aristocracy that has set the Government at defiance. The issuing power should be taken from the banks and restored to the people to whom it properly belongs.

President Thomas Jefferson[2]

From the Life-Code of Value to
the Logic of the World-System Crisis

The value program of the global market does not emerge ready-made. It mutates through master principles of value-gain over centuries. There are two master principles of value-gain that underlie the long economic war expressed by history, and these can be formulated as "codes of value." These codes of value have long been confused, but the future of civil and planetary life-organization depends on their distinction. In the present period of deregulated globalization of private money-demand, these structures of value are at war beneath social recognition.

The life code of value can be formulated in simple axiom as the sequence:

$$\text{Life} \longrightarrow \text{Means of Life} \longrightarrow \text{More Life } (L \longrightarrow MofL \longrightarrow L^1)$$

In this formula *life* means organic movement, sentience and feeling, and thought. *Means of life* refers to whatever enables life to be preserved or to extend its vital range on these three planes of being alive. Clean air, food, water, shelter, affective interaction, environmental space, and accessible learning conditions are all means of life. To reproduce life-value is to hold these capacities at their established scope. To increase life-value is to widen or deepen them to a more comprehensive range.

These are the defining parameters and sequence of the life-code and sequence of value. They are experienced by all humans every moment of their lives, and to varying extent by all sentient beings. Even a very small reduction of the vital range of breath, thought, feeling, organ, or limb is directly experienced by its sufferer as "something wrong." The more of life's breadths and depths are accessible to us, the better our condition. The more they are diminished—for example, by unemployment, a polluted environment, or unaffordable higher education—the worse our condition becomes.

In the now dominant market system, in direct contrast, the value code that underlies people's normal decisions and actions is one that affirms more money revenues as good and rejects less money revenues as bad. These are a priori principles of value and disvalue of what we have called the "corporate value program," and they are now presupposed as the prescriptions of rationality itself.

In its classical, productive form, this ruling preference for more money follows a sequence of money input (investment) to money output (profit), which can be formulated as the sequence of:

Money —> Commodity for Sale —> More Money ($ —> C —> $¹)

Money is the beginning of the value sequence, and money is the end of the value sequence. More *money*, not more life, is the regulating objective of thought and action. The more money that returns to the investor of money, whatever may happen to life, the better the investment. This value system does not calculate into its judgement whether life has gained or lost by this sequence—even the vital life-range of the one who ends with more money. Its objective is to net more money from money. Money is not used for life. Life is used for money. The final measure of the Good is increase or decrease of money sums.

Since this sequence of value begins from the assumption that more money can produce and buy more goods or utilities, it supposes that more money sums are therefore always better by definition. This is a non-sequitur of the greatest moment. But this cognitive slippage at the very base of the money value program is not recognized. It ends in the failure to distinguish between wealth and money-demand *on* wealth. This fateful confusion means, in turn, that if money-demand on the wealth of life keeps increasing, but the wealth of life keeps decreasing by its demands, the market's money-sequence calculus cannot recognize the problem. According to its metric, all is well. This logic of value can lead, if it is not seen through, to the stripping of the life-world by money-demand until the life-fabric can no longer hold.

But another money-sequence of value is even more dangerous to life. It produces no commodity or use-value at all between its investment and profit moments. It becomes more money by merely paper transactions of speculative turnovers or by debt-service that contributes no function to production. Money investment that seeks to become more money without production of any life-good or service in between has been known as long as usury. But what is historically new today is that this money-sequence of value has become the dominant decision-structure of global life-organization. From 1950 to the present, for example, in the United States net revenues from compounding interest-payments have multiplied by almost three hundred times. This is more than ten times the rise of GNP over the same period, and nearly twenty-five times the rise in the total farm income of the world's greatest food-producing economy.[3] Elsewhere interest demands on national economies have been even more extreme in their exponential rise. Between 1980 and 1994, real interest demands on less developed countries multiplied by sixteen-fold from their 1975-79 average.[4] If we reflect on these figures, we see the darkening outline of an ever more serious world disorder. Turning money into more money for money-lenders and speculators has invisibly become the ruling imperative of the planet.

The lethal mutation in the money-sequence of value occurs when money-demand is no longer a phase within the circuit of the production of society's goods, but is exclusively committed at every stage of its growth only to the multiplication of itself. Instead of any productive function in the metabolism of money through the medium of use-value to more money, there is only the metabolism of money to more money without any conversion to use-value in the circuit.

This closed money circuit mutation now emerges in many ways. Primarily, it multiplies and invades life-productive circuits by means of compounding interest demands. U.S. financier J.P. Morgan once wrote: "I couldn't name the Seven Wonders of the World, but I can tell you what the Eighth Wonder is—Compound Interest."[5] Since Morgan said these words, real interest rates on public debt in Canada, for example, exponentially escalated nearly eight-fold between 1962-81 and 1982-95.[6] At the 1967 to 1987 rate of the usury share of the U.S. national income, it will take all of the national income to pay compound interest demands within twenty-five years.[7]

Bank loans and interest loads are the drive-wheel of this money-to-more-money circuit. This pattern of extracting money from debtors with an ever wider siphon of interest demands is most ruinous in the poor developing countries of Africa and Latin America. But it is draining the countries of the First World as well, bankrupting their public sectors within a decade and increasing the debt-to-income ratios of small businesses and ordinary citizens to historically unprecedented highs. Small businesses in the United States expend an average of 22 per cent of their total incomes on interest demands, while average householder debt in Canada and the United States is now almost 100 per cent.[8]

The defining principle of the money-to-more-money circuit is that it is not bounded by any national base of control or by any requirement to commit itself to any life-serving function. It demands only to acquire maximally more money with no conversion into sustenance or service to life in between. The formula for this decoupled money-sequence can be expressed as follows:

$$\text{Money} \longrightarrow \text{More Money} \longrightarrow \text{More Money } (\$ \longrightarrow \$^1 \longrightarrow \$^2 \longrightarrow \$^n)$$

This sequence of money-demand expansion is now the master of global economies. In its most comprehensive form, it includes not only compound-interest circuits, but currency and derivatives speculation, arbitrages, and leveraged takeovers to liquidate assets. Most "foreign investment" now takes this form, and its entries and flights from societies can strip those nations of their built value overnight—as we have seen most recently in the "meltdown" of the "Asian Tigers." What all these expressions of the money-sequence of value have in common is that they transform money inputs into increased money outputs with no productive contribution required in between. Once former "barriers" to speculative inflows and outflows of unproductive money flows are removed, as the global market program demands, no society can be free from these economic predations. Together, they daily destabilize or deplete public and private sectors, with interest rates on their speculations written off public taxes on their revenues. Market leaderships now demand, indeed, that governments withdraw any attempt to regulate them. "In the face of efforts to regulate or control capital flows," warned the financial giant Goldman Sachs to the U.S. Senate Committee on Banking, "the marketplace will treat harshly even the largest nations."[9] A major New York money manager speaking to a national radio audience adds, "We are like the supranational government of the world. Where we see that politicians are doing things that are inappropriate, we hold their feet to the fire. And the way we do that is by moving a lot of money. Politicians [society's elected representatives] are *irrelevant* to the process."[10] The *Washington Post* reports, "The growing consensus among the G-7 members [the governments of the United States, Japan, Germany, France, Britain, Italy, and Canada] is that *the G-7 cannot influence events much anyway*. Immense flows of private capital have intimidated the G-7 officials from any efforts to counter them."[11]

This state of affairs has many consequences. One is the dismantling of democratic structures that might inhibit the increasing redistribution of wealth to the money-to-more-money circuits and to the banks, financial institutions, and speculators that control them. "The disposable income of the majority is being reduced," observes an internationally known economist who approves of the world trend. "The big question of the coming decades is how to find an acceptable means of scaling back democracy."[12]

The invasion has spread from the financial sector to the multinational sector of the productive economy. General Motors and General Electric, for example, both make more profits from their financial subsidiaries lending credit money at compound interest than they do from all of their production of automotive and electrical manufactures put together.[13] This practice now forms a typical pattern.

The spiralling debt and deficit circuits bankrupting governments and social infrastructures across the world are a primary vehicle of this ruling money-sequence of value. For example, the total debt of less developed countries to banks doubled from approximately $819 billion in 1982 to $1,712 billion in 1993, after over $14 trillion had already been appropriated from those poorer societies by the money-extraction cycles of major banks.[14] The damage was sufficient to collapse these societies into a growing chaos of malnutrition, illiteracy, morbidity, and destitution. Tens of millions more children are hungry, diseased, or illiterate as a direct consequence of IMF "restructuring programs" to pay international money-lenders, while the stripping of social infrastructures is now a general fact across the globe.

Third World government debts were themselves typically contracted by agents within the society placed into rule by U.S.-supported military seizures of ruling power. These regimes were sustained in rule by external military and financial institutions that assisted in channelling the original government debt money loans into major foreign banks to lend back at compound interest or to speculate and run.[15]

No such process can continue for long without devastating the invaded host societies. But if social bodies fail to convert their life-fabrics to the interest-extracting circuits, more "restructuring" and "structural adjustment" programs are imposed on them. Ever more sacrifices are demanded of societies to pay "debt-servicing" loads beyond debt and to "attract foreign investment" that is for non-productive takeovers. But no sacrifice is ever asked of these money-sequence demands themselves. They are sacrosanct, and none dares to say they are "unaffordable." Here is the evidence that the money-sequence of value is regarded as absolute, while service to the life-sequence is treated as dispensable. Thus societies have been given "shock treatments" to ensure their "hard adjustments." The means of existence of people are turned into money to serve the demands of the money-sequence for still more. No limit has yet been imposed on this holocaust of life on the altar of the money-to-more-money-sequence. The food, water, shelter, and heat energy available to more and more of society's members are reduced to service debts or to provide cost competitiveness to money investors. Unemployment rises; social services are axed. Absolute and relative impoverishment increases, more youth are without life-prospects, and more children everywhere are left without enough to eat. These are the "necessary adjustments" to the new order, in which money's reproduction and gain, not life's, is the regulating value code of the globe.

There is a conjuncture of historical conditions that has made this increasing occupation of societies by the $ \longrightarrow \$^1 \longrightarrow \$^n$ sequence possible. But currently driving the process is the centralization of investment decisions under the control of major banks, whose every choice of value is structured by the $ \longrightarrow \$^1 \longrightarrow \$^n$ imperative. In Canada, for example, from 1984 to 1994 banks have increased their market share of total assets held by investment dealers from zero to 70 per cent and by the trust and loan industry from 30 per cent to 69 per cent.[16] Governments have also rapidly redistributed public revenues to banks by making interest payments to them tax-deductible on loans that advance the money-to-more-money-sequence of both banks and their money-leveraging clients, which now include doctors, teachers, and others "adapting to the new reality." We see here a pattern of restructuring society's value system on every level to serve the growth not of humans or their environments, but of money-demand on both.

Sacrificing Life to the Money-Sequence

World society's investment decision-structures have thus been increasingly restructured towards a self-multiplying metabolism of money to more money, with social life-organization as the consumed host. Because this now dominant sequence requires ever more decoupled money growth to reproduce itself, it invades more and more life-sites of public sectors and private sectors across the world for more money returns, each cycle growing on the basis of a larger money base than before "to stay profitable and competitive." One of the primary symptoms of this mutation of productive and social capital into delinked and borderless money multiplications is that virtually no national life and health security infrastructure in the world is now safe from its invasion and demand for more "efficiency" in converting all life into moments of its self-expansion.

The rationale for this process of depriving the social body of the circulation of money it requires is to "preserve the value of money." Thus the U.S. Federal Reserve System and the Bank of

Canada in the 1980s both increased the money-for-more-money rate of interest for all lending institutions to historically unprecedented rates above inflation, up to 21.5 per cent prime—thereby systematically bankrupting productive companies, disemploying citizens by the hundreds of thousands, and, in Canada, reducing national productivity by between $40 billion (the estimate of Bank of Canada economic planners) and $140 billion (the estimate of the former president of the Canadian Economic Association) for each point drop in the national inflation rate.[17] Each rise of unemployment, in turn, increased the death and morbidity rates of society by now known correlations, again explicitly sacrificing life to the money-sequence as the ruling decision-structure of society.[18]

Here we see in stark terms the displacement of the value of life as the organizing principle of society by the mutated principle of "the value of money" as its ruling aim. Cutbacks to all social supports to the life-sequence—assistance to the poor, public education, and environmental protection—are declared "necessary" to ensure that the one sequence of value overrides the other.

Such systematic overriding of life requirements is now clearly evident from the most undeveloped to the most advanced societies of the world. In the case of Canada, again, infant mortality rates, the quintessential indicator of social health, rose an astonishing 43 per cent in the 1995 Statistics Canada figures, the first recorded rise in over thirty-one years, while child poverty had increased by 46 per cent since 1989.[19] In Africa an estimated 500,000 more children died from the imposed restructuring of their countries' economies to ensure increased flows of money to external banks, while spending on health care declined by 50 per cent and on education by 25 per cent since these structural adjustment programs began.[20]

The new modes of mutating revenue circulations within the social body are numerous. None produce any good. All serve to redistribute wealth and resources from the poorer to the richer. All are bank-driven or assisted:

· turning bankrupt governments into receiver states enforcing the money-sequence's ever-growing demands on ever poorer public sectors;

· demanding ever more tax breaks for investment in debt over equity and in non-productive speculation instead of job-creating enterprises;

· attacking national currencies by speculative buying and selling in multibillion-dollar profit accumulations that create no use-value and cripple social and economic orders overnight;

· transforming productive enterprises into broker-and-lawyer-dismantled assets for sale by leveraged buy-outs that pay for themselves by unproductive appropriation of the liquid capital of the bought firms;

· deregulating high-interest savings and loan institutions so that their principals can expropriate up to $500 billion from taxpayers to pay for their speculative money-into-more-money circuits;

· transferring tax obligations to pay bail-out costs to productive members of society with ever less income to extract;

· directing citizens' saved money stocks to billion-dollar, hostile buy-outs and to round-the-clock arbitrages and speculations on derivative market and currency values disconnected from any productive function; and

· channelling vast mutual and pension funds that now bear the privatized old-age security of the First World's middle class into socially delinked stock-market transactions.

The resulting overall pattern is historically unprecedented. Business journals have estimated that the U.S. monthly electronic trade in currencies, futures derivative instruments, stocks, and bonds, all operating beyond effective government regulation, exceeds the country's entire annual GNP; that of the $900 billion of currencies traded every day in U.S. stock exchanges, only one out of every seventy dollars of effective demand actually pays for trade in goods or services; that the financial sector's annual volume of trading is at least thirty to forty times greater than the dollar turnover of all production and distribution of goods and services; and that over one hundred times more is now expended on stocks and bonds than is invested in plants and equipment.[21] As these mid-1990s indicators disclose, the escalating money-for-more-money circuit with no commitment to life-function now overwhelms the organization and reproduction of civil society itself.

The question thus arises: If the money-sequence has now displaced the life-sequence across the world's social bodies, what can be done to stem and turn back its advance?

Towards a Cure: Relinking Banks to the Public That Charters and Funds Them

If we consider the paradigm case of private banks as an exemplar of the money-to-more-money code overriding the life-requirements of society, we can see that we have every reason to expect regulation of these banks in the common life-interest. They are government-chartered and protected institutions. They live off the government-granted right to demand minimum compound-interest payments on the lending of other people's money stocks and on money they privately create by the issuing of new debts. They have been permitted to take over the quintessential government function of controlling and creating society's money supply itself.

As long ago as 1982, it was estimated that 96 per cent of all new money entering the United States and Canada is created by private money-lending institutions. In 1982, when the market frenzy of "deregulation" began in the United States, the eminent economist Lester Thurow observed, "The Federal Reserve Board announced that it was giving up on its attempts to control the U.S. money supply on the grounds that [banks and other lending institutions] ... had essentially *taken over the government's nominal role as the printer of money*."[22] Banks and other institutional lenders have thus become "private mints" controlling and adding to society's money supply as

they please to maximize their profits. All this they do with no requirement in their charters to lend the money to productive investments or
to enterprises in the public interest.

Banks have increasingly shed previously accepted obligations
to the larger social interest, while simultaneously appropriating to
themselves ever more social powers properly belonging to public authority. They have acquired one lucrative privilege after another,
with no connection back to their host society's life-needs.

This expanding regime of money-to-more-money disconnected from society's life-requirements must eventually deprive society of its life-lines of revenue on every level; and, over time, it has.
Hence banks' loans and investments go ever more preponderantly to
non-productive and destructive uses: asset-stripping buy-outs,
disemploying mergers, destabilizing speculations in currencies, gam-
bling on stock-market derivatives, predatory repossessions, financing
takeovers of successful domestic firms by foreign multinationals, and
privatized, compound-interest loans bleeding public governments
dry. These unproductive and depletive loans and investments on the
basis of domestic savers' money and society's charters and support
services are, moreover, leveraged to high ratios of demand to cash to
escalate the volume and velocity of depredatory effects on social life-
organization. These implementations of the money-code decision-
structure constitute, in David Korten's words, "a parasitic predator
that lives off the flesh of its host—the productive economy."[23]

Clearly, this pattern of behaviour, increasingly globalized
across boundaries and segregated from the home societies that fund,
insure, and protect private bank operations, mounts a systemic assault on the life of societies and their citizens. Along with the other
principal bearers of financial operations in society—the stock markets, insurance corporations, and financial institutions and arms of
corporations, which all conform to the same value program in every
moment of their decision-sequences—the banks are the ruling
money-demand bearers and, thus, success-stories of society. In
Canada, since the government removed their reserve requirements
and privatized its debt for banks to hold instead of the publicly owned
Bank of Canada, the private banks have made record profits while

Canadians have suffered the worst and most prolonged unemployment crisis since the Depression. Indeed, the Big Five banks cut thousands of their own workers as they reaped billions more in profits. Such a social pattern in no way serves the life-sequence.

What prevents us from seeing this pattern is that the facts are kept from the public at every level, while a non-stop campaign of propaganda from both banks and corporate-financed politicians reassures us with rationalizations that have no connection to the evidence of reality. "When the public bashes the banks they are really bashing themselves," the CEO of the Bank of Montreal stated, himself expressing the disorder.[24] His position assumes that the money-stock investors in the banks are "the public."

How can these bearers of the money-sequence of value be made responsible to society's common life-interest?

Given that banks receive from society the privilege of a legislation-created charter, the use of others' money stocks and deposits, the right to create society's money supply through the continuous issuing of new debts, the instituted power to charge minimum rates of interest for producing no good, the benefit of publicly subsidized deposit insurance on their high-risk and non-productive speculations—and the protection within society of all these special privileges and operations by the force of law—we can deduce that the private banks owe a massive obligation back to society. The entitlements they have been given to create and supply society's money for their unproductive profit should either be reappropriated by public authority or, at the minimum, be made contingent on the *strict condition that society's money supply is credited, loaned, and invested in ways to protect and enable society's most basic life-interests.* This may seem an extremely modest requirement of obligatory return for such regal privileges, but if its minimal obligation was required to be fulfilled, this step would significantly transform our now rapidly deteriorating life-condition.

Once we recognize that banks owe society for every power of money-demand they have, a dependency long concealed by solemn secrecy and the presence of dominant bank temples at the centre of the world's cities, it is not difficult to identify appropriate requirements to make them accountable to society's life. If a market society clearly needs more effective demand for jobs to resolve its problems of unemployment, for example, banks should be required to introduce very low, long-term interest rates for new domestic enterprises that create secure jobs. The requirement here is so obvious that it may strike the reader as incredible that such a bank obligation has not long ago been recognized. That private banks have managed to escape any such minimal obligation becomes still more remarkable given that this arrangement has already been long implemented in the form of special development banks and public enterprises in the most competitively productive economies over three centuries. All that is required is a regulation compelling banks to set aside a substantial level of their overall loan and investment portfolios to such accounts to continue qualifying for their government charters, special entitlements, and right to lend and leverage others' money stocks.

Otherwise, all money-creating powers should revert to public authority, be tied to the rate of real economic growth, and lent solely to enterprises producing goods serving the life-sequence of value. Private banks would in such a situation be returned to the normal rights of private market agents. They could continue to lend their money stocks as their stockholders choose, but on the basis of 100 per cent reserves rather than the private creation of money.[25]

As long as private banking institutions are permitted the power to create money-demand beyond their reserves, their privilege can be tied to the public interest by specific conditions for exercising what is a right of government. Money creation is a foundational right of public authority, and constitutions standardly express this fact in their specification of national government control over matters of the national currency. Once such conditions are specified for all banks as obligatory in all money creation beyond 100 per cent reserves, banks can be made to comply with the common interest. Requirements of productive and job-creating loans could ensure higher employment, a more productive society, more diversified business activities, and a wider tax base to fund society's public goods. Small businesses, which create the majority of new jobs, would especially benefit—instead of being consistently undercredited and underfinanced by private banks whose decision-structure is biased against their scale of assets. Because private banks depend on special government entitlements, protection, and insurance and on domestic citizens' and governments' money deposits and loans, the usual recourse of capital flight to other jurisdictions would not be available as an instrument of social intimidation.

By the same principle of linkage of society's domestic money supply to society's most pressing life-requirements, interest rates set by the central bank can not only be calibrated lower for secure job-creation enterprises in society's life-interest, but also pegged significantly higher for speculative enterprises that do not create any social good or service at all. We must make no mistake about the banks' unlimited demand for more profits whatever the cost to the productive economy. After years of record billion-dollar profits in times of unemployment crisis, bankers in 1997 were still demanding "more aggressive" money returns for no productive performance, a further hike to "16 to 18 percent in the medium-term target range."[26]

In these circumstances of aggressive appropriation of ever more of society's revenues for bank growth, the distinction between money loaned for life-serving, job-creating enterprises on the one hand and money loaned for parasitic speculation on the other hand has not yet registered on Western governments or central banks as an issue. The determining decision-structure of the banks is now sequenced solely to turn money into more money-demand for money leveragers whatever the price to life. In the end, the problem is a value system war. The market imperative of self-maximizing choice in these circumstances systemically conflicts with the requirements of society's vital life. Such a disorder is only soluble by return to public authority, regulating in the common interest. A sane value ground seeks to enable the sequences of life. But this life-ground of value is now lost to government policy, and it unleashes the money-demand code through all of society's nodes.

Central banks now claim, ironically, to be committed to a social value—"reducing inflation." But the role that bank interest rates themselves play in inflation is ruled out of view: even though interest rates are demands for money without production, and therefore necessarily inflationary. This is the great taboo topic of banks, and indeed of market doctrine in general. The taboo is predictable. It follows from the blinkers of the money-code and money-sequence of value, which rule out from view whatever exposes them.

Relating rates of interest to society's most basic life-requirements, by distinguishing between enterprises that are job-creating and productive and enterprises that are not, would help banks to be less inflationary. It is policy that would also enable domestic economies to significantly overcome unemployment. Although such policy and choice may be self-evident to a decision-structure grounded in the life value code, it is repelled by the current market value set. We are dealing here with the systemic delinkage of the money-sequence from the world of life.

Differential interest rates set for economies by central banks need not be confined to the basic social interest of an increased productive and employment base. Some enterprises fulfil society's foundational life-interests in other ways. Here too, a preferential interest rate would only apply so long as the defined function for society was being demonstrably served. For example, another self-evident life-requirement of societies is to preserve the air, water, soil, and atmosphere from continued despoliation by market operations. Every society across the world is suffering from the pollutions and toxic effluents of industrial processes and products. But no banking system in the world, although now in command of society's creation and allocation of money, has yet been required to direct any of its bank-enriching loans and investments to the development and production of pollution-abatement instruments. Given that the entire world requires such devices for social and environmental life-protection, and given that no financial institution anywhere has yet been required by any public or intergovernmental authority to ensure preferential funding for any such product of survival, we can again observe another bellwether marker of the disconnection of society's money-credit system from reality. Even the most well-known means to preserve the very conditions of life on the planet are blocked from view as preferred objects for money investment.

Here too, an amount equivalent to a small percentage of the overall loan and investment accounts of private banks, or indeed of the overall money-investment portfolios of tax-deductible pension funds, could be required as a condition for their charters and tax deductions. In this case, a collective fund for a specialist Innovative Product Development Bank, or the like, could be mandated to ensure that such basic life-requirements of society are met and not evaded by consciousness enslaved to the money-sequence of value. Coordinated financing of one kind or another offering very low and long-term interest rates to mandated projects in the public interest has already been the basis of most market successes in developing infrastructure, from nineteenth-century North America to recent Asian "market miracles." But these financial plannings of capital investment in the public interest have focused on industrial production. In keeping with the money-sequence program's blindness to environmental and health requirements, they have predictably ignored life-protective products. Here as well, the connection back to life's underlying organic requirements has not been possible for the narrow lenses of the money-sequence program.

Once the mind is permitted to remove the blinkers of this disordered value regime, vital life-requirements of many sorts come to view. All of these too can be recognized, articulated, and mandated into the decision-structures of society's money-creation and allocation process, which are a long-traditional jurisdiction of sovereign governments.

There are many calls of life for public intervention on behalf of life-needs and against life-destruction by the money-to-more-money-sequence: for noiseless machines to still the ever expanding motor-racket businesses pervading the planet; for high-protein vegetarian fast foods to reduce the many times less efficient use of arable land by industrialized agribusiness and the earth-wide slaughterhouse of fellow creatures; for priority research and development of physical systems to convert wastes of every sort into reusable manufacturing forms; for more efficient water-recycling processes to convert waste water and seawater into redeployable or potable forms. It is self-evident from the life-ground that all these products qualify at the highest level of need. But, once again, few or none is invested in by the market's decision-structure. Market preference operates in accordance with one overriding goal, and that is adding money value to private money invested by self-maximizing money-lenders and investors. If there is no private money-demand for what is in the shared interests of planetary or human life, it counts as of no value to this ethic. The way in which money-demand can be reconnected to the shared life-interest of societies and their environments is to require that the private creation of money by debt-creating loans corresponds to this common life-interest.

The simplest immediate measure to effect this correspondence is for government to mandate a rising leveraged percentage of bank loans and tax-sheltered investment funds to publicly monitored job-creation, pollution-abatement, and other activities in society's common interest as a condition of their continued public subsidization.

Money Creation and Public Accountability

Money, we need to keep in mind, is the bearer of all value in the global market value system. So universal, presupposed, and overriding is the demand its units bear that even value theorists, ethicists, and philosophers avert their eyes from examination of it. They defer, on the contrary, to sovereignty of its social demand as a given more assumed than the testimony of the senses. But if we seek to regulate what exists so that it does not destroy us, we need to reassert social control over money-demand's social creation and unearned returns. To do this public policy must reground the nature of the money unit itself in the social systems of life upon which every power it has entirely depends.

Understood in its global market form, money is a society-created right to demand whatever exists on the face of the earth as the money controller's, in direct proportion to the units of money that are controlled. It is the socially investitured licence to demand, in effect, ever more of the life-world in all its forms as an object to be used or consumed as its possessor chooses. There is in the current market value system no limit to the demand that the money possessor can exercise of this sovereign entitlement to consume and command life.

What is totalitarian, in the strictest sense, about this unlimited money-demand right is that it increasingly transforms all that exists on the planet into the object or refuse of the money-sequence, with no bound of law or custom to what can be appropriated and destroyed by it. Money-demand has become in this way the world's transcultural idolatry. Its commandments exercise a shock-treatment rule over all life, with even universities, pontiffs, and heads of state falling to their faces before its prescriptions as their final law on earth. Yet without round-the-clock sustainment by social institutions, the awesome sign of money would have no more power than children's play bills. Yet as its socially manufactured, protected, and subsidized powers of demand become increasingly more absolute and monopolized, market enthusiasts perceive no problems. The final game of existence is only to compete for ever more of it. Even Marx talked only of "commodity fetishism." But this misses the real fetish of the money-sequence behind the appearances of commodities.

There is a remedy, and it requires no violent takeover of society's productive forces. The creation of money is already a first power of public authority, followed by the power to allocate it, and then to receive more from it in unearned returns. But at this ground level of society's process of money-demand creation and allocation, prior to any use of it for any productive purpose, and prior to any claim to deserve its rights of social demand, sovereign public authority has long-recognized rights to determine its creation, supply, and rates of interest return. This right is already declared in constitutions wherever they refer to the government's jurisdiction over currency and coinage. But bankers and money managers over years of financing and lobbying political parties have plied and pulled away these powers, while public servants have come to identify with these private financial interests as their future employers. This culture of complicity has subverted government itself and requires public recognition if society is to regain control over its life.

As in other enslavements to ignorance and superstitious awe, here too servitude to invisible hands and smokescreens can be quickly dispatched. It is as reversible by policy decision as is sacrificing people to please the gods. To be specific, national banks are subject to national governments. They can be told what they need to do to serve the public interest or be replaced in executive personnel by statutory direction. For example, the Bank of Canada Act already has, under Article 18, a sixty-year-old constitutional authority to lend money to the federal government at low interest rates up to one-third of its revenues. The Bank of Canada also has this constitutional mandate in regard to the country's provinces for up to one-quarter of their revenues at any rate of interest it chooses. It has, moreover, the further established right to draw upon mandatory money reserves deposited by private banks, up to 100 per cent of their loans, to use for its own purchase of government bonds without inflationary effects. The Bank of Canada is, moreover, specifically obliged by its general provisions to "mitigate fluctuations of employment." It is, finally, publicly owned, responsible to the public interest, and its chief executive is a government-appointed public servant. All interest payments to it revert to its sole shareholder, the government. In short, all the instruments for serving the common interest of society's life-requirements are already encoded in existing law.

How is it, then, that these legally instituted measures have not already been adopted to meet the declared "public debt crisis" that has systematically defunded and dismantled society's health, education, and social-security systems? The answer is that what is self-evident to the *life* value ground we bear as human beings does not and cannot compute to the *money* value ground that propels bank agents and their global market program in general.

How can a regime so prejudicial to the public good persist with so little public opposition? The answer is that what is not seen is not opposed. Significantly, the global market's international co-ordinating body that has led the substitution of privatized government bonds for bank reserves is the Swiss-based Bank of International Settlements, a socially unaccountable, private-banker committee that plots the world's norms of money creations and supplies outside of the public's gaze. The Bank of International Settlements, originally set up to bring German war reparations under banks' control before the 1929 crash and Great Depression, later handed over Czechoslovakia's gold to Hitler after his invasion of Prague in

1938.[27] Today it leads a policy of abolishing all reserves for bank loans, a carte blanche secretly passed into law in Canada in 1991. The banks' view is that everyone else must have collateral for loans but banks themselves do not need to have cash reserves to back up loans to governments and individuals. Cash reserves are called an "unfair tax," an Orwellian conception that central bankers cheerfully repeat.[28] The logic of the bankers' code exempts them from the principles they prescribe as inviolate to everyone else. This is another symptom of our social disorder.

One could hardly ask for a more revealing example. Governments' staggering debts have remained fixed on the public's back to ensure that the money-for-more-money sequence to money-lenders continues and grows. Nations' systems of public health, higher learning, unemployment and social assistance, environmental monitoring and protection, public broadcasting, and civil commons have been rapidly reduced, dismantled, or privatized to "pay down the public debt." The overriding of the life value code by the money value code within the process of public government itself could hardly be more exemplary and tragic.

The justification for this destruction of the civil commons is that "society is living beyond its means." But this phrase implies that the new money that society needs belongs to someone else—that is, to the interest demands of private money-lenders, which are now about equal to all expenditures of government on all of its social programs put together. Yet governments have managed greater public debts with no such crisis before. Canada, for example, paid back a far higher debt as a percentage of GDP after the Second World War, experiencing at the same time a robust growth rate. In exact contrast to the recent life-stripping sequence, central bank policies rapidly reduced foreign debt from 30.4 per cent to 6.3 per cent in just seven years. They also reduced overall debt from 140 per cent of GDP to 26 per cent of GDP, all the while increasing government expenditures on health, education, social security, and other civil commons infrastructure.[29]

Money creation, supply, and allocation in the global market system have been "unfettered" from accountability to society's life-requirements because governments have abdicated their function of safeguarding the common interest. A rogue value code has reprogrammed their decision-structures, policies, and implementations to serve its demands instead. The distinction between the demands of the money-code and the requirements of the society's life has collapsed. The unseen master-switch of this subversion of government's proper function on behalf of the common interest has been the covert acquisition by private financial institutions of control over society's primary unit of value, money-demand. Its creation, allocation, and interest returns have together been subjugated to the decoupled money-sequence of value as the sovereign ruler of society. But the reversal of this usurpation of government in the common interest is not beyond reach. The lawful grounds and instruments of accountability to society's shared requirements of life have already been won and are available for use by governments if publics demand it.

It is disturbing in this context that even as the long-in-opposition Labour Party of Britain was swept into government on May 1, 1997, the policy it instituted immediately on entering office was to assign to the privately owned Bank of England the sole authority to regulate national interest rates.

Notes

1. Quoted in *Monetary Reform*, Summer 1996, p.16.
2. Quoted in William F. Hixson, *Triumph of the Bankers: Money and Banking in the Eighteenth and Nineteenth Centuries* (Westport, Conn.: Praeger, 1993), p.94; and *Monetary Reform*, Summer 1996, p.16.
3. These figures are from William F. Hixson, *A Matter of Interest: Re-Examining Debt, Interest and Real Economic Growth* (New York: Praeger, 1991), pp.xiii, 230.
4. John Dillon, *Turning the Tide: Confronting the Money Traders* (Ottawa: Ecumenical Coalition for Economic Justice and Centre for Policy Alternatives, 1996), p.67.
5. Quoted by Ed Finn, *CCCPA Monitor*, July/August, 1996, p.4.
6. Dillon, *Turning the Tide*, p.42.
7. Hixson, *Ibid*, p.177.
8. Ibid., p.176.
9. Eric R. Peterson, "Surrendering to Markets," *The Washington Quarterly*, Autumn 1995, p.113.
10. Monsor Ejazz, "Economic Forecasting," *Sunday Morning*, CBC-Radio, Sept. 25, 1995; emphasis added.
11. Fred Bergsten, "The Corpse at the Summit," *The Washington Post*, June 11, 1995, p.C-4; emphasis added.
12. Ian Angell, a professor of information systems at the London School of Economics, quoted by Richard Gwyn, "Voice of Angell Provides Hard Truths," *The Toronto Star*, Oct. 6, 1996, p.A17.

Note that the newspaper headlines the "acceptable" redistribution of wealth from "the majority" and the consequent need to "dismantle democracy" as "hard truths."

13. *CCPA Monitor*, October 1995, p.5.

14. Ecumenical Coalition for Economic Justice, *Economic Justice Report*, vol. 5, no. 2 (1994), p.7.

15. Nate Laurie, "The Economy: How Third World Debt Goes in Circles," *The Toronto Star*, Feb. 27, 1987, p.A19; R.T. Naylor, *Hot Money and the Politics of Debt* (Montreal: Black Rose Books, 1994). Manuel Pastor reports that interest extractions from capital flight amount to 40 per cent of debt payments in Argentina and Mexico, and about 70 per cent in Venezuela. Manuel Pastor, "Latin America, the Debt Crisis and the International Monetary Fund," *Latin American Perspectives*, vol. 16, no. 1 (1989), pp.79-100.

16. Canada, *Report of the Auditor-General*, Ottawa, May 26, 1996.

17. McQuaig, *Shooting the Hippo*, pp.87-88.

18. The 1997 Alternative Budget of the Canadian Centre of Policy Alternatives reports that a reduction of unemployment from 10 to 6 per cent would lower mortality rates by 3.6 per cent, the homicide rate by 5.7 per cent, the suicide rate by 2.1 per cent, the number of arrests by 12 per cent, and the number of people in prison by 18 per cent. "Unemployment Inflicts High Social Costs," *CCPA Bulletin*, March 1997, p.9.

19. Alanna Mitchell, "Rising Deaths among Infants Stun Scientists," *The Globe and Mail*, June 2, 1995; Statistics Canada News Release, Ottawa, June 1, 1995. Isaac Prilleltensky, "Propaganda Works: Economic and Social Policies Are Not Beyond the People's Control," *The Record* (Kitchener-Waterloo), Dec. 11, 1996, p.A13.

20. Susan George, *Proceedings of the World Congress of the International Physicians for the Prevention of Nuclear War*, vol. XI (October 1993), p.239; Ecumenical Council for Economic Justice, *Recolonization or Liberation: The Bonds of Structural Adjustment and Struggles for Emancipation*, Toronto, 1990, p.12. For regional analysis of this problem from a health-care perspective, see Marc Epprecht, "The World Bank, Health and Africa," *Z Magazine*, November 1994, pp.31-38.

21. Ecumenical Coalition for Social Justice, "Cooling Hot Money," *Economic Justice Report*, vol. 5, no. 2 (1994), p.2; Ted Fishman, "Our Currency in Cyberspace," *Harper's*, December 1994, p.54; Kevin Phillips, "The Tyranny of Traders," *The Globe and Mail Report on Business Magazine*, November 1994, p.65; Dillon, *Turning the Tide*, p.2.

22. Quoted in William Henry Pope, "The Re-Nationalization of Money," *Options Politiques*, February 1992, p.33; emphasis added.

23. David C. Korten, *When Corporations Rule the World* (San Francisco, Cal.: Berrett-Koehler Publishers and Kumarian Press, 1995), p.193.

24. *The Globe and Mail*, Jan. 25, 1997, p.B2.

25. It is little known that the creation of money by government at low interest rates for private and public enterprises whose debt-service payments revert to public ownership is a long-established device of prosperous growth: upon which, for example, the success of the pre-revolutionary American colonies depended, and over whose prohibition by the British government the revolution itself was precipitated. See, for example, John Kenneth Galbraith, *Money* (Boston: Houghton-Mifflin, 1975), pp.45-89. Even less known is the argument of the arch monetarist Milton Friedman that government should retain sole right to money-creating powers and private banks should be kept out of the money-creating business by the requirement of 100 per cent reserves. "The chief function of the monetary authorities [of the federal government would be] the creation of money ... [and] would leave as the chief monetary function of the banking system the provision of depository facilities, facilities for check clearance, and the like." Milton Friedman, "A Monetary and Fiscal Framework for Economic Stability," *The American Economic Review*, vol. 38 (1948), pp.245-64; see also John H. Hotson, "Ending the Debt Money System," *Challenge*, March-April, 1985, pp.48-50, and "Professor Friedman's Goals Applauded, His Means Questioned," *Challenge*, September-

October 1985, pp.59-61. This is a position on which Friedman has remained silent in the present circumstances of power.

26. The words are those of Charles Baillie, CEO of Toronto-Dominion Bank, after the third record year of profits for "the Big Five" at 16 per cent. John Partridge, "Toronto-Dominion Posts Record Profit," *The Globe and Mail*, Feb. 28, 1997, p.B9.

27. William Krehm, "The Hidden Dossier of the BIS," *Economic Reform*, May 1996, p.4.

28. For a fuller story of the more or less complete subjugation since the 1980s of governors of the Bank of Canada to the private interests of large banks and bondholders, see William Krehm, *A Power unto Itself: The Bank of Canada—The Threat to Our Nation's Economy* (Toronto: Stoddart, 1993).

29. William Krehm, "Genie Out of the Bottle" and "Let's Talk Bonds," *Economic Reform*, January 1996, pp.1, 5.

The Economics of
Life and Death

Growth, Development, and the Mutations
of the Money-Sequence

The market and the pursuit of money profit are no longer, as with Adam Smith, understood as the means to achieve the "wealth of nations." On the contrary, nations, people, and environments are now understood as the means of stockholders' money profit. Whereas Adam Smith construed the market and its rule of monetary self-interest as being servants of the public good, his ethic has now been reversed. Today in the market doctrine all that exists is conceived of as a servant of corporations competing against one another in the global market to maximize capital returns. Life has become the instrument of private capital expansion, rather than investors' capital being a means to enable human life. The world of value has been turned upside down.

The now dominant concepts of "development" and "growth" clearly reveal this radical inversion of value ground. When market agents use the words "development" and "growth," they do not mean *life*'s development and growth. They mean, rather, the opposite. When, for example, the Club of Rome introduced its now everyday concept of "the limits of growth" in the 1970s, it was not life's growth that its members were concerned about setting a limit to, but "economic growth" or, to be more precise than the Club of Rome, the increase of money-measured market growth. That is the problem that is the threat to global sustainability. Growth of life in a comprehensive sense—the increase of its range of sentience, active movement, and mental reach—is the value, in contrast, that a sound human ethic conceives as ultimate. Growth and development of life in this inclusive sense are the good of all goods that other values presuppose as their ground. Already in the 1970s, however, "growth" had come to be equated not with life's growth, but with market gains in money value.

The same tell-tale shift in the meaning of "development" has occurred with the pervasion of public vocabulary by market language. When we think of "development" now, we do not think of the life-sense of "development"—the unfolding and expression of life's capacities for articulation, diversification, and increased vital powers. Rather, we are taught to think of an opposite process—the levelling of life-habitats and natural environments for the building of profitable strip-housing, highways, and shopping malls. The idea of development is no longer linked to more comprehensive ranges of being alive. Development means how much money value has been added to an economy by marketable activities. These are now opposed ethics of existence. For increases of commercial development continuously result in life-depleting outcomes. More and more the air cannot be safely breathed, the earth's aquifers are more fouled, the fresh and sea waters are more lifeless, the atmosphere is more polluted and depleted, and larger numbers of citizens and their children are malnourished. Development in the market and capital-investor sense has come increasingly to mean the destruction of evolved forms of life to produce commodities that can be sold. Many other values are invoked here, but in reality only how much money can be extracted in money outputs above and beyond money inputs governs current market decision-structures.

A revealing example emerged at the beginning of this decade from a central office of the global market program. The money-sequence of value as a regulating structure of decision for the world was leaked in a memorandum from the chief economist of the World Bank—now the deputy secretary of the U.S. Treasury. On December 12, 1991, he recommended to his colleagues that the LDCs (less developed countries) achieve "welfare enhancement" by the increased migration of "dirty industries" and "toxic wastes" to their societies.

His reasoning was exactly in accordance with the money-sequence of worth, and it consisted of three arguments. Firstly, the costs and liabilities of destroying people's health were far less in these countries, because "the foregone earnings from increased mortality and morbidity" were far less than elsewhere. Secondly, the already existing pollution in non-industrialized countries, such as those in Africa, was now "vastly, inefficiently low" compared to other countries, and so posed a comparative advantage to them to pollute much more by increased economic activities in storing toxic wastes. Thirdly and finally, the "demand for a clean environment" had "very high income elasticity," meaning that money-demand for it varies with people's money income. Since, the argument went on, "consumption of pretty air" is non-tradable for poor countries, pollution of it by importing dirty industries and wastes from other countries would be the rational option to increase the less developed societies' money revenues, which is equated to their "welfare" in this value system. In accordance with this reasoning, the World Bank's chief economist concluded that the "economic logic" of dumping poisonous wastes in the Third World was "impeccable."[1] His conclusion follows from this model's chain of logic. Life itself in this calculus is conceived as being of worth only to the extent of its price, and with no price received it is counted as being worthless. Disease and death are of no concern except as they cost money. Pollution and toxic wastes are not to be prevented, but assigned a money value to increase the output of the money-sequence. The poor are to be poisoned by the richer for their own welfare of more revenue, which they now lack. Health and life themselves are to be sacrificed to a higher good, an advanced place in the money order of worth.

All of these implications follow strictly from the money program of value that now regulates global life's restructuring to a "more efficient form." The logic is perfectly consistent with its premises and yields a set of consequences that are normally imposed without a pause. The problem is not in the expression of this "economic logic" of the global market value system by the World Bank's lead economist. It is with this accepted program of value itself.

In short, we have come to a point where people, societies, and the planet itself have been so subjugated to the rule of the money-sequence of value that the most life-invasive and morally grotesque consequences of its system of reasoning appear "rational" and "impeccable" to its logic. We may spontaneously recoil from such implications when they are spelled out for us, but the value program has been permitted to elaborate in the way it has precisely because these implications have remained out of view. From the standpoint of the life-code of value, we can readily recognize the disorder. But the life-ground of value has been expelled from the global market as an ethical reference point from which such judgements can be made. Only what fits the market's value metric is computed by it or deemed "economic." If the protest to such thinking does not proceed through the value system of the market by the sovereign entitlement of money-demand, it is repudiated. There is now no other recognized ground of value to guide or override this ruling goal of money becoming more money, because it is now conceived as "the public interest" by governments across the globe.

This global market sequence of choices and exclusions may be a socially instituted insanity. But precisely because it is the construction of human decision and normative institution, it is open to alternative. Indeed it contradicts the theoretical ground on which its founder's ethical position rested. Smith assumed that maximizing money returns to oneself was a market-confined virtue and only good so far as it produced tangible goods. Now money-maximizing behaviour is conceived as the very meaning of "rational choice," and its connection back to what society needs is no longer thought consistent with market "freedom." Smith, in contrast, conceived of money as bearing value only in "circulating consumable goods, provisions, materials and finished work," that is, as a means of serving human needs and wants.[2] Now money-demand is, in pathological inversion, conceived as an end in itself, and all life is valued or rejected for its usefulness to larger circuits of it. The "meaning of life" is thereby conceived as increasing money-demand for those investing money. Reflective awareness of this inversion of value has, however, not yet occurred even to those who make ethics their object of higher research. They are inclined rather to value themselves as others in this value system do, in terms of how much money is assigned to their lives. Such is the power of a social value program to set and control minds.

Since this sequence of value begins from the assumption that more money can produce and buy more goods or utilities, it therefore follows from its value system that more money sums are always better. This suppresses distinctions of the greatest moment, as we have seen throughout this investigation. But this cognitive slippage at the very base of the money value program is not recognized. It ends in the failure to distinguish between wealth and money-demand on wealth. This fateful confusion means, in turn, that if money-demand on the wealth of life keeps increasing, but the wealth of life keeps decreasing by its demands, the market calculus cannot recognize the problem. According to its metric all is well, and prosperity and development are being won. This can lead, if its logic is not seen through, to the stripping of the life-world by money-demand until the life fabric can no longer hold.

The Pathologization of the Money-Sequence: From Means of Life to Means of Life Destruction

As we know from the earlier analysis here, the original money value program undergoes fundamental mutations in its sequence over time. In its classical capitalist form, it invests in buying factors of production (labour, instruments of labour, and natural resources) and organizes them to produce means of life (such as clothes, foods, and shelter). Then, to complete the code's sequence, these commodities are converted back into money again with the "value-added" of profit by sale to buyers in the market. We have represented this classical profit sequence by the formula:

Money —> Commodity —> More Money or $ —> C —> $[1]

This sequence of the money-code of value mutates, however, insofar as its middle term is no longer a means of life, but a means of life-destruction. This is a mutation of the investment sequence that is not registered in market theory or practice, but it is by its nature disastrous to life.

There are two principal forms of this mutation of the money-sequence into a means of destruction as its middle term. The primary form is to invest in producing and selling means of life-destruction that directly harm, maim, or kill fellow human beings. The market commodity that qualifies for this second general sequence of value that the money program assumes is intentionally contrived to attack life. In its paradigmatic form, it is constructed to do so in the most efficient and annihilative ways that the sciences can discover (with an estimated 50 per cent of all public research money in the world assigned to military research for the private profit of market firms). The weapons commodity, which began its truly modern history with the study of falling objects and projected missiles by Galileo, consists of highly developed instruments that can in moments kill and maim whole cities of people and destroy their infrastructures of life. The armaments commodity has long been at or near the top of the global market in money value of manufacture and trade, and international competition is intense to produce and market it. Even as wars between nations have ceased, weapons to deliver the most efficiently lethal systems of attack on human life and its built means of survival have continued to be developed and marketed, although the object of their threat and attack is now internal populations rather than foreign armies.

But the market's mutation towards a means of destruction as a principal venue of sale does not end with armaments. Other commodities have been contrived to cause disease to, injure, and kill human beings by their consumption. The cigarette commodity, for example, is a market good whose smoke bears an estimated 4,000 to 5,000 chemicals into its consumers and those around them, although many of its ingredients have long been known by their manufacturers to be addictive, disease-causing, and deadly. Unlike the weapon commodity, its life-assaultive properties have until recently been militantly denied rather than asserted by its manufacturers. The feeling that its consumption produces of a chemical "high" is the alarm-response of the body's immune system to deadly toxins entering the life-system. Here as well, the commodity sold between money input and money output is a means of life-destruction. Again, money becomes more money by production and then sale for profit of a product that directly attacks and destroys life.[3]

We can represent this second type of the money-to-more-money sequence in contrast to the first money-sequence in the following form:

Money —> Means of Destruction—> More Money or $ —> D —>$[1]

Means of life-destruction are not yet recognized as a mutant commodity because there are no normative resources within the market paradigm in terms of which they can be recognized. So over time they have become increasingly important as commodities in the global market's circuits of monetized "value-adding." Another such commodity is also overlooked in the market value system, and it is now consumed by virtually everyone in the world. Here what is produced and sold is the representation of the destruction of life rather a means to effect that destruction. The middle term in the money-sequence of value is an image of life-assault instead of an instrument to perform that assault. The pervasive production and marketing of films, live contests, video games, and other portrayals of terrorizing, harming, and murdering people have become the global market's major "entertainment industry." It has many branches of manufacture and sale, including production for viewers of "the real thing" in snuff videos and real-injury sports. This is the global market's means of life-destruction in the form of a communications commodity. The purpose of its product is not, like the weapon or commercial cigarette, to attack human life. Rather, the purpose is to manufacture and sell graphic depictions of the attacking and the obliteration of human life.

We classify this form of commodity production and sale as falling within the $ —> D —>$[1] investment sequence because it too encodes in its middle term of transforming money into more money the negation of life as its logic of money gain. Although the global market's first money-sequence of value can also systemically lead to reduction and destruction of life in consequence of its operations, this primary money-sequence may still have the means of life as its saleable object. In contrast, the second general sequence of the money-sequence of "value-adding" has vehicles of life-destruction as its middle term of money gain. We might call this second form of the money-sequence, then, its death-sequence of value.

As for non-human life's place in money's death-sequence of value, the systematic destruction of the environmental life-host and of members of other species at the rate of billions of individual beings a year is another vaster and many-levelled operation of the global market. Its ever more efficient transformations of the organic into the inorganic is a process that requires, for example, the levelling of forest ecosystems to raise domestic animals for killing for meat, a practice that erodes and depletes topsoil, water supplies, and natural ecosystems. This operation alone slaughters six million animals a year in the United States, has resulted in the destruction of 260 million acres of its forests, appropriates half of all U.S. water supplies, and extinguishes an estimated 1,000 species a year across the world.[4] There are many such planes of mechanized conversion of the organic to the inorganic in the global market system. They also include industrial extraction of natural resources—metals, timber, fish, aquifers—that leave behind them obliterated ecosystems above and below the earth and the water and typically pollute the life-systems remaining with the effluents of their processes. But normally this reduction of life to death is not built into the end-state commodity as its purpose. Rather, it is the way by which other creatures and ecosystems are made into packaged commodities, which then serve as priced goods for people to consume.

Still, there are straightforward death-sequences of value within this original $ \longrightarrow C \longrightarrow \$^1$ circuit. These are means of destruction that are produced and sold as sub-sequences within the $ \longrightarrow C \longrightarrow \$^1$ circuit that have no other function than to kill or demolish life-systems. They are, therefore, bona fide commodities of the death-sequence of value. The ever more efficient instruments for tearing natural life-systems apart—bottom-scraping nets, gas-powered chainsaws and tree grapplers, earth-surface bulldozers—in order to extract or gain access to their marketable elements is one such commodity type. Factory slaughterhouses that process live animals into meat products is another. These large-scale market instruments develop alongside the armament commodities for deliberately destroying life, and they become similarly efficient in their life-destroying capacities. They rip up soil communities, demolish forest worlds, and strip aquatic ecosystems in minutes. They cage, kill, and process animals into an inorganic state at the rate of billions a year. Since they are a means of life-destruction that are produced and sold within the money-sequence of value as its middle term between investment and profit, they too qualify for the money death-sequence of value.

Finally, there is the third general money-sequence of value. As we have seen in chapter 8, the profit-sequence also mutates when it bypasses the production of any usable commodity altogether. In this elaboration of the money-sequence, the investment circuit merely transforms money into more money into still more money in a self-multiplying sequence. We represent this pattern of money begetting money as Money —> More Money —> More Money —— or $ —> $^1 —>—— $^n. Because this third general sequence of the money program of value appropriates ever more money revenues from the production and distribution of means of life in society—for example, from budgets for social infrastructures to compound interest payments to international money-lenders who produce nothing of life-value—it too systemically negates life by its investment circuit. But it does so indirectly. It does not destroy life in the same way as the first or second general money-sequence of value. It does so by incrementally depriving social life-organization of its social life-means—rerouting, for example, former expenditures on public health, education, social welfare, pensions, civil arts, and communications to payments to the expanding $ —>$^1—> $^2 —$^3—$^n sequence. The rapid depletion of the social life-fabric by this increasingly dominant global market money-sequence is another mutation of capitalism whose underlying, systemic assault on life is not registered in any version of the global market paradigm.

In these expanding sequences of the money value program, their sequences of "value-adding" come into ever sharper and more destructive contradiction with life's requirements for protection, nourishment, and growth. Either the life-code of value is reasserted against these mutant sequences of the money-code, or human and planetary life is systemically dismantled, attacked, and depleted. The greatest threat in this entire development of the money-sequence is that it continues to leave us with life reduced to a means and cumulatively destroyed as well, with no clear recognition by its agents or public authority of this inner logic of its value system. Thus the all-important choice out of this process by regulating it is not recognized.

It would be naive to argue that these pathological money-sequences are merely a deviation from the original theory and practice of the market propounded by John Locke and Adam Smith. For from the outset, private property in money and its acquisition without limit have been uncritically presupposed as necessary structures of the "free market." These sequences of value thus occupy a long-implied logical space within the framework of the market value system. Over time the theoretical openings for such mutations have been filled in. As we have observed in earlier analysis, the market's money-sequence of value has from the outset taken the form of global trade in human slaves and continuous genocide of indigenous peoples to expand market sites and resources. But the mutation of the value code since to a single and unconditional absolute of maximizing money returns for those who have money with no commitment to any life-function is a post-Marxian and post-Keynesian development. It now challenges the long-term survival of world life-organization itself.

Banks for and against the Public Interest: The Market Lessons of the Asian Tigers

Since the money-sequences of the corporate market have mutated so as to strip the life-ground itself, there must be some intervention to restore our economic condition to reproductive health. This value correction begins with a basic recognition. Human value and life value are not a means for adding money value to economies. The market is a means for realizing human and life values. Once we recognize this lost ground of our value bearing, a second step follows. The market cannot be managed or followed so that it merely maximizes the money-to-more-money sequence as society's ruling value. If it is not to systemically destroy life, the market must be made consistent with the social and environmental life-requirements that it now blindly overrides. This may seem as obvious as the seasons, but it is a life-and-death truth that cannot be recognized by the value system of the global market paradigm.

Once we take these first two steps of the life-system of value, we are in a position to take a third great step. Growth of the money-sequence is not to be directed or permitted to occur in decoupled circuits of rapid expansion that do not contribute to or produce satisfaction of any life-requirement. Wherever these money-to-more-money circuits appropriate life-lines of money-demand only for their self-expansion itself, they must be recognized and responded to. As we have seen in debt-destroyed social infrastructures across the world, the money value program proceeds with no inhibition about stripping social life-organization itself, solely to return more money-demand to money-lenders and speculators. In seeking to reverse this value code back to life's realization as our end, and investment capital as its means, we will see that the program we are struggling to reverse is now systemically invasive. It aggresses against social life-systems as a segregated law unto itself, and it demands that societies across continents subordinate themselves to its autonomous growth. We have observed that this pattern is cancer-like in its characteristics. We now need to consider how this mutating variation of the market value-code can be prevented from further stripping society's common ground of life-sustenance and differentiation.

The "miracle economies" of East Asia, prior to their abandonment to unregulated financial inflows and outflows in recent years, reveal a required basis of solution. For a long period they were very successful at designing their societies as national production machines. But they were successful at this game—against free market mythology—by government co-ordination of the supply and allocation of money for long-term productive investment. In their pre-1990 periods of double-digit growth, their ministries of finance and economic affairs controlled and regulated investment capital, its price and its productive placement, across the economy. They selected key sectors of the economy of peacetime production and growth to invest in, pegged interest-rates at low levels for preferred investment sectors, extended loan time-horizons to fund strategic infrastructure, formed and reformed capital pools and concentrations to ensure money allocation to industrial needs, and even arrested and imprisoned corporate profiteers who exported private capital or appropriated profit for themselves instead of reinvesting it in the nation's productive enterprises (for example, South Korea's Illicit Wealth Accumulation Act).[5]

These governments at the same time variously planned and funded long-term product development and exports, subsidized energy and human-capital inputs, allocated foreign capital investment under strict government control, instituted and guided industrial conglomerates, planned light and heavy industry periods of development, prescribed products to corporate producers, held domestic prices high, managed access to raw materials, nationalized infrastructures, and, overall, managed the national economy's monetary and planning inputs and outputs, all within the choice structures of a market economy.

The People's Republic of China, the latest "market miracle," is following this government-management route today, with even more government intervention and direction of market forces than the neighbouring Asian Tigers. The outcome of planning the market's growth by government means has been year after year of double-digit market growth, as well as security from the 1997-98 Asian "meltdown" afflicting the financially deregulating economics next door. Indeed, only those economies that disobeyed global market dogma and continued to regulate the inflows and outflows of foreign capital managed to stay solvent—a lesson totally lost on IMF and U.S. economic leaderships, which sought to solve the crisis by demanding still further financial and investment deregulation. In contrast, the Chinese government still regulates its 1.2 billion-member economy under the unlikely and distinctly non-capitalist name of "the Communist Party." It is true that this latest "market miracle" of commodity production recklessly fouls the air, destroys society's historically built heritage, pervasively pollutes and restructures the environment and the countryside, rules out freedom of decision-making beyond consumer choices, and has more or less expunged biodiversity on every level of life-organization.[6] But it is, in terms of the market's value-code, peerlessly successful, a paragon of sustained "market growth and development." It boasts the world's most rapidly expanding economy, with a continuous 12 per cent average of money-rated growth and a doubled Gross Domestic Product for four years in the mid-1990s.[7]

An unseen advantage emerges here that the global market ethic still routinely deplores. Central government planning and co-ordination of a market economy not only can work by the market's own most basic criteria of value-judgement, but have also worked much better than unregulated market economies, which rail against "government interference" and "intervention." The U.S. market, which is held up as a model, is declining in its growth of wages, imprisons the highest proportion of its population in the world, and condemns over 20 per cent of its children to absolute poverty. But even given the purely market criteria of money-rated growth, the doctrine's own yardsticks have shown the foundational market myth that government planning is "inefficient" and an "obstacle to the engine of private enterprise" to be false. Economies with government-planned investment have grown much faster in monetized terms. Emancipation of the mind from the long taboo against government intervention in the economy is a release from a doctrinal gridlock whose importance cannot be overestimated. Recall how many programs and initiatives of government economic planning in Western capitalist societies have been attacked into extinction by the declared certitude of market policy leaders that all such "government planning of economic activities must end in disaster."

Once the myth of "disastrous government planning" is set aside, replaced by the facts of performance, the room for government on behalf of life rather than money maximization for money investors is opened. A central example is the issue of government regulation or deregulation of banking and other money-lending institutions. The control of private money-lending institutions over 95 per cent of the creation of money supply in the United States and Canada represents an appropriation of a central instrument of government sovereignty by leveraged debt creation. This effective private licence to print money by the creation of credit with no money reserves to back it carries with it the further right to demand compound interest, which multiplies the money sums owed over time far beyond what is available to pay them back. Banks and other institutionalized money-lenders receive, in addition, the free enforcement of this arrangement by governments against themselves and other debtors, whatever the costs involved. Financial leveragers of others' money stocks are then further assisted by minimum—but no longer maximum—rates of interest to be charged for lending this debt-created money. In Canada the money reserves that must be at hand to back up loans to the public is zero, and compound interest on this money has increasingly bankrupted citizens and governments. The previous fractional reserve required as collateral for loans was steadily shrunk to 4 per cent and then, in 1991, covertly abolished altogether by the federal government, which receives bank financing at election time.[8]

In the United States this minimal reserve of money still exists at about 4 per cent, but it is not much needed by the banks. This is because the U.S. government, like other governments, requires its taxpayers to pay for major bankruptcies of deregulated financial institutions—for example, the private savings and loan institutions whose speculations for fast money have been covered by U.S. taxpayers to up to $500 billion in bailouts. More recently, the U.S. government, along with the IMF, transferred another $47.5 billion to bail out major U.S. banks, such as Chase-Manhattan, which had been "exposed" by their speculations to the Mexican currency crash in 1995.[9] This welfare scheme of multibillion-dollar bailouts of private financial institutions reached historic heights in the late 1997 crash of foreign-loan-ballooned Asian economies. These costs to governments to serve the money-sequence and its special private interests are, however, not talked about by critics of government overspending and never represented as "expenditures that raise government deficits" or as "unaffordable handouts." This structured bias is predictable, for it follows from the global market program. What serves the money-sequence of value is good. What serves the life-sequence of value is "living beyond our means."

Although dependent on this government protection of credit-created and leveraged loans for foreign and other speculations, reserve requirements are still denounced as "a discriminatory tax" against banks. This may be a breathtakingly false claim, but it is faithfully repeated as litany by even government finance ministers, who resolutely "stay the course" of the ruling paradigm of value. With this licence to avoid backing up their loans with cash on reserve, private financial institutions create money as they please, and governments take care of their speculative shortfalls on the far end of the money-sequence, by raising interest rates again, by direct bailouts, or by privatizing publicly held bonds.[10] None of this is registered in contemporary theories of justice or even by opposition political parties. What is not permitted to be seen remains unseen.

One may wonder how this tacit acceptance of the decoupled rounds of the money-lending system can continue so intact when its damages to the civil fabric only increase over time. The answer may be found in the following line of reason, which underlies contemporary political and economic thought. Since the market is good and government interference in the market is bad, and since the money-lending system is a basis of the market, therefore it is not to be interfered with by government. Since, more deeply, this deregulated money system creates ever more money-demand, and more money-demand is good, there cannot be anything wrong with it. In this way, reason collapses, and the common life-interest is made into its opposite by construing it being as identical to "the market," which is whatever this increasingly unaccountable system demands.

As for the debtor governments, small businesses, consumers, and students who are bled dry from ever more interest demands on their lives, they are to have their financial regimes restructured with sterner terms. Thus they all grow more indebted by the day to the highest levels on record, just above the ratio of the 1929 crash.[11] This is how the money-sequence of value is sustained and expanded.

Watch the money-sequence of value for the lenders and investors and for those who are lent to and invested in. The one circuit grows; the other circuit is used to make it grow. The one circuit has money as its beginning and end terms; the other has public services and people. The one circuit is unaccountable to any life requirement; the other is grounded in the needs of social and environmental life-protection.

If the bank-debtor does not pay usury and principal on time, the debtor forfeits to the bank the home, farm, or whatever has been put up as collateral. We see here the moral template of the current market order. Those who do not have any money transfer what they earn to the money-sequence of value as continuously and volumi-nously as this value program can manage to extract over time.[12] This instituted structure of social decision-sequence ensures continuous redistribution to the money-to-more-money sequence and predictably results in the deepening system of impoverishment and enrichment that we see around us. Both governments and individuals have record levels of debt. Those who invest and lend money have record levels of assets and profits. This is called, with little respect for the produc-tive origins of the market, "market discipline." Enforcing its appro-priations across national boundaries is called "protecting national in-terests abroad."

In this overall value system of money allocation and returns, private banks exemplify the money-for-more-money circuit that in-creasingly saps the life of domestic economies, governments' ability to pay for their social infrastructures, and citizens who are now at historically high debt-to-income ratios. In contrast to this pattern of banks siphoning as much money as they can extract from the real economy, individual citizens and public sectors with no accountabil-ity to the societies that host them, banks in the most productive economies, past and present, are not decoupled from the social life-organizations that sustain and protect them. This was true of postwar Western economies and true also of the high-growth Asian econo-mies in their take-off periods of economic ascension. In the cases of the Asian Tigers and, earlier, Japan, their loans and investments were, so long as they were successful, disciplined by the host econo-my's requirements. Thus government agencies and regulatory regimes directed the policies of banks—their capital loans, their interest rates, their time frames of investment, their allocation of capital, and their involvement in foreign takeovers, their capital exits, and their major mergers. This was the master pattern from the founding of Japan's prototype Development Bank working in co-ordination with its Ministry of International Trade and Industry and its Economic Planning Agency, to the internal development banks of current mainland China.[13]

Western economies have had no counterpart to these financially regulated success stories. But the most stable economy during the 1990s in Latin America, Chile, alone remained free from foreign-capital invasions and haemorrhaging flights by the simple device of the national government requiring all incoming capital to deposit funds equivalent to 30 per cent of the total in the country's central bank, where it had to remain interest-free for a year. But all such regulations of investment flows, whether in Asia or post-Pinochet Chile, have been denounced by the IMF and international money managers as "restrictive barriers against efficient capital flows," even as they have proved to be societies' only effective protection against the ruinous deluges of delinked money tides. The global deregulation program merely becomes more demanding the more disastrously it bleeds its social hosts.

Although the successful society-capital linkage was eventually unravelled in every Asian economy that caved into the global market prescription of "liberalization of investment policies," banks and foreign money speculators were not permitted to become a law unto themselves for over a quarter-century of spectacular growth. All were, on the contrary, required by various instruments of government to serve public policy requirements related to productive performance, technological advance, employment levels, and new investment initiatives for the host economy. Hence their very great economic success in market-rated terms. One of these instruments was and remains the bank charter itself, upon whose special privilege banking operations depend. Once we recognize that money creation, allocation, and returns do not express a law of nature, but are a social construct admitting of many different forms, we unlock the chains of conditioned dogma that now hold society in a course of cumulative self-destruction.

A bank charter confers a social power to appropriate, lend, and invest others' money wealth while producing no good for "the real economy." It bestows on an institution in society the extraordinary right to leverage and loan out other people's savings at interest rates it chooses, with multiplier effects that increase the money created into higher and higher aggregate amounts. This government-granted right to, in effect, use others' money to create further money for still more money returns with no tangible good produced implies a very onerous obligation to the society that has conferred this lucrative entitlement. A mind-set that can ignore such a social obligation has not yet achieved the moral level of exchange. For centuries, a far less exploitative form of exacting unearned money gains was denounced as a usurious demand and a sin against God's law. Against the law of God or no, the right to use other's money to extract unearned payments from further others by itself implies a substantive obligation to the society that grants and protects this special right to banking institutions.

Reasoning by the most elementary axioms of human exchange, we can see that this special right to use and create society's money with no contribution to the value it is a demand on implies a profound social responsibility that must be discharged to remain within the circle of moral sanity. Private banks are socially provided with the revenue life-lines of credit and loans upon which the members and other non-lending institutions of society depend—public sectors, social infrastructures, small and large businesses, creative enterprises that do not yet exist, and individuals in need of loans. This great social responsibility is obviously not fulfilled by the current market value code of maximizing money returns for money-lenders, and nothing else. Banks now operating in accordance with this money-to-more-money value program violate their implied trust of social responsibility in virtually every decision they now take: by biasing their loans towards the already wealthy; by allocating money resources in complete indifference to employment creation and loss; by financing the foreign takeover of the domestic economy with domestic savers' money; by exporting local savings into monopolist mergers and speculative foreign adventures creating no use-value; by seizing the farms, homes, or productive operations of debtors in hard times; by lending very large sums of money for leveraged buyouts to disassemble undervalued businesses; and by demanding that the government privatize the holding of no-risk bonds to receive billions in interest rates for storing them as reserve equity in their vaults.

The current global market code, which the banks now pursue as routine, is exclusively self-serving and socially destructive in the most demonstrable ways. Yet governments have succumbed to these increasing depredations of society's life-organization over time in an invisible and historic capitulation with perhaps no match in a millennium of exploitations. At the end of the game, governments have come to refuse to hold any part of this money-sequence and its elaborations accountable to any interest beyond itself. To the extent that this occurs society is left defenceless against these licensed depredations of every level of the civil fabric.

It is in this socially decoupled control, circulation, and return of social money-demand and creation that we confront the mutating value sequence of the global market system. As the examples of market-evaluated success stories in East Asia show, the uncontrolled behaviour of foreign and domestic financial institutions in exclusive pursuit of their own money maximization was long not allowed to override the requirements of the productive economy. But as national boundaries have fallen in the global market system, the mutating market code of banks and other private corporations has led them to conceive of their new global prerogatives as being tantamount to exemption from any social obligation at all. In return for their vast prerogatives and host-society support systems, their one and only ruling value is to competitively appropriate ever more money revenues and leverages across the world in any way they can. This is the structure of money creation allocation they have been permitted to contrive, with every decision and payoff granted and protected at society's expense. Without all of this infrastructure of social institutionalization and protection, there would be no special access to others' money stocks, no right to interest demands, no compound rate of its accumulation permitted, no enforcement of all of this possession and demand, and no right to create money further by credit for society's means of exchange without 100 per cent reserve to back it.

The success of "golden age" market economies, however, reveals a so far hidden fact. The money life-lines of society were in every case substantially co-ordinated by government as the basis of these societies' subsequent market competitiveness. Such a basic truth of market success, is, however, a basic truth that the current market order is programmed to repel.

"Capitalist rationality," wrote Joseph Schumpeter, the eminent chronicler of capitalism's historical tendencies, "does not do away with sub- or superrational impulses. It merely makes them get out of hand by removing the restraint of sacred or semisacred tradition."[14] The "subrational impulse" here is what more and more of society's citizens recognize as "blind greed," without fully understanding its underlying cause. Loosed from any object of purpose except money or money equivalent without limit, this investment behaviour seems to morally sane people to be avarice run mad. But more deeply it is a disorder of the mutated market system itself, a far profounder problem than the avarice of individual persons. It is the set point of a cultural insanity now increasingly locked by "trade agreements" and IMF terms into an obligatory economic system for all societies of the world.

Its internal justification is, as we know, the convenient belief that money maximization for the self must produce the common good by the miraculous workings of "the invisible hand." So the "sacred" or "semi-sacred tradition" at work here appears to be, in truth, the market theology itself. From a non-market religious standpoint, this theology is plainly idolatrous at the crudest level, deifying a social token of demand on others as God. Money turning into more money is worshipped as a final law of existence to which all else has become a servant, including society itself. No idolatry has ever been so despotic.

The prespeculative economies of the East from Japan on were, in contrast, bound by a more traditional form of sacred tradition. Confucian forms of hierarchical command and obedience, within which society's members were trained to function, limited the demands of the money-sequence of value decoupled from social obligation. The individual social cell in such a Confucian ethic is conceived as a function of a larger whole, from the family to the state or race, to which subordination of purely selfish interest is a given of social life-organization.[15] Private banks and corporations operated within this larger regulating framework. So long as the money-sequence was not delinked from society in speculative run-ups of prices and foreign money liabilities, these societies did very well at the global market game with government planning and obedience to authority as automatic. These are clearly comparative advantages for mass-scale productive efficiency in machine-production economies.

Asian social orders were in this way favoured for economic success in the corporate market—a success that only faltered when their economies permitted domestic and foreign financial speculations to become their drive-wheel. But although the values of cultural homogeneity and rank-order organization conferred competitive advantage to Asian societies in the global market, they are values that violate basic requirements of the life-code of value. Values of breathable air, of personal life-space, of preservation of biodiversity, of protection of cultural differences, and of people's participation in the decisions governing their lives are not taken into account. Other values—education and artistic expression for its own sake, green surroundings of natural habitat, work to create or do what is not a saleable commodity, and free time to think and to play—are not values that enter into this program of value as being of worth.

We might recall here *Asia Week*'s homily on market virtue: "Establishing holidays, work-day limits and overtime pay is passing laws making low productivity compulsory."[16] So although the East Asian economies succeeded at satisfying corporate market goals of value, they were by the narrowness of this achievement a reductionist parody of human values. What we need to bear in mind in this turning-point period of human civilization is that the global market selects for a machinal social system. A less disturbing lesson of the Asian market successes is that the market doctrine's claim that "government planning" or "interference in the free market" is "inefficient" and "obstructs economic growth" has long been proven spectacularly false by the measures of the market's own yardsticks. It is extraordinary that such a themal falsehood could have been so long propagated as certitude, especially given the continuous covert interventions of governments in Western markets—not by planning for the social interest, but by compulsory minimum interest rates to be paid by debtors, by endless discriminatory tax expenditures on corporations, by vast subsidy outflows, by guaranteed markets and profits to armaments industries, by incentives and reduced interest rates for favoured products for export, and by large-scale financial bailouts of major firms and banks that fail in the market. After all, the market principle of "freedom from government interference" has been, in reality, a code phrase for opposition to government in the common interest.

In the summing up of these differences in the regulation of money investment in the market societies of the East and the West, one general lesson is clear. Asian economies have demonstrated that government planning of capital investment, products, and processes works in the long term to achieve industrial efficiency and growth so long as it is not abandoned to decoupled financial sequences unrelated to real productive achievement. But even this is not a final value for a healthy society. If we seek to enable people and their environments to become more vital and comprehensive, we must look more deeply for value guidance. Pollution, congestion, uniformity, environmental desertification, and authoritarian relations are never a pattern to be construed as social success. The Brundtland Commission implied this general point, but did not identify the money-sequence program behind the unsustainability of the current human relationship to the planet.[17]

Pension and Mutual Funds: A Hidden Market Keel

As we have seen, money's social creations and returns can be regulated to serve society's life-requirements. But it is not only the banks whose program of self-enrichment without accountability must be encoded with requirements to protect and enable life. On the circuits of the money-to-more-money sequence, other pathways of money multiplication deprive society of its financial life-lines of support. An example is the vast private pension funds dependent on the earned wages and salaries of workers of all kinds. These funds have been created downstream from the banks by government tax write-offs to their contributors. Running parallel to those funds are very large mutual-fund holdings, also created by government tax write-offs to their contributors, this time as registered retirement savings. Together these private pools of capital amount to over \$4 trillion in North America alone, and the biggest suppliers of capital in global markets are expected to be the Western world's swelling pension and mutual funds.[18]

This is a threshold development, because it indicates the extent to which this value program has been universalized in its hold. Pension and mutual funds are invested as the assets of the salaried and wage classes, whose memberships do not resist or even observe this co-option of their savings and future by the market money-code. The program in this way becomes a trans-class pathology not only in mind-set and motivation but also in actual monetary stock growth. The massive volumes and velocities of these collective pension and mutual funds now drive markets and investment across the world. They will move in any direction for maximum money returns. All that the investment managers who control them are programmed to do is to add to the money value of their command. In turn these financial managers—increasingly society's highest paid and most rapidly growing money possessors—operate exclusively in accordance with the money-sequence of value, seeking only and openly to turn money into more money for themselves and the funds they control by foreign speculations, currency and derivative trading, bond purchases and sales, and a complex variety of unproductive exchanges. This is known in the business as "fiduciary trust to stockholders," and within the closed program of the money value system it is the ruling ethic of global market culture.

Only by accident do any of these manipulations of money movements relate back in any way to the life-requirements of the society that has tax-financed them into existence. Their investment, on the contrary, can go into low-cost foreign sweatshops to compete against and undercut the very working groups contributing to the funds, invade the public sector of their country with privatizing takeovers, sell out their own nation's currency, and speculate in foreign transactions that produce no goods or services at all.

There is no limit on any such uses of these vast funds, even as they are subsidized by tax expenditures, and even as they attack the home society itself. This is the nature of this value program. The sole criterion of money allocation and return in this program is more money value for the fund and the fund dealers. The actual owners of the fund, the prospective pension beneficiaries themselves, have no access, say in, or control of the nature of their investment. Fund managers assume as their sovereign right the money growth of the fund, the corresponding money commissions that flow from it. Beneficiaries accept it as the structure of their future security of existence. Again, we observe the autonomous sequence of this value program in which people become servants to its functions in the illusion of "market freedom." Though created by government tax policies themselves, these domestic social funds are deployed entirely in compliance with the borderless money-code of value and its sequence of seeking to become ever more without any linkage to the home society's common interest of employment, social security, education, or environmental preservation.

On the surface these funds appear to serve future pensioners in a private capacity. While they do have this payoff to those who are fortunate enough to have had long-term secure jobs and to have benefited from decades of tax write-offs from government, this is not a benefit to society when it serves a decreasing minority of all future pensioners, over 60 per cent of whom already live in poverty in North America in the wake of "the golden age" of high-paying, secure jobs.[19] If decent pensions for the society's retired citizens and workers are sought, why then is only a rapidly shrinking minority of society afforded such concern? Why is the "security of future pensioners" planned and paid for by government tax expenditures targeted at a decreasing fraction of the population?

The reason is that the objective being served by these pension and mutual funds is not financial security for even privileged old-age pensioners. Rather, it is the opposite. As the global market advances, old-age security by universal pensions is rapidly eroding at the same time as society's sector of full-time, permanent jobs and pension benefits is contracting.[20] The claim that these vast capital pools autonomously traversing the money-code sequence in ever greater volumes and velocities are for "old-age security" is so partial and misleading an account of what is occurring that it turns social reality into the illusion of its opposite—an ideological operation to which we are now accustomed.

Pension and mutual funds are another money-into-more-money circuit created by government tax-money flows and increasingly unaccountable to any social life-requirement. They are monolithic inputs into the segregated money-code sequences of the global market—altogether, $9000 billions, in North America alone, thirty times the total worth of the United States' sixty richest people.[21]

Instead of these thousands of billions of dollars of tax-created mutual and pension funds remaining unaccountable to any requirement of the society that has financed them, they can be redirected to socially beneficial ends. In this way, they would "pay their way" as tax expenditures—a value maxim that is instead quoted against the poor. Such options, however, are not open in this system of freedom, even to those who own the pension fund. Their voice in and even knowledge of how their pension funds are invested are denied to them by an administrative control of these capital pools that is, in effect, as distanced from their agency as someone else's private property. Financial managers, for whom the money-sequence of value is the set point of body and soul, exercise unilateral decision-making authority over the investment of these vast capital accumulations; and they do so with no other goal than to transmute them into more money value with no accountability to even the social security of the collective bodies who own the funds (for example, the unionized and public-sector workers whose positions are eliminated by the demands of the same value program).[22] This is the peculiar "democracy" of the current market order. But it is a regime against which hardly a murmur is raised, even by those union and public-sector leaderships who decry the "social irresponsibility" of the corporate capital of which their pension funds are major holders. Here again, we see the value system's ultimacy of hold, overriding even the traditional principles of property right and class division to fulfil the money-sequence's reified demand of maximum returns. This is the underlying dictatorship of the money-code and its uniform decision-sequences at work. It grips all in its diktat as does the instinct-sequence of the conditioned beast.

Programmed by this value format, governments have expended massive and increasing volumes of forfeited tax revenues to favour private pension and mutual funds. These private funds clearly owe back to the society that has paid much to finance them some return investment in enterprises that reproduce and extend society's life capacities. Such socially beneficial enterprises are not difficult to identify: for example, secure job-creating enterprises that enable the sector of society with old-age pension benefits to rise, or the mandated purchase of government bonds that would enable society's pension and other social services to be maintained. It is unlikely that still thinking contributors to these funds would object if this service to the common interest in return for tax reductions was instituted as a rebate condition. Certainly they could have no coherent reason to object unless in automatized enactment of the global market program. But the mounting armies of money-code firms and managers now in control of ever more of others' pension and retirement funds would predictably resist with the fury of the money-sequence they are driven by. But such disconnection from the principle of exchange itself upon which the market is founded is not coherent.

Is there "enough money" to serve the requirements of civil life? First World societies are overstocked with capital funds. But they are programmed only to enrich those who possess them. These occupants of benficiary roles in the money-sequence, in turn, demand even more tax-expenditures on their acquisition of foreign speculative investments as well (already 20 per cent in Canadian Registered Retirement Savings Plans).[23] Here again, we see telling illustrations of how radically delinked from its social life-host this government-financed money-sequence has become.

Taxing Money-Demand: The Unseen Principle of Justice

A more aggressive form of the money-into-more-money program is round-the-clock currency and bond speculations. As we have seen, currency speculators and bond raters and dealers who manage these tidal flows of the global market's money system publicly dictate to governments what they must do to "reassure the market." They "attack"—a term they normally use for this operation—national currency and bond values if governments do not comply with their money-code prescriptions. "Attack" is a revealing term, corresponding to the diagnostic label for the behaviour of a viral advance within the life-body. Although such attacks can destabilize and disable a society as seriously as a military invasion, as in the case of Mexico's or Indonesia's "financial meltdowns," which disemployed and impoverished tens of millions, these financial transactions operate tax-free, an exemption for which not even market ideology has manufactured a plausible pretext. Under the new global market regime, society's systems of self-defence are now opened wide to external money-sequences to plunder and exit them as the undeclared ruler of the "new world order."

Once again, this condition of social subjugation to the dominion of external and internal agents of the money-code is not "inevitable" or "beyond the powers of government." A financial transaction tax could easily be imposed on all short-term, speculative deployments of money accounts by digital tracking of their movements in major financial centres. Governments could, as with trade agreements, administer a common regulatory regime. The idea is not new. It has long been proposed by one of the world's most eminent economists, James Tobin, who won the Nobel Prize for his analysis of financial markets.[24] That a policy instrument of precise and calculable social benefit sponsored by a world-leading expert has been excluded from electoral and policy debate for over twenty years reveals, once more, the lock of the market value program on public authority itself.

G-7 meetings refuse to discuss it. Finance ministries and departments, in now standard subjugation to market demands, inveigh against the tax and misrepresent it.[25] The standard position of market agents is, predictably, that it is impossible because it would "interfere with the free movement of capital," which this program of value prescribes as a final good in itself. That this view favours speculative transactions above all other economic activities that relate to the needs of society and are nevertheless taxed is taken for granted. The program computes nothing that does not accord with its acquired demands.

It therefore follows from the money-sequence program of value that a tax on its decoupled circuits would be "unenforceable." This position entails that market agents are willing and able to violate the law on behalf of the money-sequence of value, another sign that this value order now places itself above the law with confidence of its impunity. These market responses are, at bottom, more predictable manifestations of the underlying money-code. Its program of transforming money into more money for money leveragers is, like a cancer, a sequence that overrides any barrier of life-function or legal regulation that impedes it. Fairness or justice, social survival or life-requirement, and democratic accountability or the rule of law are assumed as unable to deter it.

When we link this global market response to an infinitesimal tax with the broader pattern of increasing repudiation of taxes of any kind on unearned financial returns to money investors and lenders, we discern the same overarching pattern observed throughout this investigation. The money value code is increasingly unaccountable to law, the society that hosts it, and the requirements for survival of human and planetary life itself. Rather, law, society, and human and environmental life are now accountable to the money-code and will be attacked and stripped if they do not conform to its ever-increasing demands. The consequences of this usurpation of life by an idolatrous code may seem deranged to normal consciousness. But normal consciousness now averts its view, as the slave casts down her eyes. For those merely programmed by the code, all that occurs is in accord with necessity.

In the money-code, necessity has as one of its expressions the abhorrence of all obligations to pay towards support of the common life-interest. But taxation, at base, regulates circulation of money-demand through the social life-host. At best, it "takes from the excessive to give to the insufficient," to cite the ancient wisdom of Lao Tzu.[26] Yet government taxation across the world has increasingly assumed a new redistributive pattern. Instead of taxing the rich to give to the poor, the pattern of redistribution since the Reagan divide of 1980 has reversed this supplementation of the lesser by the opulence of the richer. Government taxation policies now increasingly operate to enrich the rich, and to do so they take from the poorer, the middle class, and the civil commons.

In general this pattern consists of tax expenditures of countless kinds to corporations and the richest income recipients by the redirection of more and more government revenues to tax reductions, write-offs, and subsidies. At the same time, government taxes on the poor and the middle classes of society have risen to pay for these tax benefits to the wealthiest by regressive sales taxes, higher real tax rates, and loss of social entitlements. Most significantly of these redistributive patterns, government spending on universally accessible infrastructures of education, health care, social security, environmental protection, family benefits, public transit, and non-profit communications have been reduced or eliminated to make up for the public revenues lost to pay for corporate and high-income tax reductions. In this redistribution of wealth from the civil commons to the money-sequence, corporation taxes have been cut to a fraction of their former rates and are now globally far below the tax rate on a subsistence wage.[27] Capital-gains and inheritance-tax revenues have, simultaneously, been repeatedly decreased without a floor to their reduction. What government revenues remain have been, all the while, increasingly directed towards compounding interest rates for private money-lenders. Remaining government activities have then been refocused on serving business corporations. This underlying metapattern of government taxation and of increasingly subsidizing, protecting, and serving already rich corporations and individuals, while dispossessing the public spheres and less affluent, has been thoroughly documented. It is a worldwide tidal shift of the instituted value system of society to a new structure of ultimate concern: to, as the now ruling value program represents it, "attract investors" and "succeed at international competition."

This overall structure of money-demand redistribution by government taxes and expenditures is not "unavoidable." It is the robotic elaboration of the money-code of value within the executive offices of governments themselves. This money-code of value does not conform to, but systematically violates, the historically instituted function of government, which is to serve the common interest. It overthrows government's declared ground of legitimacy and function and is on this account truly called a "market revolution." In response, the legal means of government taxation need to be applied to redirect government to its legitimate function. What is required is straightforward—to recognize the money-sequence disorder behind the appearances proclaimed by market ideology and to regulate this money-sequence's operations to conform to the protection and enablement of society's life.

Money is a socially constructed unit of demand on society's labour, resources, and goods. It is, put another way, what its users demand from society. Not only is it the demand of its users on society's past and present members' work and their resources, proportionate to the money they control to so demand, but in this form it is also dependent for every part of its demand on the public sector and its tax-based resources—on its laws, its enforcement systems, its costly infrastructures, its literacy and numeracy dissemination, and its many instituted guarantees and defences of the money unit's possession and worth.

Without this vast underlying social groundwork of defence and guarantee of the money token's worth, and without the actual content of goods and services produced by others to serve its socially created entitlement, money would be no more than empty signifiers without worth. Unlike private possession in real goods for use, money is in every particular and quality a social construct entirely dependent on society and its ongoing expenditures, supports, and protections. This total dependency of the money token on society's patronage for all the value and power it exerts is the market value program's deepest secret. The doctrine's layers of presupposition conceal much, but no truth is more concealed than the absolute and helpless reliance on society and government of every iota of the value and power of private money-demand. This tutelage of the God-like command of money is, therefore, a recognition that the market's program of value must repel. For once recognized, all of its vestments of authority and independent freedom dissolve into air as the emperor without clothes.

Because money's governmental ground of value and demand is not accessible to the mind-set of market believers, they everywhere fetishize its socially dependent token as a god-like power to which society itself is to be a servant. The money-code is a cosmic metaphysic, and it is more totalized by far than the deluded naiveté of past manna cults. But what scientist or philosopher today examines or lays bare its system of assumptions and fabrications? From a standpoint not locked into this cult, we are in a position to understand a basic truth. *Money-demand on society is precisely the measure of what is received from society and, therefore, the exact and proper object of its taxation.*

Approaching society's taxation of its members from a reality-grounded view, we can see that taxation needs to fall precisely on money's demands from society. The most imperious money-demands on society, on the contrary, now ride tax-free. Working from the bottom level of money-demand up, we can reasonably grant that there is a minimum level of money-demand up to which there ought to be no taxation—for example, for those who have less than an above-poverty income. Up to the level of above-poverty subsistence, then, those who exercise only a "tight-belt" level of money-demand should, to allow them minimum range of life, be left tax-free. This follows from the logic of the life-sequence, which we adopt here as the ground of tax right and liability.

Beyond this minimum level of freedom from taxation, to enable life that would otherwise go into life-deficit, taxation appropriately falls on all money-demand transactions at whatever level society requires to sustain itself. The more money-demand one exercises, therefore, the more tax revenues one ought to pay. Obligation to society is reconnected to demands from society. If one makes very great money-demands on society over a year—by stock transactions, currency speculations, investment fund activities, flip real-estate deals, private clubs, restaurant use and holidays, jet and auto purchases and uses, luxury-good consumptions, or hiring of servants and services—one would thereby be obliged to remit correspondingly high tax payment in return. Less demanding citizens would be obliged to pay correspondingly less. The overall rate of taxation could be much lower, however, because all money-demand transactions would be taxed—unlike now, where most money-demand transactions are not taxed at all (for example, in the currency, bond, and stock markets, banking operations outside these markets, and countless tax exemptions and write-offs to large money-demand bearers). We need to keep in mind here how free-riding and subsidized these money-demands on society have become. Society's currencies, infrastructures, undervalued productive businesses, employment rates, public debts, educational and health systems, and social security have all been destabilized across the world by tax-exempt transactions opportunistically seeking instant conversion into still more money-demand with no productive contribution to society at all. An automatic tax on all such impositions of unproductive money-demand is the most basic responsibility of governments to protect and enable the common life-interest of societies that have granted these monoliths of money-demand every power they exert.

A steeply higher rate of taxation on money-demand that seeks only to become more money-demand with no contribution to society follows as a self-evident principle of social value judgement once we adopt the life-code and its principle of reciprocity as our value guide. A still higher tax on money-demand that causes direct damage to human or environmental life—as with the production, emission, or purchase of toxic commodities or effluents, follows as well by the entailment of the life value code and its requirements of growth sequence. In other words, money-demand on society without return to society, or money-demand on society with known direct harm to its life, is taxed by the measure of what it costs society, with higher rates calibrated throughout by this principle. To do the right thing is to protect and enable life, in taxation as in all else.

As to how all money-demand can be taxed, the concept of a financial transaction tax has already been thoroughly researched, and implemented, in part, in some European countries. Most importantly from the standpoint of practicality, a financial transaction tax requires far less administration than existing taxes. All that is required is an automatic deduction levied on every transaction in every financial institution through which all cheques, withdrawals, transfers, credit charges, stock or bond purchases or sales, or speculative loans travel in digitally trackable flows. A money-demand taxation regime can be far more easily implemented than any taxation scheme now in place. Electronic, automated systems of money transaction are now more or less universal, and centralized in processing, across the world. The global market's base of social policy implementation is already established in transnational trade treaties. The mechanism for a direct taxation of money-demand on society's life is available for the first time in history. It requires no red tape or bureaucratic mediation by time-consuming forms, and financial loopholes are ruled out by the direct form of the taxation. The system is set for a rapid evolution out of systemic tax evasion, out of the collapse of public revenues that serve the common interest, and out of a feudal order of special parasitic privileges sapping the life-resources of society. All that is required is recognition of our condition and its existing capacities for exact intervention and correction. What stands in the way of diagnosis becoming cure is the disordered value program of the global market paradigm that is assumed as the structure of reality.

Unlike current schemes, taxation of money's demand on society does not permit most money-demand transactions to ride tax-free. More so, its small rates bite hard on large-scale, fast-flip transactions specialized in by the "paper economy" and its proliferating speculative machinations. Taxation of money's demand itself is the governing principle. The more large-scale and short-term, the more tax remittance flows to the public sector. Directly damaging money-demand usually occurs downstream in the unpaid-for consequences of pollution, labour and consumer diseases, natural resource depletions, and, in general, society's loss of vital capacities of human and environmental life by the unaccountable effects of the money-code sequence. The more severely such life-destructive effects are taxed to deter and to prevent them from recurring, the less serious their harms will become. The slide-scale of taxation can be correlated to the life-code's requirements in as developed a protocol of life-responsibility and obligation as intelligent public policy can evolve. But it is guided by two general principles of taxation throughout, which in turn are based on the life-code of value: first, the taxation of all money-demand (except that by below-poverty-line income recipients); and second, increased rate of taxation to paper-economy transactions, and, by degrees, to harm-causing money-demand not prohibited by law.

Such a money-demand tax regime in favour of life's protection and more comprehensive range will be repudiated *a priori* by the money-code mind-set, which excludes life value as such from its metric. The rejection of any value but itself to regulate the economy is a predictable consequence of its value program. Even when such a taxation principle ensures, as no other tax system can, strict proportionality between demand and obligation, non-evadable application, minimal rate, and the lowest possible administrative costs, we can know in advance that any tax at all on the money-sequence's transmutations will be attacked as "government interference in market freedom." This is why this value code is not rational, but mechanical in nature, requiring an act of mind to unlock from it.

Taxation by government that is impartial and in the common interest need not be limited to money-demands on society alone. As already observed, the life-code entails that money-demand for any process of production or product that results in harm to human or environmental life requires a higher level of taxation so as to deter and pay for such harms. *Harm* is identified in accordance with the reduction or destruction of life it imposes; which, in turn, is a principle that admits of degrees, dependent on the range of vital life that is disabled or destroyed. By its metric we can tell, for example, that destroying a forest or marine ecosystem is a permanent evil, while harvesting its resources so that all its habitats and species are enabled to reproduce is a good for the human use-values it extracts and not a harm to the life-system it draws from. There is no difficulty in recognizing by the life-code the extreme and systematic harms that have been normalized by money-sequence operations with their costs to life excluded from view as "externalities."

As we know, the market value metric counts only what is sold as a value, and only money price gained is its measure. Harm to life outside this calculus, however devastating and wasteful, does not compute. In consequence, there is a systemic proliferation of continuous, cumulative harms by global market processes and products that market prices in no way reflect. For example, the automobile product continuously kills and maims people in very large numbers. Its aggregate supplies also overrun civil space everywhere so that community life-spaces are paved over and cannot be walked in. The fossil fuels used by proliferating motor vehicles on land and water pollute the atmosphere and air we breathe, cause acid rain, despoil pristine wilderness by their extraction, deplete a preciously durable resource, and power a pervasive noise-making that violates the sentient ranges of human and environmental life across the globe's surface. Such an uncontrolled deluge of harmful products, deprivations, and pollutions to fulfil and extend the money-sequence requires government response to protect the common life-interests that government is mandated to represent. This conclusion follows straightforwardly from the life-code of value, and its implementation is in accord with traditional legal and political conceptions. But it too remains excluded *a priori* by the market value program. A life-protective tax built into the price of such commodities is a minimal measure for the life-code, both to redirect money-demand from destructive invasion of life's fields and to pay for the very great costs incurred by the public (by, for example, building roads and highways everywhere for fossil-fuel-driven commodities and providing medical facilities to treat their millions of victims). But, again, what relates to life-demands rather than money-demands does not compute to this system.

Because the market value program recognizes only money-value increases and decreases, it is structured to repel any and every limit placed on minimizing money inputs or on maximizing money outputs. If pollution by market processes, for example, becomes no longer deniable by the senses, it follows from the program that cost-adding controls on emissions imposed by public authority will be repudiated as "ineffective," and only what serves the money-into-more-money program will be interpretable as "realistic." Thus in the current period, as market pollution of the life-elements threatens the very conditions of human existence, "pollution credits" are pronounced as the sole workable solution. These pollution credits confer new monetized equity on the polluters, allow for profitable trading of their assets where no money value existed before, and maintain purpose and decision within the market's money-expanding sequence. The value of life remains as before subordinated to the maximization of money returns to corporate investors, and the actual goal of pollution reduction is thought certain to be realized by the magic of the invisible hand, which transforms private money acquisitiveness into the public good. We see in such remedies the closure of this paradigm of thinking to any reality but itself. Even when the failure of its logic has finally registered as fact, its recourse to solution remains confined within the very principles of calculation that have caused the problem.

To connect taxation in an appropriately calibrated way to society's requirements of life-protection leads in the opposite direction. We know well enough what is harmful to life, and what is not. The whole of medical science is a historical articulation of the answer at the level of the individual organism, and the principle of decreased range of vital life applies, as we have seen, universally. The problem is not one of being unable to tell the difference between good and bad, between what disables and what enables life. The "burden of proof" has been borne by millions of known victims and ecosystems and is exactly known by the relevant sciences in countless areas of life-harm. We know as well that market agents avoid costs like the plague and that a strict and unevadable tax on their pollutive products known beforehand will steer them from such product lines to the precise extent that its tariff continuously and fully reflects the extent of their pollution. Only a peculiar bias of the mind-set can blinker out these home truths, but just such a structure of outlook has been demonstrably at work in this case, as we find not a single product tax that is set fully to reflect and pay for the harm the product imposes on life.

The key to finding our life-rudder here is, in the end, to recognize a general fact. The money-demand circuits of the contemporary global market are unaccountable and are not connected back to the needs of any life-host that supports them. A disinterested gatekeeping of these money-demand circuits and their consequences is required for the safety of social and environmental life and to enable their vital expression and differentiation. Government taxation is another level of opening and narrowing the passages of money-demand to ensure that self-interested market behaviour and its money-code do not overrun the life-ground. Taxation operates at the level of money-demand itself, not by the heavy-handed and selectively applied state mechanisms of the judiciary, the command economy, or armed force. These are cruder mechanisms geared for more primitive conditions. Here the problem to be confronted is socially normalized and organic and requires correspondingly normalized and organic response. The problem has been that public taxation has not yet been coherently linked to the common interests of life itself, and so these life-interests are violated with impunity. Life-calibrated taxation is another way in which the socially institutionalized power of money-demand, now mindless, can be impartially and exactly steered towards vital goods and away from what depredates and destroys the planet's conditions of health and existence.

Until we recognize that money is not wealth, but demand upon wealth, we will continue to strip the life-world according to its ever more decoupled demands for more life to feed on. The still evolving principle of justice—to tax money-demand in proportion to all of it and, in particular, in proportion to its disabling of human and natural functions—is the long-missing link between money and its accountability to life.

Beyond the Mega-Machine to the Civil Commons

The global market system is, in the end, competent at only two kinds of functions. But because these functions are so central to contemporary life, they are thought to be all of it. First, the market system organizes the production and use of machine-made goods in a more internally cost-efficient way than known society-wide alternatives.[28] Yet at the same time, as we have seen, if it is not precisely subordinated to the rule of law in this function, it is systemically life-irresponsible in the "external" costs it imposes on workers, environments, and life in general. The global market regime is also, relatedly, competent at calculating every conceivable elaboration of the money-code and sequence so as to maximize added money returns to stockholders. This competence is, however, a danger to social and planetary life if it is not confined to the domain of machine-made commodities as its sole realm of proper use.

The ultimate reason why the market's methods are wholly out of their depth in such life-spheres as education, health-care, communications, and pensions is really quite straightforward. The market's regulating objective is to enrich market stockholders and managers rather than to serve and enable human life. As we have observed in pattern form across various levels of life-organization, the market code rules out whatever does not count towards and add to private money profit at the end of each sequence of its growth process. Life's capacities as values in themselves are of no account within this value code. Only so far as life, environmental or human, can be instrumentalized for money gain does life have any value for its decision-structures. This inverted value program is destructive enough to life when life is merely a means or factor of production. But in the realms in which life is a value in itself—the realms of education health care, art and communication, playing fields, wilderness parks, and the civil commons in general—the market's preference-structure violates the shared vocation of public service to life by its very nature. Here lies the greatest threat of its derangement, because the civil commons is also the defence system of society's life. Without its shared capacities of life-provision and response to the money program's disorder, there is little to stop the program's systematic depredation of the life-body of the world.

When the market subordinates life to its program of "value-adding," it imposes a regime of value alien to life's function—mechanical, homogenizing, and respondent only to money stimulation. But in the realm of life and the civil commons, it is not money whose fulfilment is mandated by codified policy and law. Thus as managers of privatized public sectors apply their money-to-more-money method to the realm of the community's shared life, they behave in absurdly inappropriate ways. First, they "double or triple their own salaries and award themselves extravagant bonuses and share options," to cite a national business magazine on the general course of market privatizations of the public sector in Britain.[29] The public's water supply may be "so leaky that 29 percent of treated water is lost," but "the shareholders enjoy record profits."[30] The national coal mines may be transferred to "more efficient private control," but the serious accident rate rises by 18 per cent and deaths more than double.[31] The country's privatized gas corporation may shut off gas heating the homes of people during periods of high demand in the winter cold, but this "saves money"—so that a 75 per cent raise can be awarded to the corporation's stockholding chief executive.[32] Note the program of value at work here, its sequence of value rule overrunning the requirements of life. "Private generators do not feel it is their responsibility to keep the lights on in Britain," summarizes a political scientist onlooker, and his description expresses the underlying problem.[33] Reducing money inputs to maximize money outputs is the final, ruling goal. The reduction or loss of people's lives in the process is not relevant to this sequence of value-adding.

Such a program of value to rule the realm of a community's shared life is contradictory in principle and destructive in consequence. But this does not deter the market program's leaders and followers. If there is not enough money for a majority of pensioners to pay for private plans, says a prominent investment representative advising government to end public pensions, then those left without support must "have lots of children."[34] If for-profit clinics are appropriating financial and medical resources from the public health-care system and undermining universal access to medical treatment, this is no problem, argues an eminent business newspaper, because "private clinics actually add to the proportion of GDP devoted to medical care."[35] If the nation's world-leading civil commons are rapidly liquidated to pay interest rates on privatized government bonds, this is as it should be, says the minister of finance. "It's really important," he says, reciting the currency speculators' war cry, "to have government's feet held to the fire."[36]

Here in plain view are the symptoms and signs of the collapse of the distinction between life and money values. The life realm is subjugated to the money-sequence of value, and all that does not fit as a means of its growth is expendable or to be sacrificed to its higher good. This makes perfect sense to the value-set, because the money-sequence subsumes all that is of worth. As long as the money-sequence expands to become more money, all is as it should be. As for government ministers presiding over the reduction of the public life-realm to the means or refuse of the money circuit's growth, they too are programmed by its demands. The common life-interest as distinct from the demands of the market dissolves into air. Since this structure of value judgement conceives the public good to be already served by the market, then whatever the market demands must be in the common interest. Life is expelled from any right of its own in the requirements of "the growth of the economy," and public servants themselves hasten to serve the new sovereign. In this annihilative identity, money value is the only term of value. This is how a carcinogenic circuit is established at the level of social life-organization: not as an object of metaphor, but as a clinically diagnosable attack on the life-fabric of society. At this stage of its systemic spread, the code and sequence of the disorder are reproduced by the nodes of the public sector itself.[37]

It is not difficult to discern in such instantiations of the money-code that the market program cannot, in principle, serve the realm of life as a value in itself. But just as its blind calculus increasingly fails to provide for the requirements of employment, sustenance, and environmental stewardship in the private sector, its prescriptions are all the more aggressively imposed on the public sector. The market's universal imperative for protecting value is automatic in this value regime: reduce whatever costs money to the money-sequence. Whatever serves life as a value for itself is, it follows, repelled as "unaffordable"—environmental regulations, unions defending workers' living standards, government-set minimum wage levels, the next generation of teachers in schools and universities, universal healthcare benefits, mandatory safety conditions and monitored industrial toxins, social assistance to the unemployed and their children. The list is long, and it reveals a single underlying pattern, which now metastasizes into all regions of social life and demands that the same market prescription be fulfilled or the social body will suffer more fund starvation. The possibility that this ruling value program itself is what is unaffordable to life is unspeakable, beyond this mind-set's range of comprehension. Instead, its pattern of life-stripping is broadcast as a "transformation from a bloated and deficit-ridden social democracy into a lean market economy"—to use the words of the *Washington Post* for just such a dismantling of the social infrastructure of Canada in its richest and most populous province.[38]

There is another tell-tale sign of the market's value program disorder. While it everywhere seeks to cut costs on life within the life realm itself, its costs of administering and enforcing the rapidly expanding money-sequence become ever more top-heavy. There are now, according to the late David Gordon of the *New School of Social Research*, 17 million monitors and supervisors of the global market's regime in the United States alone, not counting their secretaries, assistants, and office staffs. They cost the economy $1.3 trillion in 1994, or four times the total cost of all U.S. social security programs.[39] This cost of "efficient" market administration is estimated to now be, on average, 20 per cent of the cost of all market goods produced. Thus, "cost reduction" in the market means, in effect, decreasing the costs of the security of citizens' lives and allocating the revenues instead to administrative controls on workers serving the money-sequence.

At the same time as the costs of administratively enforcing the global market regime exceed all that is spent by government on protecting the life of society's members, still more unproductive expenditures are allocated to armed forces to back up this bureaucratic imposition of the value program with mechanisms of organized violence. This is a global pattern. Globally, military budgets exceed the total life-income of half of the world's population.[40] These administrative and armed force structures of essentially global market enforcement are complementary, and neither serves to enable life. The corporate bureaucracy organizes it into obedience to the money-sequence's imperative of increasing stockholder money value. Its military arm threatens or deploys the force of killing and maiming human bodies that resist the program's imposition. Neither provides any good from which people can live and grow. We can test this general description of the global market's configuration by seeking to find significant exception to it.

The corporate market order's "efficiency" in cost reduction is, then, extravagantly expensive, once we take into account what is spent on unproductive enforcement of its sequences of extracting money value. Such extravagant costs should not, perhaps, surprise us. The corporate market's unproductive costs of profits for non-working shareholders, of advertisements and sales forces to create and incite demand, and of high-salary management hierarchies to maintain a regime of instrumentalizing people are all costs from which the public sector is in principle free. The public sector does not require profit payments to external investors. It does not require creation and incitement of demand by advertising expenditures and sales forces. And in areas of life-service (for example, medical care, education, cultural communications, and scientific research), it does not require non-contributing administrations to prescribe to practitioners when the art they practice is autonomous by its nature.

But freedom of the public sector from these non-productive costs is not its most important value advantage. If we compare the market's capacities to serve the life-realm to the public sector's capacities to do the same, we find a still more dramatic inferiority. Public-sector programs of health care, education, research, arts and communication, libraries, parks and playgrounds, and landscaped city centres are in every case universally accessible. They provide to all citizens alike, as each qualifies and chooses, the life-services that all people at some time need and can benefit from. This is the inner logic of the civil commons and its evolved structure of life-care. The difference in outcome is dramatic. For example, for-profit "health maintenance organizations" in the United States cost $1,000 more per capita than the public health scheme of Canada, leaves 40 million citizens completely uninsured and another 38 million grossly uninsured, and results in more deaths from medical malpractice than all deaths due to car accidents, murders, and fires put together.[41]

The organized provision of life-goods for all as they need and choose is, if we reflect upon it, an achievement that marks the evolution of human culture towards ever fuller realization of the life-code. The market is, in principle, incapable of such achievements because it is restricted to exchange on the basis of money-demand. This underlying evolution of the civil commons goes beyond the imagined systems of justice that philosophers and theorists have conceived over millennia. It is a creation from the ground up of a consciously shared life-ground out of the killing fields of history, a slow and almost imperceptible construction of a form of social life that enables the health, expression, and thought of all citizens alike, which undergirds the lives of all individuals and not just those possessing or ingratiating themselves to rank or money-demand.

Consider the depth and scope of this evolution. What higher achievement of life yet exists in history? Is it not odd that this issue is never raised, never noticed in market culture, not even by justice theorists? This is what a value program does to thought. It impedes recognition of whatever does not fit the value program. And the development of the civil commons has not only occurred outside the market's drive-principle of monetized exchange for private profit, but is also, at bottom, history's greatest threat to the market system by the alternative it offers to market relations. For every sphere of life characterized by the civil commons' higher order of social relations—universal accessibility to life-goods—is the negation of the market its core. Even as it builds within a mixed economy in areas in which the corporate market is clearly incompetent, the civil commons hedges in and, by the test of experience in such areas as health care, shows the market up as an inferior system in serving life. Histori-cally, the international corporate market has always been intolerant of any competing mode of social life-organization. So it should not surprise us that its conscious or unconscious program is now to liqui-date the civil commons by defunding within domestic borders, once the menace of external alternative has been dispatched.

Confronting the Death Spiral of the System

The most disturbing contradiction between the life realm of the civil commons and the money realm of the market has still not been exposed. As we know, everything in the market has its price. This is the nature of the market. Every price, in turn, presupposes scarcity, for we cannot sell anything if it is freely available in nature or from the community. Scarcity is always required for a price to be de-manded. This is a universal precondition of price and purchase that is presupposed in the market, but not examined. Its implications are more far-reaching than we imagine. For it follows from the relation-ship of price to scarcity that the more scarcity there is, the more prices can be had. Otherwise put, the more scarcity there is, the more market opportunities there are.

The implications of this relationship between market opportu-nities, on the one hand, and human scarcities, on the other, are disqui-eting. If, for example, society's members no longer have access to clean air or drinking water, because it has been polluted or exhausted, or have no biodiverse environment to live and walk in, because it has been clear-cut and paved over, or receive no care from others except when it comes with a money price attached, or cannot stand out in the sun without the mediation of market products to mediate it, all of this is good for the corporate market. If health and social security no longer exist, or if public transit, culture, and communication lose the revenue support they require to continue, all of this is good for the corporate market. For it opens ever new sectors of human need and want to sell priced products to. Bear in mind that a basic axiom of this paradigm is that the market must have a limitless supply of wants to sell to as a necessary condition of its continuance. Wants must never be all satisfied, or there is no basis for a priced exchange. The more life's conditions are destroyed, the more markets are assured, the more commodities can be sold and the more profits can be gained. This is the death march of the system.

The perpetual search for new markets has characterized the global market since its origins. This is its quest and adventure and the underlying profile of its historic movement over centuries across all the borders of the outer and inner worlds. But what is not recognized in the logic of this omnivorous search for new market sites is that ever more value gains are offered to the market by ever more value losses in the community and nature. Losses of goods freely available in society and nature are, by definition, diminutions of life. But they are, inversely, always pluses for the market insofar as they promote new conditions of scarcity that are, in turn, new doorways to price and profit.

This implication of the market doctrine's first premise of scarcity exposes the global market culture in a new light. The corporate system now sweeping across the world is reinforced and extended by the life-destructions it causes. But the end game cannot be seen by a value regime in which only maximizing monetized sums counts. Everywhere the documentation points to a spreading and deepening pattern of life-destruction and loss of our life-goods—the air we breathe, a safe sun to move in, the climatic stability we require, the social security we rely on, the university education our children need, the biodiverse environment we long for, the health care we require when sick, the safe and accessible walkways and transportation we need as citizens, the clean and attractive social surroundings without which we are degraded. We see across the world a systemic depredation and depletion of life. But what is most profoundly unknown about this cumulative wasting of our life-grounds is that the global market is propelled forward by every loss of life condition from the commons that it affects.

What would normally provide a corrective feedback of life and death fact to stimulate recognition of the mounting danger is here, in contrast, the establishment of ever more toeholds for the global market's continued expansion. For whatever has been laid waste in the environmental or civil commons now requires a priced good to satisfy the new demand. There is no line that the doctrine specifies or implies against this downwards spiral of life. All that can be seen are new market sites for "private enterprise to invest in for the benefit of consumers." The system thus feeds on its dysfunctions as the renewing principle of its advance.

This metapattern of the market can be represented simply: *Destruction or Deprivation = Scarcity = Market Opportunity*. It follows from this pattern that, as long as the corporate market can still go on functioning with whatever life-base is left, it serves its requirements as a system that there is ever more scarcity of the shared goods of society and nature. This is not a conscious plan. It is an unintended effect that strips the life-world without comprehension of its drivewheel. This propelling demand of the system for new markets helps us to comprehend why marketeers tirelessly attack the civil commons' provisions for human needs. For every good provided to all without price that could be sold for a profit cuts private corporations off from a valuable market. At the same time the metaphysic of the doctrine assumes that nothing, including the escalating deterioration of the earth's ecosystems, is not resolvable by the market's price mechanisms and profit motive (hence the new rage for trading in pollution credits). But the civil commons and the natural environment are alternative providers for life. They are thus competitors against market share. As the life fabrics of the civil commons and the environment are both deliberately and unintentionally dismantled by social cutbacks and industrial pollutions and looting, the profit picture remains bright because a host of new surrogate and compensatory products can "come on the market to satisfy consumers"—from virtual reality, entertainment, and travel getaways to stand in for a lost world, to financial planners to ensure more money-demand for such substitutes. The market system can in this way grow from the life-deficits it causes. "Demand stimulation" by advertising the shortcomings of people's lives that only priced goods can satisfy is a century-old tradition of the corporate market. Consumer demand is here more effectively ensured by real life-deficits to proliferate demand on deeper levels. Market opportunity for the sale of commodities is promoted on both planes, which opens market horizons ever wider.

To sell "security" in this increasingly insecure world, the corporate market has a twofold solution. First, there is the commodity of all commodities, the commodity that turns money into more money, stocks, and bonds. "Financial services" are now hawked everywhere and to everyone, with public pension funds themselves being reallocated from home-government financing to the global market. In this way, ever more trillions of dollars of money-demand seek to become still more money-demand on life's resources in a global condition that offers ever less from its community and life commons. In a time when the life-fabric of civil society is being dismantled, when ever fewer money-earning jobs can be counted on for long, and when no established life-security can any longer be relied upon from the larger community—"You are on your own, no one will help you," as the financial service ads advise us—the possession of money becoming more money is the only value in which even governments now trust. This is "the new reality" that this value system has brought us to. As the market program becomes universalized, converting all who seek to "survive in the global marketplace" into its compliant functions, we are being given an offer that cannot be refused.

Money-demand is good for anything, crosses borders at the flash of an electronic signal, and gains more money value without limit. "Money makes the world go round," as God was once said to have done. That money is solely a social fabrication and dependent for every aspect of demand on elected-government protection and investiture is not recognized. The denizens of the global market worship it. Everywhere it is prostrated before and adored. Only money measures real worth, and only money can deliver anyone from the threats looming all around. Your parents, your children, your old age, your home, your job, your future, the very air you breathe and the food you eat are no longer secure. Without money, and ever more of it, the darkness will swallow you.

What is known as "greed" is only a symptom of a deeper disorder. The money commodity, like the weapons commodity, expresses an underlying value program. Where the weapon delivers "security" by powers of life-destruction, the financial product delivers "security" by powers of money-demand over life. Together they stand as the two great pillars of the global market's new order.

The Life-Ground of the Civil Commons

Underneath the global market's conversion of life into commodities and money gains, humanity is moved by a deeper sequence of value, long ago described by a Chinese philosopher, Wang Yang-Ming. He demonstrated the motivation-structure of what we call "the life-ground" in an argument that developed an ancient tradition now over 2,500 years old. Wang Yang-Ming wrote:

> Even the mind of the small man is no different. Only he himself makes it small. Therefore when he sees a child about to fall into a well, he cannot help a feeling of alarm and commiseration. This show that his humanity (jen) forms one body with the child. It may be objected that the child belongs to the same species. Again, when he observes the pitiful cries and frightened appearance of birds and animals about to be slaughtered, he cannot help feeling an "inability to bear" their suffering. This shows that his humanity forms one body with birds and animals. It may be objected that birds and animals are sentient beings as he is. But when he sees plants broken and destroyed, he cannot help a feeling of pity. This shows that his humanity forms one body with plants.[42]

Wang Yang-Ming could have gone further in his demonstration of the life-code within us. For humans identify not only with the young of their own species, but also with the young of other species, even those that could be dangerous to them. This structure of concern for life beyond our skins is spontaneous to humanity, and it underlies even our most conditioned blindnesses. It joins us most compellingly to the young of all species who bear the future of the planet's life.

The traditional term for this ontological substructure is "human-heartedness." It is what connects us at an ultimate level to life external to us—for we react in alarm whenever we see that life or lives are about to be killed. Only the most conditioned mind can bear the watching of another's unnatural death without profound disturbance. But even within the limit of death, we find the same identification with others' life at work. Our response is aroused to any sudden loss of life's vital range. Underneath the hardened shell of our conventional egos occupying the roles of this or that value program lies a deeper life-code. It is what moves us to shrink in resonance with the person we see starving in front of us, or with the sight of a limb being cut off, or at people diseased before our eyes, or even at a person "getting the axe" at work. In all these cases, it is not life itself that people are losing, but a vital part of their lives. The contraction in our shared life is in proportion to the extent of the life destroyed. If we see, for example, that children are malnourished by cuts to social assistance, or coral reefs are dying from toxic runoffs, or young people are bereft of any life vocation, these desolations of the life-realm strike at the level of the life-code underneath the money program we have been indoctrinated to. Even the person who has become a mere function of the money-sequence will deny, or look the other way, in order not to see.

The sliding scale of value and disvalue, good and bad, in the life-metric is very exact and very developed—a few degrees gain or loss in the radius of a limb, the increase or decrease of infant mortality in a society, the movement of a national literacy rate, an incremental rise in the UV-index or average temperature over the Earth, the loss of forest cover and aquifers, the regaining of a society's civil freedom from torture or disease—there is no limit to the instances or applications of this ultimate yardstick of value loss and value gain.

The life-code always confronts a systemic block to its normal sequences and elaborations. For example, today those who stand against life's destructions and deprivations are dismissed as "bleeding hearts." Those who defend the integrity of nature's ecosystems are thought of as "tree-huggers." Government ministers who do not jump to enforce the money-code against the life-code are criticized as "not tough enough." What is at work here is a conditioned mind-set that affirms money-sequences rather than life-sequences as its logic of good. With pervasive repetition of this value regime as "necessary to compete," the life-code that defines our humanity is driven underground.

In contrast to the money-sequence of value, the life-code of value begins and ends with life as its value terms. We can represent this life-code by a simple formula, expressed in two basic sequences:

(1) Life —>Means of Life (e.g., food) —> Life (survival)
     or L —> M —> L

(2) Life —> Means of Life (e.g., education) —>
     More Comprehensive Life (i.e., growth of life's range)
     or L —> M —> L^1

We can see how these lower and higher sequences of the life-code oppose those of the money-sequence. As these opposed codes are elaborated in their growth and development, they confront each other ever more frontally. Their opposition has become, at this juncture of history, a war of life against death at many levels.

The higher form of the life-code we bear as human beings seeks more life, not more money, as the end of its sequence. It is a socially evolved form of the original life-sequence that seeks only to reproduce. We call the higher life-sequence that seeks not only to reproduce but also to become more comprehensive life by the name "civilization." What is required for civilization's planes of vital life to broaden and deepen their horizons is what we have named "the civil commons." The civil commons is the middle term between life and more comprehensive life. It enables life by the basic resources of life being available to all its members.[43] These universally accessible life-goods take many forms, and they increase with the development of society. What unifies them all as spheres of the civil commons is that all enable life's growth of range, all are available to whoever chooses or needs them, and all are grounded in the first premise that life and life's comprehensive growth are ultimate values.

Today the civil commons includes many aspects. Public education to higher research levels, public arts and broadcasting, progressive healing and scientific medicine available to all, better resources of life for the aged and handicapped, open play areas and games for every age, and accessible environmental spaces in the community are all variations on the civil commons. Democratic government itself is the civil commons in one of its most powerful capacities of shared growth. The civil commons, by definition, enables life to become ever more comprehensively vital life for society's citizens.

Language itself is only the civil commons in its most basic and underlying form and is its vehicle of mediation for other life-goods. It has, as we know, been monopolized by priests and other castes over history. But by its nature language is open to all, enables all, and is humanity's greatest contribution to the life-realm of value. Overcoming monopolies of language is much of the story of civilization's development. Democracy—the self-government of a society by its people in participant decision-making—is the civil commons in collective thought and action. The civil commons, in all, defines a society's true level of life evolution.

The civil commons must be distinguished from the government or state, and also from civil society as such. Civil society is defined through its property divisions, which the civil commons underlies. The state's resources may sustain and organize much of the civil commons, but the civil commons can also be at war with the state (as in, for example, third-world dictatorships). Government, at its most developed stage, becomes one with the civil commons, but is as yet far from achieving this full representation of the common interest. In this period of government as mere servant of the money-sequence of value, on the contrary, the state's decision-structures dismantle the civil commons to reroute their revenues to private market interests.

The civil commons is, in truth, being stripped across the world. But just as the mind of a human being "cannot bear the child about to fall down a well," so the mind of the evolved human being cannot bear to see the civil commons so dismembered.

The first step of the life-code's sequence of value is always to prevent the death of the life that is in danger. Prevention begins with recognition of the threat to life, whether it is an individual organism or the social life-fabric. If we conceptualize the civil commons as the life-body we share as a society enabling all citizens and their environments to grow and develop individually and together, we can clearly see the profile of its reduction at every level across the global market. There is clearly a pattern of expropriation and destruction that is as significant and far more rapid in execution than the clearances of peoples from the traditional commons in earlier stages of the global market order. There is now no place in the world, indigenous or industrialized, in which the civil commons is safe from corporate market invasion.

This is a generalization that can be tested. We measure the deficits of a society's or the globe's human and environmental life by the reductions and destructions of its evolved vital ranges below their prior state. If the wages of the workers do not rise but fall, and more people become life-insecure and unemployed; if more people fall below the poverty line and become malnourished; if the homeless and the destitute increase instead of declining; if the illiterate grow in numbers and the resources of higher education decline; if the gap between rich and poor grows rapidly and the poor become absolutely poorer at the same time; if the air we breathe does not become cleaner, but more fume-filled and toxic; if the water life it depends on to live does not increase or become purer, but depletes and becomes polluted, even underground; in short, if life's vital ranges do not hold or grow, but are systemically reduced and disabled by money-sequence operations, we face a global life decline on all levels. Here again we can test every general pattern of life reduction, one by one, to see for ourselves. "Even the mind of the small man" cannot but respond to such a loss of life.

In the global market value system, however, deficits of life do not compute. Only money gains and debits register in its "bottom line." Since human beings and their environments can be degraded to ever lower ranges of vital life, and the market's metric of value does not identify the debits, there is no limit to the life-losses that can be incurred. Unpriced and shared life-goods that disappear from nature and the commons merely open by their scarcity "more market activities." The circle of the money-sequence widens as the circle of life contracts. This fateful problem has a human solution—to recognize the problem, and to respond to the disorder. This effective response, in turn, must be borne by an organized, unified, and consciously operating vehicle of the common life-interest. This agency, in further turn, is not restricted to class or party or period or the state, but is the civil commons that has evolved from the beginning of human society. We face grim realities. Malnutrition and hunger now afflict 1.8 billion people as food-security programs are slashed, and community water supplies have gone brown for over 1 billion citizens across the "developing world."[44] As these and other indicators of life-assault and decline across the globe confront us, the market program closes off effective response. "The wealthy," observes a scientist of the military solution, "seek to maintain their security as a short-term law of reaction."[45]

These last words, from Paul Rogers, professor of peace studies at Bradford University, are an apt rendering of the money-sequence program. It reacts to perceived threats to money bodies instead of threats to life. Just as the life-sequence bearer responds to loss of life before it to prevent it, so the money-sequence bearer reacts to loss of money in its expansion. It is money's gain or loss, not life's, which is the Good and the Bad of this value code.

It may be thought that it is merely the possession of money that ultimately counts to its bearer, not the money's gain or loss as such. But here the case of the money-sequence's chief international representative is revealing. Faced with the following cascade of consequences from the money-sequence's imposition on the world's poor, the IMF director-general warned against the "moral hazard" of reducing compound-interest burdens. He did so in the context of the following consequences of IMF prescriptions:

> The United Nations report [at the Habitat II Conference, Istanbul, 1996] says one of the main reasons for the rapid deterioration in world cities in the past 10 years is economic structural adjustment programs that have been imposed by the International Monetary Fund. These, it is said, have increased poverty, homelessness and unemployment in more than 50 countries, including some of the poorest of the world. Structural adjustment programs ... devised in the 1980's ... have de-

manded that developing countries privatize and deregulate industries, cut public spending, and reduce or eliminate health and education subsidies.... The world's aid agencies and development banks give low priority to ... sanitation, housing, air pollution, and waste.[46]

This is the money-code and money-sequence in action. It expands itself as the moral good whose prescriptions must be obeyed. The IMF is its vicar of command. But there is another way that fights against it, and its code of life is as ancient as humanity. Its evolving vehicle across the ages is the civil commons. The roots of the civil commons spread deep and wide. Its realm has long been borne by the great unpaid social infrastructure of all society and the monetized economy—woman's daily work. Women do an estimated two-thirds of the world's work to enable a larger community—domestic work since the beginnings of historical time, and now a great part of the market's work too.[47] Woman's traditional work is the undergirding ground of all work. It brings up humans through nature's longest maturation period, while sustaining humanity's graduated producers at the same time. Most paradigmatically, woman's service to the preservation and growth of life beyond herself is not for money. Her work is to sustain and develop life. She has long been humanity's great bearer of the shared life-sequence of value. Woman is the mother of the civil commons.

Males too can live for life, not money growth. They too can use money solely to serve life. They too can reduce money-demand to realize life's capacities without making demands on others' work. Men can, and do, bear the life-code as well. But they do it against the grain of the corporate culture they have been conditioned and confined to. Their tradition is now to show how much money they can acquire rather than how they can enable other life. The money-code is not gender-specific, but one gender is held by it. It has become male identity-structure within the corporate value program.

In the case of the Indian state of Kerala, one of India's poorest states in per capita money wealth, the life-sequence of value has achieved higher levels than far richer states. One reason for this during the period of success was a government policy of educating all women to basic levels of literacy. This simple civil commons device resulted in exceptional advances in the society's life expectancy, reductions of infant mortality, and a general rate of literacy two times India's average. This pattern was summarized Amartya Sen in 1993: "Kerala, which has one of the lower gross national products of the country [India], has high literacy rates for both sexes. Despite extreme poverty, public commitment to education and health as well as to improving the status of women has in general made the population of Kerala literate and long-lived."[48]

The text concludes: "This fact alone shows that certain measures of economic success such as GNP can be incomplete." The statement is true, but is itself incomplete. A more adequate statement is that GNP cannot compute the preservation and growth of life at all, because it reports only what is sold for a money price. The entire life-transformative process of universal education for women at home is therefore excluded from view. There was in this case no indication or expectation in the market economy of any increase of profits or sales of commodities or additional export earnings. Since the market's metric of value-added computes only money gains, and there were none, the education of women here therefore counts as being of no value. Calculating by the market's measures, therefore, the education of women outside the market and for no money-making activity is a "wasteful government expenditure." It is "wasteful" because:

1. it does not increase the total money revenues generated by that society's priced goods and services; and

2. it costs government tax expenditures to support, which must be extracted from market revenues.

The conclusion follows easily, then, that such a program is "unaffordable." If it does not add value to the money-sequence, its cost burden cannot be justified. Therefore it, or other like services of the civil commons, clearly qualify within the market value system as targets for "necessary cutbacks" and "government savings."

The Civil Commons and the State

The civil commons is not yet recognized for what it is, but traces of it have been called names of all kinds: "communism," "government waste," "handouts"—the list is long. But the civil commons has existed for millennia before any of these slogans were invented. It has a precise and bounded meaning, one that market ideology has never recognized: *The civil commons is the organized, unified, and community- funded capacity of universally accessible resources of society to protect and to enable the lives of its members as an end in itself.*

The "public good," "the general interest," "national security," and "the common weal" are all established phrases to describe what the "state" and "statecraft" stand for. But the reality of the common interest to ground these phrases has always remained obscure. So much that contradicts "the public good," "the common interest," and "national security" has been done in their name that these concepts have been deformed out of recognition. We no longer know, in effect, what they mean.

The civil commons, in contrast, is precise and long-tested in its meaning and is what any legitimate state or government properly serves and supports. But there is much more to the civil commons than we yet recognize. It is an open conversation in a public place, a neighbourhood network of mutual life assistance, a health-care visit, an educational classroom, a public gallery or library, an information broadcast or common knowledge, an old-age or disability pension, a park, a democratic election, a city playing area, a path in the wilderness, a community day care, a mass transit system, a home for the homeless: All these unpriced public goods are life-means of the civil commons. All are universally accessible, community supported, and consciously enable the vital life of a society's members to flourish and grow. All in a contemporary society are also normally government-funded, because none can be provided by the market's system of value production and distribution.

In direct attack on this evolved structure of the actual common weal, the global market doctrine demands that all that is spent by government becomes accountable to the market's decision-structure of money transactions and profits. The voices of the market's money-sequence interests are loud, and we will not repeat their arguments again here. What we can conclude is:

1. The functions of government to protect and expand the money-code program of the market cost many times more than the entire civil commons.

2. Those who derive the money profits from these operations pay an ever smaller fraction of their costs.

3. These costs are increasingly paid for by defunding the civil commons.

This redistribution of wealth from the people and the civil commons to the market's money-sequences is what, at bottom, "the market revolution" means.

These redistributive operations have bankrupted the common interest. Public debt along with "reducing costs to compete in the marketplace" have been the two pincers of pretext. As the civil commons has been deprived of its resources in this way, its life-service functions have, ironically, been equated to Big Government, and Big Government itself—that is, its armed forces and bureaucratic and repressive functions—has meanwhile grown. Media pundits have, simultaneously, blamed the sacrifices of social programs on the public's need for them. "We must learn not to depend on government." "We must pay our own way." "A substitute for government is needed." "We must stand on our own two feet."

The reality that banks, corporations, the wealthy, and senior government officials themselves depend more than anyone on government is not mentioned, nor are their expenditures slashed. Business infrastructure, inflated contracts, protection, and representation across borders around the clock never arise as a cost issue. "All of us must learn to do without government assistance" is code for the principle that all but the money-sequence must be cut from public funding. Life-functions of the civil commons are "beyond the capacity of government to support." As with the IMF in the Third World, so with the market program in the First World. Government's function is no longer government, but service to the global market's demands.

The justifying claim for the common life-interests of the people is that "the market has proved itself more efficient in producing goods and services." But this claim is calamitously false from the standpoint of life's preservation and development. And, as we have seen, the market system is demonstrably incompetent in the realm of service to life. The market's ruling money-sequence of value has a special capacity to serve society, in the end, only in the sphere of *machine-made goods*. Even here it is life-blind to the external consequences of machine manufacture and commodities. The civil commons can, in contrast, provide its evolved framework to rectify the market's life-blind sequences. It can, more directly, enable the vital life of human beings and their environmental host by providing universally accessible life goods.

The problem society is said to have is a "shortage of money" to pay for its life. Yet there is a huge surplus of money-demand committed to no life function at all. It is many times greater in daily turnover than all expenditures on life-preservation and growth. Monetary levers, product taxation, conditional tax deductions, financial transaction taxes, and the rule of life-protective law are more than sufficient to fund any society's civil commons at a high level. Then there are the vast revenues that government has given away in the last decade to dominant market agents—banks, corporations, military-industrial contactors, capital-gains speculators, and the top one per cent of income recipients. These expenditures too exceed the total costs of a highly developed and securely funded civil commons.

What is in short supply is government in the common interest. Here we confront what is traditionally known as a "revolutionary situation." John Locke's concept of a revolutionary condition, we might recall, was "a long train of abuses, prevarications and artifices, all tending the same way," which "make the design visible to the people."[49] What is missing in our current condition is the final step— "make the design visible to the people." That is the function of this study. That such a design can be recognized in our current predicament can hardly be doubted. That it increasingly invades the life-security of peoples across the world has been demonstrated. That it represents a tyranny to those increasing masses of social populations terrorized and dispossessed by it is all too evident. The problem has been in the act of understanding. As the civil commons is globally stripped of its life-functions, the invading market program is represented as an emancipation from the nation-state. In social life as in cellular life, the carcinogenic code evades detection by representing itself as benign.

Given that the civil commons is distinct from government, the traditional "change of government" is not adequate. But the civil commons is the core of government insofar as it acts in the common interest of society. Government today, however, is not government in this sense. It has been subjugated to the private interests of the market, or, more precisely, the distinction between the common interest and market demands has collapsed. In consequence, government has become programmed to the money-sequence as the common interest.

In other words, the deep-structural problem confronting us is a decision-structure of value by which the whole regulatory web of society has been taken over. Yet because it has been encoded across classes as "necessary," "global," and with "no alternative" to it, it operates as what is normal even as it abolishes the grounds of normality. The hold of the money-code of value on society is finally a problem of comprehension. Impelled to implement its sequence to survive in the game, peoples and governments move in lockstep to it. The symptoms of a mental and physical disorder are all too evident.

"What sustainable development really is is a smokescreen for socialism," thunders *Forbes* magazine, a commercial guide to the U.S. business class. "Sustainable development—economic development that does not exhaust the resources of a host country'—is fundamentally fascist."[50]

"A low-grade civil war is being fought every day in the world's urban centres," says the secretary-general of the UN's Habitat II Conference. "Big numbers are risking their lives every day. Cities are collapsing. We must wake up to the fact that it is no longer business as usual."[51]

Life-organization is being warred on by the money-sequence march. But the breaking of the life-structure is not recognized by the people who are its victims. The trance-breaking step, the end of the end game, the waking up from the ceremony of the transubstantiation of life into money, is there to be taken. But the capable are afraid of losing their place in the next round of the money circuit's expansion. The "design has not been made visible to the people." The functions return to work and their assigned role in the sequence, and return home to observe the money game on TV.[52]

Deep in the intuitive repositories of the life-code of value that lies within, the global crisis is felt in premonitions and fears. But it is not yet recognized in the design of what drives it. As the cumulative life crisis moves to more threatening thresholds, the basis of its resolution is dismantled at the same time. Since the civil commons is at once the substance of government's functions in the common interest of society and the sole protector of society's environmental life-host, the historic attack on its life-lines of funding is simultaneously an attack on social and global life themselves. But the magic numbers of increasing GDP, trade, stock, profit, and export gains keep the mind in thrall.

Because the civil commons is not recognized as what it is, but is designated by code terms for attack like "wasteful government," "structural rigidity," and "obstruction to trade and development," the crisis of global life-degradation and the social agency of its resolution continue their slide. Still, there is no end of slogans to sell substitutes for life to an increasingly insecure public: the dream of self-multiplying gains in the "dynamic growth of the global market," the promised land of "future prosperity," the technical magic of electronic signals creating the "virtual reality" of the consumer's choice. In this imaginary world of market substitutes for life, "the consumer" replaces the citizen, and the market's "self-regulating laws" replace evolved life fabrics. This is the final delusion of our millennium. But as long as people are jobless and social sectors are being axed, certain conditions still pose a political problem. These conditions are managed, when the mood is charitable, by market invocations of the "social safety net." The social safety net is a ceremonial deferral to the stubborn realities of citizen deaths, destitutions, and ruins, which cannot be altogether blamed on the victims. For these, one must move outside the market's money-sequence to get re-elected. Some two hundred years of history have accomplished this much. Mortal realities can still register as social problems where once the hard facts of life's starvation were sanctified by market explainers as the workings of the invisible hand.

It is worth reflecting on the social safety net. It catches bodies before they hit the cement of the market's harsh consequences for those who fail to keep themselves in its competition. On the one hand, this is a great step upwards from the past of "merciful starvation," as marketeers called it in earlier days and are whispering again. On the other hand, the concept and device of a safety net miss the life-code's civilized sequence. This sequence is to enable life to become more comprehensive life. It is not to keep it from dying merely to re-enter the wheels of the system again as a temporary wage-and-consumption function. The civil commons is devoted to the growth of life's vital range as an end in itself. To prevent life's fall from hitting the killing floor of starvation, malnutrition, disease, and death is not truly enabling life. It is a passive catch of a human body falling to the floor. The civil commons, in historic contrast, is the living bonds of community organized to transform the life of all its citizens to a more comprehensive, vital being.

The Civil Commons and Real Capital

The civil commons is not, as it may first seem, "social capital" in the sense of the term promoted by avant-garde economists. It is, admittedly, certainly better to have such a concept and the social connectedness it designates than to merely ignore society's role in capital formation altogether. But the civil commons is obscured by such conceptions, because what social capital means is that society is taken account of only so far as its collective factors of cohesion, trust, and community have productive value to the market's transformation of life and matter into money gains in sales and profits.[53] If the social values are intrinsic, but they do not contribute to sales and profits, as in, say, trust among citizens as such, then these values do not count as values to the market metric. They are not social capital under the doctrine's version of the concept.

Capital is the generic Lord of the global market system, "the almighty dollar," as it is called in its visible signs. Thus citizens have become habituated to value in all its forms being subordinated to it as the bottom-line of life. What does not serve it is of no worth. Because capital and its growth designate the ultimate value in the global market system, one may not publicly say "capital" or "capitalist" in a pejorative way. The word is not used on mass media except in approbation. Just as the deity of other world religions cannot be offended by use of the Name in any but reverential signification, so the words "capital" and "capitalist" receive the modern version of such adoration in the global market culture. Given this power of sanctifying investiture, the term "social capital" is the linguistic costume of observance in which the civil commons must be dressed to allow it entry through the gates of market freedom.

Capital's career as a value term, however, is far more venerable than the corporate market. It recapitulates the three great eras of history—"cattle" value, "chattel" value, and "capital" value—each term a variation on one root concept. Capital, in truth, means "wealth that produces more wealth."

This true meaning of capital is not appreciated. For if it were, the term "capital" would not be used to designate what is not wealth that produces more wealth. It would not be used, as it now is in the global market, to denote the opposite—the systematic attacks on the bases of wealth by the money-into-more-money sequences. This is a conceptually seismic point. For it enables us to distinguish what is not yet distinguished: real capital from what masks itself as capital, but is not. *False capital* is money input that becomes more money output not by producing more stock of wealth, but by producing more money-demand on wealth, while depleting or destroying already existing wealth. The mutated money-sequences analysed earlier (for example, the armaments industry and bank usury) qualify as such false capital; that is, they create more money-demand, but create no wealth. At the same time they destroy or deplete wealth by destroying natural and physical capital and by taking away from the wealth of the civil commons to serve their non-productive demands. Once we understand this distinction between real and false capital, we can recognize our disorder from the standpoint of capital itself. But this life-and-death distinction leads further than we know.

Even when the more farsighted of the market congregation use the term "social capital," no one presumes to mean by social capital anything except what enables private capital to grow by private profits. Even then it is not a category of value that is accepted in market doctrine beyond the avant garde. This is because the use of the term to designate the quality of social relations raises embarrassing issues of capital not produced by the market. In the market theology, this is like creation that is not produced by God. If social capital is admitted into the lists of what has value, then social cohesion, trust, and ties of community have important worth in the global market system after all. This seems innocent enough for a mind still connected to reality. Worth that is not produced by the market, however, is not worth that market orthodoxy likes to acknowledge.

The same refusal to grant value to what is not produced by the market holds for "environmental capital" or "natural capital." Either one of these categories designates the economic value of land, water, timber, subsoil assets, mineral resources, and whatever else can be turned by extraction or use into money profit in the productive money-sequence. But, as we have seen, "natural capital" not produced by the market still has no actual standing in the orthodoxy of market doctrine. The market God is a jealous God. It abhors whatever is not itself. No market-led government, therefore, dares calculate its holdings of "natural capital." The practical ground of the market's intolerance here is that if nature's stock were recognized as capital, its use would have to be paid for like other capital, and its capital value would have to be preserved on pain of repayment costs. Such costs would impose new obligations and liabilities on corporate users and destroyers of nature's stock, for which they are now unaccountable. Thus the concept of natural capital is one that remains confined to the rhetoric of the market's *avant garde*.

Nevertheless, wider-lensed value calculators realize that if natural resources have no market value or price attached to them, they will be depleted and destroyed by reckless extraction, pollution, and deregulation. So natural capital or environmental capital, like social capital, has emerged as a vanguard concept to lead the global market to a more sustainable order. The category remains on the margins, but its introduction recognizes values of capital not produced or distributed by the market that must somehow be included in its price system if it is not to self-destruct.

Although the emerging concepts of social capital and natural capital are of great importance in opening the market doctrine to realities of life, they still presuppose that life is only a means to the money-sequence's fulfilment. Life itself has value only insofar as it provides the instruments of achieving more money revenues. This continued assumption of the money-sequence as the market's ultimate regulator of value remains unchanged in even the "new economics."[54] This presupposition, which grounds the market paradigm in all its forms, has two fateful consequences. First, whatever is perceived not to serve the sovereign goal of money gain is not recognizable as of value within the system. It is blinkered out as non-value (for example, unexploited nature, or the love of performing non-paying work of value for others). Second, what is perceived to have value to investment sequences is conceived of as being of instrumental value to it and of no value as such (for example, education and health).

In the civil commons, social capital and natural capital are oppositely conceived. To be precise, any kind of capital of the civil commons is stock that enables the maintenance and growth of life, not money, from one investment period to the next. Its universally accessible goods are not consumed, used up, or wasted by its members, but are preserved and accumulated to provide continued and growing life-goods to subsequent generations (the written culture, accessible wilderness, and life-serving infrastructure, for example). Once we understand capital in this deeper sense of "wealth that is used to produce more wealth," the world of value turns right-side up again. Life's growth is the ethical sovereign, and its capital base upon which the margins of life's increase depend is to be protected and developed as the first priority of society.

Only a grounding in the life-sequence of value can penetrate behind the money-sequence's mask of "development" to reveal its delinkage from the common life-ground. Only the civil commons, which bears this life-code in universalized form, can protect and enable what the unregulated market is value-blind to. Beyond the natural capital of society, which the civil commons protects by its regulatory restraints and autonomous spheres of parks and wilderness, there are also its produced assets or "physical capital."

We have seen throughout this book how the produced assets of the public sector have been subserved to the special interests of the market, including military-industrial structures, commercial arteries to serve the transport of market products, megapower projects geared to corporate producers, trade-promoting diplomatic infrastructures and judicial apparatuses for business adjudication and protection, public buildings, and assets of all kinds to specially serve the market's needs. Physical capital in the civil commons, in contrast, is the socially owned, built structure of society that preserves and enables the lives of its members over generations. Much of the public sector's infrastructure does do this, and it does so in life-and-death ways: its clean water supply systems, its garbage, sewage-disposal, and recycling operations, its electrical grids and lighting systems, its hospital buildings and equipment, its public transit structures, its housing for the poor and resources for the handicapped, its school classrooms and facilities for teaching members of the community of all ages, its statistics-gathering systems and public libraries, its science and public arts facilities, its roads and sidewalks that make possible the safe travel of pedestrians, bicycles, and powered vehicles, its public broadcasting centres, its laboratories for food and drink inspection and public disease prevention, and its public play and environmental free spaces for interaction and enjoyment of shared life.

There is, however, a straightforward way in which to distinguish in principle between the physical capital and personnel of the government, which serve only the money-sequence of the market, and the physical capital and personnel of the public sector, which serve the life-sequence of society and its environmental host. This distinction is found by posing the following question: If this physical capital or personnel expenditure were no longer to continue in this or that society, would society's members or their life-environment suffer a reduction of any vital life-range by its defunding? As we have observed, systematic privatizations and defundings of public sectors have already occurred across the world, but in no case on record has this criterion of selection been applied. One might very plausibly argue that the pattern of reduction and elimination of the public sector's goods has been the opposite: everywhere targeting expenditures on citizens' lives and needs and everywhere avoiding cuts of expenditures on the demands of the market.

Consider this poignant example. In Canada, while higher education and social assistance transfer payments were being slashed towards zero, and health care, environmental protection, public broadcasting, train transit, unemployment insurance, and old-age pensions and municipal transfers were being reduced in unprecedented major cuts, the federal government, which represented itself as "saving the country's social infrastructure," continued to build, upkeep, staff, and deploy certain produced state assets and personnel: purchasing and equipping military jet bombers in ever greater numbers of flights and bombings over new and expanding bombing ranges, 7,000 to 18,000 times each year in low-flying invasions of Innu traditional lands and wildlife breeding and nesting grounds of caribou, ducks, and other species.[55] Clearly, these unnecessary public expenditures were serving the special interests of the Canadian and NATO military establishments in service to the security of the money-sequence across the world and, more directly, the profits and sales of major weapons-producing transnational corporations. At the same time, no usable produced assets were thereby conferred on the life-needs of the population or its environmental host. On the contrary, these government expenditures assaulted both citizens and environment. Although the designated foreign enemy at which all of this public money was directed had not existed for years, the life-world—the atmosphere, the quiet, the wild creatures, and the environment of the Innu people—was duly invaded every twenty-eight minutes by bombing schedules, while the old and the young of all species of this civil commons were terrorized or vexed continually within a 500-square-mile area. But during this period, no market representative, corporate spokesperson, or mass media campaign ever targeted these life-destructive expenditures of the public sector as "unaffordable."

This example illustrates that the civil commons criterion for required government expenditures is very different from the market's, and the criterion leads in an opposite direction. The same principle holds for all the physical capital of the public sector. There are, for example, public city spaces and streetscapes designed for people —their movement, their interaction, and their aesthetic enjoyment— that are the genuine built assets of society. There are other far more expensive physical assets paid for by the public purse that do little but increase the speed and volumes of market commodities delivered to sales sites. The principle of distinction here is so deep-seated that, once recognized, it transforms the understanding of government itself.

The point here is not to call for abolition of, say, polluting and hazardous market-made vehicles from public spaces, lakes, and rivers, although this is already done in the most advanced sites of the civil commons, and it marks a truly civilized society. The point is, rather, to understand clearly that government expenditures of taxpayers' money on the physical assets of public spaces is now structurally biased towards physical capital that subsidizes and enforces private corporate interests at the cost of civil and environmental life. Since the immense public expenditures devoted to these market outlays can hardly be said to issue in "wealth that is used to produce more wealth," but are rather the temporary props of the market's circuits of money-to-more-money gain, the concept of "capital" here is again a misnomer.

This criterion of distinguishing between physical structures for the shared life-interests of society's members, on the one hand, and corporate market sequences that degrade the life-range of public spaces, on the other, can be applied across society's publicly owned assets. Public play areas and facilities for all-seasons sports, for example, meet this criterion. But the current pattern of reducing or eliminating these facilities, while subsidizing palatial stadiums for commercial marketing sites, violates this criterion. By the same token, government financing of the infrastructure and policing of private logging operations for major corporations to clear-cut publicly owned old-growth forests, while simultaneously not funding urban sewage treatment and policing of toxic polluters, is a life-destructive pattern of the same type. Yet "physical capital" remains a term applied indiscriminately to these opposite kinds of outlay paid for and owned by the public. In one case, the term is fraudulent. In the other case, it is true. But the distinction between these state infrastructures is not yet made, although it marks the dividing line between life and what attacks life. If the distinction is not recognized, the fraudulent physical capital paid for by the public will continue to grow, while the life-enabling physical assets of the public sector will continue to be defunded and degraded. Here again, we see the incapacity of the market paradigm to guide us in the public sphere. Instead, it misleads us, to the point of self-destruction.

Another concept of the market economics is "human capital." Here too, the term provides an important tool for broadening the market's metric of value to include more than money capital. Again, however, human capital—like social capital, natural capital, and physical capital—is presupposed to be a means to increase monetary capital and never resupposed as a value in itself. Life matters only to the extent that it provides resources for the market's money-sequence of value. Its value is purely instrumental. The market, it is recognized, depends for its level of productivity and profitability on having healthy and trained human beings to fulfil its money-sequence requirements. People's education, nutrition, and freedom from disease count as contributory values to the market's monetized growth, but the market's conceptions cannot break out of this closed circle. All that exists is of value only so far as its input can be used to turn money into more money output for money investors. Market value remains the sovereign and ultimate value on which all values depend, including humanity itself. No value can escape this iron cage of the system.[56] Human capital or human resources are what humans must make themselves into in order to be valued as a means for the market.

They must be properly trained and educated for it, and so, it follows, public education too must be "restructured" and "rationalized" for this purpose or be defunded as "unaccountable." Accountability always goes one way. The education and future of the next generation must be made accountable to the market, but the market is accountable to nothing.

From the standpoint of the civil commons, humans are not merely a means of something else. That would make humans into slaves—in this case, into slaves to the rule of the corporate market, whose investment circuits increase the money holdings of a fraction of the population. The ethic of the life-code is in direct contradiction with this value program, even when its value calculus takes into account the education and organic functioning of the human instruments it still needs to employ. As for those humans the market does not employ, their training, health care, and nutrition can have no worth to this value system at all. Here the market paradigm of value reaches its limits. Those who are not of value as a means to the market, whose "human resources" cannot be sold, cannot escape being worth nothing in this metric, even if they are mothers, artists, or saints enabling life to flourish across generations. In this way, at the most progressive margins of the doctrine, those who are not employed to add value to the money-sequence are faced with a blind alley. They cannot by the doctrine's logic be legitimately provided with education, nourishing food, or medicine because there are no money returns for such investments. They are a "cost burden" with no gains for stockholders and investors to justify the expenditures on them. At this point the market system's doors of value slam shut on human life itself, with a political struggle required to provide a survival stipend to those for whom the market cannot find employment.

The human capital of the civil commons is oppositely conceived. A person is human capital if she or he is "wealth that produces more wealth," one whose life adds value to life's stock so that it can, in turn, enable others across generations in a growth of humanity and its life-world to ever more comprehensive compasses of being alive. From the wider and deeper ethical standpoint of the civil commons, human life and its health or education are not values made conditional on some external value, like money profit or market growth. They are goods in themselves, intrinsic goods. As a shared value of the life-ground that is of worth in itself, the civil commons' vocation is to ensure access to them for all. As these goods progressively enable the members of the community and their environmental life-host in each's life capabilities and diversity of being, we observe the growth of what we might call "life capital." This growth, we might say, provides a purpose of being alive that has been with us all along.

Conclusion: The Way Ahead

The overriding problem is that the market's value system has not been recognized for what it is. Even when it recognizes natural, social, and human capital as values, it remains a monstrous system of value. What I mean by "monstrous" is that it subjugates and sacrifices ever more life to its demands—if not by destruction and consumption, then by instrumentalization or starvation of what does not serve it.

The question that remains is how the life-code and the civil commons that enable its sequences of elaboration can register to society as the way ahead. The civil commons is a solution that evolution and history have long prepared, over the tried and true bodies of countless predecessors who have lived and died for it from the earliest records of humanity. There is now a deepening contradiction between life's most basic requirements of survival and growth, on the one hand, and the global market's program of subjugating, reducing, and destroying life in increasingly unregulated sequences of money expansion, on the other. The life-and-death choice now confronting us has as its resolution the sovereignty of the life-sequence of value and its vehicle, the still evolving civil commons. The problem is in the end one of human self-comprehension. We do not yet know what great malaise afflicts us. The market's international leadership itself recognizes the symptoms. For even the transnational Organization of Economic Co-operation and Development publicly declares that there is a "global feel-bad factor," but it cannot explain it.[57] Those whose lives and communities are directly assaulted by the system's invasions are more explicit. They declare that a war is being waged against their very existence, and they rise up against it. The battle is being waged across the globe, and it is everywhere against the assault on life and the civil commons by the money-sequence in its multiple forms.

The design is not clear to the people, and it is least of all reported in the corporate advertising vehicles of the mass media. But the sites of the struggle at this moment are many: in Chiapas, Ogoniland, southern Brazil and the rainforests of Ecuador, East Timor and West Papua, Burma, the First Nations reserves of North America, Tibet, the Philippines, Central Africa, the cities of India, Germany, France, and Canada, South Korea, Israel, Peru. The pattern of insurgency is not observed in the media, because that recognition would confront the global corporate market with its systemic invasions of human and environmental life. Such a deep-structural problem the commercial media are structured to rule out of view. Our historically new predicament is that we are bordering on exponential life-reversal, as one threshold after another of life-fabric destruction is normalized and one life condition after another is depleted.

"Earth is experiencing an unprecedented extinction of life," says a 1996 United Nations report. The report Taking Action says the overall quality of life is deteriorating in nearly every category—from air and drinking water to the oceans and forests that sustain life—"It is an open question whether the human species can survive," observes Elizabeth Dowdeswell, head of the U.N. Environment Program.... But if humankind can find the will "the world community is quite capable of finding solutions."[58]

The World Health Organization says that one fifth of the 56 billion people in the world live in extreme poverty, almost a third of the world's children are malnourished.... "The scale of the human global human tragedy," observes the WHO's Director-General, Hiroshi Nakajima, is devastating."... The challenge is to prevent health catastrophe."[59]

Sixty percent of growth is going to one percent of the population," observes MIT Professor Noam Chomsky. "Half of families have an income that is going down. Entry level wages have declined by 30 percent for men since 1980, and 18 percent for women.... The richest suburb in America gets the most public funds of any community.... Remember systems are not firm. They can collapse."[60]

Many people who are not closed into specialized functions or mind-locked in the market value program recognize the grave challenge now faced by the world's civil and environmental life-organizations. Underneath the slogans and citations of money-transaction numbers, the realities of the accumulating life deficits do not go unnoticed. For those to whom nature and people are not merely throughputs of the money-sequence to ever higher aggregate numbers, social and planetary life matter. For those for whom the earth is understood as an interrelated web of vital being that is felt as their true body, an outlook as old as the First Peoples, this deep slide of life is a matter of life and death more important than their own survival. There are many levels of the dawning recognition.

Unreported by the corporate media, tens of thousands of bearers of the life-code fight to hold the life-fabric together. They feel the breakdown of the shared life-ground across the world. They know intuitively that humanity's joint agency of the civil commons must respond. But, as we find again and again, the life-code and life-sequence of the true common interest is obscured and repressed in the dominant culture. The life-blind adversary that invades the shared body of life is confused with the common interest. The "hard decisions" that must be made continue to be prescribed not for, but at, the cost of the life-host. Development and progress are still understood as the growth of money-sequences to ever higher accumulations.

But like a slow brush fire across the globe, ever more people feel what is happening, sense the pattern that is unfolding, intuit the urgency to restore the life-code to rule. They have begun to join for and across the civil commons of the world as an emergent ground of shared life and agency—through government for the common interest and against government for corporate administration, outside the institutions of oppression but storming them for instituted rules to protect life. It is coming up from the ground. The ancient vocation of protecting the common life-interest is at work within and across the most apparently disparate intentions. It is in defence of life and the civil commons across struggles. It is demanding government for the commonweal beyond bureaucratic evasion and opportunism. And it is beginning to lay bare the closed corporate money-sequence that invades all of life to turn it into itself. The uniting of the servants of life's freedom is as old as historical movements, but never more challenged than now. Assistance to the hungry, the homeless, the poor, and the powerless is as ancient as human vision, but has never been more equipped than at the present. It is no exaggeration to say that we are at a turning point of the world's history.

The epochal evolution out of a life-destructive value program will, as in the past, be led on the basis of and by the agency of the civil commons. Our concepts of social justice, the commonweal, national security, the sovereignty of the people, and the rule of law are a nexus of maturing ideals whose inner meaning is this shared life-ground of humanity in organized co-operation to overcome threats to individual, social, and now planetary life. The civil commons has been developing and has traversed many stages towards more comprehensive community for thousands of years. At the end of this era, an abyss looms of an increasing depredation of the evolved webs of life by a life-blind program of value whose mutated logic invades everywhere, seeking to grow money in place of diverse environments and people. The demand of money over life, instead of money as a means of exchange to serve life, is the inner thread of our predicament, which has now globalized across borders. Only the long-evolved resources of the civil commons in its local, national, and international forms, using governments and institutions at all levels as its framework of collective agency across time, are capable of recognizing and responding to the planetary disorder.

The footings of the civil commons are everywhere, developed over generations and fought for across the world from Mexico to China. There is hardly an existing government-funded institution that does not somewhere elaborate the civil commons' inner principles of protecting life from harm or of enabling citizens' universal access to some vital life-good. The life-code and life-sequence are somehow recognized in these codifications of civil purpose, found somewhere in the immune fabric of society beneath the deformations and misrepresentations overlaying them. These inner, codified grounds of civilly recognizable response on behalf of life's requirements are instituted decision-structures crystallized out of past struggles. They are the established bases on which action can be mobilized by any conscious bearer of the civil commons to confront the pathological program. They all inscribe at some level their recognition of the life-sequence that registers the evolution of the society within which citizens live. Without their already shared ground of value and prescription, there is a crisis of conflicting interests and perspectives that may be unresolvable except by organized violence and force. This is the condition of lawless societies and civil war into which much of the world has in the past, and now again, descends.

On the level of institutional, municipal, regional, and national government, the encoded grounds of civil commons response are present to be built upon at every level. Even at the most remote and life-blind sites of the global market program, the banks, corporations, and money pools of investment are still subject to civil commons response in exact ways, including bringing current lawless trade treaties under the rule of international law. At even the immediate sites of an individual person's life and work, there are codified imprints and inlets of the life-ground and life-sequence of value that can be activated to make the money program more accountable to it, from mission statements and charters to founding and regulatory statutes.

What is missing is the social body's recognition of the life-invading value program that disables it. Public communications monopolies misrepresent reality as "getting the fundamentals right" and "developing global prosperity," even as environmental and civil life-fabrics demonstrably unravel. Monetary co-ordinates of value can only judge monetized sequences of value. The prison of habituated value program blocks political recognition and response to the accumulating crisis of life conditions for social and ecosystem reproduction and growth, although it is now detectable at all levels of the biosphere and global commons. The constitutional bases, the rule of law, the statutory provision, the untested professional oath, the contractual opening, the public platform to speak, the electronic pathway not yet entered, and the footings of the social immune system are all around. The world now moves for the first time in history to a global struggle between knowledge and misrepresentation as the finally contending forces. Even the police state we see re-entering to quell publics cannot contain the new, connecting stage of the global mind.

On this emerging field of contest between knowledge and misrepresentation of the common life-interest, the bearers of humanity's life-code of value may be stigmatized, kept out of view, ranted at, dismissed, or dispossessed, but their mass murder is no longer politically acceptable. Transnational market media at least bears this form of understanding of an emerging global civil commons. The comprehension of a common body of life is growing across societies as a shared condition of future survival. The fight for life at its greatest crossroads ever can finally, perhaps, be played at the human level, by means of the civil commons' first common ground: the word and the sign that all can understand.

Notes

1. The text of the World Bank's chief economist, now the U.S. Deputy Secretary of the Treasury, is reproduced below. I am indebted to Terisa Turner for the full text of this memorandum, part 3, Dec. 12, 1991.

"Dirty" industries. Just between you and me, shouldn't the World Bank be encouraging more migration of the dirty industries to the LDCs? I can think of three reasons:

1) The measurement of the costs of health-impairing pollution depends on the forgone earnings from increased morbidity and mortality. From this point of view a given amount of health impairing pollution should be done in the country with the lowest cost, which will be the country with the lowest wages. I think the economic logic behind dumping a load of toxic waste in the lowest wage country is impeccable and we should face up to that.

2) The costs of pollution are likely to be non-linear as the initial increments of pollution probably have very low cost. I've always thought that underpopulated countries in Africa are vastly under-polluted, their air quality is probably vastly inefficiently low compared to Los Angeles or Mexico City. Only the lamentable facts that so much pollution is generated by non-tradable industries (transport, electrical generation) and that the unit transport costs of solid waste are so high prevent world welfare enhancing trade in air pollution and waste.

3) The demand for a clean environment for aesthetic and health reasons is likely to have very high income elasticity. The concern over an agent that causes a one in a million change in the odds of prostrate [sic] cancer is obviously going to be much higher in a country where people survive to get prostrate [sic] cancer than in a country where under 5 mortality is 200 per thousand. Also, much of the concern over industrial atmospheric discharge is about visibility impairing particulates. These discharges may have very little direct health impact. Clearly trade in goods that embody aesthetic pollution concerns could be welfare enhancing. While production is mobile the consumption of pretty air is a non-tradable.

2. Smith, "Of the Accumulation of Capital," book II, chapter III, *Inquiry*, p.286.
3. International epidemiologist Richard Peto of Oxford University estimates that smoking is responsible for 3 million deaths per year worldwide, which will likely reach 10 million in three decades. Peto estimates that in China alone 50 million people will eventually die from smoking-induced diseases. Former U.S. Surgeon-General C. Everett Koop observes: "I feel the most shameful thing this country did was to export disease, disability and death by selling our cigarettes to the world." Clayton Yeutter, the U.S. trade representative, however, exults on the increased U.S. trade figures and exports in the global market: "I just saw the figures on tobacco exports here a few days ago and, my, have they turned out to be a marvelous success story." Here we see in clear expression the global market's "death sequence of value" affirmed as an optimum good. Figures and quotations are cited in Glenn Frankel, "U.S. Aided Tobacco Firms in Asia Conquest," *The Washington Post*, reprinted in *The Guardian Weekly*, Dec. 1, 1996, p.15.
4. M.I.T. Vegetarian Support Group, "How Our Food Choices Affect Life on Earth," World-Wide-Web, Nov. 22, 1996, p.1.
5. See, for example, George C. Lodge and Ezra F. Vogel, *Ideology and National Competitiveness* (Cambridge Mass.: Harvard Business School Press, 1987); R. Wade, *Governing the Market* (Princeton, N.J.: Princeton University Press, 1990); Will Hutton, "Why the Asian Tigers Burn So Bright," *The Guardian Weekly*, April 6, 1995, p.12.
6. Marc Renaud, at his photographic exhibition *40 Ans de Photographie en Chine, 1956-96*, the Centre National de la Photographie, Paris, reports:

The market reorganization has all taken place in a frighteningly brutal way.... The wife is forced to prostitute herself with the mother's consent to pay the rent.... There's terrible corruption. There are no more bookshops, no free speech, no free press, no right to stake. There's no such thing as town planning.... There are no checks and balances.

Renaud also reports "a higher standard of living." *The Guardian Weekly*, July 14, 1996, p.A14. Amnesty International's 1996 report on the People's Republic of China reads, "Across China, people from all walks of life and from many ethnic backgrounds are imprisoned for the peaceful expression of their opinions: those who speak out for the human rights of others face harassment and imprisonment. All detainees are at grave risk of torture and ill-treatment. Thousands of people are executed every year. Independent religious groups face harassment. Inadequate legal safeguards allow for arbitrariness and abuses of power." Amnesty International Worldwide Petition on Human Rights Violations in China, November 1996.
7. Keith B. Richburg, "Neighbours Watch Warily as the Giant Stirs," *The Guardian Weekly*, March 16, 1996, p.19.

8. William Krehm, "The Committee on Monetary and Economic Reform Responds to the 1996 Bank Act Review," October 1996, pp.4-5.

9. Alex Cockburn and Ken Silverstein, "War and Peso," *New Statesman and Society*, Feb. 24, 1995, p.A.

10. William Krehm, "The Anatomy of Deceit," *Economic Reform*, March 1996, p.1.

11. The ratio of private debt to income is reported in Canada, for example, as 800:522 billion, or 169 per cent. In 1929 it was 160 per cent. Roger Schmitz, "The Interest Is Killing Us," *Monetary Reform*, Fall 1996, p.16.

12. The U.S. financier J.P. Morgan described the power of this money-to-more-money sequence via interest demand in this way: "I couldn't name the seven wonders of the world, but I can tell you what the eighth is—Compound Interest." Quoted by Ed Finn, *CCPA Monitor*, July/August 1996, p.4.

13. See, for example, George C. Lodge and Ezra F. Vogel, *Ideology and National Competitiveness: An Analysis of Nine Countries* (Boston: Harvard Business School Press, 1987).

14. Quoted in Greider, *Secrets of the Temple*, p. 20. It is of interest in this connection to recall Yeshua's prescient advice: "You cannot be the servant of both God and money." *Matthew*, chapter 6, verse 24.

15. Confucius, for example, states: "The superior man understands righteousness; the inferior man understands profit." Wing Tsit Chan, ed., *Sourcebook in Chinese Philosophy* (Princeton, N.J.: Princeton University Press, 1968), p.28.

16. *Asia Week*, April 14, 1993, p.23.

17. World Commission on Environment and Development, *Our Common Future* (the Brundtland Report) (New York: Oxford University Press, 1987).

18. Jacquie McNish, "Bankers' Brawl," *The Globe and Mail Report on Business Magazine*, January 1996, p.82.

19. Maude Barlow, *Council of Canadians Petition on Pensions*, Sept. 20, 1995. These figures will only increase as the percentage of low-paying, non-pensioned jobs increases. By 1993, the percentage of male workers in low-wage, non-pension jobs had nearly doubled since 1975, and 85 per cent of all employed workers in the 18-24 age-bracket were in such jobs. Bruce Little, "Income Disparity on Rise, Study Says," *The Globe and Mail*, July 12, 1996, p.1. In Britain a similar trend exists in employment patterns, with part-time workers up 50 per cent between 1981 and 1986. Richard Thomas, *The Guardian Weekly*, June 23, 1996, p.15.

20. "Young Canadian families," reports *The Globe and Mail*, "saw their family income plunge 20 percent from 1980 to 1990." Edward Greenspon, "The 68¢ Government," Sept. 28, 1996, p.D1. As we have seen, this plunge in income for recent market entrants in the last two decades is similar elsewhere.

21. Ed Finn, "Why Don't Our Own Unions Flex Their Pension Muscles?" *CCPA Monitor*, February 1996, p.4.

22. When concern was raised in 1996 about the use of $70 million of the Ontario Teachers' Federation Pension Plan to invest in the Toronto Sun Publishing Corporation, owner of an antiunion tabloid that invariably attacked teachers during contract or other disputes, the response of the financial manager of the teachers' pension fund was predictably in accord with the absolute rule of the money-sequence of value. He said that not even the governors of the Ontario Teachers' Federation could instruct him as to his obligations of investment. "In essence, I don't think we're bound by anything," he said. "Our responsibility is to make money for the plan." See "Ontario Teachers Peeved over Sun Bid," *The Globe and Mail*, Aug. 24, 1996, p.B3. Although the massive pension plan fund of over $40 billion provided ample leverage to the Ontario teachers and their leaderships to correct this delinked rule of their own pension capital, there was no further opposition reported to this independent reign of the money-sequence of value over its contributors.

23. As those who read investment newsletters will recognize, this 20 per cent limit on tax-deductible investments in countries outside the country paying for the tax deduction is attacked by investment

dealers and financial advisers as an intolerable limit on individuals' investment rights and future security.

24. James Tobin, *The New Economics One Decade Older* (Princeton, N.J.: Princeton University Press, 1974); see also Tobin, "Tax on International Currency Transactions," in United Nations Development Programme, *Human Development Report 1994* (New York: UNDP, 1994), p.70.

25. Thomas Homer-Dixon reports: "I discussed the Tobin Tax with a senior bureaucrat from the Canadian Department of Finance. She heatedly rejected the proposal, claiming [falsely] that Tobin has repudiated the idea." See "How to Put a Brake on Currency Volatility," *The Globe and Mail*, July 8, 1996, p.A13. Here we have a quintessential expression of the social value program: (1) the confusion of public servants between the public interest they are paid to represent and the private demands of the market; (2) confusion of the special interests of financial speculators with both the market and the public interest; and (3) on the basis of these layered, metaphysical confusions, a false claim of fact to confirm them.

26. Lao Tzu's words, in chapter 77 of *Tao-te Ching*, are: "The Way of Heaven reduces whatever is excessive and supplements whatever is insufficient/The Way of man is different/It reduces the insufficient to offer to the excessive." To be more specific than Lao Tzu, "the way of man" is a social value program that can be consciously revised.

27. Maude Barlow and Tony Clarke, "Canada: The Broken Promise," *The Nation*, July 15-22, 1996, p.16.

28. This is an arguable point. The Mondragon co-operatives of Basque Spain and the Emiliano Romagna co-operatives of Northern Italy employ hundreds of thousands of worker-owners at competitive rates of productive efficiency and with a fraction of the rate of social unemployment and poverty in their regions. See, for example, Alistair Campbell, Charles Keen, Geraldine Norman, and Robert Oakashott, *Workers-Owners: The Mondragon Achievement* (London: Anglo-German Foundation for the Study of Industrial Society, 1976).

29. Madelaine Drohon, "Perils of Privatization," *The Globe and Mail Report on Business Magazine*, May 1996, p.39.

30. Ibid., p.40.

31. "In Brief," *The Guardian Weekly*, July 21, 1996, p.19.

32. Drohon, "Perils of Privatization," p.41.

33. Ibid., p.40.

34. Bruce Little, "The Pension Squeeze," *The Globe and Mail*, June 8, 1996, p.B4. Financial manager Malcolm Hamilton, a principal of W.M. Mercer Ltd., is the source of this moral counsel.

35. "Considering Medicare," editorial, *The Globe and Mail*, June 1, 1996, p.D6.

36. Canadian Finance Minister Paul Martin, speaking to the Canadian Federation of Labour, Ottawa, June 6, 1996.

37. This carcinogenic pattern of the global market value system is repeated in government ministries and central banks managing public policy by the money-code and money-sequence in many ways: assisting evasion by billionaire capital of tax obligations (as in the Bronfman movement of $2 billion to the United States to evade Canadian taxes, a loss of public revenues advocated and defended by this same ministry); abolishing all cash-reserve requirements of private banks as an "unjust tax" on their unrestricted use of money-creating powers (as performed by Canada's central bank with no public or parliamentary notice in 1991); declaring the over-50 per cent ownership of all newspapers in Canada to "not substantially lessen competition" (as determined by the Federal Competition Bureau of Canada in response to Conrad Black's Hollinger takeover of Canada's largest newspaper chain).

38. Ann Swardson, "Canada's Slimline," *The Guardian Weekly*, July 14, 1996, p.17.

39. Jack M. Beatty, "What Election 96 Should Be About," *The Atlantic Monthly*, May 1996, p.118; David M. Gordon, *Fat and Mean: The Corporate System of Squeezing Americans* (New York: Simon and Schuster, 1996).

40. A telling fact that helps to disclose the operational function of the global armaments industry is that one-fifth of the countries are now at war against their own peoples, but not one nation-state is at war with another. Ploughshares Monitor, *A World at War: The 1996 Armed Conflicts Report* (Waterloo: Conrad Grebel College, 1996), p.12.

41. Cited by Ralph Nader, "Stop Americanizing Canadian Medicare," *CCPA Monitor*, February 1996, p.16; and "It's Time to End Corporate Welfare as We Know It," *Earth Island Journal*, Fall 1996, p.37.

42. Wang Yang-Ming, "An Inquiry on the Great Learning," in *Sourcebook in Chinese Philosophy*, ed. Wing Tsit Chan (Princeton, N.J.: Princeton University Press, 1968), pp.659-60.

43. I have introduced the concept of "civil commons" to distinguish it from the traditional "commons"—the shared natural lands upon which an agricultural village economy depends. I mean by the civil commons both the traditional commons and all other universally accessible goods of life that protect or enable the lives of society's members. The traditional village commons was the ancient mode of both protecting and managing the lands between the wilderness and the individual farm plots of the village. It consisted of the community's building materials in their natural state and was continuously used as a shared pasture for the livestock of the community's individual households. Universal access to its essential and shared life-goods was regulated by a set requirement that the commoner could only turn out to range as many head of livestock as he could feed over the winter in his own corrals. Once the international wool trade became the progenitor of the global market from the fifteenth century on, the commons were forcibly fenced off by the landlord class for large-scale sheep herds with the support of the urban mercantile guilds and the state in the great privatization movement called the "enclosures," which centred in Britain but afterwards swept across the world in some form. This enclosure movement dispossessed commoners and subsistence farmers and provided, across the continents, the basis of the landless working class, who ever after had to sell their labour to others to survive. Meanwhile this privatizing, market clearance of the people from their common lands opened up the land and forests to for-profit and eventually industrial lumber and mining operations, which began the great modern assault on the environment that continues to grow in force today. In this overall pattern of privatization and marketization for world trade, landless labour, and environmental exploitation is a historic conjuncture of planetary consequences for the life-sequence at every level of survival and growth, which continues unregulated today. This planetary pattern too is not seen or discussed, even as its process of clearance and appropriation of communal lands continues in the present from North and Latin America to Africa and Asia. Much of the history of our time is the history of the continuing clearance of communal farm and tribal lands across the world—the inner story of First Peoples uprisings from Oka to Chiapas, from Ogoniland Nigeria to the Tibetan plateau of China. At the same time, the civil commons of shared social resources in the form of public-sector provision of food subsidies, health care, free education, and so on has been systematically attacked by Structural Readjustment Programs imposed by the IMF and other institutional money-lenders across the Third World since the 1970s, a program of stripping the civil commons that has recently moved, in turn, to the Second and First Worlds since 1989. These patterns are discussed in detail elsewhere, but here it is important to emphasize that the concept of civil commons subsumes both the traditional commons and the built commons of universally accessible social goods evolved by public sectors since the Industrial Revolution and, in particular, since the end of World War II. A clear description of the traditional commons is provided by Gary Snyder, "Understanding the Commons," in *Environmental Ethics: Convergence and Divergence*, ed. Susan J. Armstrong and Richard G. Botzler (New York: McGraw-Hill, 1993), pp.227-30. The destruction of the commons in this traditional sense is discussed by Karl Marx in *Capital*, vol. 1, Part VIII. The massive social protests and rebellions against contemporary destructions of the civil commons by structural adjustment programs are the subject of a valuable study by, inter alia, J. Walton, "Debt, Protest and the State

in Latin America," in *Power and Popular Protest*, ed. Susan Eckstein (Berkeley: University of California Press, 1989).

44. These figures were reported by the United Nation's Global Habitat Conference, Istanbul, 1996, and the UN's Development Programme respectively. *The Guardian Weekly*, July 16, 1996, p.24, and July 21, 1996, p.1.

45. John Vidal, "The Global Formula for Dynamite," *The Guardian Weekly*, reprinted, *The Globe and Mail*, June 15, 1996, p.D4.

46. The facts in this paragraph are cited in Kevin Watkins, "IMF Holds a Gold Key for the Third World," *The Guardian Weekly*, June 16, 1996, p.14.

47. Ariel Salleh, "Working With Nature: Reciprocity or Control?" in J.E. Engel, *Ethics of Environment and Development*. Tuscon: University of Arizona Press, 1990.

48. Amartya Sen, "The Economics of Life and Death," *Scientific American*, May 1993, p.40.

49. Locke, *Second Treatise on Government*, Section 224, p.126.

50. Brigid McMenamin, "Environmental Imperialism," *Forbes*, May 20, 1996.

51. Quoted in "Global Warning: Cities Harm People," *The Guardian Weekly*, June 16, 1996, p.24.

52. A finding that discloses the enmeshment of the population as a whole in the value system disorder is that 82 per cent of a prebudget poll in Canada "said they would want to see a cut in government spending even if the deficit wasn't a problem." Canadian Press, Aug. 10, 1996. This result depends on both pollsters and public not recognizing the base-line distinction advanced in this investigation between government for the life-sequence of value and government for the money-sequence of value. The inability to make distinctions between the requirements of life and the demands of a ruling value program is a paradigmatic problem of any pathological social value system.

53. This is a point not recognized by those who are glad that the World Bank's 1996 proposal of a "new system to measure the wealth of nations," which includes "social capital." They do not distinguish, that is, between "social capital" of the market-instrumental kind and "social capital" of the intrinsically valuable kind. See, for example, Ismail Serageldin and John O'Connor, "World Bank Develops New System to Measure Wealth of Nations," *The Guardian Weekly*, Sept. 17, 1995, p.2.

54. Here, as earlier, I mean by the "new economics" or the "more farsighted" of market theorists those who propose that economic measures must take into account non-monetized forms of wealth as well as monetized wealth (that is, money income) if they are to comprehend the real wealth of nations. The earlier reported initiative of the Environmentally Sustainable Development division of the World Bank is representative of this "new economics." Here the categories are Social Capital, Natural Capital, Human Capital, and Produced Assets Capital, but elsewhere they can be conceptualized somewhat differently with the same referents. What is common to these widened conceptions of capital is the unexamined assumption that all such wealth or forms of capital have their value as capital value insofar as they "promote development" or are "determinants of growth" conceived in terms of conventional money-income measures. In other words, the recognized means of increasing the money-sequence of value are broadened, but the sovereign value of money gain that they must serve remains the same.

55. These facts are derived from personal testimony and letters from "The Friends of Innu," the most recent June 12, 1996.

56. All of the current value audits of the new economics seem to suffer from this presupposition of human and other life as values only insofar as they are contributing factors to economic growth or the money-sequence of value. This presupposition underlies not only the World Bank's "new wealth accounting system" but also the OECD, European Union, and IMF protocols for integrating social and environmental statistics into national accounts.

57. OECD, *Press Release*, June 20, 1996.

58. "Extinctions Unprecedented, U.N. Says," Canadian Press, April 20, 1996. Elizabeth Dowdeswell's leadership of the UN Environment Program was publicly attacked within days of this statement by the U.S. government as "ineffective."

59. "Poverty Is World's Greatest Killer," *The Guardian Weekly*, May 21, 1995, p.1.

60. I am indebted to Tara Cullis, who transcribed these words of Noam Chomsky's public lecture in Vancouver, May 5, 1996.

Index

Books Of Related Interest From Kumarian Press

When Corporations Rule the World
David C. Korten

Shows how the convergence of ideological, political and technological forces is leading to an ever-greater concentration of economic and political power in a handful of corporations and financial institutions. Korten shows how the interest of the corporation is separate from human interest leaving the market system blind to all but its own short term market gains.

US $19.95 Paper: 1-887208-01-1
US $29.95 Cloth: 1-887208-00-3

Creating Alternative Futures
The End of Economics
Hazel Henderson

This book has been the catalyst for many of today's debates on ways to reformulate economic theory to help industrial societies follow healthier paths toward more equitable, ecologically sustainable human development. As a renowned futurist and human ecologist, Henderson's recommendations are as valuable and as timely as ever.

US $17.95 Paper: 1-56549-060-6

Mediating Sustainability
Growing Policy from the Grassroots
Editors: Jutta Blauert and Simon Zadek

This book explores how mediation between grass-roots and policy formation processes can and does work in practice by focusing on experiences in Latin America in promoting sustainable agriculture and rural development. The contributions to this book draw on the work of researchers, activists, farmers and policy makers through concrete evidence and appraisal.

US $25.95 Paper: 1-56549-081-9
US $55.00 Cloth: 1-56549-082-7

Kumarian Press
14 Oakwood Avenue
West Hartford, CT 06119

Phone: 800-289-2664
Fax: 860-233-6072
E-Mail: kpbooks@aol.com
Web: www.kpbooks.com

AGMV
MARQUIS
Québec, Canada
1999